TM

References for the Rest of Us!®

BESTSELLING BOOK SERIES FROM IDG

Are you intimidated and confused by computers? Do you find that traditional manuals are overloaded with technical details you'll never use? Do your friends and family always call you to fix simple problems on their PCs? Then the *...For Dummies*® computer book series from IDG Books Worldwide is for you.

...For Dummies books are written for those frustrated computer users who know they aren't really dumb but find that PC hardware, software, and indeed the unique vocabulary of computing make them feel helpless. *...For Dummies* books use a lighthearted approach, a down-to-earth style, and even cartoons and humorous icons to diffuse computer novices' fears and build their confidence. Lighthearted but not lightweight, these books are a perfect survival guide for anyone forced to use a computer.

> *"I like my copy so much I told friends; now they bought copies."*
>
> — Irene C., Orwell, Ohio

> *"Quick, concise, nontechnical, and humorous."*
>
> — Jay A., Elburn, Illinois

> *"Thanks, I needed this book. Now I can sleep at night."*
>
> — Robin F., British Columbia, Canada

Already, millions of satisfied readers agree. They have made *...For Dummies* books the #1 introductory level computer book series and have written asking for more. So, if you're looking for the most fun and easy way to learn about computers, look to *...For Dummies* books to give you a helping hand.

TM

IDG BOOKS WORLDWIDE

4/98

CREATING WEB PAGES FOR DUMMIES®

3RD EDITION

by Bud Smith and Arthur Bebak

Foreword by Kevin Werbach

IDG Books Worldwide, Inc.
An International Data Group Company

Foster City, CA ♦ Chicago, IL ♦ Indianapolis, IN ♦ New York, NY

Creating Web Pages For Dummies® 3rd Edition

Published by
IDG Books Worldwide, Inc.
An International Data Group Company
919 E. Hillsdale Blvd.
Suite 400
Foster City, CA 94404
www.idgbooks.com (IDG Books Worldwide Web site)
www.dummies.com (Dummies Press Web site)

Library of Congress Catalog Card No.: 98-84489

ISBN: 0-7645-0357-X

Printed in the United States of America

10 9 8 7 6 5 4 3

3O/SS/QZ/ZY/IN

Distributed in the United States by IDG Books Worldwide, Inc.

Distributed by Macmillan Canada for Canada; by Transworld Publishers Limited in the United Kingdom; by IDG Norge Books for Norway; by IDG Sweden Books for Sweden; by Woodslane Pty. Ltd. for Australia; by Woodslane Enterprises Ltd. for New Zealand; by Longman Singapore Publishers Ltd. for Singapore, Malaysia, Thailand, and Indonesia; by Simron Pty. Ltd. for South Africa; by Toppan Company Ltd. for Japan; by Distribuidora Cuspide for Argentina; by Livraria Cultura for Brazil; by Ediciencia S.A. for Ecuador; by Addison-Wesley Publishing Company for Korea; by Ediciones ZETA S.C.R. Ltda. for Peru; by WS Computer Publishing Corporation, Inc., for the Philippines; by Unalis Corporation for Taiwan; by Contemporanea de Ediciones for Venezuela; by Computer Book & Magazine Store for Puerto Rico; by Express Computer Distributors for the Caribbean and West Indies. Authorized Sales Agent: Anthony Rudkin Associates for the Middle East and North Africa.

For general information on IDG Books Worldwide's books in the U.S., please call our Consumer Customer Service department at 800-762-2974. For reseller information, including discounts and premium sales, please call our Reseller Customer Service department at 800-434-3422.

For information on where to purchase IDG Books Worldwide's books outside the U.S., please contact our International Sales department at 650-655-3200 or fax 650-655-3295.

For information on foreign language translations, please contact our Foreign & Subsidiary Rights department at 650-655-3021 or fax 650-655-3281.

For sales inquiries and special prices for bulk quantities, please contact our Sales department at 650-655-3200 or write to the address above.

For information on using IDG Books Worldwide's books in the classroom or for ordering examination copies, please contact our Educational Sales department at 800-434-2086 or fax 817-251-8174.

For press review copies, author interviews, or other publicity information, please contact our Public Relations department at 650-655-3000 or fax 650-655-3299.

For authorization to photocopy items for corporate, personal, or educational use, please contact Copyright Clearance Center, 222 Rosewood Drive, Danvers, MA 01923, or fax 978-750-4470.

is a trademark under exclusive license to IDG Books Worldwide, Inc., from International Data Group, Inc.

About the Authors

Bud Smith is a computer book author with over ten years of publishing experience. *Creating Web Pages For Dummies,* 3rd Edition is one of a dozen books Bud has written; his IDG Books Worldwide titles include *Push Technology For Dummies* and *Marketing Online For Dummies.* In addition to writing books, Bud has been a computer magazine editor and product marketing manager.

Bud got his start with computers in 1983, when he left a promising career as a welder for a stint as a data-entry clerk. Bud then moved to Silicon Valley to join a startup company, followed by work for Intel, IBM, and Apple. His work and interests led him to acquire a degree from the University of San Francisco in Information Systems Management.

Arthur Bebak received a degree in Computer Engineering at the University of Illinois, which he attended on a fencing scholarship. He has designed mainframes, managed large engineering projects, and studied business administration. Arthur is founder of Netsurfer Communications, Inc., a highly successful electronic publishing company. Arthur has done a lot of writing, which has led to his current "surprising" (though only to him) role as coauthor of this book.

At Netsurfer, Arthur oversees a large staff of people who create Web sites for numerous clients. They also write, edit, and publish several Web-based electronic magazines, popularly known as "e-zines."

ABOUT IDG BOOKS WORLDWIDE

Welcome to the world of IDG Books Worldwide.

IDG Books Worldwide, Inc., is a subsidiary of International Data Group, the world's largest publisher of computer-related information and the leading global provider of information services on information technology. IDG was founded more than 25 years ago and now employs more than 8,500 people worldwide. IDG publishes more than 275 computer publications in over 75 countries (see listing below). More than 90 million people read one or more IDG publications each month.

Launched in 1990, IDG Books Worldwide is today the #1 publisher of best-selling computer books in the United States. We are proud to have received eight awards from the Computer Press Association in recognition of editorial excellence and three from *Computer Currents*' First Annual Readers' Choice Awards. Our best-selling ...*For Dummies®* series has more than 50 million copies in print with translations in 38 languages. IDG Books Worldwide, through a joint venture with IDG's Hi-Tech Beijing, became the first U.S. publisher to publish a computer book in the People's Republic of China. In record time, IDG Books Worldwide has become the first choice for millions of readers around the world who want to learn how to better manage their businesses.

Our mission is simple: Every one of our books is designed to bring extra value and skill-building instructions to the reader. Our books are written by experts who understand and care about our readers. The knowledge base of our editorial staff comes from years of experience in publishing, education, and journalism — experience we use to produce books for the '90s. In short, we care about books, so we attract the best people. We devote special attention to details such as audience, interior design, use of icons, and illustrations. And because we use an efficient process of authoring, editing, and desktop publishing our books electronically, we can spend more time ensuring superior content and spend less time on the technicalities of making books.

You can count on our commitment to deliver high-quality books at competitive prices on topics you want to read about. At IDG Books Worldwide, we continue in the IDG tradition of delivering quality for more than 25 years. You'll find no better book on a subject than one from IDG Books Worldwide.

John Kilcullen
CEO
IDG Books Worldwide, Inc.

Steven Berkowitz
President and Publisher
IDG Books Worldwide, Inc.

**Eighth Annual
Computer Press
Awards ≥1992**

**Ninth Annual
Computer Press
Awards ≥1993**

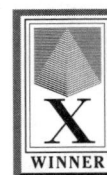

**Tenth Annual
Computer Press
Awards ≥1994**

**Eleventh Annual
Computer Press
Awards ≥1995**

IDG Books Worldwide, Inc., is a subsidiary of International Data Group, the world's largest publisher of computer-related information and the leading global provider of information services on information technology. International Data Group publishes over 275 computer publications in over 75 countries. More than 90 million people read one or more International Data Group publications each month. International Data Group's publications include: **ARGENTINA:** Buyer's Guide, Computerworld Argentina, PC World Argentina; **AUSTRALIA:** Australian Macworld, Australian PC World, Australian Reseller News, Computerworld, IT Casebook, Network World, Publish, Webmaster; **AUSTRIA:** Computerwelt Osterreich, Networks Austria, PC Tip Austria; **BANGLADESH:** PC World Bangladesh; **BELARUS:** PC World Belarus; **BELGIUM:** Data News; **BRAZIL:** Annuário de Informática, Computerworld, Connections, Macworld, PC Player, PC World, Publish, Reseller News, Supergamepower; **BULGARIA:** Computerworld Bulgaria, Network World Bulgaria, PC & MacWorld Bulgaria; **CANADA:** CIO Canada, Client/Server World, ComputerWorld Canada, InfoWorld Canada, NetworkWorld Canada, WebWorld; **CHILE:** Computerworld Chile, PC World Chile; **COLOMBIA:** Computerworld Colombia, PC World Colombia; **COSTA RICA:** PC World Centro America; **THE CZECH AND SLOVAK REPUBLICS:** Computerworld Czechoslovakia, Macworld Czech Republic, PC World Czechoslovakia; **DENMARK:** Communications World Danmark, Computerworld Danmark, Macworld Danmark, PC World Danmark, Techworld Denmark; **DOMINICAN REPUBLIC:** PC World Republica Dominicana; **ECUADOR:** PC World Ecuador; **EGYPT:** Computerworld Middle East, PC World Middle East; **EL SALVADOR:** PC World Centro America; **FINLAND:** MikroPC, Tietoverkko, Tietoviikko; **FRANCE:** Distributique, Hebdo, Info PC, Le Monde Informatique, Macworld, Reseaux & Telecoms, WebMaster France; **GERMANY:** Computer Partner, Computerwoche, Computerwoche Extra, Computerwoche FOCUS, Global Online, Macwelt, PC Welt; **GREECE:** Amiga Computing, GamePro Greece, Multimedia World; **GUATEMALA:** PC World Centro America; **HONDURAS:** PC World Centro America; **HONG KONG:** Computerworld Hong Kong, PC World Hong Kong, Publish in Asia; **HUNGARY:** ABCD CD-ROM, Computerworld Szamitastechnika, Internetto online Magazine, PC World Hungary, PC-X Magazin Hungary; **ICELAND:** Tolvuheimur PC World Island; **INDIA:** Information Communications World, Information Systems Computerworld, PC World India, Publish in Asia; **INDONESIA:** InfoKomputer PC World, Komputek Computerworld, Publish in Asia; **IRELAND:** ComputerScope, PC Live!; **ISRAEL:** Macworld Israel, People & Computers/Computerworld; **ITALY:** Computerworld Italia, Macworld Italia, Networking Italia, PC World Italia; **JAPAN:** DTP World, Macworld Japan, Nikkei Personal Computing, OS/2 World Japan, SunWorld Japan, Windows NT World, Windows World Japan; **KENYA:** PC World East African; **KOREA:** Hi-Tech Information, Macworld Korea, PC World Korea; **MACEDONIA:** PC World Macedonia; **MALAYSIA:** Computerworld Malaysia, PC World Malaysia, Publish in Asia; **MALTA:** PC World Malta; **MEXICO:** Computerworld Mexico, PC World Mexico; **MYANMAR:** PC World Myanmar; **NETHERLANDS:** Computer! Totaal, LAN Internetworking Magazine, LAN World Buyers Guide, Macworld Netherlands, Net, WebWereld; **NEW ZEALAND:** Absolute Beginners Guide and Plain & Simple Series, Computer Buyer, Computer Industry Directory, Computerworld New Zealand, MTB, Network World, PC World New Zealand; **NICARAGUA:** PC World Centro America; **NORWAY:** Computerworld Norge, CW Rapport, Datamagasinet, Financial Rapport, Kursguide Norge, Macworld Norge, Multimediaworld Norge, PC World Ekspress Norge, PC World Nettverk, PC World Norge, PC World ProduktGuide Norge; **PAKISTAN:** Computerworld Pakistan; **PANAMA:** PC World Panama; **PEOPLE'S REPUBLIC OF CHINA:** China Computer Users, China Computerworld, China InfoWorld, China Telecom World Weekly, Computer & Communication, Electronic Design China, Electronics Today, Electronics Weekly, Game Software, PC World China, Popular Computer Week, Software Weekly, Software World, Telecom World; **PERU:** Computerworld Peru, PC World Profesional Peru, PC World SoHo Peru; **PHILIPPINES:** Click!, Computerworld Philippines, PC World Philippines, Publish in Asia; **POLAND:** Computerworld Poland, Computerworld Special Report Poland, Cyber, Macworld Poland, Networld Poland, PC World Komputer; **PORTUGAL:** Cerebro/PC World, Computerworld/Correio Informático, Dealer World Portugal, Mac*In/PC*In Portugal, Multimedia World; **PUERTO RICO:** PC World Puerto Rico; **ROMANIA:** Computerworld Romania, PC World Romania, Telecom Romania; **RUSSIA:** Computerworld Russia, Mir PK, Publish, Seti; **SINGAPORE:** Computerworld Singapore, PC World Singapore, Publish in Asia; **SLOVENIA:** Monitor; **SOUTH AFRICA:** Computing SA, Network World SA, Software World SA; **SPAIN:** Communicaciones World España, Computerworld España, Dealer World España, Macworld España, PC World España; **SRI LANKA:** Infolink PC World; **SWEDEN:** CAP&Design, Computer Sweden, Corporate Computing Sweden, Internetworld Sweden, it branschen, Macworld Sweden, MaxiData Sweden, MikroDatorn, Natverk & Kommunikation, PC World Sweden, PCaktiv, Windows World Sweden; **SWITZERLAND:** Computerworld Schweiz, Macworld Schweiz, PCtip; **TAIWAN:** Computerworld Taiwan, Macworld Taiwan, NEW ViSiON/Publish, PC World Taiwan, Windows World Taiwan; **THAILAND:** Publish in Asia, Thai Computerworld; **TURKEY:** Computerworld Turkiye, Macworld Turkiye, Network World Turkiye, PC World Turkiye; **UKRAINE:** Computerworld Kiev, Multimedia World Ukraine, PC World Ukraine; **UNITED KINGDOM:** Acorn User UK, Amiga Action UK, Amiga Computing UK, Apple Talk UK, Computing, Macworld, Parents and Computers UK, PC Advisor, PC Home, PSX Pro, The WEB; **UNITED STATES:** Cable in the Classroom, CIO Magazine, Computerworld, DOS World, Federal Computer Week, GamePro Magazine, InfoWorld, I-Way, Macworld, Network World, PC Games, PC World, Publish, Video Event, THE WEB Magazine, and WebMaster; online webzines: JavaWorld, NetscapeWorld, and SunWorld Online; **URUGUAY:** InfoWorld Uruguay; **VENEZUELA:** Computerworld Venezuela, PC World Venezuela; and **VIETNAM:** PC World Vietnam.   5/7/98

Authors' Acknowledgments

The authors thank Mike Kelly, acquisitions editor, and the staff that helped produce this book: Kathy Cox, Kelly Oliver, and Kelly Ewing, project editors; Ted Cains, copy editor; and Mike Lerch, technical editor, as well as the many people involved in page layout, proofreading, indexing, and graphic art.

The Web was built more for love than money, and that tradition was continued by the many people who generously gave their time and support for this book. We especially thank the providers of Web tools who supplied us with an excellent set of programs for the CD-ROM and the Web authors who agreed to let us use their sites for the figures in this book.

Publisher's Acknowledgments

We're proud of this book; please register your comments through our IDG Books Worldwide Online Registration Form located at http://my2cents.dummies.com.

Some of the people who helped bring this book to market include the following:

Acquisitions, Development, and Editorial

Project Editor: Kathleen M. Cox

Acquisitions Editor: Michael Kelly

Media Development Manager: Joyce Pepple

Permissions Editor: Heather H. Dismore

Copy Editor: Ted Cains

Technical Editor: Michael Lerch

Editorial Manager: Colleen Rainsberger

Editorial Assistant: Paul E. Kuzmic

Production

Project Coordinator: E. Shawn Aylsworth

Layout and Graphics: Lou Boudreau, Linda M. Boyer, J. Tyler Connor, Angela F. Hunckler, Todd Klemme, Jane E. Martin, Anna Rohrer, Brent Savage, Deirdre Smith, Kate Snell, Michael A. Sullivan

Proofreaders: Michelle Croninger, Mildred Rosenzweig, Rebecca Senninger, Janet M. Withers

Indexer: Sharon Hilgenberg

Special Help

Copy Editors Linda Stark and Paula Lowell; Associate Technical Manager Joell Smith, and Access Technology, Inc., for producing the CD; and Supervisor of Graphics and Design Shelley Lea

General and Administrative

IDG Books Worldwide, Inc.: John Kilcullen, CEO; Steven Berkowitz, President and Publisher

IDG Books Technology Publishing: Brenda McLaughlin, Senior Vice President and Group Publisher

Dummies Technology Press and Dummies Editorial: Diane Graves Steele, Vice President and Associate Publisher; Mary Bednarek, Director of Acquisitions and Product Development; Kristin A. Cocks, Editorial Director

Dummies Trade Press: Kathleen A. Welton, Vice President and Publisher; Kevin Thornton, Acquisitions Manager

IDG Books Production for Dummies Press: Michael R. Britton, Vice President of Production and Creative Services; Beth Jenkins Roberts, Production Director; Cindy L. Phipps, Manager of Project Coordination, Production Proofreading, and Indexing; Kathie S. Schutte, Supervisor of Page Layout; Shelley Lea, Supervisor of Graphics and Design; Debbie J. Gates, Production Systems Specialist; Robert Springer, Supervisor of Proofreading; Debbie Stailey, Special Projects Coordinator; Tony Augsburger, Supervisor of Reprints and Bluelines

Dummies Packaging and Book Design: Robin Seaman, Creative Director; Jocelyn Kelaita, Product Packaging Coordinator; Kavish + Kavish, Cover Design

◆

The publisher would like to give special thanks to Patrick J. McGovern, without whom this book would not have been possible.

◆

Contents at a Glance

Cartoons at a Glance

By Rich Tennant

page 195

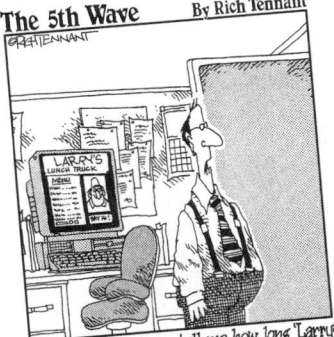

page 283

page 293

page 7

page 129

Fax: 978-546-7747 • **E-mail:** the5wave@tiac.net

Table of Contents

Foreword

*I*f you're reading this book, chances are that you fall into one of three categories:

The Webophile. You're already convinced that creating your own Web pages will help you win friends, influence people, find true love, improve your business, and get that nasty marmalade stain out of your favorite fez. You may have even made a few tentative attempts at creating your own Web pages, but you still think HTML stands for "Hard To Master Lingo." Now you've bought this book, and you're sitting in front of your computer hoping this Foreword doesn't ramble on much longer so that you can get to the good stuff about how you can design your own World Wide Web pages.

The Browser. You're thumbing through this book in the "Computers" or "Internet" section of your favorite bookstore. Perhaps someone else found this book in the store and decided to buy it for you as a gift. Or maybe you actually bought this book yourself, even though you aren't yet convinced that it will help you lose 30 pounds in three days and show you why the Internet and the World Wide Web are the biggest things since hula hoops. Unfortunately, you were voted "Most Likely to Remain Passive" in your high school yearbook. You've heard about the Internet and the World Wide Web, and you may already have an account with a commercial online service or an Internet service provider. You think you want to create your own Web pages, but you're not quite sure what to do or why.

The Webophobe. You feel like roadkill on the information superhighway. You may be accustomed to using a personal computer and even to surfing the Internet, but the thought of trying to write your own Web pages fills you with inexplicable dread. Sure, your propeller-head friends have their own Web sites, but you don't have a Ph.D. in computer science and quantum physics. You're not even sure what you could possibly put on your Web page that other people might want to read.

So, for whom is this book appropriate? All of you.

Regardless of your level of computer expertise, you can benefit from becoming a Web publisher. People who have heard of my *Bare Bones Guide to HTML* — a concise index of the language used to create Web pages — often ask why they should invest time and effort in publishing their own pages on the World Wide Web. Why should they spend their time fiddling around with some arcane computer codes just so they can stick a bunch of flashing doodads around their name and send it over the Internet?

Because you can do so many things, and it's so easy. This book shows you how easy it is to create Web pages. Here are some reasons why creating your own Web pages is something you might want to do.

The Web is your platform to say, do, or show whatever you want to the millions of people with access to the global Internet. You can talk about yourself, your hobbies, or your business. You can publish a short story or a collection of jokes. You can display pictures of your dog or pictures of your company's latest product. Your own imagination is the only limit to what you can put on the Web.

The World Wide Web is truly a web in the sense of being an endless set of criss-crossing interconnections between an ever-growing number of points. It's a community in the truest sense of the word.

In short, the Web brings people together. And you can participate in bringing people together by creating your own site on the Web. No matter what you're interested in, if you design a good Web page about it and publicize it well, lots of people with similar interests will visit. You may be the only person in your town who thinks O.J. is innocent, and 99.9 percent of the people on the Internet may disagree. Normally, in that situation, you would wind up a troubled loner. But one-tenth of one percent of the people on the Internet still means tens of thousands of people who can get to your Web page with a click of a mouse. You don't need special permission or special qualifications, and you don't need millions of dollars of venture capital and special equipment to spread your message to the far corners of the Earth. All you need is a bit of knowledge about how the Web works and how to design Web pages.

The Web has grown tremendously in recent years, but there's still as much space for new Web pages as there are people with Internet access. No one else has quite the same interests, ideas, and talents as you do, and, therefore, no one else will create the same Web page as you. As you move into the world of Web publishing, you'll find that, just like you, thousands and thousands of people are learning how to create Web pages, and they're often happy to share ideas and experiences. The most important thing is to take the plunge and get started.

Good luck, and have fun!

— *Kevin Werbach*

(Kevin Werbach works in Washington, D.C., at the Federal Communications Commission, Common Carrier Bureau, as an attorney in the Policy Division. He has written orders on issues ranging from the regulation of 800 services to the provision of enhanced services, such as voice mail. He is the author of The Bare Bones Guide to HTML, *a popular Web site that is a resource for Web authoring. For more about* The Bare Bones Guide to HTML, *see Appendix C.)*

Introduction

*I*t may be hard to remember, or it may seem like only yesterday, but just 30 years ago, the personal computer was introduced. The rise and rise *and rise* of the personal computer — with maybe an occasional stumble but never a real fall — seemed certain to be the most important social and technological event leading into the new millennium. From Wozniak and Jobs's Apple II to Bill Gates's Windows 95, it may have seemed as though nothing could ever be bigger, or more life-changing and important.

But, people do talk. In fact, talking is one of the main things that people are all about, and in the beginning, the personal computer didn't let you do that. However, first with modems, and then with networks, and finally through their combination and culmination in the Internet, personal computers became the tools that opened up a new medium of communication. The most visible, graphical, and fastest-growing part of the Internet is the World Wide Web. Now communication, not computation, is the story. Computers are still important but mostly as the means to an end; the end result is further enabling people to interact.

If the most exciting channel of communication is the Web, the means of communication is the Web page. Ordinary people have demonstrated amazing energy and imagination in creating and publishing diverse Web home pages. And although ordinary people have a *desire* to create Web pages, businesses have a *need* to set up shop on the Web. So the rush to the Web is on, often with the same people expressing themselves personally on one Web page and commercially on another.

So you want to be there, too. "But," you ask, "isn't it difficult, expensive, and complicated?" Not any more. As the Web has grown, easy ways to get on the Web have appeared. And the best of these ways are discussed in the pages of this book.

About This Book

It's *about* 370 pages.

Seriously, what will you find here? Almost every easy way to get published on the Web that we could find or think of. Plus the information you need to go beyond your first Web page and create a multipage personal or business Web site. And tools — described in the book, or provided as demos or in full versions on the CD-ROM — to help you go as far as you want to go in creating a Web site.

Foolish Assumptions

Lots of good information is in this book, but no one is going to read all of it — except our long-suffering editors. That's because we cover Web page topics from beginning through intermediate levels, including how to publish a Web page via Web-based services and the major online services, how to use half a dozen different tools, and some Mac-specific and Windows-specific stuff. No one needs all of that!

But what *do* you need? We assume, for purposes of this book, that you have probably used the Web before and that you want to create a Web page. We further assume that you are not yet a Web author or are fairly new to the process. To use the information in this book, you need access to a personal computer running MacOS, Windows 3.1, or Windows 95, and you need access to the Web — either through an online service or a direct Internet Service Provider (ISP). You should be running a Web browser such as Netscape Navigator, Microsoft Internet Explorer, or a browser provided by an online service. If you have a UNIX system and an Internet connection, much of this book will work for you, but you won't have access to any of the online service or Web page creation tools described in this book.

If you don't have Web access from your personal computer, see Appendix B for a list of service providers who will help you get it. You should have already spent some time surfing the Web, or be willing to do so as you gather information and examples for your Web page. In other words, if you're wired, or willing to get wired, you're in. With that, the door to this book is open to you, whether you want to create your first Web page or add new features to one you already have.

The figures in this book show Macintosh and Windows 95 screen shots. The instructions and steps in this book are written to work equally well for the Macintosh, Windows 3.1, and Windows 95.

Jump around in the book and go straight to information you need. Later, you can back up and read something that interests you, page through the tools sections, try using one of the tools on the CD-ROM, and then go look at something on the *Creating Web Pages For Dummies* home page (created by one of the authors) at the following address:

www.netsurf.com/cwpfd

CD (-ROM) for Me, See?

The CD-ROM that comes with this book is a rich source of software for creating World Wide Web pages. You can find plenty of software for either Macintosh or Windows. For details about what's on the CD-ROM, see Appendix E. For details about how to use specific programs, see the chapters and sections of this book. For information on how to install the software on the CD-ROM, see the instructions in Appendix E.

Conventions Used in This Book

When our publisher first told us that this book was going to have *conventions*, we got out our silly hats and our Republican and Democratic paraphernalia, but it turns out that she meant that we had to be consistent. The conventions in this book are standard ways of communicating specific types of information, such as instructions and steps. (One example of a convention is the use of italics for newly introduced words, as with the word "conventions" in the first sentence of this paragraph.)

Here are the conventions for this book:

- Things that you, the reader, are asked to type are shown in **bold.**

- New terms are printed in *italics*.

- Information used in specific ways is formatted in a specific typeface. In this book, one of the most common kinds of information displayed this way is HTML *tags;* that is, formatting information used to create Web pages (see Appendix A for a more complete definition). An example of a tag is `<TITLE>`.

  We also use a special typeface for *URLs* (Uniform Resource Locators), which are the addresses used to specify the location of Web pages. For example, the URL for IDG Books' Dummies Press is as follows:

  `www.dummies.com`

- The Web is fast-paced and evolving. Some of the URLs listed throughout this book may have changed, may have become inaccessible, or are not supported through your local Internet Service Provider.

- Related, brief pieces of information are displayed in bulleted lists, such as the bulleted list that you're reading right now.

- Numbered lists are used for instructions that must be followed in a particular sequence. This book has many sequential steps that tell you just how to perform the different tasks that, when taken together, can make you a successful Web author.

To make the steps brief and easy to follow, we use a specific way of telling you what to do. We don't use a lot of formatting because of the need to provide instructions that work equally well on the Macintosh, Windows 3.1, and Windows 95. Here's an example of a set of steps:

1. **Start your Web browser.**

2. **Go to the Web site**

   `www.freestuff.com/`

   Note: This is not a real site, just an example.

3. **Click the link that matches the type of computer you have: Macintosh, PC, or UNIX.**

In the chapters in Part III and Part IV that cover specific Web authoring tools, we provide general steps for tasks, such as formatting a word or phrase, followed by the details that show how to create a specific example illustrated in that chapter's figures. In this way, you have access to both general procedures and specific examples.

Part-y Time: How this Book Is Organized

This book was written to a carefully plotted, precise, *unvarying* plan, with the predictable and predicted result: the book you're holding in your hands now. And the CD-ROM? Same thing.

Wait a second. Isn't it true that the Web is changing every day, that Web sites appear and disappear like so many jacks-in-the-box or whack-a-moles, if that's a more familiar example to you, and that Web companies go from opening their doors to public stock offerings — and sometimes back — in weeks? So — what was that about a plan?

Well, okay, we did change things a little along the way. Maybe a lot. But there *is* a plan behind the book, even if it was finalized in a conference call at 5:00 this morning. The following sections explain the parts that make up the book.

Part I: Get Started with Web Publishing

Those of you who, like us, are comforted by the idea that you have a plan will like Part I. Go to this part to understand the ideas and buzzwords behind the Web. Then learn how to plan your Web site and how HTML, the underlying language behind Web pages, shapes what you can create on the Web.

Part II: A Home Page in a Day

In Part II, you'll surprise yourself; you'll move very quickly from wondering how you are ever going to create a Web page to having one up and working. Use Part II to create your first Web page in a few hours — directly on the Web using the free Web publishing service provided by GeoCities or with free tools from America Online or CompuServe. The cost: free for the Web-based services, or included in the usual cost of your online service. The reward: You'll be telling friends your Web address tomorrow!

Part III: Better, Stronger, Faster Sites

Most businesses today need a presence on the Web; but how do you create a site that's attractive and informative without spending too much time or money? This part shows you how to build and publish a basic business Web site quickly and easily. Then you add graphics and multimedia and publish your full-featured Web site. This part shows how to get to the next level of coolness with simple but powerful additions to your Web pages.

Part IV: Web Publishing Tools

If you're creating and maintaining a multipage Web site and you really want the most creative capabilities with the least exposure to HTML, you should consider one of the Web publishing tools that are transforming Web page authoring. Part IV introduces the cream of the crop of full-featured, easy-to-use, Web authoring tools.

Part V: The Part of Tens

A Top Ten list is a great way to make complex information fun and easy to remember. Our Top Ten lists show you some DO's and DON'Ts of Web publishing.

Part VI: Appendixes

Appendixes in books are usually like appendixes in people: funny little things that get taken out of the patient in a hurry if they act up. But for this book, we packed in great information that can really help you. In Appendix A, a complete glossary defines the Web and Web publishing terms that may be confusing to you. You see information about Web service providers and Web page developer resources. Best of all, we secured permission to use a great Web resource, *The Bare Bones Guide to HTML,* as the starting point for rearranged tables that show just what parts of HTML you can use to create different kinds of Web pages.

Icons Used in This Book

 Tells what is on the accompanying CD-ROM.

 Marks information that you need to keep in mind as you work.

 Points to things you may want to know but don't necessarily need to know. You can skip these and read the text, skip the text and read these, or both.

 Flags specific information that may not fit in a step or description but will help you create better Web pages.

 Tells you things to go try yourself.

 Warns you of effects that take a long time to appear.

 Points out things that may cause problems.

Part I
Get Started with Web Publishing

In this part . . .

This part orients you to the key ideas behind the Web and Web publishing. It also gives you the basics about HTML (HyperText Markup Language), the specification from which Web pages are built.

Chapter 1

Web Publishing Basics

The Internet and the Web have such a high profile that almost everyone knows what they are. But to do a proper job of publishing on the Web, you need to know more than the casual Net surfer. In this chapter, we map out the territory that you, as a Web publisher, are about to enter. You can start Web publishing without most of the information in this chapter simply by following the steps we provide in this book. However, knowing the basics makes it easier to go beyond the steps and create a Web page that really does what you need it to do.

If you can't wait to get started with Web publishing, go straight to the end of this chapter for the seven secret steps to publishing on the Web.

The Internet Begets the Web

Many people think that the Web seems to have busted out of its host, the Internet, and taken over. The fact is, however, that the rest of the Internet is alive and well. To understand the Web, you need at least a basic understanding of the Internet.

What the heck is the Internet?

The *Internet* is a giant computer network that connects other computer networks. More and more of the world's computer networks are being connected to it. Think of the Internet as a giant octopus with a million tentacles. Each tentacle is grasping another, smaller octopus — that is, the networks that are connected by the Internet. And many of the smaller octopuses are grasping even smaller ones because many university and company networks have several levels of connections within them as well.

The Internet hosts several different services; the one used by the most people is *e-mail*. Just a few years ago, you couldn't send e-mail to someone unless both you and the recipient were on the same online service. But with the Internet, you can send a message to anyone on any online service or on any other network connected to the Internet.

In addition to e-mail, some other popular Internet services are FTP and Gopher. *FTP* is not a misspelling of the name of a flower delivery service; it stands for *File Transfer Protocol,* which is a method for transferring files from one computer to another. You use FTP for a few of the procedures in this book. *Gopher* is a steward on *The Love Boat,* an old TV show — whoops, sorry, wrong book. Gopher is another relatively well-known Internet service and is sort of a precursor to the Web. It allows text searches, like the Web, but does not have built-in support for graphics. We don't use Gopher in this book.

The Internet accesses different resources that are stored in different kinds of services by using a special kind of address called a *URL (Uniform Resource Locator* — which sounds like something the Armed Forces invented to track down clothes). The address that you type to get to a Web page is a URL. For example, www.geocities.com/Yosemite/Rapids/7538 is the URL for Bud's home page. The URL is made up of the three following parts, which are shown in Figure 1-1:

Figure 1-1:
URLy to
Web, URLy
to rise.

The *protocol* is the name of the communications language that the URL uses: HTTP (HyperText Transfer Protocol, used on the Web), FTP, Gopher, and so on.

The *domain name* is the logical name of the server that the file is on.

The *pathname* tells how to find the file to be retrieved.

What the heck is the World Wide Web?

The *World Wide Web,* now approaching its first decade of use, is the newest of the widely popular services on the Internet. The Web combines text, graphics, multimedia, and links between files to create a giant "web" of easily accessible information.

How to picture the Web? Imagine that a single copy of every magazine in the world was laid on the floor of a huge building. Imagine that pieces of string connected specific locations in each magazine to relevant information in other magazines. The result would be a giant web of text and graphics. That's pretty much what the Web is like. People who can move smoothly through that web — that is, through the Web — are empowered. People who can add their own information to the Web and tie the information to other related material are *very* empowered. The purpose of this book is to help you become very empowered.

The Web has several key features that make it popular. Each document on the Web, a *Web page,* is based on a text file. Just as e-mail is made up of text files, so are the basic underpinnings of the Web. This makes it easy to create, edit, and transmit Web pages. But the Web is flexible; you can include a graphics or multimedia file in a Web page by linking it to the underlying text file. You can also link the page to other Web pages.

The Web is the most popular and fastest-growing service on the Internet. Why? Because the Web is graphical and easy to use and because it has so much great stuff on it. And why does it have so much great stuff on it? Because publishing on the Web is surprisingly easy, as we show you throughout this book.

Webs that exist "behind the firewall"

These days, people are doing more and more Internet and Web work out of public view, "behind the firewall" within a company or other organization. The term *firewall* brings up an image of a thick, impregnable barrier protecting part of a building. But in computing, a firewall is just a combination of hardware and software that work together to prevent outsiders from entering a private network that is connected to the Internet.

A private web, or intranet, is an effective and useful way to make information available to people who need it. The best of the private webs work just like the World Wide Web, only they are smaller. Firewalls protect private webs and other proprietary information on a company network from most of the outside world, and on balance do a decent job.

Getting Webbed

This book talks a lot about the Web but doesn't discuss how to get on it. And even if you're on the Web already, perhaps through a connection at work, you may also want to get on the Web from home. How do you do that?

The quickest and easiest way to get on the Web is to join one of the big online services and use their Web software (for information about getting on the Web through an online service, see Chapter 5). America Online (AOL) and CompuServe (now owned by AOL) both offer Web access and Web publishing services. Microsoft Network has Web access and is promising Web publishing services soon. All three services have phone support people to help you get connected and thousands of users in online forums who are eager to help you learn the Web.

Although firewalls help protect against unwanted tampering, no protection system is foolproof. If you ask a resourceful and proficient hacker (a person who — malevolently or not — tinkers with others' computer systems) whether a firewall provides as much protection as its name implies, stand back and hope that he doesn't hurt himself laughing.

The techniques in this book work for publishing on a private web as well as on the World Wide Web. Just find out from the local Webmaster (the person in charge of your private web) about the policies and procedures for publishing on the private web, and then go for it!

I link, therefore I am

The most exciting features of the Web are based on *linking* — that is, clicking a specific spot on a Web page to see a graphic, hear a sound file, or jump to another page. For example, from a Web page on the United Nations, you can view images of flags from countries around the world, hear people say "hello" in their various languages, or jump to additional information on related topics, such as other international organizations or worldwide news.

How does this magic work? A Web page is stored on a special kind of computer called a *Web server* (which is not to be confused with a *Web surfer,* the name for someone who uses the Web — though both surfers and servers can wipe out spectacularly!). A Web server is a computer that is connected to the Internet and can answer requests made in a particular communications language, or *protocol,* called HTTP.

When you use the Web, your machine is acting as a *Web client,* a machine that downloads information from the Web. When you access a Web page, your machine fires off a request over the Internet for a Web file specified by a URL. Your machine connects to the machine that has the Web file. (So every time you get another file from the Web, even a little bitty graphic, the process is called a *connection.*) The Web finds the file and downloads it over the Internet to your machine. Your *Web browser* (the program used to look at World Wide Web documents) then displays the file. This request/receive cycle, shown in Figure 1-2, is repeated every time you surf the Web.

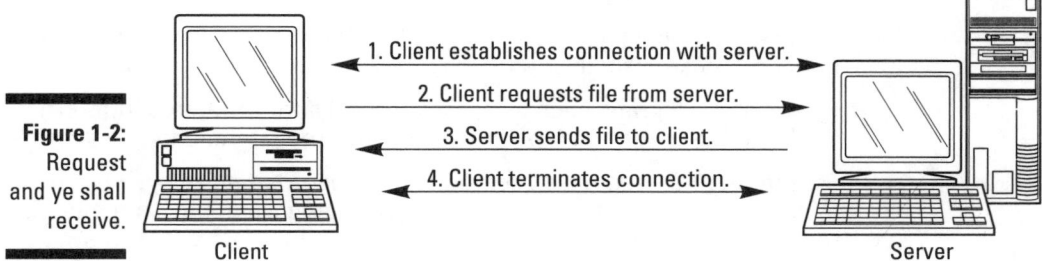

Figure 1-2:
Request
and ye shall
receive.

1. Client establishes connection with server.
2. Client requests file from server.
3. Server sends file to client.
4. Client terminates connection.

Client   Server

Access several Web sites and watch the process of downloading the text and graphics in each site. Each file downloads separately; you can watch as each graphic or multimedia file appears in turn.

Being a Player on the Stage of the World Wide Web

As a World Wide Web user, you're part of the audience for a constantly changing drama. After you put your own page on the World Wide Web, you're actually one of the players in the drama. To play your part correctly, you need to know a bit about the *dramatis personae* that make the Web work.

Getting to know the cast of characters

GIFs and JPEGs and Web sites, oh my!

The Web is so new that people can't even completely agree on how to define it. So in the list below, we define a few basic terms that you need to understand to become a Web publisher. In the process of reading the definitions, you find out a little more about how the Web works. Although people don't yet completely agree on how to talk about the Web, most accept the following definitions:

- ✔ **Web page.** A text document on the Web that includes formatting information and pointers to graphics files, multimedia files, and other Web pages. Some of the graphics and multimedia files are displayed immediately when the Web page is downloaded; other files are displayed by clicking a link to download them.

- ✔ **Home page.** A Web page that you intend users to come directly to.

- ✔ **Web site.** A home page plus, optionally, additional pages. These additional pages are usually intended to be accessed from the home page.

- ✔ **Browser.** A program, such as Netscape Navigator or Microsoft Internet Explorer, that's used to look at World Wide Web documents.

- ✔ **Search engine.** Web-based services that help you find things you're looking for. (The Web is so popular that finding what you want among the millions of Web pages online is a huge problem.) The authors' favorite search engines include Yahoo!, which has a hierarchical listing of many Web sites, and OpenText, which has a Power Search option that lets you search for text in URLs. You can find these search engines at the following URLs:

  `www.yahoo.com`

  `index.opentext.net`

- ✔ **Inline image.** A graphic that's displayed as part of a Web page.

- ✔ **Downloadable image.** A graphic that's displayed only when the user clicks a link (defined in the following section) to download and display it. Figure 1-3 shows the home page of Vigra, a San Diego-based division of VisiCom Laboratories. It has both an inline image — the photograph — and downloadable images, which are available by clicking the underlined terms GIF or JPEG.

- ✔ **GIFs and JPEGs.** Two common types of graphic files on the Web. GIF files — known as *GIFs,* pronounced like "jiffs" by some, and sound like *gifts* by others — are more common and easier to create. JPEG files, known simply as *JPEGs* (jay-pegs), are more compressed and can produce the same size image while taking up less disk space than GIFs. All currently available browsers that support graphics support GIFs and JPEGs as inline images that you can view embedded in the Web page.

If everything in the preceding list just seems like a bunch of words, stop reading and surf around the Web a little bit; look for examples of the terms used in the list. They are easy to find! You can even look up the terms with the Yahoo! search engine by using this URL:

`www.yahoo.com`

Inline image   Downloadable images

Figure 1-3:
Image-ining
a home
page of
your own.

Examining the HTML script

We keep saying that a Web page is a text document that almost always
includes formatting information and links to other files. But how is that
special formatting and linking information stored in the text document? It's
stored in special strings of text called *tags*. The format of these tags and
what each tag means are determined by a specification called *HTML,* or
HyperText Markup Language. You'll find that having a basic understanding of
how HTML works is worthwhile before creating your own Web page,
whether you use a Web page creation tool that hides HTML from you most of
the time, or whether you work directly in HTML, typing in the tags yourself.

If you want to see an example of HTML code for a simple Web page —
including formatting, an inline image, and a link — see the Cheat Sheet at the
front of this book.

Take a closer look at the term for which HTML is an acronym, HyperText
Markup Language. You may already know that hypertext is text that has links
in it. A *link* is just a connection to another document. So far, so good. But
what's a *markup language?* (It's not that confusing language that car dealers
speak when they decide how high to jack up the price!) A markup language
is simply a way to put information about a document — for example,

information about hypertext links and formatting — in the document itself. Markup languages often use tags — labels placed within text that give display instructions. So Hypertext Markup Language — HTML — is a specific way of using tags to convey information about a document.

Most tags come in pairs: One starts a change; the other ends it. In the following example sentence, the first tag, `<B>`, means start displaying text in a **bold** typeface; the second tag, `</B>`, means stop using bold.

Here's how the sentence looks when "marked up" with HTML tags:

```
That's a <B>bad</B> idea.
```

Here's how the sentence looks when displayed on-screen:

```
That's a bad idea.
```

The browser reads the original, text-only sentence — `That's a <B>bad</B> idea.` — and says to itself, "I'll display `That's a`, turn bold on, display `bad`, turn bold off, and display `idea`." The person who created the original sentence puts in the HTML tags, the browser interprets them, and the user only sees the effect — in this case, the word *bad* displayed in boldface type.

The idea of a machine or procedure that reads a piece of input, uses that input to make a decision, carries out the decision, and then reads some more input is centuries old and thoroughly studied. Such a machine or program — a browser, for example — is called a *finite automaton*. (Pronounced to rhyme with "flynight ought-omaton.") Try dropping that term into your conversation the next time the Web comes up!

The `<B>` and `</B>` tags are *formatting tags* that describe how a browser should display text. The other kind of tag in HTML is the linking tag. *Linking tags* specify outside information to be brought into a document. Here's some complicated-looking HTML text that shows an example of linking tags:

```
To learn about <I>avatars</I>, online representations of
people, go to the Web site for <A HREF="http://
www.communities.com">Electric Communities</A>.
```

The text appears on-screen as follows:

```
To learn about avatars, online representations of people,
go to the Web site for Electric Communities.
```

The `<I>` and `</I>` tags specify that the word `avatars` is to be displayed in italics. The `<A>` and `</A>` tags specify that `Electric Communities` is displayed as an *anchor* — that is, the start of a link. On most browsers, as here, anchors are underlined. So what does the extra text — `HREF="http://www.communities.com"` — inside the `<A>` tag mean? HREF is short for *Hypertext*

REFerence. If you click the anchor, your browser looks for the URL that serves as the hypertext reference, which in this case is the Electric Communities Web page address that appears after the equals sign.

Other tags work the same way: They tell the browser either how to format text or where to look for more information. We go into further excruciating detail about what the most commonly used tags do in Chapter 3.

Building the set with image maps and forms

Two of the most important elements that affect what you can do with the Web are image maps and forms.

An *image map,* or *clickable image map,* is a graphic that has hot spots built into it. A *hot spot* is an area inside a graphic that acts as a link to another URL, the same way that the underlined text in a Web page acts as a link. These hot spots do different things when you click them. Clicking a hot spot usually invokes a URL, which causes the user to go to a different page. Used this way, an image map can serve as a map or guide to different parts of the Web. The Apple home page, shown in Figure 1-4, is an example of this kind of clickable image map. To paraphrase Buckaroo Banzai: Wherever you click, there you are.

Advances in HTML

Since the Web first became widely (and wildly) popular in the mid-1990s, several advances in HTML have taken place. These advances build on the solid base of the original HTML specification and add new capabilities. However, they also make HTML much more complicated and add many more issues for those designing Web pages.

The biggest changes are the addition of tables, frames, and Dynamic HTML. *Tables* not only display information in table form, but also are used to help precisely position text and graphics. Tables are widely used. *Frames* allow a Web page to be divided up into independently controlled sections. They are somewhat widely used, but not as popular as tables.

And *Dynamic HTML* is a new addition to the original HTML specification that allows moving elements to be included in a Web page, among other changes. It's not widely used yet.

What all these features have in common is that they add a great deal of complexity to your Web pages if you use them, and they aren't usable by all the Web browsers out there. (Tables come close to this ideal.) We describe how and when to use these advanced features in Chapter 6 (tables and frames) and Chapter 7 (Dynamic HTML). However, you can go far with the original HTML specification that is usable by all browsers, and we stick with that version for most of this book.

Figure 1-4:
An Apple
with hot
spots —
including
the three
square
images and
the "Apple
Store"
rectangle at
the bottom
of the page.

Image maps are hard to create, and users who turn off graphics in their browsers while surfing the Web can't see them. But image maps are very attractive and easy to use. Chapter 7 describes how to create a simple image map.

A *form* is just what the name implies: a place where a user can enter data, such as name, address, and telephone number. Figure 1-5 shows a form used by the Monster job search database from TMP Worldwide. On the part of the form shown in the figure, you enter data by clicking your choice from a scrolling list.

Seeing HTML

When Tim Berners-Lee invented HTML at CERN (the European particle physics research facility) a few years ago, he probably never imagined that so many people would be interested in seeing it. Today, most browsers include a command that enables you to see the actual HTML source that makes the page look and work the way it does (see the figure in this sidebar for an example).

For example, in Netscape Navigator, you can open the View menu and then choose the Page Source option. Netscape displays the underlying HTML file. You see all the HTML tags that make the Web page look and act the way it does.

You can also save the page to your hard disk, and then open it in a word processor and view the HTML tags. You can even edit the text and the HTML tags, save the file, and then open the file again in your browser to see how it looks with the HTML changes. In Netscape Navigator, open the File menu and then choose the Open File option.

Editing a Web page that you've saved on your hard disk doesn't change the page stored on the Web; only the local copy stored on your hard disk changes.

```
                            (untitled)

<HEAD>
<TITLE>Version 2.0b1-95279</TITLE>
</HEAD>
<BODY BGCOLOR="#C0C0C0" TEXT="#000000"
LINK="#0000EE" VLINK="#551A8B" ALINK="#FF0000">
<TABLE CELLPADDING=3 WIDTH="100%">
<TR>
 <TD ALIGN=CENTER><A HREF="about:authors"><IMG ISMAP SRC="about:logo" ALT=""
border=0></A></TD>
<TD>
 <CENTER>
 <B><FONT size=5>Netscape Navigator
   <SUP><FONT SIZE="-1">(TM)</FONT></SUP></FONT><BR>
 <FONT size=4>Version 2.0b1</BR></FONT></B>
 Copyright &copy 1994-1995 Netscape Communications Corporation,
 All rights reserved.
 </CENTER>
<P>
<FONT size=2>
This software is subject to the license agreement set forth in the
<A HREF="about:license">license</A>. Please read and agree to all
terms before using this software.
<P>
Report any problems through the
<A HREF="http://cgi.netscape.com/cgi-bin/auto_bug.cgi">
```

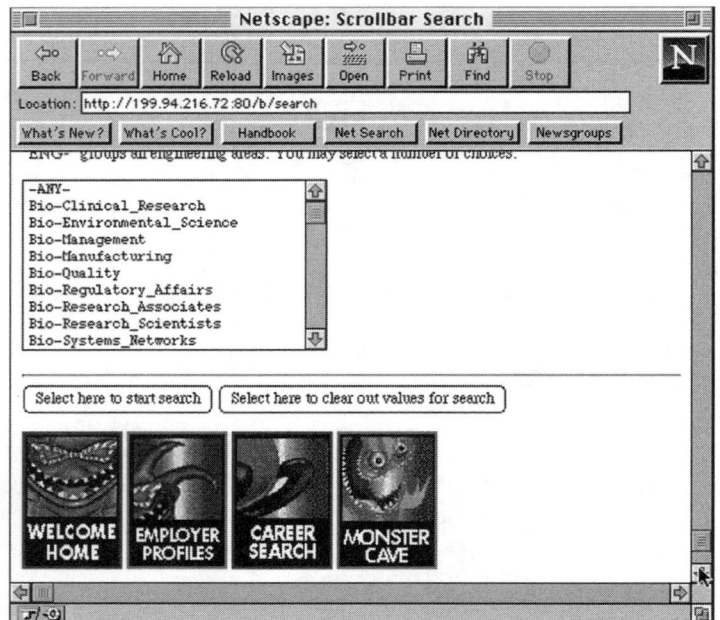

Figure 1-5:
A Web
page form.

The form has elements for entering data and for choosing from a list of predetermined options. Although forms are easy to set up in a Web page, the Web page doesn't automatically know how to handle the data that is entered in the form. You have to write a computer program or use some other kind of tool to receive the data and store it or otherwise act on it. Because of this difficulty, we mostly ignore forms in this book.

Putting Your Name in Lights on the Web

You already know that the Web is a great and exciting thing, and you want to be part of the excitement by publishing your own Web page. But you might run into a few potholes on the road to fame and fortune on the Web. What does it take to be a Web publisher? You find out in this section.

Stumbling blocks on the Web

For all its great things, the Web has some problems from the point of view of a publisher:

✔ **Differences in browsers.** Different browsers display the same HTML tags differently. And some browsers support newer or nonstandard tags, so pages displayed in them look better — or at least different — than they look on other browsers. This inconsistency can drive you to distraction.

✔ **Faster and slower connections.** Some users have fast network connections to the Web, whereas typical home users dawdle along at 28.8 Kbps — ten times slower than a typical corporate connection. So a graphics-rich page that comes up fast on one machine downloads *very s-l-o-w-l-y* on another.

✔ **Those darn users.** Users have different screen sizes, and they can reconfigure their browsers to use different fonts, different window sizes, and so on. So even users who connect to the Web through the same network and run the same browser can see the same Web page quite differently.

✔ **Getting on a server.** For your Web pages to be on the Web, they have to be on a Web server. This means that you have to find either a volunteer or a vendor with a Web server and some space to spare. Luckily, space for a small Web site is usually either free or cheap, but finding server space and getting your files to the server can be a big hassle.

The first three problems are related to inconsistencies in the Web, and you might have run into them as a user. Now that you're a beginning Web publisher, the answer to all these problems is the same: Keep it simple! In this book, we use simple Web page layouts and stick almost completely to the basic HTML features available in all browsers.

The problem of getting your Web page on the server is a little different — the kind of hurdle that can stop neophytes cold but that experienced users clear with ease. In the next few chapters, we show you enough varied server solutions to meet any needs — and some of them are even free!

Kirk versus Spock in Web publishing

Reading this book is going to make you a Web publisher — anyone who puts up even a single, simple home page is a publisher on the World Wide Web. Congratulations!

You can take two approaches to this role: the spontaneous approach that Captain Kirk — the risk-taking leader of the Starship *Enterprise* — would use, or the careful approach that the more logical Mr. Spock would prefer. The spontaneous Captain Kirk approach can be summarized in the popular Nike slogan "Just Do It." You can get a simple page up on the Web with just a few hours of work, without paying any money.

In contrast to Captain Kirk's quick-and-dirty approach, Mr. Spock's more logical method requires you to do the following:

✔ Set goals for your Web site.

✔ Plan the contents of your site to meet those goals.

✔ Storyboard your site to specify what's on each Web page and how the pages fit together.

✔ Compare your planned site to similar or competing sites and revise your plans accordingly.

✔ Create your site on your own machine first and test it thoroughly.

✔ Carefully choose a Web service provider who will do the best job of hosting your site.

✔ Get your site up on the Web and begin an ongoing cycle of testing and revision.

Whew! That's a lot of Tribble — I mean, a lot of trouble!

Either the spontaneous or the careful approach is just fine, but you should match your approach to what you want to do on the Web. We recommend that you try the spontaneous approach first. Don't put out a great deal of effort, and don't use your initial page to try to start a Web-based business empire. Just create a personal or business home page that says something about you or your organization.

If you don't own or run your organization, make sure that you have the permission you need before putting up a Web page that represents the organization. Otherwise, you could find yourself on an unexpected, rapid transition off your current career path. (The Monster bulletin board mentioned earlier in this chapter is a great help in looking for a new job!)

If that one page is all you ever publish on the Web, fine. A lot of the fun of being on the Web is seeing the Web pages created by individuals who are just trying to have fun and share their interests. But if you go on to create a Web presence for a business or even create a Web-based business of your own, the experience that you get when you "just do it" may prove invaluable. Table 1-1 suggests when to use the careful versus the spontaneous approach to Web publishing.

Table 1-1	The Kirk (Spontaneous) and Spock (Careful) Approaches to Web Publishing				
	Have Fun	*Learn Now for Advanced Work Later*	*Small Business Web Presence*	*Larger Business Web Presence*	*Web-Based Business*
Spontaneous	X	X	X		
Careful			X	X	X

Seven Steps to Successful Web Publishing

Once you understand the different parts that make up the Web, you're ready to become a Web page publisher. Here, we roughly break down the steps to becoming a publisher on the Web:

1. **Create your HTML-tagged text files.**

2. **Create or otherwise obtain graphics files.**

3. **Put links to graphics files and to other Web pages into your HTML files.**

4. **Test your soon-to-be Web site on your own machine.**

5. **Find Web server space.**

6. **Transfer your files to the Web server, thus creating your Web site.**

7. **Check that your new Web site works the way you want it to work.**

Although these steps sound simple, they can become complicated. In fact, some people make a good living handling just parts of each of these steps. The "simple" step of creating your HTML files, for example, includes deciding what you want to say; deciding how you want your page to look; choosing whether to use HTML directly or use an HTML editing tool; learning HTML, the HTML editing tool, or both; and more. The different parts of this process are the reasons for most of the chapters in this book.

Making simple things simple

If all you want to do is create a simple "I exist" Web page, either for yourself or for your business, you shouldn't have to go through the rigmarole of learning HTML or a tool, finding server space, and so on. Part II of this book, made up of Chapters 4 and 5, describes easy ways to get on the Web. Chapter 4 describes free services for putting a simple personal site on the Web. GeoCities, the Web's biggest personal Web page publishing site, not only gets you on the Web quickly, but also includes free server space for personal Web pages. That's right — no need to set up your own Web server or pay for space on someone else's. If you use GeoCities, your Web space is free.

Chapter 5 describes the Web publishing offerings of the major online service publishers. If you're a customer of America Online or CompuServe, you can probably get Web publishing tools and a limited amount of server space for a personal Web page "free" — that is, it's included as part of the fees that you already pay. (The Microsoft Network plans to have this kind of service "real soon now.") If you don't already use an online service, you're probably just as well off to start with the Web-based services described in Chapter 4.

But if you already use an online service, the advantage of Web publishing through your service is that customer service and support — and probably even free critiques of your Web page — are available in the online community you already know how to communicate with.

To see how easy it is to publish on the Web, just turn to Chapter 4 or 5 and get started. You'll be a Web publisher with just an hour or two of effort.

Making difficult things possible

The free services and online services differ in how far they allow you to go without outgrowing the free Web site. If your site gets too large or gets too much traffic, they'll probably ask you to start paying for it. Also, you may want a new site with your own easy-to-find URL, especially if your site represents a business. And if you know from the start that you want to create a relatively large or busy Web site, to go with your real-world business or personal activities or to start something exciting online, you may want to start planning now for something that goes beyond the limited support available for a free Web site.

The rest of Part I describes the basic strategy you can follow to get your first site up on the Web and just enough of the HTML language to help you get there. Part II describes how to create your initial site on a free Web-based service or an online service.

After Part II, this book is all about creating or expanding your Web site so that it's right up there with some of the most interesting and attractive sites on the Web. But we've said it before, and we'll say it again: Even if you want to do something big on the Web, it's well worth getting some hands-on experience by first creating a personal or simple business Web page by using one of the free approaches mentioned in Chapters 4 and 5.

Chapter 2
Your Web Publishing Strategy

Creating an initial Web page is easy, especially if you use the Web page creation services described in Chapters 4 and 5. But creating a *good* Web page or multipage Web site is more work. Doing the extra work is what makes you a real Web publisher — someone who can go beyond saying "I've done that" to knowing that you created a Web page that gets a point across, helps people, and contributes something positive to the Web.

If you're a person who gets all your ducks in a row before proceeding — a Spock, as we said in Chapter 1 — or you are creating a more advanced Web site, read this chapter in its entirety before creating your first Web page. But, if you're more spontaneous — more a Kirk type — or are just in a hurry, we suggest that you go to Chapters 4 and 5 and use the instructions you find there to create your first home page right away. Then come back to this chapter and the next one for the information you need to make your Web page something to be proud of.

This chapter condenses our experience in paper publishing and Web publishing down to a few principles and steps that can make your early Web work a success and lay the foundation for making your site even better in the future. Following these guidelines can help you get your message across more effectively.

Web Page Design Guidelines

A Web page or Web site is basically a publication, though an interactive one. Thinking through a few simple principles now before you start will help make your Web site much more interesting and useful to the people who see it. Or you can revisit this section after you put up your initial Web home page and revise your page to make it even more interesting and useful!

Ask "Why am I doing this?"

We talk soon about the purpose of the Web site itself. But a good question to ask yourself going in is "Why am I doing this?" (As you do more and more work on your site, your answer to this question may come to have some degree of profanity in it.) That is, why are *you* creating the site, and not having someone else create it for you? The answer helps you determine some important things about the site. The following are the most common reasons for creating a Web site:

- ✔ **For work.** More and more people are being asked to create Web sites as part of their jobs; for example, they use Web sites to communicate with people inside or outside their companies. But unless you are going to be a full-time Webmaster, you need to balance the time you spend developing your site with the time you spend on the other demands of your job. Be modest in your initial goals, and plan to learn more about Web publishing so that you can keep your site useful and interesting by building on what you already created. And be sure to keep records of each step in creating and adding to your site so that you — or the person who takes over for you — can refer to them later.

- ✔ **For fun.** Fun sites are good, and they are a lot of what makes the Web worthwhile. But if you create your site for fun, you may find time to work on it only after you spend time on other things, such as work, school, or time with friends and family. So don't be too ambitious in your initial plans, or it may be quite a while before you can get your site done and published.

- ✔ **As a career move.** So you want to be a full-time, or nearly full-time, Webmaster; or you want, in some other way, to make the Internet or Web your career. In this kind of situation, you can afford to plan an ambitious site that uses advanced tools, tracks use, and otherwise gets close to the cutting edge of the Web. Create your initial Web site by using the accessible and broad-based tools and approaches described in this book to gain experience, and then take your page closer to the cutting edge by using more advanced techniques described and taught elsewhere, such as using Java programs as described in *Java For Dummies*, 2nd Edition, by Aaron Walsh (IDG Books Worldwide, Inc.).

Web terms to know

As in Chapter 1, we want to clear up, and also reemphasize, how we use some Web terms that are only vaguely agreed on:

✔ **Web page.** A text document published on a Web server that has HTML tags in it; almost always includes links and often includes graphics. When you click the Forward and Back buttons in your browser, you move chronologically through Web pages you already visited.

✔ **Home page.** The Web page that you try to get people to access. You let people know its URL (address) and try to get others to provide links to it. Your home page is the starting page for your Web site, and it contains links to other pages in your site.

✔ **Web site.** A collection of Web pages that are usually accessed through the site's home page and that share a common theme and purpose. Some Web sites have only a home page; others have many pages and even multiple home pages for people to access.

✔ **Site versus page.** You can use these terms almost interchangeably, as we do in this book. Just remember that a site can have more than one page in it.

✔ **Who knows?** To mimic a line from the film *Risky Business,* sometimes in life you just have to say, "What the heck." You may not have a specific reason for getting on the Web, but that doesn't mean you shouldn't do it. You may figure out a good reason after you have a little Web experience under your belt. Start simple, so you can score an early success in getting a basic Web page up, and then go from there.

Don't spend too much time on design

Designing a Web page is not like designing any other kind of publication because you don't have as much control over the look and feel of Web pages as you do with other types of publications. Modem and network connection speeds, browsers, screen sizes, and the font settings and other settings within a browser vary so much that users can have very different experiences with your Web page.

HTML is often used as a page-layout system, but the goal of HTML is to mark the documents in functional bits. For example, you mark a piece of text as a headline to indicate that it's significant, not to specify exactly how it displays. This is an underlying principle of using HTML. Remember that you use HTML to describe the function of different parts of your document; the HTML tags enable search engines and Web "spider" programs to help users find your Web page. It's up to the Web browser and specific settings that can be changed by the user to determine how your document appears on-screen.

With the latest versions of HTML, it's possible to control more aspects of your Web page's appearance. However, many aspects of these new versions of HTML are not yet standard across different Web browsers. In this book we stick with HTML 2.0, which is less flexible but which works the same way for nearly all Web users.

These seemingly subtle points lead to a single, bottom-line conclusion: Keep your design simple and don't spend too much time on it, initially. Then build it up as you learn more about Web publishing, generally, and more about how people use your page, specifically.

Put your work on the panel

To a writer who is used to creating work that's printed, the Web can seem pretty neat. Unlike a printed page, Web browsers have scroll bars that enable you to create a page that's as long as you want it to be — just like an old-fashioned scroll. But when you design a Web page, more is less. The more you put on a page, the less likely someone will look at all of it.

Instead of thinking of your Web page as an infinitely extensible page, think of it as a series of panels, such as those in a comic strip. Each panel is the size of the browser window on the user's screen. Upon arriving at your Web site, a user sees the initial panel — the top part of your home page. The next thing the user does — scrolling down, clicking a link, or hitting the Back button on the browser — depends entirely on the user's reaction to what is in that initial panel. Similarly, every link destination in your Web site is experienced first as a panel, and the user decides what to do next based on what's in that panel.

The top portion of each Web page is always seen as a panel. But don't forget that if you provide links to a spot within a page, the area around the link destination — the spot you arrive at when you click the link — is experienced as a panel too.

As an example, think of most of the big corporate sites you see. Many have a graphic that fills some or all of the top of the site's home page. Why? To make a good impression in that first panel. Pages that aren't well-designed tend to start with text at the top and just keep going, ignoring the notion that the user, upon seeing all that text, may immediately go somewhere else.

As you design and test your Web site, think of the panels that the user sees and what actions the user may choose to do next. Which choice looks most interesting? What do you want the user to do? What would you do if you were the user? Then have a few friends try your site. Which path do they follow through — or out of — your site and why? If you find the answers to these questions before you publish your site and revise your site accordingly, you're way ahead of most Web publishers.

Surf around some of your favorite Web sites. What brings you back to them? Is the information you want easily accessible? Do you enjoy the site as a whole, or just check one or two things before leaving? Keep your answers in mind when you design your own site.

Put the good stuff first

Imagine the Web as a giant magazine rack and the person surfing the Web as someone scanning the front covers of all those magazines. People who see your Web page decide whether to stay at your site or go elsewhere based largely on what they see when your page first comes up.

Big issues for big sites

This book focuses on the needs of people who are creating a single Web page or a small Web site, and who are doing so on their own. Larger sites, or sites that need to be put up quickly or changed rapidly, need to have additional people working on them.

If you want to create a larger site down the road, start thinking now about what resources may be available to put into it. How many people in your company or other organization work on advertising, public relations, and marketing? How many people question whether those jobs are real work? (Just kidding — the author who's a marketer wrote that!)

You may reasonably suppose that your company may retarget some fraction of its advertising, marketing, and PR funding efforts to support a presence on the Web. And what about sales? As Web-based business transactions take off, some portion of a company's sales effort will be Web-based, necessitating a suitable up-front effort to bring returns down the road.

Or your company may already have suffered from Web burnout. Classic symptoms of Web burnout are massive early investment to create a beautiful site, months of failure to update or maintain the site, followed by finger-pointing about who wasted all that money. The real problem is usually that no one set goals for the site, so no one managed the design and construction of the site with those specific goals in mind. Often, too few financial and human resources are designated for maintenance and improvement of the site. If this has happened in your company, you know the problems that result, so be sure to have clear goals for your own Web efforts.

The most important element in adopting any new technology in business is a successful pilot project. As someone creating a smallish Web site, you're developing important skills and knowledge about the all-important intersection of the needs of your business and the opportunities afforded by the Web. Set specific goals, strive to meet them, and record both the problems you encounter and your successes. You will then be in a good position to justify the investment of further resources as the Web grows in importance for your company.

If your purpose is to provide information or links, put that information first or, at most, one click away. For example, if you create a site that provides information about your company, make it easy for people to get contact information: your company name, address, phone number, and fax number. For a personal site, if part of your purpose is to appear attractive to employers, make it clear what employment field you're in and make your résumé easy to access.

If your purpose is to draw people into your site to entertain them, educate them, or expose them to messages from advertisers — these possibilities are not mutually exclusive — then the first part of the page should make a strong impression and invite the user to go further into your site. This is where creating that clickable image map we talk about in Chapter 1 may prove worthwhile — even though it can take a long time to download. Figure 2-1 shows the Kaua'i Exotix Web page, certainly one that catches your attention. It's at the following URL:

```
planet-hawaii.com/~exotix
```

But, like the Kaua'i Exotix Web page, your home page should also help people who seek a quick "hit" of information; they're more likely to come back later if you don't waste their time during their first quick visit.

Figure 2-1:
Buds for
your buds.

Think twice about download times

Putting lots of graphics in your pages is time-intensive for you because creating or finding good graphics and then placing them takes a great deal of time and effort. It's also time-intensive for those who surf your site. So plan to use spot graphics (small images that download quickly) at first and think twice before creating those large clickable image maps or attractive opening graphics that you find on sites such as Netscape's, Apple's, or SGI's (Silicon Graphics, Inc.).

You may find a good deal of coverage in the computer press, and even in mainstream newspapers and newsmagazines, about ongoing efforts to make faster access available to ordinary users. But for all the talk about ISDN, cable modems, satellite downloads, and other advanced techniques, the only higher-bandwidth solution to reach a significant number of ordinary end users so far is 56K modems, which are somewhat less than twice as fast as the previous modem champs, 33.6 Kbps modems. So ignore the hype — the speed at which the average person accesses the Web is creeping upward slowly, not leaping ahead. (That may change, however, if Digital Subscriber Line technology is standardized and made widely available in the near future.) For now, be conservative in how much data you put in each page, and test the download times of your pages yourself before you publish them.

Know your audience

According to Web researchers, Web users are overwhelmingly English speakers, as either a first or second language, because the great majority of Web content, Web creation tools, and Web browsers are in English. North America is still the "center of gravity" for Web access. A survey from the University of Michigan (available at www.gvu.gatech.edu/user_surveys, courtesy of Georgia Tech Research Corporation and the Graphics, Visualization, and Usability Center of the University of Michigan) gives a lot of useful information on these topics. It indicates that two-thirds or more of the Web audience is male, the average age is just over 30 (few kids are on the Web, and even fewer grandmothers), household incomes are high (more than half are over $50,000 a year), and most of the audience has graduated from college. Several surveys report that only about 10 percent of North Americans surf the Web regularly; the percentage is lower elsewhere.

Why are these people online? The University of Michigan survey indicates that the top reasons people use the Web are for gathering information, work, education, communication, and entertainment. A small but growing number of people shop. Which of these purposes do you intend for your site to meet? How do you appeal to such people? How do you help them find you? The answers to these questions will help you enhance the appeal and usefulness of your site.

Finally, what kind of browsers are your users running? Surveys indicate that about two-thirds of Web users run Netscape Navigator; most of the rest use Microsoft Internet Explorer. Both of these browsers, and most others that make up the remaining user base, support graphics and tables, and most users run their browsers with graphics turned on (which doesn't mean that they appreciate waiting for complex images to load — unless those images are pretty cool!).

For more details about who's online, what they do there, and what it means to you if you're creating a business Web site, see *Marketing Online For Dummies* by Frank Catalano and Bud Smith (IDG Books Worldwide, Inc.).

Use text bites

As we say earlier in this chapter, when preparing a Web site, less is more. Saying something with less text makes it more likely to be read and more likely to be remembered. A *text bite* is like a sound bite. It's a short, clearly written piece of text that makes a single point.

Although you can overuse text bites, they are very important in Web page design. Text bites help you convey as much information as possible in the limited amount of time users spend looking at each Web page. And they help you balance the basic elements of Web page design: text, links, and graphics.

Consider using non-English Web pages

One of the most limiting factors to the spread of the World Wide Web is that it's nearly all in English. This situation is changing; already, some sites, such as the OpenText search engine, offer their services in other languages. But the amount of non-English content is small compared to the size of the Web.

To create Web pages, you need to know enough English to learn and use HTML and Web tools. But what about your audience?

First, find out how many people in your target audience speak a specific language and how many of them have access to the Web. Then consider the cost of translating your content to each language in which you're interested; then compare that cost to the size of the potential audience. Be optimistic; having native-language content really distinguishes your site in each language into which you translate it. At this point in the Web's growth, you're better off having the Web's best list of movies in Farsi (Iran's predominant language) than yet another list of movies in English.

At the least, if you have printed materials already translated into other languages, either put those materials on the Web or publicize them there. Using non-English languages on the Web offers the same kind of ground-floor opportunity that the Web as a whole offered when its popularity started a few years ago.

If you want to put long documents on the Web, consider rewriting them as a series of text bites. If rewriting them isn't a good idea, at least provide short, clearly written blocks of text that present navigational information for your Web site and introductory and summary information for the documents themselves. Put this information at the beginning and end of long documents. Add headers to break up the flow of text and provide pointers to key areas. Without such guidance, users may well give up in frustration without reaching the information they're looking for.

Look at sites you like

With the principles described in the previous section in mind (if you've read them), look at sites you like and at sites whose purposes are similar to your own. What's good about them? What's not? Imitate successful elements and avoid unsuccessful ones — without copying, which would be a violation of copyright laws. As the development of your site progresses, keep checking it against the sites you previously identified and widen your search to get additional ideas — on what not to do as well as on what to do. Very few original ideas are on the Web, and your initial site is likely to contain one or two new ideas at best. The rest of your site will echo things readers have already seen, and you're better off if your site brings to mind other good sites, rather than bad ones. (But be careful. If you start yelling "Bad! Bad site!" at your computer screen and swatting it with a rolled-up newspaper, you may not be allowed around sharp objects much longer.)

Plan for ongoing improvements

As you plan and implement your Web site, you will, no doubt, find yourself creating a "To Do" list of things that you can't fit into the original site but want to add later, when time allows. (Creating this list is great protection against trying to create a supersite right off the bat, getting stuck in the creation process, and never getting to a point where you can actually publish.) This list is the start of a plan for ongoing improvements.

Some things that you put in a Web site need to be kept current. For example, if your business Web page has your company's quarterly results, be ready to update it quickly when the next quarter's results come out. If it has a list of company officers, update it as soon as a change takes place. (Unless you're one of the people changed — then it'll be your successor's problem!)

What about hiring out your Web work?

If you work in a large organization, you or your boss may be considering hiring out all of the Web work for your company. This arrangement would be unfortunate. Although using consultants to help introduce and use new technology is a good idea, having a reasonable amount of expertise in-house is also a good idea. So don't hire out the entire process; have a mix of employees and contractors working on your company's Web site. A good way for you to get the necessary experience to be a useful member of such a team is to create a couple of small Web sites yourself.

Having information that is obviously out of date is one of the best ways to leave a bad impression of you or your company overall and steer visitors away from your Web site.

Beyond this obvious updating, avoid using "Under Construction" signs and otherwise apologizing for things that aren't there yet. Everything on the Web is under construction, which is half the fun of using the Web and creating pages for it in the first place. You get only one chance to make a first impression, and an "Under Construction" sign does not count in your favor.

Be sure to give users a place to see the progress of your Web page and find out about your plans for it. Some sites have a "What's New" page to describe recent additions, and such a page would also be a good point to describe your plans for expansion (but avoid giving specific dates unless you're very sure of them). Be sure to convey excitement about what you already have up and what you're planning to add, not embarrassment about what's missing.

Define and measure success

Before you design and create your Web page, define what you believe will make it a success. For an initial effort, simply having something up on the Web that clearly conveys basic information is probably enough. For follow-up work, get more specific. Are you trying to reach a certain number of people or type of people? Will measuring *hits* — the number of times that people access some piece of your site — be enough, or do you need some other measure of response, such as having people send e-mail or call an 800 number? Do you want the site to be seen as a top, leading site in terms of bell-and-whistle features like fancy graphics and animation — and if so, are you willing to invest the time and money to make this happen? Talk to people who do advertising and marketing in the real world as well as people who work on the Web, and get a sense of what goals they set and how they measure success in meeting their goals.

Types of Web Sites

The Web offers examples of nearly every communications strategy known to humanity, successful or not. But not every example will apply to your situation. For one thing, the resources of different Web publishers vary tremendously. For another, several different types of Web sites are out there, and not every lesson learned in creating or inspecting one type of Web site applies to the others.

The major types of Web pages are personal, topical, business, and entertainment sites. In the next sections we describe some of the specific considerations that apply to each type of Web page and not to the others. Decide in advance what type of Web page you want to create. When you look on the Web for examples of what to emulate and what to avoid, focus mainly on pages that are the type that you want to create; examples from other genres are as likely to be misleading as helpful. Don't be afraid to integrate elements of one type of page into another; just make sure that in doing so you're helping to meet the overall purpose(s) of your Web site, instead of detracting from it.

Personal sites

Personal Web sites can have many goals. Often, your goal is simply to share something about yourself with coworkers, friends, family, and others. Personal Web pages are a great way for people to learn about others with similar interests and for people in one culture to learn about other cultures. A representative example of an initial home page is the personal home page shown in Figure 2-2. (A brand-new home page that already has a counter and is verified with three browsers — pretty cool!) See it at:

`www.geocities.com/Athens/Olympus/5648`

Creating a personal Web site is a great deal of fun and great practice for other work. But personal Web sites are often left without additions or updates after the initial thrill of creating and publishing them fades. Be different — add to your Web site today! To the extent that personal Web sites evolve, creators tend to add more information about a single key interest, in which case the pages may become topical Web sites, or they add more information about professional goals and accomplishments, in which case the pages resemble business Web sites.

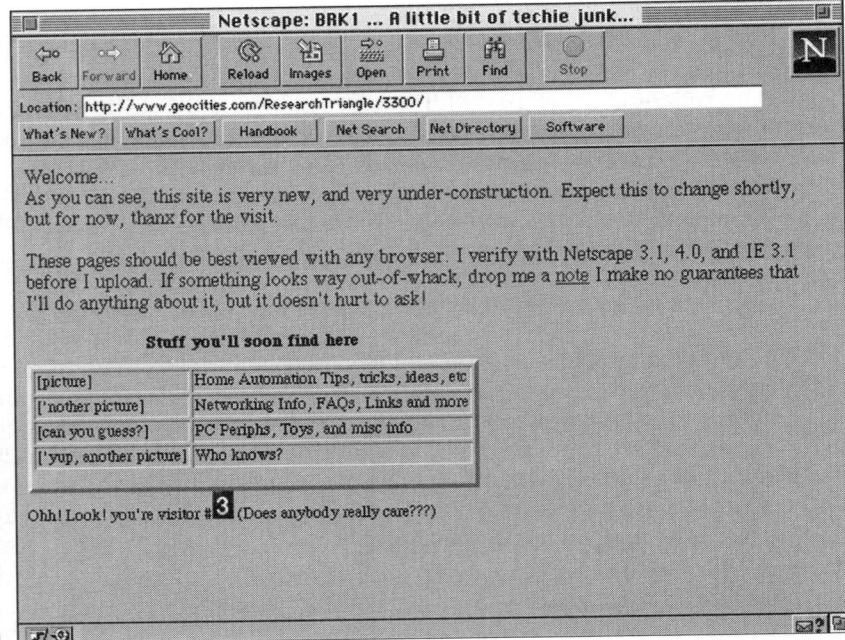

Figure 2-2:
Hurry up
and
become the
next visitor.

Following a few simple rules helps make your personal Web site more fun and less work:

✔ **What's on first?** No, no. What's on second. . . . The first panel, or screenful, of your personal Web site's home page should make the main point of the site clear. If the main point is just "you," the first screenful should have links to Web pages about some of the things about "you" that are in your site. If the point is a topical interest, business interest, or professional self-promotion, you should make that clear, too.

✔ **Keep it simple.** Start with modest goals and get something up on the Web; then create a To Do list of ways in which to extend your site. Consider spinning off commercial and topical pages that reflect your desires and interests, each with its own access point, rather than funneling everything through your personal home page.

✔ **Provide lots of links.** One of the best ways to share your interests is to share information about Web sites that you like, as well as books and other resources. If you develop one or more thorough, carefully up-dated lists of links around a specific interest area, you've created a very valuable resource for others.

✔ **Consider your privacy.** A Web page is just like a billboard — except that 30 million or more people can see it, not just a few thousand. Don't put anything up on your Web page that you wouldn't want on a bill-board. And think twice before putting up information about your kids, especially pictures; there are weirdos in cyberspace, too.

Are personal Web sites still relevant?

Recently, a tremendous amount of interest has developed in Web-based commerce, corporate intranets for internal company communications, and extranets for private communications between organizations. Personal Web sites have somewhat gotten lost in the shuffle as well-funded corporate sites get all the attention. Never fear; personal Web sites are still fun, easy to create, and — did we mention that they're fun?

The GeoCities Web site, which pioneered the free hosting of personal Web pages and is described in detail in Chapter 4, is consistently ranked in the Top 10 most-visited Web sites — an enviable distinction indeed. Personal Web pages on other sites continue to proliferate as well. Part of what's driving the continuing interest in personal Web pages is that more and more people are on the Web. The chances are better than ever that a high percentage of your friends, family, and colleagues can visit and appreciate your site. So don't be put off by the tremendous growth of business on the Web; the personal and fun side is growing, too, it's just getting a little less media attention than the commercial side.

Topical sites

That's "topical," not "tropical." (See the Kaua'i Exotix home page earlier in this chapter for an example of the latter.) A topical home page is a resource on a specific topic. A topic can be an interest or volunteer group to which the author belongs, in which case the page may grow over time into something much like a business Web site. (Creating a Web site for a group is a tremendous contribution, but watch what you may be getting yourself into!) Or it can be about any interest, cause, concern, obsession, or flight of fancy that you have. In this sense, the Web is like an out-of-control vanity press, allowing anyone to go on and on about anything — sometimes offering something of great value, sometimes not.

The best-supported topical interest area on the Web is on Web publishing itself. One such page is the Useless Pages page, shown in Figure 2-3, which started as a pet project of one of the talented employees of Primus Consulting, Inc. (The fun part is to guess which of the Useless Pages were designed badly just to get on the Useless pages list!)

Making a second career out of maintaining and extending a topical Web site is easy, but the pay is usually nil. This is especially true if you create a Web site for an interest or volunteer group that is, of course, delighted to be on the Web — and, by the way, will have just a few little ideas of additional things that they'd like to see you put on the site. Here are some things to consider when you create a topical Web site:

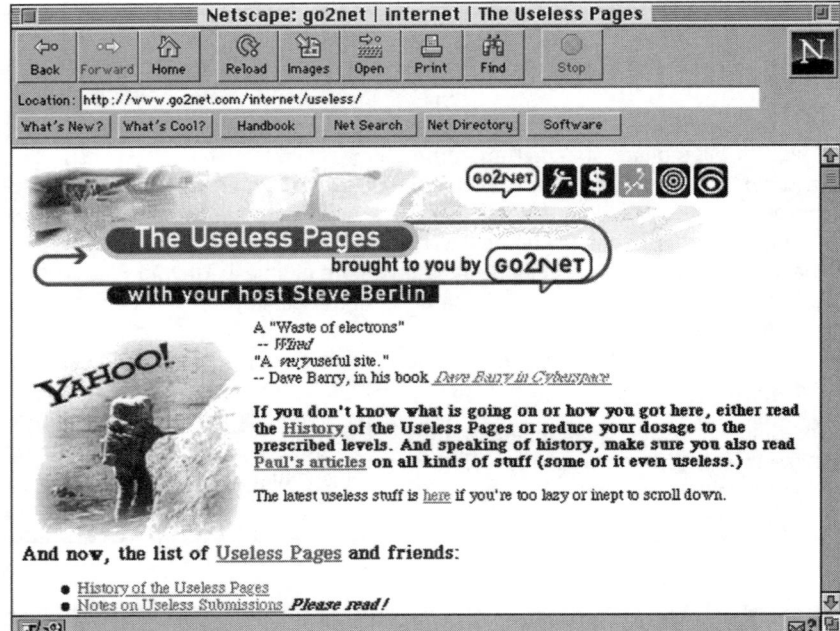

Figure 2-3:
A unique
take on
Web
publishing.

- ✔ **What's on first?** As with a personal Web page, the title of a topical Web page and the first screen need to make unmistakably clear what the topic is. And, to the extent possible, it must describe what resources on the topic the Web site offers.

- ✔ **Keep focused.** A topical Web site loses value if it goes beyond a single topic. How many of the people who share your love for Thai cooking also share your abiding interest in rotifers? (Which are too small to use in most recipes.) If you have two interests that you want to share on the Web, create separate sites.

- ✔ **Create a succession plan.** If your Web site grows beyond your capacity to maintain and extend it properly, find someone to take it over. The first person you should ask about taking over is anyone who's complaining that you're not extending the site fast enough! If your site supports a specific organization, then people in that organization are the logical ones to take it over. Decide what role you can handle and then ask for help in doing the rest.

Commercial sites

Business Web sites, also known as commercial sites, have become the 50,000-pound gorilla of the Web, with a tremendous amount of time, energy, and money being devoted to them. Business Web sites cover a wide range of styles because their goals and the expertise and the resources behind them vary so much. This book provides enough information for you to create a competent "Web presence" site with several pages of contact and company information. But even these kinds of sites vary quite a bit, and you need to be sure that your company's page is well executed. Figure 2-4 shows the Netsurfer home page created by Arthur's business.

Go surf around the Netsurfer site (www.netsurf.com/) to see what a site designed and implemented by one of the authors (Arthur Bebak) looks like.

The first question to ask about a business Web site is "Who can access it?" Some sites are intended for the World Wide Web and everyone on it; others are on the World Wide Web but are password-protected or otherwise restricted in access; still others are on private networks that are inaccessible to outsiders. These inaccessible networks are "behind the firewall," as we explain in Chapter 1. Any Web page that isn't accessible to everyone is considered an internal or private Web page, even if the list of people who can access it includes thousands of people.

Despite the wide variety of business Web sites, following just a few rules can help you create a page that meets your goals:

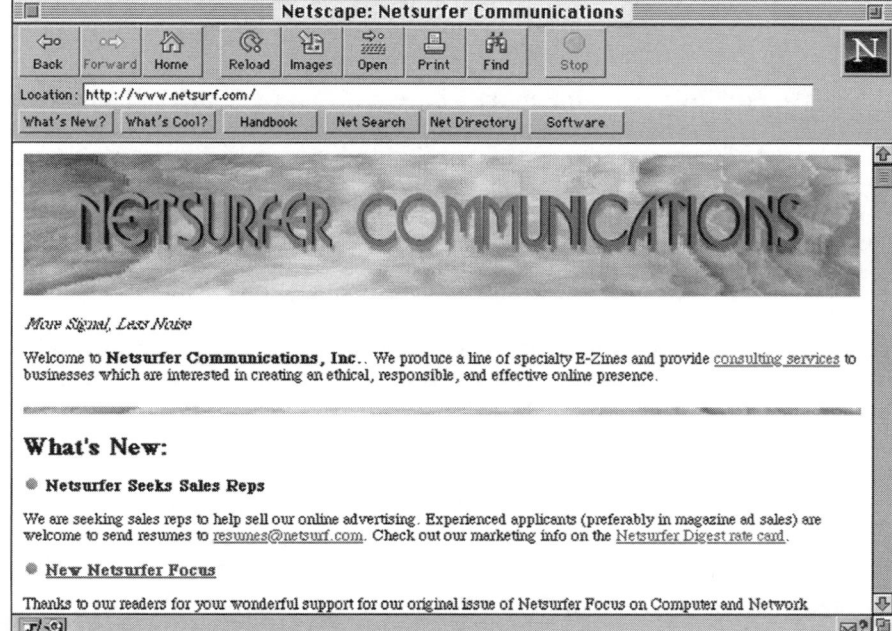

Figure 2-4:
Netsurfer Communications' motto: More signal, less noise.

✔ **What's on first?** Again, a business Web page should make the name and purpose(s) of your business immediately clear. Also, it should provide information on how to contact the business and what resources the site offers.

✔ **Get permission.** Unless you own the business, you should ask for permission before putting a company page on the open Web. If you don't, after you publish, someone may give you a hard time to the point that you wish you'd gotten permission or hadn't published at all. For internal pages on your company's intranet, you may not need permission. Make sure that you have any permissions that you need before you publish your Web page.

✔ **Inside or outside the firewall?** Deciding who gets access is tricky. For example, a small amount of confidential information can make a site more valuable, but the presence of confidential information also prevents you from opening up the entire site to the broader public — including people who may benefit from it. Implementing access decisions can also be difficult. Investigate how to password-protect a site, or ask a network administrator at your company whether you can physically control access. For instance, you may be able to prevent access based on what network the user connects from.

✔ **Find experts.** It's likely that businesses similar to yours — or even coworkers, if you're in a large company — have Web sites that have a purpose similar to yours. Look to the creators of those sites for guidance and inspiration.

✔ **Pursue uniqueness.** Who wants to be a clone? Find specific ways to make your site different from — and better than — others, without compromising broad usability. People who do this well are the ones you see getting "Cool Site of the Day" and similar tokens of recognition from other Web users.

✔ **Monitor usage.** Investing time, energy, and money in a business Web site requires a trade-off among the Web site and other things that resources could go to. One of the crucial questions you may be asked in order to justify maintenance or expansion of a Web site is how much the site is being used. Investigate ways to measure the use of your site. A basic hit counter, as described in Chapter 14, is a good way to start.

✔ **Seek out additional resources.** This book is focused on hands-on creation of simple personal and business Web sites. For a larger business site, you need access to additional information to help you with the planning, hosting, and maintenance of the site. Consider purchasing *HTML 4 For Dummies,* by Ed Tittel and Stephen N. James, for more information on the HTML specification, and *Marketing Online For Dummies,* by Frank Catalano and Bud Smith (both from IDG Books Worldwide, Inc.), for more information on planning and creating a business Web site with a marketing bent.

Entertainment sites

Being entertained is one of the top three reasons that people use the Web, and the number of such sites is growing. Humorous pages and services such as multiuser dungeons (MUDs) and shared games on online services are now expanding onto the Web. Figure 2-5 shows an interesting entertainment site from Service Tech, Inc., at the following URL:

```
www.angband.com/towers/core.html
```

A MUD is an agreed-on environment in which users interact. It can be anything from a medieval adventure to a shared experiment in running a fictitious country. So if someone tells you he spent the morning "wandering around in the MUD," you may have to look at his shoes to determine which kind of mud (or MUD) he means.

Entertainment sites are usually for more than "just" entertainment. For one thing, many include advertising or intend to at some point down the road. Ad sales and advertising support for sites are among the trickiest issues on the Web, because until a couple of years ago the Internet was a noncommercial environment. Educational elements are often included in the entertainment

Figure 2-5:
A site for
sore eyes.

mix, covertly or overtly. These complicating factors and the high expectations that people have of entertainment sites can make these sites some of the most demanding ones to create. Here are a few suggestions for creating entertainment sites:

✔ **Don't start here.** Don't try to learn Web authoring by creating an entertainment site. It's a very demanding task. Try another type first and edge your way into entertainment.

✔ **Keep it fresh.** How funny is a joke the second time you hear it? You have to either rapidly update the content or allow participants to provide the content through their interaction with one another — neither option is easy.

✔ **Push the technology.** Interactivity is also key to entertainment, and that means going beyond HTML and static graphics. You need to learn and use at least one advanced Web technology to make a fresh and interesting entertainment Web site.

✔ **Let the technology push you.** The technology can give you ideas that are in themselves pretty funny. Try using Java to create a Three Stooges-type animated routine, or use VRML (Virtual Reality Markup Language) to create a virtual reality environment that includes funhouse mirrors. (Both Java and VRML are described in Chapter 8.)

Is your page cybersmut?

For most Web page publishers, the best policy as far as putting anything potentially offensive in your Web pages is to keep your site clean. The use of gratuitous sex and violence in your Web pages will simply put off many people and put the Web site itself in a bad light.

But what if the sex or violence is not gratuitous and is actually central to your point? Then send the authors your URL so that we can see it for ourselves — but be sure to make the first page a home page that warns readers that they may find your content offensive and lets them gracefully opt out before they view whatever you show.

Even that enlightened approach may not be enough, however. Some Web server owners will drop your page if it violates their rules, and several countries have laws that may directly or indirectly specify what can and can't be on a Web page. Be sure to find out about the rules and laws that apply to you before you put anything questionable on your Web page.

The ...For Dummies Way to Web Publishing

Getting an initial Web page up on the Web is easy, but making a good, useful Web site is more work. For anything beyond an initial home page, we highly suggest the following decision-making process:

- ✔ Determine the purpose of your site.
- ✔ Decide the structure of your site.
- ✔ Decide the layout of your pages.
- ✔ Decide what links to use between pages in your site.
- ✔ Decide what links to external Web sites to include.
- ✔ Create the text for your pages.
- ✔ Convert the content to HTML.
- ✔ Create the graphical elements in your pages.
- ✔ Test your site.
- ✔ Put your content on a Web server.
- ✔ Publicize your site.
- ✔ Bask in the glory of being a Web publisher. (Then start again at the first step. . . .)

These detailed steps fall into three larger categories: planning your site, creating the content for your site, and publishing your site. Though most information about Web publishing focuses on the content-creation part in general, and HTML authoring in particular, all parts of the process are important. For a good, more advanced book that includes design information, pick up *Creating Cool HTML 3.2 Web Pages,* 3rd Edition, by Dave Taylor (IDG Books Worldwide, Inc.).

Plan your site

The only tools you need for this part of the Web publishing process are a Web browser, for doing research, and either a word processor and draw program, or a pencil and paper — whichever is more comfortable — for sketching your plans and taking notes. A few extra hours up-front can save you a great deal of time later and help you produce a better Web page. Yet the planning step is the most overlooked part of the Web publishing process. To plan your Web site, follow these steps:

1. **Determine the purpose of your site.**

   Decide which type of site you want to create: personal, topical, commercial, or comical. (We could also call the last two "business" and "entertainment," but those don't have alliteration.)

   Each type of site, and some specifics about how to design for it, is described earlier in this chapter. See those specifics, research existing sites, and research other media that serve the same purpose (magazines, brochures — even television). Ask what it is about your material, or about the Web, that makes the Web a good way to get your material out. Think some more about your own needs and interests. Then write a few goals for your initial site and for later versions of it.

2. **Decide the layout of your site and your pages.**

   The layout of your pages can make them more useful, more interesting, or more entertaining, whichever is their purpose. Here are a few general rules:

   - Decide how many pages to have and how they link to each other.

   - Put the purpose of your site near the top of your home page.

   - Indicate the purpose of additional pages near the top of each page.

   - Use bullets, icons, and other graphical elements to highlight key points.

   - Think about what graphics you need. Start the process of generating or obtaining them.

   - Use summary elements, such as a table of contents and Frequently Asked Questions (FAQs).

   - Put navigational elements — links from your home page to other pages in your site, and from other pages back to the home page — in a consistent spot at the top or bottom of each page.

3. **Decide what links to include.**

   A Web page that has no links is generally pretty boring. You already decided in Step 2 which links to include between the pages in your site. Now think about what links to include from your pages out to other sites. What links make sense? What links are fun? Use Web search engines such as Yahoo! (www.yahoo.com) to search the Web and find suitable links (see Figure 2-6). Then check the links and cut the list down to the personally significant ones, not just a laundry list. (Unless you're making a list of laundries!) Create a place to save links that you run into while using the Web so that they're available for you to use in future versions of your pages.

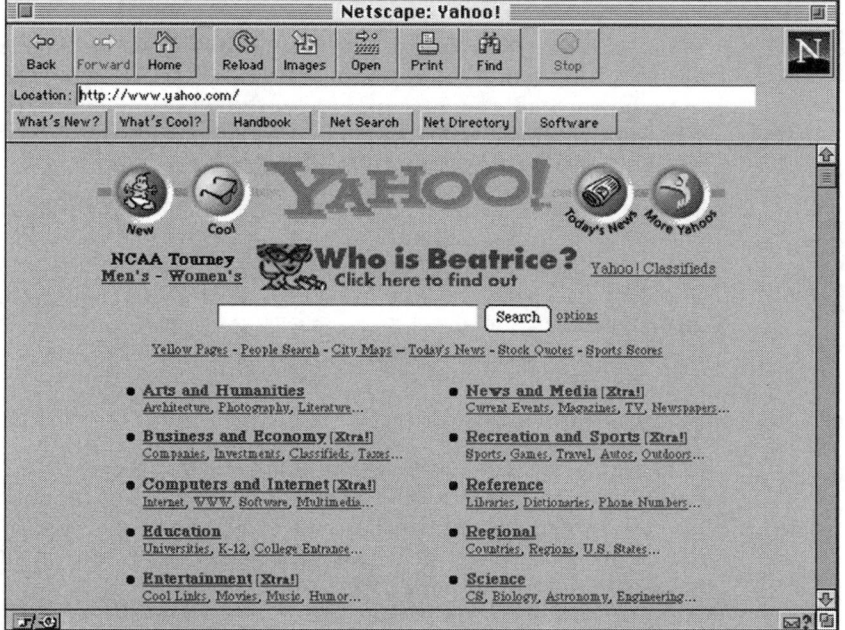

Figure 2-6:
The Yahoo!
screen.

Now think some more. Do the links that you're including fit the purpose of your page? How can you organize them? Should you group sets of key links together? Are some of the links repetitive or superfluous? Getting your links right makes your site more useful. And although no one likes to be left behind, which is what happens to you when people click an outbound link in one of your pages, a good set of links can, paradoxically, make users more likely to return to your site in the future.

Create the content

Creating content is the part of the Web publishing process where tools come in. You need tools to create HTML-tagged text (or a word processor if you want to work in HTML directly) and graphics tools to create graphics and convert them to one of the common Web formats, GIF or JPEG. (Yes, you can use other file formats for Web graphics, but, as we say in Chapter 1, GIF and JPEG are the most widely supported.) For simple sites, a single person can do all the work (but it will be a lot of work); for creating and maintaining larger sites, you need a team of people, often including consultants who have HTML expertise or other skills.

1. Create the text for your pages.

The best thing to do here, if you're new to Web publishing, is to work in a word processor without putting in HTML tags, at least at first. That way you can use a familiar tool to get the text right and to spellcheck it. Just remember that you can achieve much more precise formatting in a word processor than you can in a Web page.

You may want to consider going an extra step and creating a "dummy" of your Web site — pun intended — in your word processor before you commit to HTML. Making a dummy (a printer's term for a mock-up of a printed page) is a good way to plan what's on each page, and you can insert graphics and simulate links with underlines and colors. Compare this model to relevant Web sites you admire and see what changes you want to make.

2. Convert the content to HTML.

Next you need to convert the content to HTML. You can add the HTML tags yourself (see Chapter 3), use HTML conversion capabilities built into your word processor or use file translation tools (see Chapter 14) use a graphical Web page editor (see Chapters 10 through 12), or cut and paste the text into an HTML editor and "mark it up" with the appropriate tags (see Chapter 13). You may well end up using a combination of methods for new content and for files that you use or adapt from various sources.

Read Chapter 3 to learn how HTML works. Even if you use a tool and don't put in the tags yourself, knowing what is and isn't possible in basic HTML saves a great deal of time and effort in the overall publishing process.

3. Create the graphical elements in your pages.

Graphical elements include not only photos and computer-generated images but also mastheads, separator bars, and icons. This is also the time to create multimedia elements, such as sounds or video clips, if you really want to push the envelope. All these elements are covered in Chapter 7.

Publish your Web site

Putting your site on the Web — either an intranet or the open World Wide Web — is the most exciting part of the Web publishing process. (But watch out! Your excitement may quickly turn to anxiety as you think of people actually looking at your carefully crafted baby.) For this part of the process, you don't need any tools, except possibly an FTP (File Transfer Protocol) program to move your files to the Web server. Usually, whoever is providing your Web hosting service supports this process.

First bring the elements of your site together, then test it on your local machine, and finally publish it! Here are the steps for publishing (or republishing) your site:

1. **Put it all together and test it.**

   Check that you have all the content and links in the places that you want them and then test each Web page and the entire site. On your own machine, you can use a Web browser not only to see what your pages look like but also to follow links from your site to other sites; then you can use the Back button on your browser to return. (The only thing missing is that the people who eventually surf your site can't get to it until it's actually published on a Web server.) We describe in detail this testing process and the other stages of publishing your Web site in Chapter 8.

2. **Put your content on a Web server.**

   This is when it gets real. After you get your pages on the server, test them again. Especially, test all the links to make sure that they really go somewhere; remember, nothing is more frustrating than clicking a broken link.

3. **Publicize your site.**

   Get some users onto your site. Tell your friends, use Web resources, run ads on the Web, run ads in print and broadcast media, and, especially, get related Web sites to put in links to your site. Offer some kind of reward for feedback on your site — even if it's just taking that person's site off your "bad HTML examples" list! (For more detail on this part of the process, and the entire Web publishing process, see Chapter 8.)

4. **Bask in the glory of being a Web publisher.**

   Having a Web site up and running is something to be proud of. Sit and enjoy it for a while.

After you get your site on the Web, you'll experience a brief moment of elation and then concern as you think of all the things you wanted to do with the site before you ran out of time. Then you'll click around the site and realize that something doesn't look quite as good as you wanted. You may compare your site with others and decide to add new features. Back to square one.

Chapter 3

Just Enough HTML

Knowing a little HTML is a good thing. HTML is the link between the text file that you create in your text editor, or with an HTML tool, and what people see when they look at your Web pages with a browser. (We explain what HTML is in Chapter 1. A *text editor* is a program that lets you enter text and save it, but without visible formatting such as boldface or underlines or embedded formatting codes in the file; an HTML tool is a program that makes working with HTML easier. We talk more about these later in this chapter.)

You can add HTML tags, the formatting and linking elements described in Chapter 1, to regular text to create your own Web documents in any text editor or word processor. Or you can use a Web editing tool that hides the gory details of HTML tags from you. This chapter gives you enough background to know what you're seeing when you look at text that includes HTML tags and to make a few changes if you need to.

Trying to learn a lot of HTML right away is a *bad* thing. Spending hours and hours learning all the details of HTML is likely to slow your sprint to becoming a Web publisher. And becoming a Web publisher quickly can be a *good* thing. So don't let a bad thing get in the way of a good thing; focus on learning just enough HTML to help you create some basic pages and get them on the Web.

Ready: A Refreshingly Brief Description of HTML

This chapter gives you a basic working knowledge of HTML. We don't burden you with hundreds of pages of HTML tags, tips, and tricks. Some of the more technical details and background are in the sidebar called "The helter-skelter growth of HTML." (Try it; you'll like it.) After you publish a few Web pages, you can take the time to learn more HTML. At that point, you may want to buy that 400-page HTML book.

If you like to know everything that's going on before you roll up your sleeves and plunge into things, you may want to start by looking at *HTML 4 For Dummies,* a comprehensive guide to HTML by Ed Tittel and Stephen N. James, from IDG Books Worldwide, Inc.

Why learn HTML?

More and more Web authoring tools try to hide HTML from the user; you can use one of these tools to create a Web page without knowing a thing about HTML. But here are several reasons to learn the basics of HTML:

- ✔ **Because everyone else is.** Bad reason. Next!

- ✔ **To understand how the Web works.** This understanding is pretty valuable if you're a heavy Web user (or a light one), especially if you plan to publish on the Web. Some of the Web's limitations, such as "what you see is not what you get," are hard to understand if you don't know something about HTML.

- ✔ **To use free Web tools.** Most free Web tools enable you to enter HTML tags directly to jazz up your text. Knowing a few tags can go a long way.

- ✔ **To work directly in HTML.** Many Web pros tire of managing HTML tags by hand and start using a tool that hides the tags. Others swear by HTML. Everyone swears *at* HTML, at least some of the time. But the only way to have a choice is to know some HTML.

Working with HTML documents

An HTML document is simply a plain-text document that has HTML tags embedded in it. A *plain-text document* is a document with nothing in it but regular keyboard characters; any formatting codes in a plain-text document are visible to the person creating or editing it. (Unlike a plain-text document, word-processing documents and other kinds of formatted documents

The helter-skelter growth of HTML

HTML is a markup language that follows rules stipulated in a more complex specification — SGML (Standard Generalized Markup Language). HTML has evolved to Version 4.0, but not all browsers and tools support that version. Version 2.0 is supported by nearly all Web editing tools and browsers, and we only use HTML tags and capabilities from the Version 2.0 specification in this book unless otherwise noted.

The trouble with going beyond HTML 2.0 is that HTML is "growing" proprietary pieces on top of its standard base — kind of like the Blob, the monster in that horror movie from the 1950s. Web editors and browsers vary widely on how they handle more complex formatting, such as frames. If you want your Web pages to work equally well on all Web browsers, stick with HTML Version 2.0, as this book does. For details, see Appendix C.

---

have special formatting codes embedded in them that are not readable by other people.) The formatting in an HTML document is embedded in tags, such as the <B> and </B> tags described in Chapter 2. You need to know a few basic things to start working with HTML documents.

Viewing HTML documents

You can see HTML anytime you use the Web. Just pull up a Web page and then use the View Source command, or a similar command, in your browser. The command displays the HTML source code that underlies the Web page. This capability naturally leads to the temptation to borrow attractive documents from the Web, save them to your disk as HTML files, and then use them as templates for your own work — kind of a magpie approach to Web page building.

Borrowing someone else's material is okay for basic HTML formatting, but for more sophisticated formats that are distinctive and embody a great deal of work, get permission before you use them. Simply contact the Webmaster at the site you admire, describe how you want to use the format, and request permission. You may be surprised how many people say yes — without even exacting a promise from you that you hand over your firstborn.

Creating HTML documents

You can create HTML documents in a word processor, in a text editor, or by using an HTML tool. Each method has its advantages:

- ✔ **Word processor.** Most newer versions of popular word-processing packages include "save as HTML" capability. You can open and edit a document in the word processor and then save it as HTML-tagged text that makes up a Web page. However, this works best if you only format your document in the same ways that HTML supports directly, which you learn about in this chapter.

✔ **Text editor.** A text editor is a program that edits regular text, such as the dull, boring, plain text that most people send e-mail messages in — no fonts, no bold or italic text, and no styles. When you save a file from a text editor, it saves as plain text, with no added codes for formatting. Although most text editors lack the advanced features found in word processors, many HTML experts swear by them. (You can also create a file in a word processor, then save it as text, to achieve the same effect.)

✔ **HTML tool.** An HTML tool hides some of the details of HTML from you. But you have to go through a learning curve for any HTML tool, and few tools completely hide HTML. So the basics we present in this chapter will help, even if you plan to use a tool. By knowing the basics, in this way, you can use the tool better and have some alternatives if the tool doesn't do everything you need it to. (And what tool does?)

After you create an HTML file, save it with the extension .HTM. The extension enables the Web browser to recognize the file and interpret it correctly.

Every computer allows different kinds of filenames. But you should keep your Web filenames short, and within the 8-by-3 filename limits of DOS. (FILENAME.EXT is an example of an 8-by-3 filename; up to 8 characters before the period, up to 3 characters after.) HTML files should end in the characters .HTM. Also, leave spaces and special characters out of the name. This way, your filenames are valid regardless of the type of computer that ends up being the Web server for your pages.

Previewing HTML documents

However you create your HTML file, you need to see what it's going to look like on the Web. Some HTML tools offer special preview modes, but you can get the best idea of how your HTML file will look on the Web by using your Web browser.

While working in your text editor or word processor or using an HTML tool, simply save your file to disk. (Remember to use the .HTM extension.) Then open your Web browser. In Netscape Navigator, choose Open File from the File menu to open the file you just saved; in Internet Explorer, choose Open from the File menu and then use the Browse button to find the file.

The file appears in your browser just as it does on the Web. (Well, except that other people use other browsers, and they may have specified different fonts for displaying Web pages. But at least you get an idea of how the page looks.) If you're connected to the Internet, you can even click links in your document to see the appropriate graphic or Web page.

Navigator bookmarks as a Web page

If you have Netscape Navigator, or another browser that saves its bookmarks file as an HTML file, you can create a Web page in a big hurry. Find your bookmarks file and make a copy of it. (The bookmarks file is called BOOKMARK.HTM on the PC or BOOKMARKS.HTML on the Macintosh.)

Open Netscape Navigator. Then choose Open File from the File menu to open the file you just copied. Your bookmarks file appears as a Web page! The sidebar figure shows the use of the same file as both a bookmarks file and a Web page. You can edit the copy of the bookmarks file in a text editor or word processor and even

publish it on the Web. (Then you can always get to your bookmarks file, no matter where you're browsing from! Then again, so can anyone else; but if anyone makes snide remarks about some of the links that are there, you can always claim that the links are for research purposes.)

Look under the Help menu in Netscape Navigator for information about how to use HTML. Then follow the hyperlinks to find tools and examples. The information on the Web is a nice complement to this book and goes into great detail for those who want to do more in HTML.

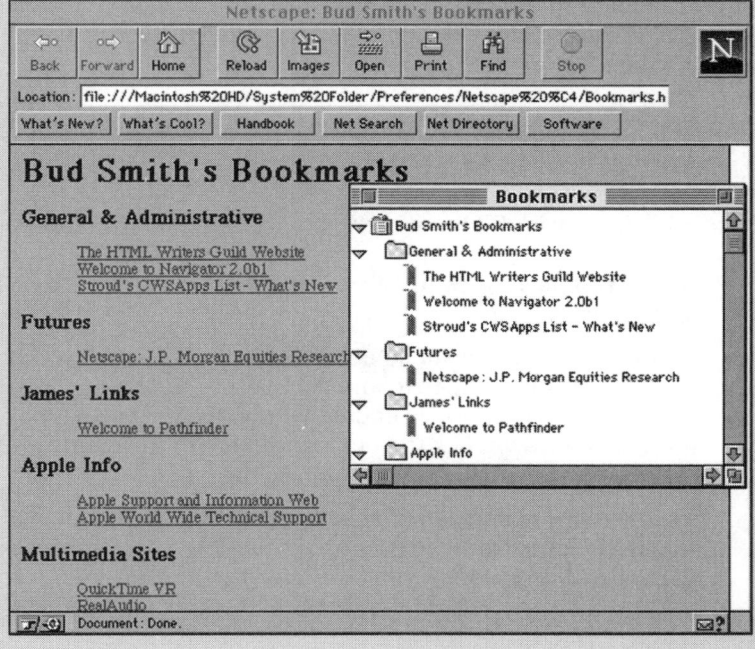

If you can run your editing tool and your browser at the same time, all the better. (In Windows, use the Alt+Tab key combination to shift quickly between applications. On the Mac, use the application pull-down menu in the upper-right corner of the screen.) You can change the document in your editing tool, save the file, and then use the Reload command or similar command in your browser to see the changes. (Kind of like those bumper stickers you may have seen on the freeway, "Keep Honking, I'm Reloading.") This way, you never need to be surprised by what you see after something you created is published on the Web.

But don't stop there. To see what your document looks like on different browsers before you publish on the Web, you can get copies of all the top browsers from the Web sites of the browser companies and preview your document in them as well.

Set: HTML Horse Sense

People used to refer to common sense as "horse sense." Most things about HTML fall under the realm of horse sense. After you see HTML tags a few times, most of the rules "feel right," and you have little trouble remembering or using them.

Basic HTML rules

Here are a few basic HTML rules and some "gotchas" to watch out for:

✔ **Most HTML tags work in pairs.** (Does that make these dynamic duos "tag teams"?)

For example, if you want some text displayed in bold, you have to put `<B>` at the front of the text, and you have to put `</B>` at the end of the text. If not, you can easily end up with a document that looks fine at the start but then switches to bold somewhere in the middle — and this bold continues all the way through to the end.

So remember to use paired tags and to check your document for unpaired tags before you publish it. And if you still end up seeing bold all over your document, you know what to look for.

✔ **HTML tags are written in ALL CAPS.**

Convention says to put HTML tags in ALL CAPS so that they stand out from the text they're embedded in. But inside an anchor, put the hypertext reference (such as a URL) in the case it would normally have (upper or lower) if you were using it elsewhere. The following example illustrates this use of capitalization:

```
<A HREF="textver.htm">Text version.</A>
```

The parts of the tag that are predefined HTML tags, such as A, /A, and HREF, are in ALL CAPS. The filename is in all lower-case letters (a UNIX convention that may save you some problems if your Web page ends up on a UNIX server). The text between the tags, which gets displayed on the Web page as link text, can be capitalized in whatever way makes sense for your Web page's readers.

UNIX machines are case-sensitive: If you call one file MyFile.txt and another file myfile.txt, they are separate files. The Macintosh and PC are case-insensitive and treat the names MyFile.txt and myfile.txt the same. Because you may end up putting your Web files on a Web server that's a different kind of machine from what you create them on, you need to pay attention to the use of upper- and lower-case. The easiest rule is that followed by UNIX users: Use capital letters as little as possible for filenames.

✔ **HTML ignores paragraph symbols and tabs in your text.**

One of the most confusing things about HTML is that the paragraph symbol in your text that you create when you press Enter is ignored, and so are tabs. When displaying HTML, the browser automatically breaks lines to fit the current window size. And the browser makes a paragraph break only when it sees the paragraph tag, ⟨P⟩, or some other tag that implies the start of a new line (such as a top-level heading tag, ⟨H1⟩).

✔ **Basic HTML looks different on different browsers.**

Basic HTML doesn't give you much control over the appearance of your document. (Newer versions of HTML allow more control, but aren't supported by older versions of popular browsers, so we suggest you avoid the new stuff.) Different browsers handle the same tags differently. For example, a top-level heading (specified by the ⟨H1⟩ and ⟨/H1⟩ tags) may look much different in one browser than it looks in another browser.

✔ **Some tags don't work on some browsers.**

Some browsers (such as Netscape Navigator) support tags that other browsers can't handle. We recommend sticking with the tags in HTML 2.0 to avoid the chance of giving users nasty surprises when they view your documents, and we use only those tags in this book.

✔ **Users configure their browsers differently.**

As if the differences among browsers weren't enough, users can configure their browsers differently. Users who have bigger monitor screens tend to look at documents in a bigger window. But because these users sit farther back from their big screens — remember your mother telling you to always sit at least six feet from the TV? — they may also specify that larger font sizes be used in displaying text. Some users like to have their browser display all graphics as the page is transmitted; others have graphics turned off. All of these idiosyncrasies can make your document look different to different users. Figures 3-1 and 3-2 show the same Web page from the Fullerton School District in Southern California, but displayed with different option settings; as you can see, they don't look the same.

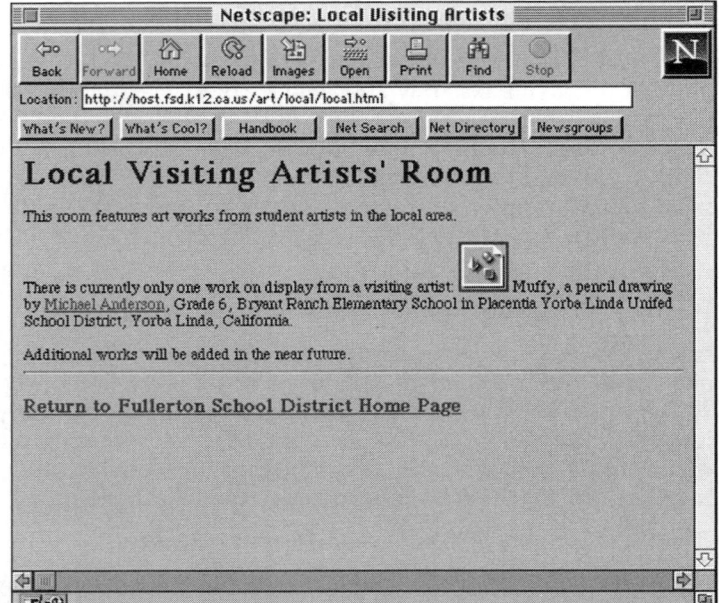

Figure 3-1: A Web document with default settings, including images turned off.

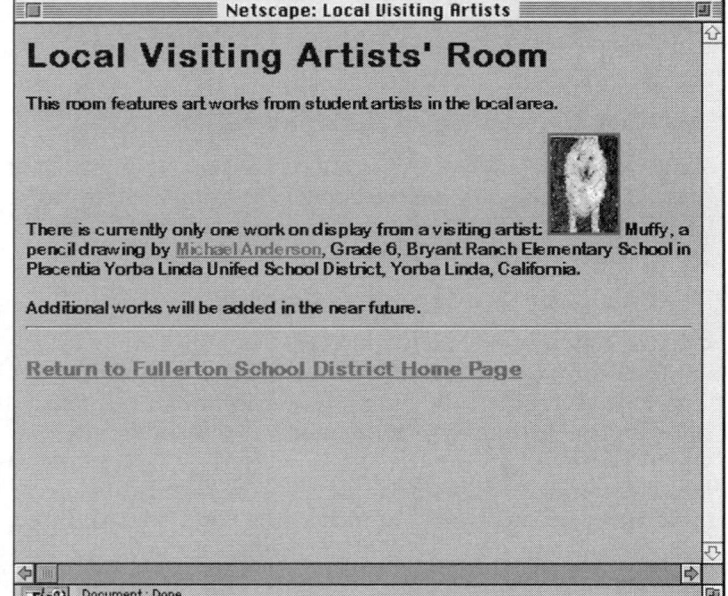

Figure 3-2: The same document shown in Figure 3-1, but with different settings.

Ten key HTML tags plus one

The Cheat Sheet at the beginning of this book shows an example of an HTML document, which is just regular text plus tags — those funny things with the angle brackets around them. If you haven't already, tear out the Cheat Sheet so you can look at the sample HTML document while you read this section.

Although looking at a complicated HTML document can make your head swim faster than Olympic medalist Mark Spitz, you don't need to know many tags to create basic, useful Web documents. Table 3-1 lists some key tags with brief descriptions; longer descriptions follow later in this chapter.

Table 3-1	Key Tags to Use
Tags	*Tag Location*
<HEAD>, </HEAD>	Put these tags around the <TITLE> and </TITLE> tags at the start of the document.
<TITLE>, </TITLE>	Put these tags around a short title that describes the document but is not displayed on-screen. (For more information about the <HEAD>, </HEAD>, <TITLE>, and </TITLE> tags, see the section "Heads — you win" in this chapter.)
<BODY>, </BODY>	After you add the </TITLE> and </HEAD> tags to end the title and header area, you surround everything else in the document with the <BODY> and </BODY> tags.
<H1>, </H1>, <H2>, </H2>,...	Put the initial heading at the top of your document between the <H1> and </H1> tags. Then use higher-numbered tags for progressively lower heading levels. You can go down six levels (<H6>, </H6>), which is a lot — this book uses only three heading levels. If a book that weighs in at 350-plus pages needs only three levels, you have to create something pretty detailed before you need five or six.
<B>, </B>	Surround text you want to display in bold with these tags.
<I>, </I>	Surround text you want to display in italics with these tags.

(continued)

Table 3-1 *(continued)*

Tags	Tag Location
`<P>, </P>`	The paragraph-break tag is not needed at the end of headings and in some other places, such as within a list, but it is needed everywhere else. Besides the anchor tags (`<A></A>`), `<P>` may be the easiest common tag to misuse. The end paragraph tag, `</P>`, is basically optional for beginners.
`<HR>`	The horizontal rule tag displays a horizontal line that is good for separating sections of documents.
`<A>, </A>`	The anchor tags define hypertext links and contain hypertext references, somewhat complicated information about where the link goes to. Link text — the text that gets underlined to indicate a hypertext link — goes between the tags. When the user clicks the underlined link text on a Web page, the display changes to show the Web page indicated by the hypertext reference.
`<A HREF="http://www.aSite.edu">My kid's site</A>`	The `<A>` and `</A>` tag pair defines an anchor. HREF indicates a hypertext reference — in this case, a pointer to a Web site's URL. The link text is `My kid's site`; the user sees this text, underlined, as part of the Web page. See the section on anchors near the end of this chapter for details on these and other kinds of hypertext links.
`<IMG SRC="BudPic.gif">`	The `IMG` tag brings in an image in a format that the browser understands, either GIF or JPEG. The `SRC` part of the tag tells the browser where to find the file. In this case, the file is called `BudPic.gif` and is in the same directory or folder as the HTML file that the `<IMG>` tag is in. (You can tell it's the same directory because the filename doesn't have any pathname information in front of it, such as `\images\BudPic.gif`.) Unlike the other "top ten" tags, which are described in this chapter, the `<IMG>` tag is described further in Chapter 7.

For an example that uses these tags, see the Cheat Sheet. For a complete list of tags, see Appendix C.

Go: Create a Web Page with HTML

Yes, you are just about ready to create a Web page with HTML. However, the whole secret of using HTML is knowing what tags to use and when. So now that you know what a tag is, what more do you need to know? Well, tags can be divided into three kinds:

- ✔ **Tags that contain *meta-information* about your document.** Meta-information, such as the title in the header section of your document, doesn't affect how your document is displayed; instead, it is used by various Web tools, such as search engines that look at the title to see what your document is about. (And we never "meta" Web tool we didn't like!)

- ✔ **Tags that format characters in your text.** These tags do nothing but modify the way your text looks when the browser displays it. (<B>, </B> and <I>, </I>, for example.)

- ✔ **Linking tags.** These tags connect the user to different kinds of information and even to other documents. The section "Look back (and forward) in anchor," in this chapter, explains linking tags in detail.

After you create and save an HTML file with text and these different kinds of tags, pat yourself on the back. You've just created a complete HTML document, and you're well on the way to being a tagger yourself! (Not the kind that puts graffiti on buildings, but the kind that expresses himself or herself electronically on the Web.)

Create a blank file for your HTML

HTML files should include only plain text — no word-processor formatting. And the name of the document should always end with .HTM. So start by creating a text-only file to hold your Web page's text and HTML tags.

To create a blank plain-text document that your HTML code will be inserted into, follow these steps.

1. **Start your text editor or word processor.**

2. **Open a new document.**

   Some programs automatically open a new document when you start them.

3. **Start the process of saving your document so that you can name it.**

   If using a word processor, use the Save As or similar command and choose Text as the type of file.

> Don't choose the Text with line breaks option; line breaks make the document harder to edit. The good old Text option will do.

4. **Name the document.**

   Put **.HTM** at the end of the name.

5. **Save the document.**

   In most programs, you click a Save button or press Enter.

The steps enable you to create a blank HTML document — which wouldn't be very interesting if you were to put it on the Web! So you want to start filling in your document by adding heading information.

Heads — you win

First, some bad news: You start your HTML documents with some tags that don't really do anything for you. In fact, the tags add a few more things to worry about. And you thought that you could finally start getting some real work done!

Now, the good news: These tags make the Web a better place. They contain introductory *meta-information* — descriptive information about your document that doesn't affect how the user sees your document. But although the user doesn't see these tags directly, the tags support search tools and other tools that make finding a Web page — hopefully, *your* Web page — so quick and easy that users can get to it directly. (Of course, looking at a lot of other things in between can be half the fun of using the Web.)

- ✔ <HTML>, </HTML>. These tags surround everything in your document and identify the document as being in HTML. As the Web supports more and more different types of files, these tags become increasingly important.

- ✔ <HEAD>, </HEAD>. These tags go around the title of your document and any other information that isn't displayed within the Web page itself. For now, that just means the title.

- ✔ <TITLE>, </TITLE>. These tags go around the title of your document. The title is a short phrase that describes your document and is not displayed in your Web page.

- ✔ <BODY>, </BODY>. These tags go around everything in your document that isn't part of the head. The <BODY> tag goes just after the </HEAD> tag, which goes just after the </TITLE> tag.

If you use a tool that creates a Web page for you, such as the free tools in Chapters 4 and 5, you don't need to put these introductory tags in because the tool does it for you.

Look at this well-mannered, albeit nearly empty, HTML document to see what the top should look like:

```
<HTML>
<HEAD>
<TITLE>A Brief Introduction to Electric Guitars</TITLE>
</HEAD>
<BODY>
Your HTML document goes here.
</BODY>
</HTML>
```

Popular Web tools use these tags. The Power Search option of the OpenText Web-searching service enables users to search specifically by words in the title. To access the OpenText search engine, go to

```
index.opentext.net
```

Netscape Navigator and Microsoft Internet Explorer use the title of your document — the phrase between the <TITLE> and </TITLE> tags — as the document description in their Bookmarks menu. (No, we don't keep mentioning these products because we own Microsoft and Netscape stock; this is just one of those cases where the best products and the market leaders are the same thing.) The title is also displayed in the title bar of the browser window when the page is displayed.

To give yourself a jump start each time you want to start a new HTML document, create a text-only document in your word processor or text editor with the head, title, and body tags already in place. When you're ready to create a new HTML document, start by making a copy of this document.

Follow these steps to create a text-only document that contains the introductory tags:

1. **Open a new document.**

2. **Save your document as a text-only document with the name you want, ending with .HTM.**

3. **On the first line of the document, enter the tag** <HTML>.

4. **On the second line of the document, enter the tag** <HEAD>.

5. **On the third line of the document, enter the tags** <TITLE> **and** </TITLE>.

   Do not enclose anything within the <TITLE> and </TITLE> tags for now. After you copy this text-only document to create an HTML document, you can enter the material that you want to use as the "title." When you are deciding what to include between these tags, remember that many Web tools use the information between these tags when searching for documents.

6. **On the fourth line of the document, enter the tag** </HEAD>.

7. **On the fifth line of the document, enter the tag** <BODY>.

8. **Leave the sixth line of the document blank.**

   The main content of the document goes here.

9. **On the seventh line of the document, enter the tag** </BODY>.

10. **On the eighth line of the document, enter the tag** </HTML>.

    Whatever else you do in your document, </HTML> is always the last tag.

Get a heading and some body

Most HTML documents start with a heading that appears on the Web page as the document's title. Headings in HTML documents are indicated with the <H#> tag, where # is any number between 1 and 6. The end of the heading is marked with the </H#> tag. Large, top-level headings are indicated by the <H1> tag at the beginning and the </H1> tag at the end. Most documents have only one top-level H1 heading. Lower-level headings are marked <H2> for second-level headings, <H3> for third-level, and so on. <H6> is the lowest-level heading. (Dante specified nine circles of Hell, but HTML specifies only six levels of headings.)

Underneath the headings, your document needs some content — just plain old words, maybe highlighted with **bold** and *italics* where needed.

Don't overuse the tags for bold and italic. Like early desktop publishers, who put three different fonts on every line of text, HTML novices tend to put **lots of bold** and *italics* in their documents. When you preview your document in your Web browser, look for areas where you overuse bold and italic formatting. And when in doubt, don't use bold and italic. Your readers will thank you.

Here's how to put a top-level heading and some basic text into your Web document:

1. **After the** ⟨BODY⟩ **tag, and before the** ⟨/BODY⟩ **tag, put in your top-level heading. Surround the heading with the** ⟨H1⟩ **and** ⟨/H1⟩ **tags so that the browser knows that the text is a level-1 heading.**

   The top-level heading is often the same as what is enclosed within the ⟨TITLE⟩ and ⟨/TITLE⟩ tags.

2. **After the heading, type some text.**

   For optimal use by Web search tools, the first paragraph in your document should be a brief summary of the document's contents.

3. **At the end of each paragraph, put in a** ⟨P⟩ **tag.**

   No matter how many times you press Enter in your document, your dense browser doesn't get the message. It only understands that you want to end a paragraph and start a new one when it sees the ⟨P⟩ tag.

4. **Surround text with the** ⟨B⟩ **and** ⟨/B⟩ **tags to make it bold.**

   Don't overdo the use of the ⟨B⟩ and ⟨/B⟩ tags! But starting out, use bold once or twice just to get a feel for it.

5. **Surround text with the** ⟨I⟩ **and** ⟨/I⟩ **tags to make it italic.**

   Don't overdo italicizing, either! But use italics a few times in your first document or two for practice.

6. **Try adding a horizontal rule.**

   Add the ⟨HR⟩ tag in one or two places to create horizontal rules. (Not to start an argument with those who think that vertical rules.)

   As with headings and other elements of your document, put the ⟨HR⟩ tag on a line by itself so that you can find it easily later to move or remove it.

7. **After you're done, check your tags.**

   Paragraphs should end with a ⟨P⟩ tag to start the next paragraph. All ⟨B⟩ tags should have a matching ⟨/B⟩ tag, and all ⟨I⟩ tags should have a matching ⟨/I⟩ tag.

   The most effective way for many of us to check this, believe it or not, is to print out the document and then cross out pairs of tags with a pencil.

8. **Save your document.**

   If you use a word processor rather than a text editor, be sure to save your document as text.

The Cheat Sheet at the front of this book shows a *simple sample* Web page.

Add a little list

One of the best ways to "break up" your Web page is to insert lists. HTML supports bulleted lists, numbered lists, and lists of definitions or descriptions. HTML makes it easy to create a list, although it doesn't give you direct control over how lists turn out. (Repeat after me, "Trust your browser, trust your browser. . . .")

- ✔ **Unnumbered lists** (often called bulleted lists). Unnumbered lists display as lists with bullets next to them and are "appropriately" indented (the indentation varies with different browsers and browser settings). The list you're reading now is a bulleted list, but it uses check marks in place of the bullets.

- ✔ **Ordered lists** (often called numbered lists). These lists are similar to bulleted lists, but with — you guessed it — numbers in place of the bullets. You can rearrange the items in the numbered list as much as you like. The browser automatically keeps things in order by putting in the right numbers when it displays the list.

- ✔ **Definition lists.** These lists usually alternate terms and their — duh — definitions. The term goes where the bullet goes in a bulleted list, and the definition goes next to it or on the line immediately below.

You create all lists in basically the same way: You start the list with a beginning tag, such as ⟨UL⟩ for an unnumbered list. You then tag each item separately to let the browser know that it's a separate item. You use the tag ⟨LI⟩ at the beginning of each item in both unnumbered and numbered lists; you don't use an end tag for individual list items. The list finally ends with a closing tag — ⟨/UL⟩ to end an unnumbered list, for example.

The following instructions describe how to create an unnumbered (bulleted) or ordered (numbered) list:

1. **Put in a tag to start the list:** ⟨UL⟩ **for an unnumbered list,** ⟨OL⟩ **for an ordered list.**

2. **Put in an** ⟨LI⟩ **tag to indicate a list item.**

3. **Starting on the same line, enter the text for the list item.**

   "Red Hot Chili Pepper Potato Chips" is a good way to start.

4. **For the remaining items in the list, enter the** ⟨LI⟩ **tag followed by the item text. Press Enter at the end of each line to visually separate the items on-screen as you edit.**

   You don't need to use an end tag for list items. Also remember that hitting Enter at the end of a line causes the cursor to move to a new line on-screen, but doesn't cause line breaks to be put in the HTML-tagged text; the browser starts a new line when it sees a new ⟨LI⟩ tag or a ⟨/UL⟩ tag.

5. **Enter a tag to end the list —** ⟨/UL⟩ **to end an unnumbered list or** ⟨/OL⟩ **to end an ordered list.**

To create a definition list, follow these steps:

1. **Enter the** ⟨DL⟩ **tag to start the definition list.**

2. **Enter the** ⟨DT⟩ **tag to indicate a definition term.**

3. **Enter the text for the definition term.**

4. **Enter the** ⟨DD⟩ **tag to indicate definition data — the description of the definition term.**

5. **Enter the text for the definition data.**

6. **For the remaining items in the list, enter the** ⟨DT⟩ **tag followed by the definition term and then enter the** ⟨DD⟩ **tag followed by the description of the term.**

   Remember — as with other list items, no end tag is needed for definition terms or definition data.

7. **Enter the** ⟨/DL⟩ **tag to end the list.**

Figure 3-3 shows an example that includes the three kinds of lists. Because people use the Web to learn new things and to look things up, lists are some of the most important formatting elements in HTML.

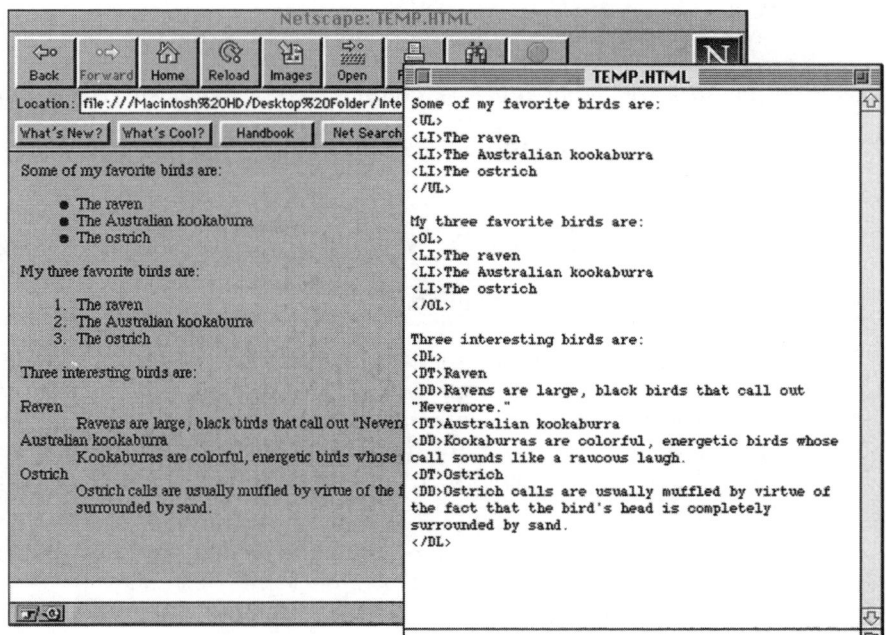

Figure 3-3:
Using lists
in your
Web page.

Look back (and forward) in anchor

Remember that HTML stands for HyperText Markup Language? Well, applying all those tags is the markup part. Now hang on to your hat: Here's everything you need to know about the hypertext part. In this section, we demonstrate how to use hypertext to create links between information in your document and information in other documents. This stuff is a bit confusing at first, but after you understand it, you'll think of many exciting ways to use hypertext in your Web pages.

In HTML, every hypertext link has two ends, which are called *anchors*. (Some people think that putting anchors into a Web page makes them anchorpersons — but sorry, no seven-figure salary.)

An anchor is the beginning of a link. It appears in a document as text that is underlined or an image that is surrounded by a border. (Usually, the underline under the text, or the border around the image, is in blue.) When you click the anchor and new information shows up on your screen, that new information is the other end of the link — the other anchor. The Back command, or a similar command, in your browser takes you back to the anchor that you started from.

When you define an anchor, you use tags to specify two things:

- ✔ The text or image that is highlighted as the place you click to follow the link
- ✔ The other anchor that you want to go to when you click the link

Anchors are among the most complicated tags in basic HTML. But you don't want to say "Anchors away," as the old movie had it. Anchors expand the possibilities of your Web page tremendously. The following is an example of an anchor:

```
<A HREF="http://www.BetterDogs.com">How to train dogs</A>
```

Here are the parts of an anchor:

- ✔ `<A>`, `</A>`. These tags go around text that you want highlighted as a hypertext link (`How to train dogs` in the preceding example). Try to use text that represents the thing that you want to link to, such as "Adobe Corporation" or "my résumé." The better this text describes the thing that you link to, the more helpful it is to the user.
- ✔ `HREF`. This information follows the `<A` within the `<A>` tag. It tells the browser to link to the information located at the pathname that appears after `HREF` when the user clicks the link text.

✔ **Hypertext reference.** These characters follow the equal sign in the `HREF` part of the anchor. They are the pathname of the document that you link to. In the example, the hypertext reference is the name of a Web site: `"http://www.BetterDogs.com"`.

When an HTML file is posted on a server, some anchors in it can point to Web documents on the same Web server as the HTML file, while other anchors point to Web documents on other Web servers. When the document is on another server, the anchor contains the document's full URL, in the same form as you type it in your browser. For example, an anchor pointing to the *...For Dummies* Web site looks like this:

```
<A HREF="http://www.dummies.com">"...For Dummies"</A>
```

When the document that's pointed to by the initial anchor is on the same machine, the anchor contains the pathname of the document. The pathname specifies where on the machine the file is to be found.

The pathname looks different depending on where the second document is in relation to the HTML document. If the two documents are in the same directory or folder, the pathname is simply the filename. But if the second document is in a different directory, you can use two methods to specify how to reach it: absolute addressing and relative addressing. In *absolute addressing,* you use the path from the root directory of the server to the second document. In *relative addressing,* you use the path from the current document to the second document.

To specify an absolute address, start with a forward slash (/) to indicate the root directory of the Web server. Then specify the full pathname from the root directory to the file. The following example shows an absolute address:

```
/photoshp/samples/sunrise.gif
```

To specify a relative address, start with the directory of the HTML document that the anchor is in and then enter the path that leads to the desired file from there. A pair of dots (..) specifies the directory one level above the current one.

For example, if you have an HTML file called sunset.gif in the directory /mysite/html, and you need a file that is in /mysite/html/pix, a subdirectory of the current directory, the relative address is the following:

```
pix/sunset.gif
```

If you also need a file that is in /mysite/trial/pix, you use the .. characters to specify the subdirectory above this one and then go back down the directory tree to the needed file. Put a slash after the dots. In this case, the relative address is as follows:

```
../trial/pix/moonrise.gif
```

Starting at the beginning of the path, ".." means "the directory above the current one." The words separated by slashes, "/trial/pix/," are the names of the directory and subdirectory in which the file is stored. "moonrise.gif" is the name of the file.

Table 3-2 shows examples of anchors.

Table 3-2	Examples of Hypertext Links (Anchors)
Destination	*Sample Anchor*
Document on a different server	`<A HREF="http:// www.mycorp.com/Job Requirements">link text</A>`
Document in same directory	`<A HREF="MyDoc2.html"> link text </A>`
Document in different directory; relative addressing	`<A HREF="Personal/ Resume">link text</A>`
Document in different directory; absolute addressing	`<A HREF="/Maya/Personal/ Resume">link text</A>`

For simple Web sites that you create, put all the documents in the same directory or folder so that you have simpler anchors.

Link for yourself

Absorbing all this knowledge about hypertext links is pretty useless if you don't actually use the knowledge yourself. Here's a description of how to create a link (note how we cleverly work several different types of links into the instructions):

1. **Open an existing HTML document.**

2. **Move to the place in the document where you want to insert a link.**

3. **Start the link by entering the opening tag, including the hypertext reference that you want the link to lead to.**

   For a link to a file in the same directory, enter the filename in quotation marks, as in `<A HREF="AnotherDoc.HTM">`. (The filename is "AnotherDoc.HTM.")

   As described previously in this chapter, you can enter a relative or absolute address for a document that's in a different directory within your Web site.

   For a link to a file in the `graphics` subdirectory of the current directory, enter the pathname: `<A HREF="graphics/ dancers.gif">Dancers</A>`.

For a document that's on a different server, enter the document's URL (for example, `<A HREF="http://www.ACoolSite.com">`).

When no specific filename is entered, the browser looks for the default file, index.htm or index.html.

4. After the opening tag, enter the link text.

5. Don't forget the closing tag!

After the opening tag and the link text, enter the closing tag.

The inner game of links

That's a lot of stuff to absorb! Just one more thing to consider: What if you want to link to a specific spot *within* the same Web page?

To link to a specific spot, you need a pair of anchors. The first is at the spot from which you want to link. This first anchor is just like the links described previously, but it has one more element — the name of the link that's at the spot to which you want to link. For example, the following anchor links to a spot that's named "Bebak," within the same file as the anchor:

```
<A HREF="#Bebak">Bud's coauthor</A>
```

The pound sign, #, denotes an anchor within a Web page. The second anchor, also called the link, is at the spot to which you want to link. The second anchor exists only to specify that spot and doesn't cause the link text to show up as underlined on the user's screen. Here's the link for the second anchor:

```
<A NAME="Bebak"> </A>Arthur Bebak
```

The link doesn't need a pathname, but the anchor that links to it needs a pathname if the anchor and link are in different files. And you don't need any text between the anchor beginning and ending.

Can your browser handle it?

An anchor can link the current document to another HTML file or to some other type of file, such as a graphic, a sound, a video clip, or almost anything else. Most browsers know how to handle HTML files and GIF or JPEG graphics files automatically. Other types of files may be handled in different ways by different browsers — automatically, or by the user's specifying a program to handle them. So for these examples, we stick with links to HTML files and GIF and JPEG files because we know that those files work with just about any browser.

Try using internal links in an HTML document on your own machine, and test the links in your browser. Experiment with different kinds of relative addresses, or pathnames. Trying different links and pathnames gives you the experience you need to easily use these features in your "real" Web pages.

Linking to specific spots in your own Web page is common. Many Web sites have long Web pages that include clever internal links that move the user around in the page. Linking to specific spots in other people's Web pages is less common. Why? Because it's hard to control where the other page's author chooses to put link anchors — and harder still to make sure that link anchors don't get moved around on you unexpectedly, rendering your anchor invalid. How would you like it if, for example, you defined a link to a serious essay on home brewing and later discovered that the essay had been replaced by a discussion of Greek philosophy? Sheesh!

Browse your own weblet

Here's the moment you've been waiting for: Whether you've followed all of the previous steps, or just some, you should now have a ready-to-use little HTML document. To see whether you did it right, all you have to do is try it in your Web browser. That's right — you can view your very own HTML document in your very own browser!

Not only can you view your HTML document from your browser, but you can even follow the links to other HTML documents on your local system and from your system out onto the Web. (We assume that your browser is connected to the Web at the time. If not, following a hypertext link to a Web URL will be a short trip!) Using the Back command in your browser, you can even return to your own document.

There's only one limitation to this testing: Other Web sites can't link to your HTML document because it's only saved on your local machine, not on a Web server. And that's because of the one thing that's stopping your HTML document from being a Web page: It's not hosted on a Web server. Details, details — we take care of that little omission in later chapters.

For now, you need to find out how to view your HTML document in your browser. This is something you do every time you work on HTML documents. Start a document; view it in your browser. Change the document; view it in your browser. And on and on. . . . (Maybe it's finally time to buy that 20-inch color monitor you've been thinking about so that you can see both documents at once as you switch back and forth.)

To view your HTML document in your browser:

1. **Start your browser.**

2. **Select the Open command, usually found under the File menu.**

3. **Find your HTML document on your hard disk and open it.**

4. **View your own HTML document in your own Web browser.**

   You can even click links to follow them. Use the Back command in your browser to return to your HTML document.

5. **Look for problems in your HTML document, or things you'd like to add.**

   So half your *document is in italics* and <u>the rest is underlined</u> as if it's all part of a link. Who cares?! Go fix it!

6. **Open the HTML document in your text editor or word processor and fix it.**

   The earlier parts of this chapter may be of some help here.

7. **Save the changed HTML document.**

   If you forget to save the document, your changes don't show up in your browser, and you wonder whether your changes "took" or whether you're losing your sanity.

8. **Use the Reload command or a similar command in your Web browser to reload the fixed HTML document.**

   If you forget to reload the document, your changes don't show up in your browser, and, again, you wonder whether your changes "took" or whether you're losing your sanity.

   If you forget to save the document after you make changes, or forget to reload the document in your browser, the changes you just made won't show up. Anytime you think that this may have happened, just go back to your text editor or word processor, save the document, return to your Web browser, and reload. The changes appear.

9. **Repeat Steps 5 through 8 until done.**

   (*Done* can mean until the HTML document is done or until the HTML document's author is done in!)

Don't forget to use the Reload command when you're done modifying your document and want to look at it again in the browser.

Next steps in HTML

The parts of HTML that are covered in this chapter are just the basics. As you create, test, and deploy your own Web pages, you may want to understand more about HTML.

If you use a tool such as the ones described in Parts III and IV, you may be protected from the gory details of HTML. But you never know when you may end up back in "raw" HTML to add a feature or fix a problem.

For more about HTML, see Appendix C, which is a quick guide to HTML tags. The appendix lists and briefly describes all the tags in the HTML 2.0 specification, plus some tags from more advanced specifications. The appendix also points to additional resources on the Web for more information on HTML. And don't forget, *HTML 4 For Dummies* (IDG Books Worldwide, Inc.) is an excellent source for more detail on HTML.

Part II
A Home Page in a Day

The 5th Wave — By Rich Tennant

"Hold your horses. It takes time to build a home page for someone your size."

In this part . . .

Use this part to create your first Web page in an hour or two, using free Web publishing services provided by GeoCities or free online Web publishing tools provided by America Online and CompuServe. Your out-of-pocket cost: free for the Web-based services, or included in the usual cost of your online service. Your reward: being able to tell your friends and colleagues your Web address tomorrow!

Chapter 4

Put a Home Page on the Web

· ·

In This Chapter

▶ Using GeoCities for personal Web pages

▶ Applying for your page

▶ Waiting for your password

▶ Building your personal home page

▶ Finding more free Web publishing opportunities

· ·

*G*etting your first page up on the Web seems like a tall order. So it may be hard to believe just how easy it is to get started. But with the free Web-based publishing services described in this chapter and the next, you can have your first Web page up within a couple of hours — and at no cost. You don't have to learn HTML, you don't have to deal with typical publishing complexities, and did I mention that you don't have to pay anything?

If you are a member of America Online or CompuServe, you can use free Web publishing tools available from those services to get a Web page up quickly and easily. These services have the advantage of built-in support for your Web page efforts from the same help resources — including your fellow online service members — that you're already familiar with. So if you're a member of America Online or CompuServe, start your Web page creation effort with the next chapter.

If not, though, you have an alternative that's just as good: GeoCities. GeoCities is a site that offers free personal Web page publishing, and has done so for more than two years. Since its inception, GeoCities has hosted the creation of more than 1,000,000 — yes, that's one *million* — personal Web pages. GeoCities has also steadily climbed the charts to become one of the Top Ten most frequently visited Web sites. This means that their service is extremely popular with visitors as well as publishers. It also means that their advertising-supported, self-publishing model is so successful that it's likely to be around for a long time to come. (Other, similar services featured, along with GeoCities, in earlier editions of this book have since disappeared, a testament to the rapid rate of change on the Web.)

Follow the instructions in this chapter to become a member of GeoCities. You'll be a Web publisher in less time than most people take to even start thinking hard about how to get their first home page published on the Web.

Start with a Personal Web Page

Getting up a personal Web page accomplishes a lot of things. For one, it's fun. Hundreds of thousands of people have gotten a real kick out of sharing information about themselves and their interests with their fellow Web users. Many personal Web pages that initially started out quite simply have evolved into large and popular Web sites focused on topics of any imaginable sort. As the number of Web users increases, more and more of your colleagues, family, and friends can see your Web page, plus (of course) tens of millions of complete strangers.

Creating a personal Web page is also very valuable in helping you learn how to publish on the Web. Until you publish something on the Web, you may find it hard to believe that you can actually do it. After you put up your first Web page, you'll find it hard to believe that anything can stop you from doing it again. The initial success of getting up your personal Web page will spill over into all your future Web efforts.

Now, you may feel that you should start out with a business Web site, a home page for a nonprofit organization, or something similarly serious. But that approach has a couple of problems:

- The "barriers to entry" — if I can use a marketing term — for a site that represents an organization are much higher because you're taking on a more complex task.

- The quality of your work will have much more impact because you're representing a larger cause than just your personal interests. So your fear of failure will be greater. And you'll be undertaking this task with no background and no experience.

- Finally, Web space for business sites costs money. So you have a buying decision to make before you can even get started — yet another barrier.

So get on the Web first with a simple, personal Web page. Learn something, have some fun, and prepare now for more ambitious endeavors later. And GeoCities is just the place to do it.

To see what other people have done with their personal Web sites, visit GeoCities right now:

www.geocities.com

The initial home page for GeoCities is shown in Figure 4-1. (Don't be alarmed if you see something slightly different; GeoCities updates its home page every few months, but the mechanics of publishing your own page using GeoCities' tools change much more slowly. So even if the GeoCities home page has changed, the instructions in this chapter are likely to still be valid.)

Visit the GeoCities site and tour the GeoCities neighborhoods to see what other people have done; look at their initial efforts, and then see what people did to spruce up the place after they first arrived! (Here's an extra tip: In any given GeoCities neighborhood, sites with lower numbers tend to be older and more complex; higher-numbered ones tend to be newer and simpler.) When you first access the GeoCities site, you may spend a couple of hours wandering around and looking at cool stuff, just as we did. But the point is to get a personal home page on the Web quickly and with a minimum of distractions. So we suggest that you follow the steps in this chapter to get your site up first; then ask questions about what others have done with their sites later.

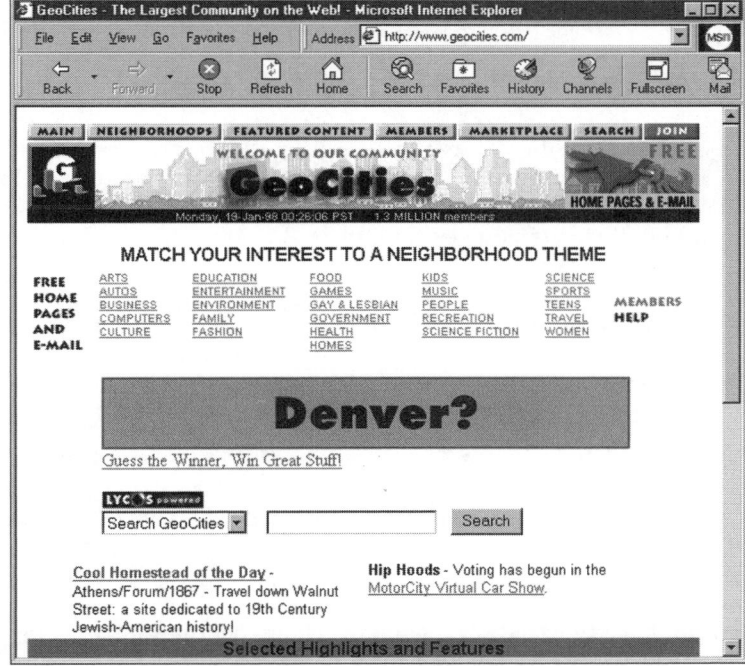

Figure 4-1:
GeoCities is the home of more than 1 million personal Web pages.

Web tools versus Web services

A Web publishing tool is a program that helps you prepare content for the Web, such as a text editor. A Web publishing service is a support function that handles part of the process of Web publishing for you, such as hosting your Web page(s) on a server. The two Web publishing services described in this chapter also include online tools for preparing your Web page(s), but because the free Web page hosting they provide is the most notable thing, we refer to them as services.

Tear out the Cheat Sheet at the front of this book and tape it to the wall! Although you don't need to know HTML to use the services described in this chapter, knowing a little bit of HTML can help you make your initial page look better. See the Top Ten list in Chapter 3 and the Cheat Sheet for a list of tags that can spruce up your initial Web page.

The Inside Scoop on GeoCities

You can use GeoCities' easy-to-use editing tool to create a simple home page quickly and easily. You can then use HTML, FTP (described in Chapter 1), and other tools to create and transfer more sophisticated pages to create any kind of Web site you want, up to 3MB in size. But you have to keep in mind these restrictions:

- ✔ **No business.** You can't use this free Web page service for a business home page, although you can mention your business on your free personal home page. (Some people use their free personal Web pages to "mention" their businesses an awful lot.)

- ✔ **No monkey business.** GeoCities does impose restrictions on what you can publish; no nudity is allowed, and anything that would get a movie an R rating is likely to be problematic. If you have doubts about something you want to publish, check out the GeoCities guidelines page at

  www.geocities.com/members/guidelines

- ✔ **No more than 5MB.** All your Web files together must occupy no more than 5MB of disk space, which is about 5,000 pages of text or about 40 to 50 large, quarter-screen graphics. This restriction is not a problem for pages created with GeoCities' personal Home Page Editor, described later in this chapter, because they are likely to be far below the limit. If you expand your page beyond the limit later, GeoCities makes more space available and gives you other goodies as part of the GeoPlus program for a mere $4.95 a month.

Choose GeoCities or online service?

If you use an online service, you can create a free personal Web page on GeoCities, on your online service, or on both. We recommend that online service users put their first Web page on their online service. Why?

A number of reasons. First and foremost is support. Online services are great sources of help for all kinds of online concerns, not least of which is getting your first Web page up and running. You can get a lot of help easily from your fellow members and from the support personnel of your online service.

Second is familiarity. You're already familiar with your online service. You're more able to take advantage of its free services than the

services in some other kind of setup, even one as friendly and open as GeoCities.

Third is community. Online services try to foster a sense of community, as does GeoCities. If you're a person who values this feeling, you probably have already developed it within your online service; you may as well take advantage of the community that you're already paying for!

So if you're a user of an online service, go to the next chapter and follow the instructions for creating and hosting a free Web page. If not, you don't need to join an online service just to get free Web hosting service; GeoCities is fast, easy, and fun.

✔ **No guarantees.** GeoCities doesn't guarantee that it will continue to provide free Web page service in the future. GeoCities has to say this to protect itself from unanticipated events, but all indications are that it does indeed plan to continue this free service for quite a while. And after you create your Web site, you can always get another host for it later if you need to. The point is to take advantage now of a unique and very valuable opportunity.

You can create a commercial home page on GeoCities to explicitly support a business. The cost is $50 for setup plus $50 a month, which is not too unreasonable, but you aren't allowed a custom domain name (such as www.yourbiz.com), CGI scripts to add interactivity, or other nice features most competing services offer. Fewer than 100 companies have taken advantage of GeoCities' commercial pages program at this time, making it far less successful than their personal publishing program. (About one-ten-thousandth as successful, to be precise.) If you want a very easy start to your business page publishing effort, consider GeoCities; otherwise, check Chapter 5 for less expensive online-service options, and Chapter 8 for other Web hosting services.

For more information on GeoCities' commercial page service, see this information page:

www.geocities.com/main/info/comm_info.html

GeoCities is constantly improving its offerings and could improve its commercial page service at any time, so do check the information page for an update if you're interested.

For a list of existing GeoCities commercial sites, check the following Web page:

`www.geocities.com/search/commercial.html`

Even if you do need to create a business page, consider creating a free personal page first. You get a lot of experience, and then you can apply that experience to creating a credible business Web page or site.

Unlike businesses, nonprofit organizations or anyone offering a free public service is likely to find GeoCities a great place to get started. The people at GeoCities may even adjust their 5MB limit upward for your site if your site is interesting and promotes a good cause.

Applying for Your Personal Home Page

Before you can create your personal home page on GeoCities, you have to apply for it. A couple of hours after you apply, you receive your permission and password. (What are you waiting for? The quicker you apply, the quicker you get your permission and password, and the quicker you can get started.) The password keeps others from editing your home page. After you receive the permission and password, you have about a week to put up at least a placeholder page, or GeoCities gives your space to someone else.

The next set of steps is long, and you should be ready to complete it in the same session in which you start it. So be sure you have about 60 minutes free to spend online before beginning.

To apply for your personal home page, follow these steps:

1. **Open your Web browser.**

    The GeoCities site works with any browser.

2. **Go to** `www.geocities.com`**.**

    You can access all sorts of cool stuff from the GeoCities home page. Try to ignore all the cool stuff for now and go to the next step. You can tour the GeoCities site further after you send in your application.

3. **Click the Free Home Pages and E-mail button, which is in the graphic in the upper right of the Web page.**

    Steps to apply for your free personal home page appear.

4. Click the Neighborhood Directory link.

Surf through GeoCities neighborhoods until you find one you like. To see a description of a specific neighborhood and access the personal Web pages in it, click the neighborhood name. Many neighborhoods highlight top pages, which you can check out as part of getting a feel for the neighborhood. (The top pages are often quite complex, but don't let that worry you; most people start simple and build from there.) See the sidebar, "Choosing a neighborhood," later in this chapter, for a list of GeoCities neighborhoods.

5. When you find a neighborhood you like, click its name to bring up its home page. Then click the Join This Neighborhood button.

A detailed description of the neighborhood appears. For some crowded neighborhoods, you also see a list of specific subneighborhoods, such as Area 51/Cavern and Area 51/Corridor.

6. Click a link to any block with vacancies. Use the address links in the left-hand frame to look at different blocks. Scroll up and down within each block to see vacant addresses.

Each time you click a link, a different page of GeoCities homesteads appears, as shown in Figure 4-2. Note that some sites are vacant; others are occupied.

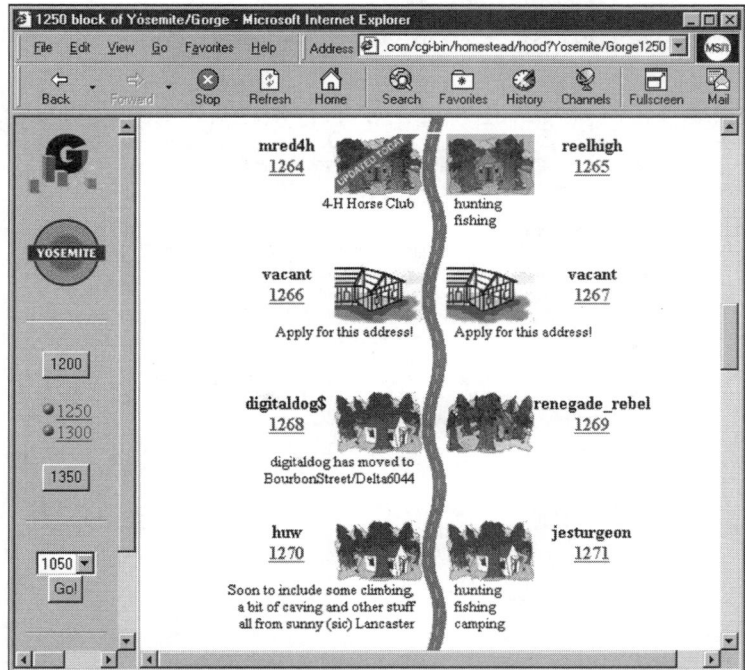

Figure 4-2:
Find a spot to build a home of your own.

7. When you see a vacant address you like, click it.

The GeoCities New Member Application appears, as shown in Figure 4-3.

8. Click the Free Personal Home Page Program radio button. Scroll down to the middle of the page and review the Member Terms of Service.

The GeoCities Member Terms of Service is not like a typical software license. It includes interesting and important information for your GeoCities membership, including restrictions on what you can put in your Web pages. GeoCities specifically excludes nudity or pornography, displaying material that exploits children, blatant expressions of "bigotry, prejudice, racism, hatred, or profanity," and commercial activity, including selling products, soliciting for advertisers or sponsors, or promoting multilevel marketing activities. Review the terms of service carefully before proceeding; if you aren't comfortable with them, or believe that the content you want to put up may violate them, use a different publishing option than GeoCities.

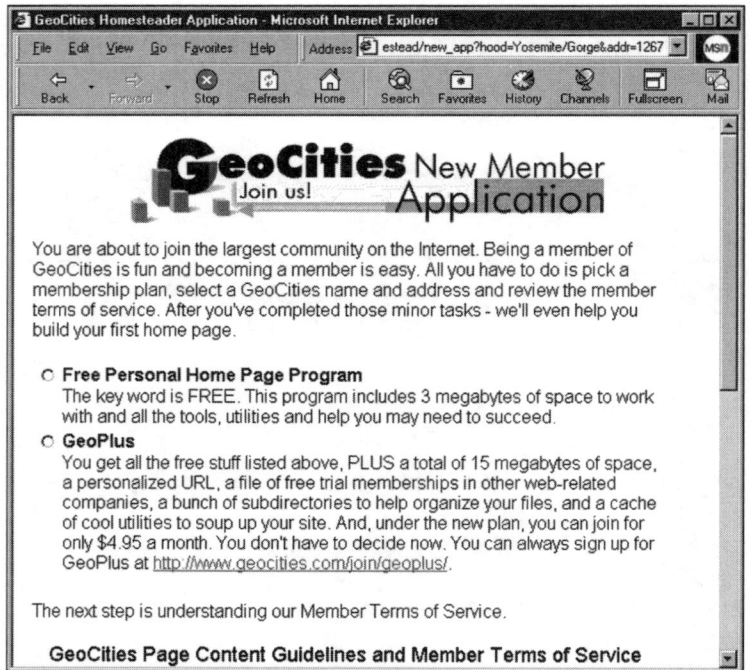

Figure 4-3:
Apply to
become a
GeoCities
neighbor.

9. **If you agree with the terms and conditions, scroll to the bottom of the screen and click the button, I Agree to These Terms and Conditions.**

   The GeoCities Membership Application Form appears.

10. **Fill in the fields in the Personal Information area of the Membership Application Form:**

    - **(Required) First Name; Last Name:** Your first and last name.

    - **(Optional) Street Address, City, State, Country:** Where you live.

    - **(Required) Postal Code:** Your Zip Code (U.S.), Postal Code, or other mail delivery code.

    - **(Required) E-Mail Address:** Your e-mail address. Double-check to make sure you enter this correctly.

    You can sign up for a free GeoCities e-mail address on this page, but you can't use your new GeoCities e-mail address in this application form; you have to give another e-mail address here. That's so you can get confirmation and instructions before using your GeoCities account. If you don't have an e-mail account of your own, ask a friend to let you use theirs temporarily; you need to ask your friend to print out for you the information they receive on how you can use your GeoCities e-mail account.

    - **(Required) Gender, Date of Birth:** Choose male or female and enter your date of birth.

    - **(Optional) Would you like to receive special offers from advertisers based on your interests:** Just say no if you don't want these offers. If you leave the answer as yes and give your real address, expect to see offers in your real mailbox by your real house or apartment. Whether or not you specify your real address, advertisers are likely to use the e-mail address you're required to give.

    - **(Optional) If yes, please check those that apply:** What kind of offers do you want to get? Check the areas that interest you most.

11. **Fill in the fields in the Home Page Information area of the Membership Application Form:**

    - **(Required) Member Name:** A name with no spaces, no capital letters, up to 14 characters long, for logging on to GeoCities. Examples: budthesmith, doronron, or helpmerhonda. Your member name will be listed next to your address.

    - **(Optional) Directory listing:** Up to three lines describing your home page, like the descriptions shown in Figure 4-3. Each line can be up to 35 characters long (you can't type any more characters into the boxes than that). Use this! It helps people find your home page.

- Don't use apostrophes in your directory listing; they won't show up on your Web page.

12. Specify whether you want a GeoCities e-mail account:

- **(Optional) Would you like to receive a free GeoCities e-mail account:** This is a good thing to have — an e-mail account not dependent on your work. Unless you already have a personal e-mail account, sign up for a GeoCities e-mail account.

13. Just say No — or Yes — to Special Offers:

- **Click No unless you want to receive special offers based on your interest.** Just say no if you don't want these offers. If you leave the answer as yes and give your real address, expect to see offers in your real mailbox by your house. Whether or not you specify your real address, expect advertisers to send offers to the e-mail address you're required to give.

- **If yes, please check all that apply:** What kind of offers do you want to get? Check the areas that interest you most; options include Automotive, Health, Sports, and more.

- **Surplus Direct, GeoPlanet, InfoBeat:** Unless you say no by clicking the appropriate button, you receive computer hardware and software advertising from Egghead Computer and Surplus Direct, and are put in touch with friends by GeoPlanet. If you want an e-mail news update from InfoBeat, click Yes and then check off your interests. If you don't want InfoBeat, click No to make sure you don't get one.

14. Fill in the fields in the Optional Information area of the Membership Application Form:

- **(Optional) Highest Level of Education Completed; Household Income; Marital Status; Occupation; Interests:** We recommend that you fill in this information to help GeoCities better understand who's using its services.

15. Specify whether to include personal information in your initial GeoCities home page:

- GeoCities automatically includes information about your interests and your e-mail address in your initial home page. If you don't want this information published for you, click No.

16. Click the Submit button to submit your application.

A confirmation page showing your information appears, like the one in Figure 4-4.

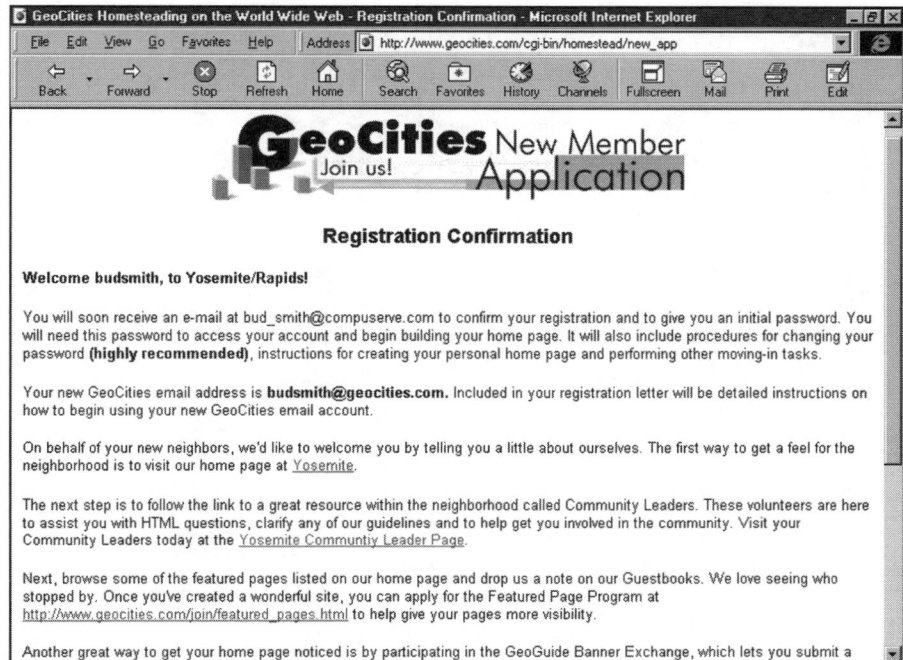

Figure 4-4:
Surf
GeoCities
until you
get your
password.

After you submit your application, your address is reserved, but you have to wait until your password arrives before you can create your home page. You should get the password in a few hours. (However, if you're excited about creating your Web page, a few hours can seem like a long time.) After GeoCities approves your application, they notify you by e-mail at the e-mail address you included in your application.

Once you get your password, hurry and move in; if you don't, your space may be released to someone else. If so, you'll be offered a new space, but you may want to avoid the hassle and just get settled in your new address quickly.

Choosing a neighborhood

Just as in real-life house-hunting, finding the right neighborhood for your personal home page can take some thought and investigation. The GeoCities neighborhoods include the following:

- Area51: Science fiction and fantasy fans
- Athens: Education, teaching, reading, writing, and philosophy
- Augusta: Golfing life
- Baja: Four-wheeling and adventure travel
- BourbonStreet: New Orleans tribute with jazz, Cajun food, and culture
- Broadway: Live theater and show business
- CapeCanaveral: Science, technology, aviation
- CapitolHill: Politics, government, and national affairs
- CollegePark: University life
- Colosseum: Sports and recreation
- Enchanted Forest: For and by kids; special content restrictions apply
- Eureka: A different kind of SOHO (Small Office Home Office)
- FashionAvenue: Beauty and fashion design
- Heartland: Parenting, pets, and hometown values
- Hollywood: Entertainment capital of the world
- HotSprings: Health, fitness, medicine
- MadisonAvenue: Advertising
- MotorCity: Automotive and racing enthusiasts
- NapaValley: Gourmet food, wine
- Nashville: Both kinds of music: country *and* western
- Paris: The arts, fine wine, and continental lifestyle
- Pentagon: Military people
- PicketFence: Real estate and home improvement
- Pipeline: Extreme sports (think X Games)
- RainForest: Environment and conservation
- ResearchTriangle: Think tank for high-tech visionaries
- RodeoDrive: Shopping and upscale living
- SiliconValley: High tech; the most popular neighborhood
- SoHo: Bohemian artists, writers
- SouthBeach: High-style hot spot for mingling
- SunsetStrip: Nightlife, adventure, personals, and more
- TelevisionCity: TV fans
- TheTropics: Vacation, resort, travel, and leisure
- TimesSquare: Computer games, video games, and interactive adventure sites
- Tokyo: Far Eastern
- Vienna: Classical music, ballet, opera
- WallStreet: Finance, business, commerce, and investing

✔ Wellesley: Women's community

✔ WestHollywood: Gay and lesbian life

✔ Yosemite: Hiking, climbing, skiing, rafting, camping

To go directly to a neighborhood from your browser, just type its name after the GeoCities URL: For instance, enter www.geocities. com/soho to access the SoHo neighborhood.

Many neighborhoods have "suburbs," areas within the neighborhood to accommodate additional settlers. Though the suburbs often have cute names — SoHo has Cafe, Gallery, Lofts, and others — suburbs exist only to create additional space in the main neighborhood and don't have any special focus of their own. The only difference is that the main neighborhood is likely to have older Web sites than the suburbs, since the main neighborhood was settled first.

Waiting for Godot (Or Whatever Your Password Is)

While waiting for your password to arrive, you can do several things:

✔ **Visit your new neighborhood.** The Web page that appears after you register includes links to your new neighborhood, to the community leaders' page in your neighborhood, and more. Follow these links to get to know your new virtual neighbors.

✔ **See special offers.** The Web page that appears after you register also includes a link to special house-warming offers, not unlike the welcome basket you receive when you move into a real-world home. Follow the link to check them out.

✔ **Learn more about GeoCities in general by clicking and navigating around the GeoCities Web site.** One thing you may not learn is how GeoCities can afford to give away free Web space. The answer is that GeoCities really wants to build true communities in cyberspace (that is, the online world). GeoCities also gets advertising revenues, clients for its custom Web work, and the fame and possible fortune of having one of the top spots on the Web.

✔ **Visit your temporary Web page.** From the Web page that appears after you register, follow a link to your new GeoCities Web homestead, like the one shown in Figure 4-5. GeoCities puts up an initial home page for you, a kind of cyberspace placeholder with your interests in it. You can check it out and also bookmark it so you can quickly get to it from within your Web browser.

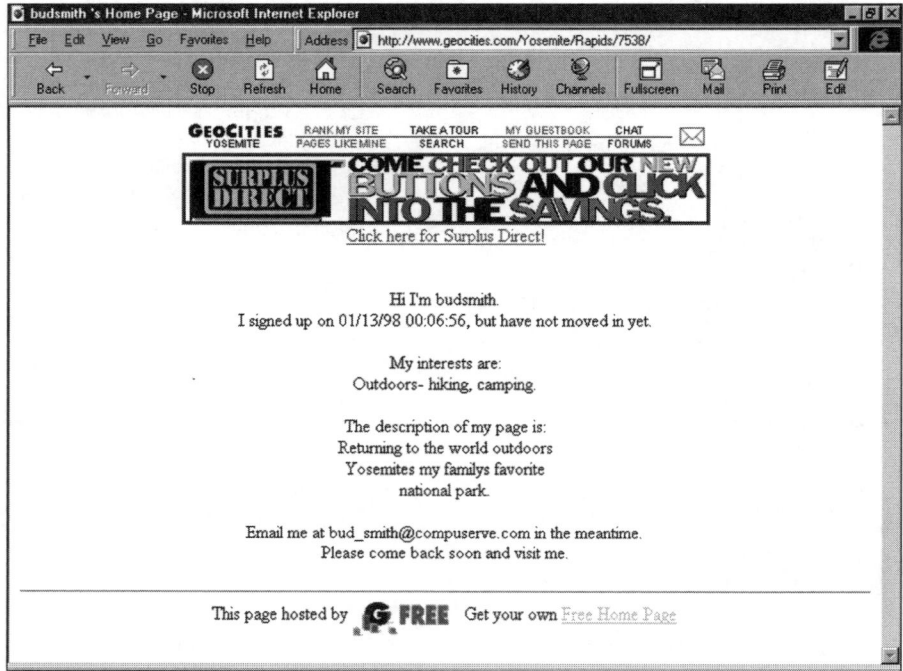

Figure 4-5:
Your initial
Web page
with your
theme info
— and no
apostrophes!

✓ **Look for the URLs of your favorite Web sites.** The GeoCities Basic Home Page Editor lets you list links to six of your favorite Web sites — but to link to them, you need the URLs. Surf around the Web and find the URLs of six sites that reflect your interests and the interests of the neighborhood you're putting your home page in. (The more obscure, the better!)

✓ **Use a word processor or a few pieces of notebook paper to plan your initial Web page.** (Use the paper for drawing only — neither origami nor paper airplanes translate well to the Web.) Just rough out what text you want to put in and what URLs to include. Then, when you get your password, you're ready to go.

✓ **Read this book.** To move ahead with Web page authoring, you're going to want to know most of what's in the rest of this book anyway. Waiting for your password gives you a good opportunity to read it.

✓ **Catch up on life.** You've probably spent a good deal of time on the Web lately, and after you get permission to create your home page, you'll probably spend even more. So take this opportunity to organize your baseball cap collection, wipe off the ink spots that are messing up your pocket protector, or call your mom and apologize for forgetting her birthday two weeks ago.

GeoCities personal home pages and banner ads

The only direct cost of publishing your home page on GeoCities is the same as the only direct cost of watching television: ads. Your GeoCities home page must have a GeoCities banner ad; selling these ads is how GeoCities makes its money. The ads are kind of annoying, but don't worry — if you create a good site, people spend most of the time on inside pages of the site, away from the ads, and not on the home page.

A Home (Page) of Your Own

After some time passes, you get an e-mail message from GeoCities with your password. Now you're ready to create your personal home page. This is the fun part! With the GeoCities Home Page Editor, you can't really cause any big problems. Just relax and enjoy yourself.

Although creating a Web page isn't difficult, it involves many steps. We have divided the steps into three groups to make them more manageable.

Like the process of signing up for your free GeoCities home page, the process of creating your initial home page takes some time. Make sure you have about 60 minutes free to spend online before beginning.

The following steps are intended to help you to successfully create a home page fairly quickly, with the idea that you can come back and improve it after achieving initial success. If you have time and feel adventurous, you can deviate from the steps to create a fancier home page right off the bat; just follow the on-screen prompts and suggestions.

Getting to the Home Page Editor

To create a Web page in GeoCities, the first thing that you need to do is get to the Basic Home Page Editor:

1. **Open your Web browser and go to** www.geocities.com/members.

   The Members page appears, as shown in Figure 4-6.

2. **Under the Tools header, click the File Manager link.**

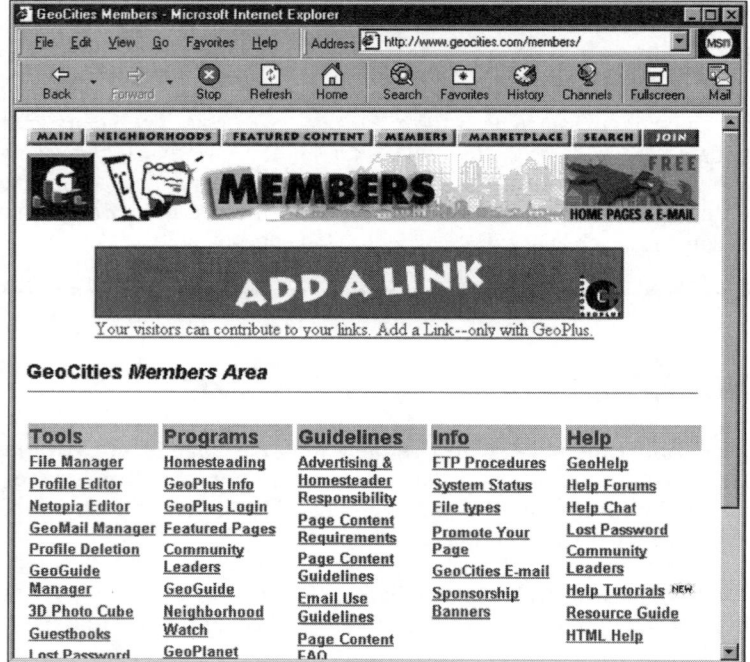

Figure 4-6:
Once you're
a member,
you can use
cool tools.

3. **Enter your member name and password, then click Submit.**

   Both the member name and password are in the e-mail message that
   you received authorizing you to use the Home Page Editor. After you
   enter your member name and password, the File Manager brings up a
   page that lets you choose what to do next.

4. **Scroll down to the middle of the page and find the Choose Your
   Editor prompt. Choose Basic Home Page Editor from the drop-down
   list.**

   This option helps you create your new Web page using the Basic Home
   Page Editor, which hides the details of HTML from you.

5. **Click the Create New HTML File button. The GeoCities Basic HTML
   Editor appears.**

   Figure 4-7 shows part of the Basic Home Page Editor screen.

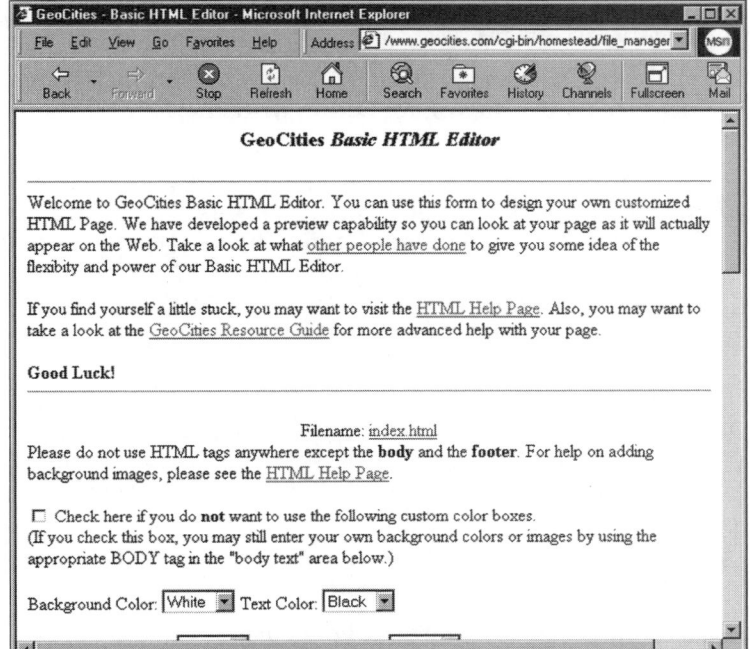

Creating a first impression

You want the first thing that people see when they open your Web page to make them want to see more, so spend some time deciding what to put on this page and figuring out how to make the page look good:

1. **Check the check box that reads Check here if you do not want to use the following custom color boxes.**

   Most Web pages use a basic color scheme in which text is black, the background is gray or white, unvisited links are blue, and visited links are purple. That color scheme is not an available option here. So check the check box to ignore custom color boxes and use the basic color scheme that people are used to until you're ready to take the time to figure out a replacement color scheme that works well.

   If you don't check the check box and leave the custom color boxes all set to Blue, your page will not work correctly. That's because the text and links are the same color as the background, which makes them invisible! So check the check box.

2. To put an icon at the top of your home page, click the Images link. A list of icons appears.

If you want to use an icon, you must choose it from among those provided by the Home Page Editor. Write down the abbreviation for the icon you want. At the time of this writing, the choices include

- Flags — dozens of flags, including af (Afghanistan); au (Australia); at (Austria); be (Belgium); br (Brazil); ca (Canada); tw (China); hr (Croatia); cu (Cuba); cz (Czech); dk (Denmark); uk (UK); fi (Finland); fr (France); de (Germany); gr (Greece); hk (Hong Kong); ie (Ireland); il (Israel); it (Italy); jp (Japan); lv (Latvia); le (Lebanon); lt (Lithuania); mc (Macedonia); mx (Mexico); nl (Netherlands); no (Norway); pa (Panama); us (USA).

- Other images: ab (abacus); am (Amber); bm (bomb); cv (Calvin); cf (Cindy Crawford); ah (Audrey Hepburn); in (info); my (money); nw (news); nt (note); os (Oscar); qu (question); rb (rainbow); sk (skull); sm (smile); sp (Mr. Spock); ss (Sharon Stone); tt (tic-tac-toe); wr (warning).

3. Click on the icon you want from the list that appears or enter the code for the icon that you want.

4. Enter the Page Title for your home page.

The Page Title does not appear in your page! It appears in the title bar of the browser window of most browsers and is used by Internet search engines and other tools to find your page. Enter your name and one or two key phrases that describe your page.

5. Enter the Title Line that you want below the Page Title, if any.

The Title Line appears across the top of your page.

You can enter long titles. A normal browser window is wide enough to display about 50 large characters across; if you don't mind having the Title Line be longer than one line, you can enter even more characters. (I was able to use a 200-character Title Line with no problem.)

6. Choose a character size and style for the Title Line, or None if you have no title line.

Choices are small, regular, large, small italic, regular italic, large italic, and none. It looks better if the Title Line is larger than the Second Title (see next step), if any; so make the Title Line regular or large if you plan to have a Second Title.

7. Enter the Second Title that you want below the Title Line, if any.

The Second Title appears below the Title Line, as shown in Figure 4-8. Like the Title Line, it can be quite long. Think of the Second Title as the subtitle of a book. Just leave this blank for now.

8. **Choose a character size and style for the Second Title, or choose None if no second title.**

   Choices are small, regular, large, small italic, regular italic, large italic, and none. It looks better if the Second Title is smaller than the Title Line, so choose a size smaller than the Title Line.

9. **Click the box after the Separator prompt to choose a Separator line to appear underneath your page's titles.**

   The default choice is blue_thin_line_2. Choose from other kinds of lines if you want; the choices include: blue_mrble_thick, blue_marble_thin, black_thin_line1, blck_beaded_line, red_thick_line_1, yellow_thck_line, blue_cool_links1, red_yel_hot_link, construct_line_1, rainbow_thinline, wave_thin_gray_1, string_tape_line, and ruler_measured_1. To view examples of each separator, click the Separators link.

All the separators are actually separate graphics. If the person viewing your home page has graphics turned off, that person sees an ugly block or another kind of marker representing a missing graphic where you intended to have a nice separator line. A way to avoid this potential problem is to leave the predefined separator lines set to None and put in the HTML tag for a horizontal rule — <HR> — at the start and end of your body text.

If you do use a separator line at any point in your home page, consider using the same separator line elsewhere as well. The visual effect of using several different styles of separator lines can be as jarring as using too many fonts on one page (which does happen during the editing process, believe us).

10. **To preview your work so far, scroll down to the bottom of the page and click the Preview button.**

    Wait a few seconds, and you see a preview of your Web page so far, followed by the editing page you are working in. You can continue working in the editing page; then, click Preview whenever you want to see how your work will look on the Web.

Don't do as one of the authors did — lose patience during the preview and start clicking other buttons or the Back button on your browser. If you do, you get confused as to what page you're working on. Just wait until the preview page comes up.

Getting your body in shape

After you look at the preview of your page, you just scroll down to keep working on your page and enter the information that you want to convey. For example, maybe you want to use your Web page to encourage people to sign up for that new self-help group your spouse suggested that you form — Web Addicts Anonymous — or to promote your favorite sport: bungee jumping in the Grand Canyon. Or maybe you just want to share some info about yourself and your more mundane interests. It's your call.

1. **Enter the body text for your page.**

   Type in the body text for your page. Include HTML tags if you want. (See the Cheat Sheet for a list of the most popular ones.) You can include several pages of text.

   You really don't have to say a lot here. If you don't have any bright ideas at this point, you can simply use the space to say hello, mention a couple of your interests, say how much you like GeoCities and (especially) the 3rd edition of *Creating Web Pages For Dummies,* and promise to provide more later.

   If you are entering more than a few lines of text, create your text in a word processor and then cut and paste it into the Home Page Editor. Ignore the fact that the line goes off the side of your screen, because the user's browser breaks the lines where needed.

   Some browsers don't display the scroll bar for the text field. Any text that you enter that doesn't fit in the text field "as is" may simply be deleted. If your browser doesn't support scroll bars, consider getting a newer browser such as a recent version of Netscape Navigator that does support scroll bars.

2. **Time to save your work! Scroll down to the bottom of the page and click Save and Continue Editing.**

   You've done the bulk of the work needed for creating your home page, and there's no sense in losing it now. Click Save and Continue Editing to save your work. After the save, the page reappears; scroll back down to the Body Text area to continue your work.

3. **If you want, choose a separator line to appear below the body text.**

   For the most consistent appearance, use the same kind of separator line that you used after the Title Line. Or ignore all this advice and choose any darn separator line you want.

4. **Enter the URLs for up to six of your favorite Web sites; enter a description for each URL.**

   Leave out the http:// that is at the beginning of Web URLs, and don't put any spaces in URLs. Also enter a description for each Web site. The Basic Home Page Editor displays the description text and makes it a link to the URL. Here are some examples:

   • URL: www.communities.com (Note that http:// is not used.)

   • Description: Avatars, Java, and more.

Most Web users have already heard of sites such as Yahoo!, Apple, San Jose Mercury News, Pathfinder, and other extremely popular Web sites. Be more creative than other people and list sites that are meaningful to you in terms of your personal interests.

You probably don't know the URLs of all your favorite Web sites off the top of your head. The good news is that you can go cruise around the Web at this point to find URLs; the bad news is, you risk losing your work if you have a system crash while surfing around. To avoid problems, use the Save and Continue Editing button at the bottom of the page to save your work before you go off Web surfing.

5. Choose a separator line to appear below your favorite URLs.

6. Enter the footer text for your page. Include HTML tags if you want.

This text appears below the URL list. It can be quite lengthy; one of the authors was able to include 12 lines over 100 characters each with no problem.

7. If you want your e-mail address to appear on your home page, put a check mark in the Include E-Mail Address on Page check box.

Most personal home pages include the creator's e-mail address. You can always put your address in and then remove it later if you get too much mail. ("Too much" is a relative term. Some people dislike getting e-mail; others live for it.)

8. If you want, choose a separator line to appear at the bottom of your Web page.

You've completed the first draft of your GeoCities home page.

9. To preview your work, scroll down to the bottom of the page and click the Preview button.

Wait a few seconds, and you see a preview of your Web page so far, followed by the editing page you've been working in. Figure 4-8 is an example.

10. Congratulations! You've completed your first Web page. To save your work, scroll down to the bottom of the page and click the button Save. Then enter `index.html` **as the filename to use.**

Your work is saved, and you return to the GeoCities File Manager.

11. Look at your home page on the Web. Tell your friends! You now are a published Web page author.

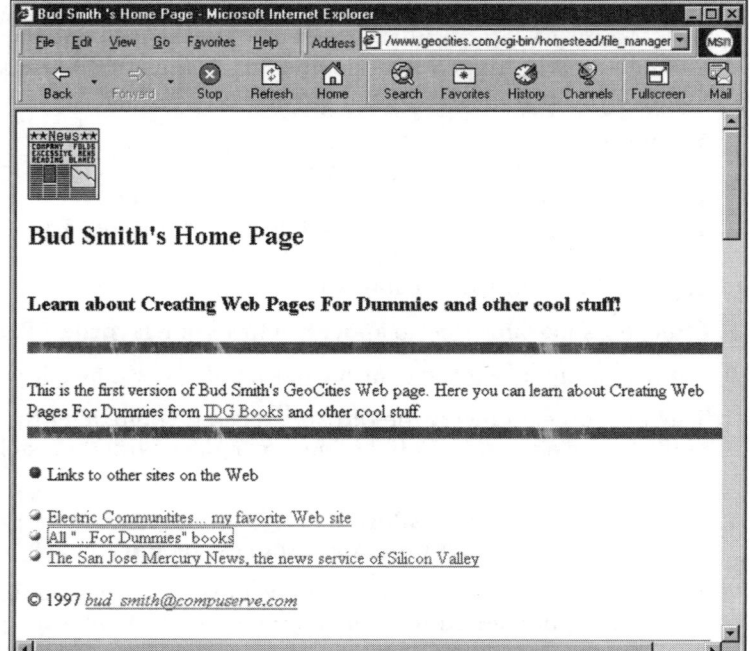

Figure 4-8:
Previewing
your first
home page
for the
Web!

Using the Home Page Editor to try HTML

You can enter HTML tags in the body text, which is a good way to see what different tags do. Try surrounding a word or phrase with some of the following formatting tags to see the effect:

- ✔ `<P>` to start a new paragraph.

- ✔ `<B> text </B>` for bold.

- ✔ `<I> text </I>` for italic.

- ✔ `<IMG SRC="URL">` to put a graphic in your home page. Until you learn more, you

have to use a graphic that's already on the Web, so make sure that you have no problems with permissions.

- ✔ `<A HREF="http://www.geocities. com">text</A>` for a link that goes to the GeoCities home page when you click it. Use other URLs for other anchors.

See the Cheat Sheet and Chapter 3 for more HTML tags that you can use in this or any other Web page you create.

You can see the underlying HTML that makes up your GeoCities home page. In the File Manager, click the check box next to the file called index.html. Then choose Advanced HTML Editor from the drop-down list. Click the Edit button. Your home page appears as HTML-tagged text. You can use the information in later chapters of this book to add HTML tags and add more capability to your home page. (*Note:* If you change and save your home page from the Advanced HTML Editor, you won't be able to edit it in the Basic Home Page Editor anymore.)

Expanding the old homestead

Once you've done the basics and gotten your first Web page up, you may want to expand your efforts. GeoCities offers support for going much further with your Web page. Here are some pointers:

- **Adding graphics.** To add a graphic that isn't already on the Web, you need to upload the graphics file to your site and then point to the graphic from within your Web page. See the GeoCities Personal Home Page Program FTP Procedures at the following URL:

  www.geocities.com/homestead/homeftp.html

- **Adding HTML tags.** You can put HTML tags in the body or footer of your Web page. To see a basic list of HTML tags, see Chapter 3, or the GeoCities "HOME PAGE Home Page" at the following URL:

  www.geocities.com/Athens/2090

- **Changing the look of your page.** Really changing the look of your page requires that you work directly in HTML. Edit your page using the Advanced Home Page Editor to do this. Go to the File Manager; choose your home page file called index.html; select the Advanced Home Page Editor from the drop-down list; then choose Edit. You can make the changes you want and then save the changes. However, after you edit your file in the Advanced Home Page Editor, you can't use the Basic Home Page Editor to edit your page any more, only the Advanced Home Page Editor.

- **Adding multimedia, Java, ShockWave, and more.** GeoCities already supports some advanced features and is working on more. Read Chapter 8 for information on these advanced features. Tour the GeoCities site for information and to find existing pages that do what you want so you can determine how to add the functionality you want.

- **Adding CGIs and other executables.** GeoCities won't support certain features that may cause problems on the server end, such as CGI (Common Gateway Interface) scripts that update databases. You need to find another Web service provider for functions like this.

More Web Freebies

GeoCities is the best way we know to get a "starter" personal home page on the Web. But offering free Web pages is becoming popular. A number of additional Web-based services that ease the process of creating a Web page are available. To find more, start by checking Yahoo! at

```
www.yahoo.com/Business_and_Economy/Companies/
Internet_Services/Web_Services/Free_Web_Pages/
```

Here are some of the best sites found there:

> ✔ **Service:** Directories
>
> **URL:** `www.yahoo.com/Business_and_Economy/Companies/Internet_Services/Web_Services/Free_Web_Pages/Directories`
>
> **Description:** These directories provide alternate listing of sites that provide free Web page services.

> ✔ **Service:** Free Homepage Center
>
> **URL:** `www.freehomepage.com`
>
> **Description:** This is a directory of free homepage sites that meet specific criteria, including several good ones.

> ✔ **Service:** Free home pages for nonprofits.
>
> **URL:** `www.achiever.com/design/freehmpg.html`
>
> **Description:** Ostriches online is a large company dealing with ostriches that has a civic-minded bent and, as such, offers a small amount of space — 150K or so — for an initial home page for non-profit organizations. Go to the URL above to apply for permission; if you get it, follow the instructions to take advantage of the free offer.

You also can look for free Web pages on your own. You can go to the Yahoo! Web site (`www.yahoo.com`), the OpenText search service (link from Yahoo!), or another search service and look for "free Web pages" or similar phrases. As in all Web searches, your chances of finding what you're actually looking for are only so-so, but your chances of finding something interesting enough to keep you online for an hour or two are great!

Chapter 5

Using Online Services for Web Publishing

· ·

· ·

*A*lthough it may seem as though the easy-to-use, open, ungovernable World Wide Web is going to wipe out traditional, closed, monitored online services such as America Online, CompuServe, and The Microsoft Network, it's not really working out that way. The online services are adapting quickly. They have become gateways to the Web and offer easy-to-use Web publishing services that include hosting your Web page for free.

If you already use an online service, that service is probably the best place for you to start experimenting with Web publishing. You already know the interface, you can find online forums and discussion boards for Web publishing, and you can use the easy-to-use Web publishing features that the major services have scrambled to provide. Even online services that aren't in the "big three" likely offer support for your Web page publishing efforts.

If you aren't yet an online service user, the quickest and cheapest way to get your first page up on the Web is to use GeoCities, the Web-based service described in Chapter 4. When you're ready to improve your Web site, your next step may be to subscribe to an online service. America Online, in particular, has strong features for intermediate Web publishing, including support for both Windows and Macintosh, 2MB or more of free server space, and (at the time of this writing) no restrictions on using free Web pages for business.

Note: Just like the Web, online services are changing quickly. The information in this chapter was accurate at the time we wrote it, but you need to check online for the latest info.

Choosing an Online Service for Web Publishing

To quote a song from Devo (a crazed and defunct rock group), "Use your freedom of choice." You certainly have freedom of choice when it comes to online services. And your choice truly is free — most online services offer free signup and a free trial period. You can try two or three services before making a long-term choice. Just remember to resign from any service that you stop using, or the $20 or so a month charge to your credit card will go on forever!

In this chapter, we describe the top three online services: America Online (AOL), CompuServe, and The Microsoft Network (MSN). Why only these three? Because they have the most variety; because they extend across North America and, increasingly, the world; and because they all offer, or soon plan to offer, some form of free Web publishing services. But you may want to consider a smaller service or an Internet service provider (ISP) instead. Compare other offerings to the big three, and if you can find something that better fits your needs, go for it.

The best online service

The question "What's the best online service?" has been asked and answered in dozens of articles, panel discussions, and personal conversations by tens of thousands of users who have tried one, two, or more of the services. The discussion focuses disproportionately on which service has the easiest and most attractive user interface, while sometimes ignoring the content and overall functionality of each service. (In online services, as in life, beauty is only skin deep — and is entirely in the eye of the beholder.) To get beyond the surface, try one or more services yourself and see how each service fits your needs.

Many professional, trade, and interest groups have a home on one of the online services. Microsoft software support finds a natural home on The Microsoft Network; AutoCAD provides support for its users on CompuServe; and America Online has a wide variety of consumer-oriented services, one of which is the very popular NetNoir service spotlighting African-American culture. All three services are trying to provide the best features for children. If you have a specific professional or personal interest to pursue online, ask around to see whether one of the online services has a clear lead in content for your interest.

As for more general concerns, all three interfaces have a modern, relatively attractive GUI (graphical user interface), but CompuServe in particular still shows traces of its text-based past. The experience of using America Online also is increasingly marred by pop-up ads that you have to click to get rid of; these ad deals are worth tens of millions of dollars to America Online, Inc., but they are just as annoying as TV ads. Figure 5-1 shows the clean and attractive interface of America Online — but watch out for those pop-up ads. Figure 5-2 shows the functional interface of CompuServe; Figure 5-3 shows the revamped interface of The Microsoft Network.

The examples show the versions for Windows. The Macintosh offerings on the Big Three tend to lag behind the versions for Windows; many Macintosh owners choose America Online, which got an early start with Macintosh users (America Online's software is based on work Apple did for its own defunct online service).

So what's the best online service? If you already use one, you should probably stick with it when pursuing your Web publishing efforts. Learning a new service is a big hassle, and each online service has decent Web publishing support — except The Microsoft Network, which promises to have it soon.

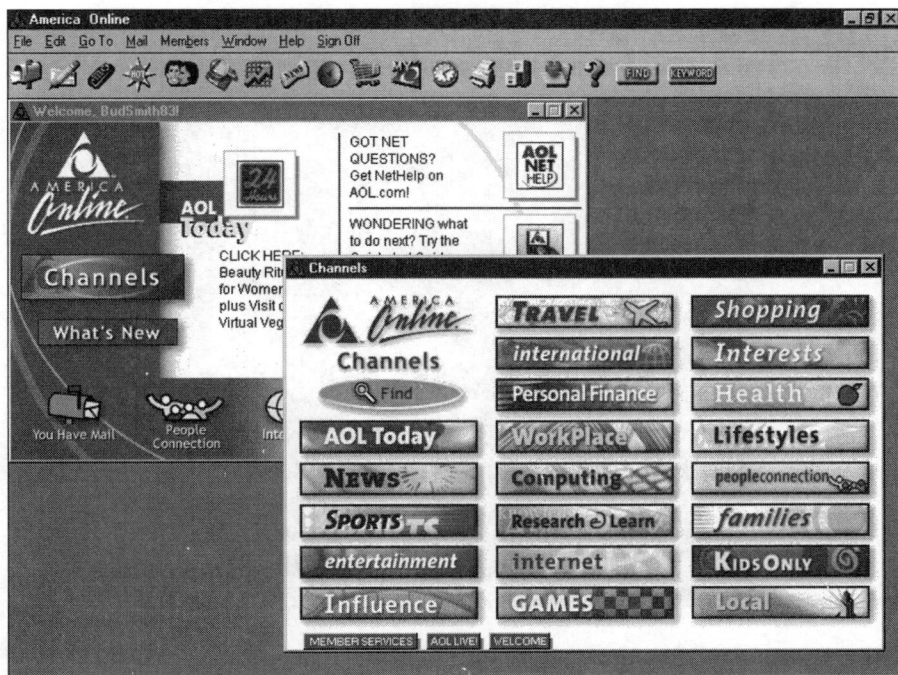

Figure 5-1: America Online is easy for everyone to use.

Figure 5-2:
CompuServe
gets more
GUI with
time.

Figure 5-3:
The
Microsoft
Network —
like a TV
network,
only slower.

But if you have not yet chosen an online service, or have been considering switching, here are the high points of each service:

- ✔ **America Online.** So far, the market has consistently voted most strongly for America Online, making it the largest and fastest growing of the services with about 10 million users. America Online also has the most Macintosh users and Mac-related content of the major services. America Online regularly suffers from growth-related problems, such as users complaining about difficulty signing on, performance problems, and even billing problems. AOL continually works hard to address these concerns, but joining the leader may cause you occasional performance anxiety.

- ✔ **CompuServe.** For business, CompuServe may be the top choice. It has a vast array of business-oriented services and millions of business-oriented users who help each other with both general and industry-specific questions, as well as robust offerings in other areas. CompuServe is also the leader outside North America, partly because its international access is so good. Though CompuServe is harder to learn and sometimes inconsistent in the way it works, its rich content and reliable access make it the top choice for many users. However, America Online has recently acquired CompuServe; it's quite possible that future improvements to CompuServe may be put on the back burner while AOL moves steadily ahead. AOL may also extend its ads to Compuserve soon.

- ✔ **The Microsoft Network.** The Microsoft Network is the smallest, but fastest-growing, of the top three. A recent revamp has led The Microsoft Network to use lots of moving graphics organized in a *channel* metaphor, which means that this can be the slowest online service to use. Also, at this writing, The Microsoft Network does not yet have its own easy-to-use Web page creation tools. Although they promise to have them "soon," The Microsoft Network will likely lag behind America Online and CompuServe in this area for a while.

- ✔ **Prodigy.** Prodigy, once a leader, has not maintained its momentum and growth while going through a change of ownership and a change of focus. Now it is relaunching itself as Prodigy Internet and plans to introduce new Web page creation services soon. Although we don't cover Prodigy Internet in this book, you may find it worth checking out.

You can find many smaller national services and dozens of local online services around the world. Each has its pluses and minuses, its fans, and its specific appeal. You may even learn about worthwhile local services by cruising one of the big services.

Some services offer language-specific support. If you want to work in a language other than English, ask users who have experience with using that specific language about available services.

Checking newsgroups for the real deal

For user feedback on online services, you may want to check Usenet newsgroups, which you may have access to at school or at work. Newsgroups are discussion groups, hosted on the Internet, that allow people to discuss shared interests. Web browsers often include the capability to read Usenet newsgroups, and the online services offer Usenet access along with Web access. Try the following newsgroups:

- alt.online-service.america-online
- alt.online-service.compuserve
- alt.online-service.microsoft

You can find current information about the services and download client software from each service's Web site:

- www.aol.com
- www.compuserve.com
- www.msn.com

America Online and The Microsoft Network sites are among the most popular sites on the World Wide Web.

The best Web access

The major online services all offer Web access, but what's offered varies dramatically. In general, if all you want is Web access, you may be better off with an Internet service provider (ISP), a company that provides direct access to the Internet and that may well be cheaper, have better browser support, or be more reliable to access than the major online services. However, Web access through the major online services offers some shared good points:

- **For occasional use, online services are cheap.** If you use the Web only a few hours a month, online services offer base rates lower than many ISPs — as little as $10 or less for five hours of use. The typical rate for online services and ISPs is about $20 a month for unlimited use.

- **Access is easy and reliable.** You can get to the Web by using the same phone numbers and access techniques that you use for the online service. If you have trouble getting a connection, you also can call an 800 number for help. If you travel a great deal or need backup Web access in addition to that offered by an ISP, easy, reliable access alone can make the online service worth it. (America Online has been notable in its occasional problems in providing reliable access.)

✔ **You'll find plenty of online support.** Given the difficulties you may encounter in learning to use and publish on the Web, who wouldn't want a few thousand friends online to help out? All the online services offer support for Web use and Web publishing. Online forums can tell you what to do, point you to good sites, and more. Online technical support helps you get beyond Web problems and problems with the online service itself.

✔ **Online services offer Web server mirroring.** Online services can *mirror* popular Web sites; that is, online services can keep a copy of the site on their own servers and offer simultaneous support of more users and faster access than can be provided over the open Web.

However, the online services also share some Web access problems:

✔ **Lack of choice.** Online services can lock you into a specific browser, usually Microsoft Internet Explorer. If you want to use Netscape Navigator, you may be able to, but only by doing extra setup work — and then you have a harder time getting questions about how to use your browser answered by your fellow online service users.

✔ **Access is slow.** As we note earlier, access to some popular pages can be faster through an online service than through the open Web. But while some pages are cached for faster access, those that aren't have extra overhead; the online service has to go get them for you from the Internet and then provide them to you, adding an extra step to the process of retrieving the pages.

✔ **Using an online service is like having training wheels.** Remember how free you felt when your parents finally took the training wheels off your first bike? Having the interface of your online service take screen space away from your Web browser, having access to online newsgroups restricted by the online service, and switching back and forth between the "look and feel" of your online service and your accustomed browser may irritate you when compared to feeling the open air of the unregulated Internet.

Along with their common pluses and minuses for Web access, online services also have their own specific pluses and minuses:

✔ **America Online.** For most users, America Online has the best combination of online service features and Internet features. (It has been named the Editor's Choice by *PC Magazine*.) Figure 5-4 shows America Online 3.0 with its built-in Web browser running. (You have to upgrade to Version 3.0 to use America Online's new Web publishing features.) But access is another story; access to America Online is periodically plagued by problems (try saying *that* three times fast) for users trying to get online.

Figure 5-4:
America
Online —
Webbed
best?

✔ **CompuServe.** CompuServe now has direct Web access from within CompuServe via WinCim, the interface software for Windows. Figure 5-5 shows the CompuServe Web browser, Mosaic. (Microsoft Internet Explorer has replaced Mosaic on both Windows and Macintosh, but hundreds of thousands of users will still be on CompuServe Mosaic for a while.) Like America Online, Compuserve has also won the *PC Magazine* Editor's Choice award. CompuServe is a little behind AOL and The Microsoft Network in integrating Web services with its proprietary content.

✔ **The Microsoft Network.** The Microsoft Network is only available on 32-bit Windows (that's Windows 95 or Windows NT) and forces you to use Microsoft's Internet Explorer browser. Though well-integrated with the browser, The Microsoft Network also limits your ability to use things like bookmarks to save pointers to your favorite Web sites. (You can launch Internet Explorer separately to get the full features.) Figure 5-6 shows The Microsoft Network browsing the Web.

Many Web users start with an online service and then move to an Internet service provider after they get going. We recommend that you use an online service to get started or for occasional use and then consider moving up to an ISP, which can be cheaper and more reliable as you increase your time on the Internet.

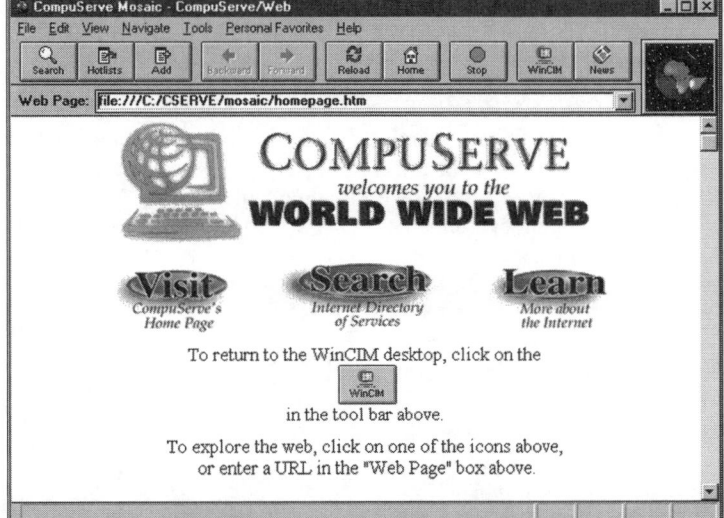

Figure 5-5:
CompuServe
— late to
the Web,
catching up
fast.

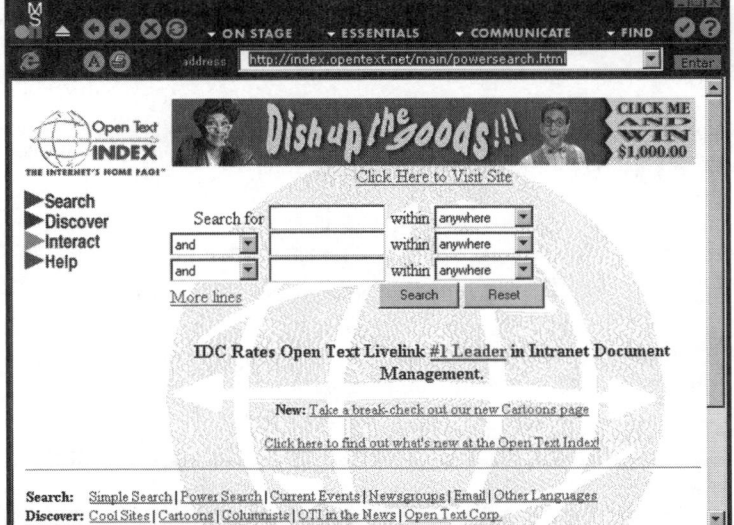

Figure 5-6:
The
Microsoft
Network —
What in the
HTML is
going on
here?

Using an Internet service provider

Internet service providers offer complete Internet and Web access, usually for a moderate price for a large number of hours. Although some ISPs provide only local service, do little to get users set up, and offer poor connections, an increasing number of "best of breed" ISPs offer regional or nationwide service, easy setup, and robust connections, including 56K or ISDN access for faster performance. (56K is a new modem standard that offers faster access; Intergrated Services Digital Network, or ISDN, is an improved kind of phone line that is even faster but is expensive, hard to set up, and not available in all areas.) Although covering the huge number of ISPs is beyond the scope of this book, the following are a few of the top ones in terms of breadth of service and ease of use:

✔ **internetMCI.** Has somewhat limited support for Internet services, but has two pricing plans — limited access at $3.00 for 3 hours, plus $1.80 for each additional hour, or unlimited access for $19.95 per month. Connections are robust and available nationwide, as one might expect from MCI, and Netscape is the browser provided.

✔ **NetCom.** Offers its NetCruiser package for $19.95 for 40 peak hours and unlimited nonpeak hours, plus decent support. You can also "go direct" and use any Internet tool.

✔ **UUNet.** A longtime leader in Internet access that provides good connections for a $25 startup fee plus $30 a month for 25 hours of access, $2 an hour thereafter. Personal Web access is not their main business; UUNet sells access to other ISPs as well.

Also, if you buy Netscape Navigator over the counter as a boxed, retail product, you get a free setup program that enables you to easily choose an ISP. When we checked, you could choose from internetMCI, NetCom, and UUNet Technologies. Internet Explorer is also available as a boxed product with Internet access. You can just buy Netscape Navigator or Internet Explorer, choose an Internet provider, and be in business! If all you want is Web access, the Netscape Navigator or Internet Explorer retail product is a good choice.

For Mac owners, Apple offers the easy-to-use Apple Internet Connection Kit and other Internet tools with a Navigator bundle.

Note: Specific prices and "deals" are subject to change, as is international availability of these and other Internet services.

ISPs make a great deal of money from users who pay a flat fee of $20 or so and then log on for only a few hours a month. If you're going to use the Internet and the Web for only a few hours a month, consider an online service.

The best Web publishing support

Online services are a good place to start your initial Web publishing efforts: low prices, good tools, lots of support — kind of like running downhill with a tailwind. Now that America Online, CompuServe, and The Microsoft Network offer Web browsers, Web publishing is the cutting edge of Web-related functionality for the services to offer. America Online and CompuServe offer the following:

✔ **No extra charge for Web page authoring.** All three services offer free support for Web page authoring (The Microsoft Network promises Web page authoring "soon"); you pay only the normal per-hour connect-time charges for creating and viewing your page and other Web pages.

✔ **Easy Web page authoring tools.** America Online and CompuServe offer easy-to-use, fill-in-the-blanks tools that help you create, quickly and easily, an initial Web page. AOL has an easy-to-use, Web-based service; CompuServe has a somewhat more powerful but more complex stand-alone HTML editor.

✔ **Free Web server space.** One of the biggest problems in creating an initial Web page is getting space on a Web server. America Online and CompuServe both offer free Web server space for personal home pages; America Online offers free space for business pages as well.

✔ **No file transfer hassle.** Getting your files onto a Web server is often a pain; the online services' easy Web page authoring tools can make it easy to get your information online.

✔ **Upgrading to HTML tools.** The services enable you to use separate HTML tools, such as the ones described in Part III and Part IV, to create your own custom Web page and to then transfer your files to their server for free hosting.

All three of the online services are rapidly evolving their Web support in general and their Web publishing support in particular, so check updates on Web services before making a final decision on which online service to use.

Each online service has different specific features and restrictions on your Web pages. At this writing, the policies and offerings of the top online services are as follows:

✔ **America Online.** The good news: Up to 2MB of free Web server space per screen name — and you can have up to five screen names per account. More good news: AOL has a very easy-to-use service called Personal Publisher for creating your Web page; support for graphics and multimedia; and no restrictions on using your Web page for business. The only bad news: America Online has historically had periods of trouble in providing reliable access to its millions and millions of users.

✔ **CompuServe.** The good news: CompuServe offers a powerful, flexible tool called Home Page Wizard for creating Web pages and a separate Publishing Wizard for getting pages onto the Web. You get up to 5MB of free server space for personal Web pages. The bad news: Powerful as it is, the Home Page Wizard/Publishing Wizard combination is somewhat complex. You can use the free service to mention or describe a business but not to promote it; you can't do an all-business Web page. For business pages, you have to pay some charges that were not yet announced at this writing.

✔ **The Microsoft Network.** The good news: The Microsoft Network is a fast-growing and determined entrant into the online services arena. The bad news: At the time of this writing, The Microsoft Network does not yet have support for personal Web pages for its users. If this is an important feature to you, check The Microsoft Network Web site at www.msn.com to see if personal Web page publishing has been added before signing up for The Microsoft Network. (I noticed from messages on an MSN user forum that many MSN members use GeoCities free Web pages, which we describe in Chapter 4.)

Publishing Your Web Page Online

In the following sections, we describe how to use the easy-to-use Web page tools and free Web server space from America Online and CompuServe. The descriptions include the following:

✔ Overall capabilities of the service's Web publishing tools

✔ Steps for creating and publishing a simple personal home page with a personal description, favorite URLs, and a photo or other image by using the online service's easy-to-use Web publishing tools

✔ Steps for copying text from your word processor or text editor to the Web publishing tool

The descriptions in this chapter are only the steps for *creating* Web pages; for ideas on how to *design* your Web page, see Chapter 2. The descriptions in this chapter also do not describe the tools that each online service has for transferring HTML-tagged text and other Web files created with other tools to its Web servers; for information on this topic, see the instructions available on each online service. The descriptions here are also just the tip of the iceberg of the Web publishing resources on each major online service. After you use the steps in this chapter to create your initial home page, use the online service itself for further help, support, and ideas.

What's a Mac user to do?

Two words: Get AOL. America Online has robust Macintosh support, including full cross-platform support for easy Web publishing. CompuServe does not support an easy-to-use Web publishing tool on the Macintosh, only on Windows. (Mac users have access to free Web server space, but no easy-to-use publishing tool.) The Microsoft Network doesn't support the Macintosh at all! So if you are a Mac user who wants an online service that supports your Web publishing efforts, get America Online.

All the Web page tools described in this chapter enable you to include HTML commands in your text. For a description of key HTML commands, see the Cheat Sheet, Chapter 3, and Appendix C. (Feeling restless? Tear out the Cheat Sheet and tape it to the wall in front of you, where you can see it!)

Get your page online with America Online

America Online has several parts to its Web publishing service:

- ✔ **Personal Publisher II.** Personal Publisher II is America Online's free, easy-to-use tool for creating a personal or business Web page. (Personal Publisher II replaces the original Personal Publisher service and is available with America Online 3.0 only.) America Online allows you to include pointers to content on both the open Web and within AOL; only other AOL members can see the AOL content, though.

- ✔ **Primehost.** Primehost is an extra-cost service from AOL for creating and hosting business Web sites with their own URL, so that your business looks "real" in cyberspace. It includes more advanced Web page creation software.

- ✔ **My Place.** My Place is the Web server space AOL provides to members. If you use Personal Publisher, AOL automatically transfers your Web page files to My Place; if you use other tools to create your Web page, you can use the Upload function to move the files to My Place.

- ✔ **EZ Scan.** EZ Scan is a service that digitizes your photographs or provides ready-to-use digital photos and art, all for use on your Web site and all at low prices.

- ✔ **Web Diner** and **Web University.** These are educational discussion areas and information sources for taking your Web page to the next level. They include support from AOL and other users.

Nothing prevents you from creating additional screen names for yourself, putting up 2MB of Web files for each screen name, and then tying all the files together through the judicious use of links between Web pages. (Just don't tell AOL we told you so!)

In addition to its other good features, such as a large amount of free Web server space, America Online is the only major online service that enables you to use your free server space to put up business Web pages. If you are already an America Online user, you need go no further to find a great home for your initial Web page. If not a user, America Online is the only online service that provides easy-to-use tools and free Web server space for a business page, so you may want to sign up today!

America Online's Personal Publisher service works well and is relatively easy to use. Here are the steps for using Personal Publisher to create a simple home page that has introductory text, a single image, and favorite URLs. We have divided them into easily digestible bites for you. The entire process of getting an initial Web page up takes 30 to 60 minutes; be sure to set aside that much uninterrupted time before starting.

Finding Personal Publisher

The first thing to do is find the Personal Publisher service among the bewildering array of choices on America Online.

1. **Sign onto America Online.**

   The Welcome window appears, with the Channels window behind it.

2. **Click the Channels window to bring it to the front.**

3. **Click the Internet button**.

   The Internet Connection window appears.

4. **To surf the Web while creating your home page, click the Go to the Web button (the button in the middle of the Internet Connection window).**

   Have your Web browser open so you can find graphics and favorite Web sites online to use in your Web page.

   You can also bring up a Web browser window in AOL at any time by clicking the globe icon in the icon bar; using the Internet Connection window also gives you access to other Internet services.

5. **In the Internet Connection window, click the Internet Extras button.**

   The Internet Extras window appears.

   To help you achieve initial success as quickly as possible, we deliberately ignore many of the choices and sources of information that America Online makes available to you. After you follow the steps given here to successfully create your initial Web page, go back and click other buttons, icons, and folders and try other options to find out more and to create a more sophisticated Web page.

6. **In the Internet Extras window, click the Personal Publisher button.**

   The Personal Publisher window appears, as shown in Figure 5-7.

7. **Click the Create a Page icon.**

   This begins the process of creating your Web page! The Select Template window appears.

Figure 5-7:
Personal
Publisher
gets you on
the Web
AOL-fully
fast.

Starting your home page

After you get to the starting gate, America Online takes you through the
process of creating your home page. By following the next few steps, you set
up the overall "look" of your Web page. Here's how to get your home page
started:

1. In the Select Template window, click the Personal icon.

The Add Title and Headline window appears.

Even if you want to create a business page, experiment with a personal
page first — it's a lower-pressure exercise in which you feel more free
to experiment.

2. Enter your page's title.

The title is not displayed in the Web page itself, but in most Web
browsers, it shows up at the top of the browser window. It is also used
by Internet search engines to find your page.

**3. Enter your page's headline. Click Align Left, Center, or Align Right to
position the headline on the page.**

The headline appears in large bold type at the top of the page. Making
the headline and the title the same doesn't hurt anything.

Centering the headline looks good, especially for short headlines. In my
copy of the America Online software, only the radio button for Align
Left appeared at first. When I clicked in the area next to the word
Center and then clicked in the area next to the phrase Align Right, the
buttons for those options appeared where I would have expected them.

4. Click Next to move to the next step.

When you click Next, the Add Background window appears.

5. **In the Add Background window, choose None, Image, or Solid Color. If you choose Image, double-click to select one of the tiled images in the drop-down list, or click Browse My Images to choose an image stored on your hard disk. If you choose Color, click the color wheel to select a color or create your own custom color, as shown in Figure 5-8.**

   To quickly get something that looks kind of cool, choose Image and then double-click one of the images in the drop-down list. Or you can use the Browse My Images button to retrieve an image from your hard disk and use it as a background image.

6. **After you've chosen a background, click Text Color to choose a color for the text on your page. Click Next when done.**

   Try to balance the background color or background image with the color of the text so they have a pleasing overall appearance.

   In some of the Personal Publisher windows, you can see a miniature version of what a page might look like, as shown in Figure 5-8. This page area shows the various stages of the Web page creation process; for instance, when you have to specify a headline, it says "Headline" across the top. However, this does *not* preview your specific home page and does *not* reflect the specific changes you make in your page.

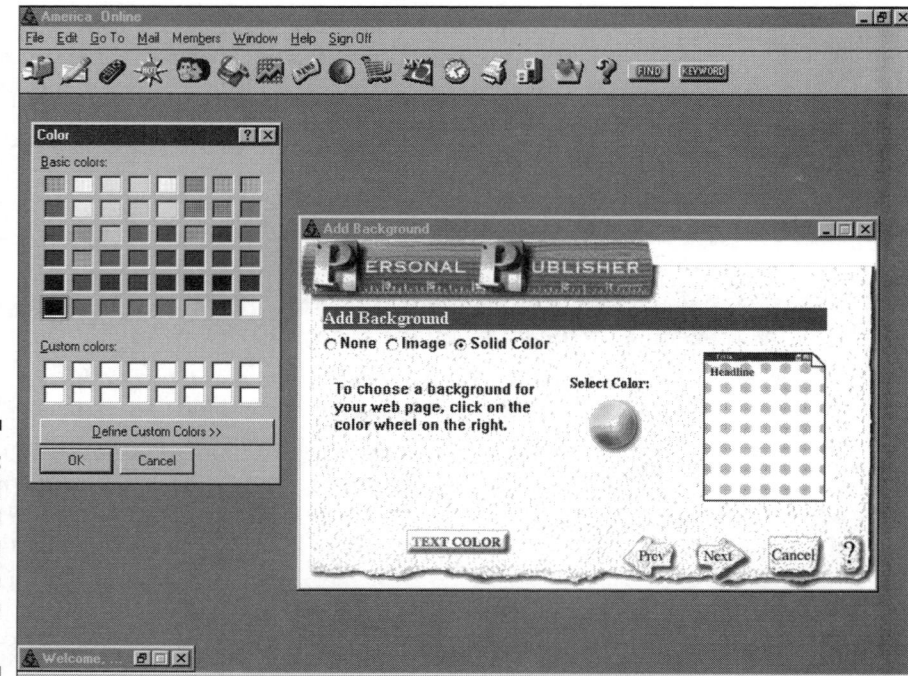

Figure 5-8:
Add background colors and images to your Web page.

Don't choose a solid-color background color and a text color that are the same — otherwise your text will be invisible against the background!

7. Click Next when you're done choosing images and colors.

When you click Next, the Add Image window appears.

8. In the Add Image window, double-click to select one of the images in the scrolling list, or click the Browse My Files button to choose an image stored on your hard disk. Click Align Left, Center, or Align Right to align the image.

To get an image quickly, double-click one of the images in the drop-down list. (Some of them are pretty ugly; choose carefully.) Or use the Browse My Files button to retrieve an image from your hard disk and use it as the image for your Web page. (If you have some time, you can browse the Web for a free image, save it to your hard disk, and then load it into your Web page.)

When you click Next, the Personal Information window appears.

Finishing your home page

At this point, you have the basic look of your Web page. Now's the time to fill it in with details — the things that really make your Web page "you." Here's how to tell the world something about yourself:

1. In the Personal Information window, click just under Name and Location and then enter your name and where you live.

This is just ordinary text that appears in the body of your Web page. You can even delete the phrase "Name and Location:" and replace it with something original. But to get closer to actually publishing your Web page, go ahead and enter your name and where you live.

Do enter your city, state, and similar location information; don't enter your home address unless you're sure you want over 30 million Web users to have it.

Getting images for your Web page

To get fancier images for your Web page, you can go out on the Web and look for free, downloadable images. One great place to start is America Online's free images site at

`www.aol.com/images/public`

To retrieve the image just click and hold (Mac) or right-click (Windows). Choose the Save Picture option and save the image to your hard disk. But make sure that the image is legally okay to copy before you do this.

2. **Click just under Hobbies and Interests and write a couple of paragraphs about things that you like to do. Click Next when done.**

When you click Next, the Body Text window appears.

3. **Click in the Body Text entry window. Enter text for your Web page. Format the text by selecting it and then clicking a button: smaller, normal, or larger font; bold, italic, or underline; left, center, right, or fully justified alignment.**

The body text can say anything you want to say: what you like or don't like about AOL, what you like or don't like about the Web, your personal history, your political opinions, computers you use and like or dislike, work interests, favorite quotes, favorite books, or anything else you care to say.

4. **To add AOL Favorite Places to your body text, select an entry under Favorite Places and then click the Add Favorite Place button.**

This feature lets you use Favorite Places that you have previously defined in AOL as part of your Web page.

People accessing your Web page who are not logged on to AOL cannot follow Favorite Places links that go to locations that represent AOL content.

5. **To add regular Web links to your body text, select some text by highlighting it. Then click the Add New Location button. Enter the descriptive text and URL for the link. The new link shows up in Favorite Places. Highlight it and then click Add Favorite Place to create a link. See Figure 5-9 for an example.**

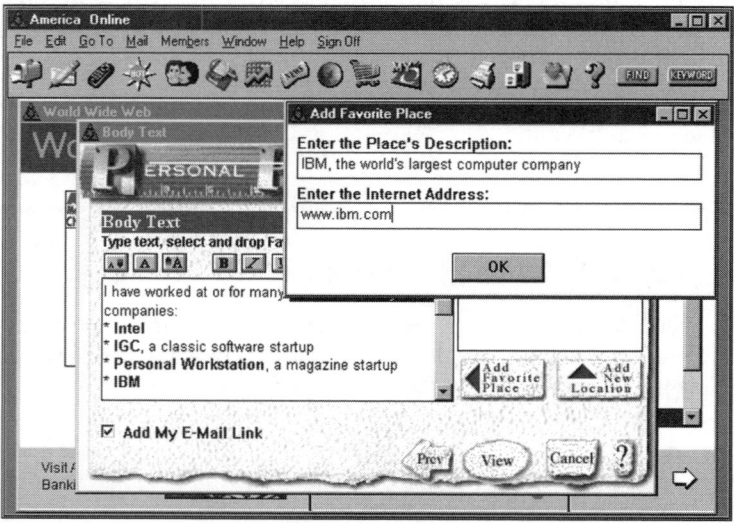

Figure 5-9:
I link,
therefore
I am.

A typical way to do this in a Web page is to write text like, "One of my favorite things is <u>Russian food</u>." The underlined text, "Russian food," is the description; it serves as a link to a Web destination such as www. russiafood.com. (That's not a real link; we just made it up.) In your AOL Web page you can either make a list of destinations, or work the destinations into text, or both.

   6. **To add your e-mail address to your Web page, click the Add My E-Mail Link check box. Then click the View button.**

   It's friendly to include a link to your e-mail address in your Web page.

   When you click the View button, the Personal Publisher window appears with a preview of your Web page.

After you click the View button, don't use the X button in the corner of the America Online window to close the view — you'll accidentally shut down AOL instead.

Publishing your home page

Now it's time to really put your home page on the Web. (You can edit it first, but why not publish it now and then edit it later?) Here's how to get your page onto the Web:

   1. **In the Personal Publisher window, click the Publish button.**

   2. **A dialog box appears, showing the Web Page File Name as index.html. Click OK.**

   This makes the name of your Web page index.html. This is the default name for the home page of any Web site. By using it, you enable your users to access your Web site just by typing the Web path and not the filename as well.

   3. **AOL transfers your Web page and any graphics files to the AOL Web server, My Place. A message then appears with the URL of your Web site, asking if you want to add it to your America Online Favorite Places list. Click Yes.**

   If for some reason you don't want to add your URL to your Favorite Places, write it down before you click No.

   4. **Check out your Web site! Click Ctrl+K for Keyword, and then type your URL:** http://members.aol.com/ . . . **(Insert your member name where the dots are.) Your Web page appears. See Figure 5-10 for an example.**

   Congratulations! You have created your first Web page. Look it over. If you see something you don't like, make a note of it.

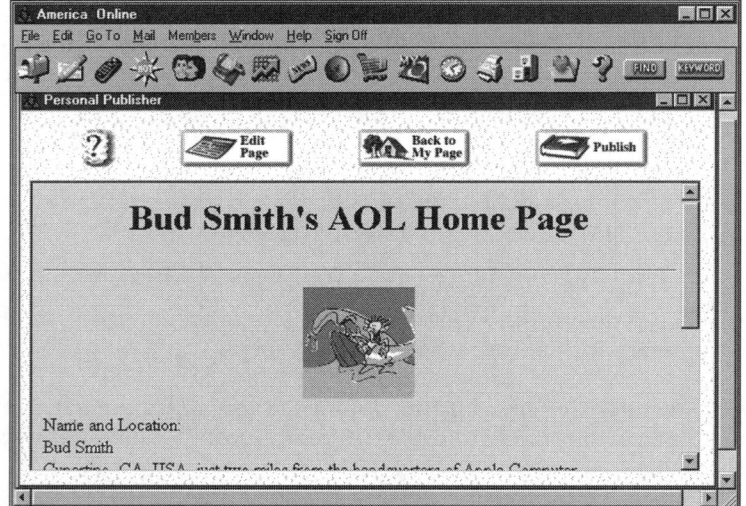

Figure 5-10:
Bud Smith joins the ranks of AOL home pagers.

The easiest way to note changes you want to make in your Web page is to print out the page and then note the changes you want to make on the printout.

5. Edit your page. In the Personal Publisher window, click Edit Page.

The Edit Home Page window appears. You can use it to add or edit the contents of your home page. Experiment; it's pretty easy to use.

6. Save your work and quit.

You can come back and edit your page anytime!

Go through the Personal Publisher area on AOL and read all the information you can about different capabilities and options; your second try at your Web page may look quite a bit different from the first!

If you previously viewed your home page during an online session and then changed the page, the version that appears may not be up to date. Click the Reload button to update the image on your screen.

Getting served with CompuServe

CompuServe offers 5MB of free Web server space to its users for their Web pages. Like America Online, CompuServe has several parts to its Web authoring support. But unlike America Online, CompuServe does not have an integrated, easy-to-use, Web-based service that enables you to create and publish a home page in a single operation. The parts of CompuServe's Web authoring services are as follows:

✓ **Home Page Wizard.** Home Page Wizard is a stand-alone tool that runs outside CompuServe and creates HTML-tagged text. Home Page Wizard may not meet all needs, and over a year after its introduction, the program is still stuck at Version 1.0. However, it's free and is bound to be well-supported by CompuServe and CompuServe users, so it's worth trying. (And check CompuServe forums for recommendations from other users about other tools that may better suit your purposes.)

✓ **Publishing Wizard.** Publishing Wizard takes HTML output from Home Page Wizard or other HTML editors and other Web files, such as GIF and JPEG graphics files, and places them on the CompuServe Web servers for you. You have up to 5MB of free server space for your personal Web site.

Mac users can use Publishing Wizard but not Home Page Wizard; the Home Page Wizard software has not been ported to the Macintosh. To download the Macintosh version of the Publishing Wizard, press Cmd+K to enter a keyword, and then enter **MACPUBWIZ**.

As with GeoCities, but unlike America Online, CompuServe prohibits you from using your free server space for a business site. You can mention your business, describe it, and give contact information for it, but you can't overtly promote it unless you pay for a business site. We don't know yet how strictly CompuServe enforces this restriction or how CompuServe interprets the difference between "describing" and "promoting" your business. One tip: If you "describe" how great The Microsoft Network is, CompuServe may "promote" your page to the Recycle Bin.

Unlike other online services and unlike the easy-to-use, free Web-based services described in Chapter 4, CompuServe's Web page creation tool is stand-alone software that you run from your hard drive. In this way, it's more like the HTML editing tools mentioned in the latter chapters of this book. Home Page Wizard is both more powerful and potentially more confusing than the Web-based services. But never fear, ...*For Dummies* is here! To get a simple home page up quickly and easily, just follow these instructions, which we divide into groups of steps to make them a little easier to follow.

CompuServe has a new offering called BusinessWeb that supports many desirable Web publishing features, but at this writing it's expensive at $50 for setup and $79 a month (which includes the cost of a regular CompuServe account). To learn more, go to businessweb.csi.com.

Grab the software you need

First get the Home Page Wizard and Publishing Wizard onto your hard disk. (Skip these steps if you already have the programs, but go ahead and grab them if you're not sure that you have the latest and greatest versions. Why use software that has old, familiar bugs when you can use software that has new, fresh ones?)

1. **Sign on to CompuServe.**

2. **Choose Services⇨Member Center.**

   The CompuServe Member Center window appears.

3. **Double-click Visit Our World from the scrolling list of options.**

   The Our World Web page appears. Our World is a Web area for CompuServe members.

4. **Click the Publish in Our World button.**

   The Publish in Our World Web page appears.

5. **Click the link, Download the Home Page and Publishing Wizards now.**

   The Author Tools Web page appears.

6. **Under the heading, CompuServe Home Page Wizard, click the link Get it now!**

   The File Download dialog box appears.

7. **Choose the option, Save this program to disk, and click OK.**

   The Save As dialog box appears.

8. **Open the folder you want the program to download to, then click Save.**

   The compressed file with the Home Page Wizard downloads to your computer. The file is about 1MB in size and takes about 10 minutes to download using a 28.8 Kbps modem.

9. **Shut down CompuServe.**

   You're going to use the Home Page Wizard for a while, which is a separate program that doesn't require CompuServe. So you may as well shut CompuServe down for a while. (Exception: If you want to use CompuServe while building your home page to surf the Web to find graphics files, favorite links, and so on, you may want to leave it running.)

Install the Home Page Wizard

Now that you've downloaded the Home Page Wizard, it's time to install the program so you can run it. Here's how to get going:

1. **Find the file** HPWIZ.EXE**. Double-click it to start installing it.**

   Use the Windows Explorer (or Program Manager, if you have Windows 3.1) to find the file. Then double-click the icon to run the program.

2. **Click OK in response to the self-extractor message and then click Unzip to decompress the file. Click OK to acknowledge that the files decompressed successfully.**

   The file self-extracts.

3. **Install the Home Page Wizard and the Publishing Wizard.**

   A Windows installation wizard prompts you through the process of installing these other wizards. Be sure to review the ReadMe file before running the program; it may have helpful information. Don't start the Home Page Wizard right now, though; we do that in the next section.

Follow the installation program's recommendation that you quit all other programs before installing, even though this means that you may have to disconnect from CompuServe. If you don't follow this recommendation, and something goes wrong while setting up the Home Page Wizard, you may lie awake nights wondering whether the problem occurred because you didn't follow this recommendation.

Put the Wizard to work

Now that you've downloaded and installed the Home Page Wizard, you can finally start creating your home page:

1. **Choose Start⇨Programs⇨Compuserve⇨Homepage Wizard.**

   The Welcome to the Home Page Wizard screen appears (see Figure 5-11).

2. **Enter the title of your home page.**

   The title appears in the title bar of most browsers and is also used by Web search engines to find your Web page.

3. **Enter a name of up to eight characters for this project.**

   A project is the same thing that we call a Web site in this book: one or more Web pages, accessed through a single home page that the user goes to first and that gives access to the rest of the site. You can have multiple projects saved on your hard disk, but you can publish only one at a time on the Web.

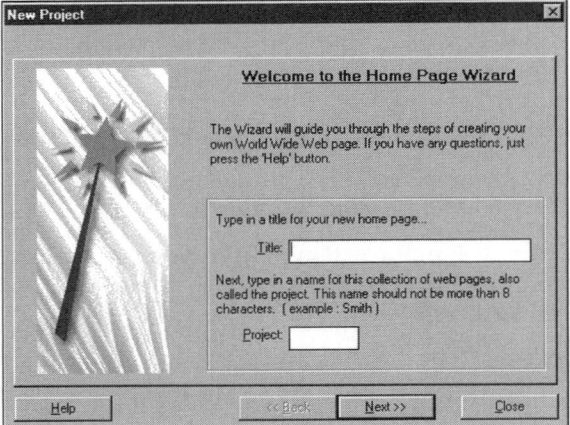

Figure 5-11:
Welcome
to the
CompuServe
Home Page
Wizard.

The project name is not displayed on your Web page. The Home Page Wizard names a subdirectory after your project and places Web pages for that project as separate files in the subdirectory.

Create your first Web page in one project and then work on its replacement in a separate project. When the new project is complete, you can replace the original Web page with the new one and keep the first Web page available as a backup in case of problems.

4. **Click the Next button.**

The Personal Information window appears.

5. **Enter your personal information.**

Some fields in the personal information area are required and some are optional. You do not have to display this information in your Web page (see Step 6). The information that you enter is available for use in future projects as well.

Personal information that you can enter includes

- **First name:** Required
- **Middle initial:** Optional
- **Last name:** Required
- **City:** Required
- **State/Province:** Optional
- **Country:** Required

- **Occupation:** Optional. Enter as a noun or noun phrase, as in: welder, carpenter, real estate salesperson, and so on. (If you include your personal information in your home page, your occupation is inserted into a predefined sentence, and a noun works best in that sentence.)

- **Hobbies:** Optional. Enter as a noun or noun phrase or a list of nouns, as in "stamp collecting, Elvis impersonation, rock climbing, Elvis sightings, rock collecting, sighting Elvis impersonators." (If you include your personal information in your home page, your hobbies are inserted into a predefined sentence, and nouns work best in that sentence.)

Do not capitalize the first letters of your occupation and your hobbies. If you do, they look strange when displayed by CompuServe on your home page in sentence form.

- **E-mail address:** Optional. CompuServe asks you to enter your CompuServe User ID followed by @compuserve.com. You can probably get away with using a different e-mail address if you prefer.

6. **To include your personal information in your home page, leave the check box named Use Personal Information in Home Page checked. To exclude your personal information, clear the check box.**

   You can include the personal information you entered in your home page. If you don't, your personal information is left out. If you do, it appears in the following format:

   ```
   Hello! My name is <First name> <MI> <Last name>. I live
   in <City>, <State/Province>, <Country>. I am a <Occupa-
   tion> and enjoy <Hobbies>.
   ```

   If your personal information comes out looking good the first time, congratulations! If not, you have to go back and change the word order and capitalization in entries such as your list of hobbies.

7. **Click the Next button.**

8. **Choose a radio button — Blank Page or Template. If you choose Template, highlight one of the choices: Career, Fun, or Nature.**

9. **Click Finish.**

   A preview of your home page appears. See Figure 5-12 for an example made by using the Fun template.

Figure 5-12:
A fun home
page from
the Home
Page
Wizard.

Gussy up your home page

The steps up to this point have helped you create a very simple, basic home page. Now you enter part of the Home Page Wizard with many options for improving your page. The nice thing is that you can publish your page at any point, come back to it, improve it some more, and republish it as many times as you want. Follow these steps to add a few features to your basic page:

1. **Click the Close button to close the Tip of the Day, if it appears.**

2. **Inspect the options available for your home page (refer to Figure 5-12 for an example).**

   The buttons across the top of the Home Page Wizard editing window make many options available:

   • **Headline** — insert or edit a headline. Choose a headline style from Headline 1 (largest) to Headline 6 (smallest).

   • **Text** — insert or edit text. Choose text styles: centered, preformatted (use existing line breaks and a nonproportional font), or bulleted.

   • **Image** — insert an image. Browse your hard disk to find images. Enter alternate text for an image. Set an image's size. Center an image.

   Alternate text for an image is text that displays if users have graphics display turned off in their browsers. Many users with slow connections turn graphics display off for speed, and providing a text description of the image helps them decide whether to download it.

- **Lines** — insert or edit a horizontal line. Choose its dimensions and alignment: left, center, or right.

- **External link** — insert or edit a link to an Internet location, such as a Web URL. Center the link, or place it in a bulleted list.

- **Internal link** — insert or edit a link to another page within your current Web project. Create a new page to link to. Center the link, or place it in a bulleted list.

- **E-mail** — insert or edit a link to an e-mail address. Center the link, or place it in a bulleted list.

- **Background** — change page properties such as the background pattern, link color, or text color.

- **Test** — automatically open your page in any browser that you have on your hard disk. (You have to use the Browse button to find the browser first; then it is added to a list within the dialog box.)

- **Publish** — starts the Home Page Publishing Wizard, which publishes your Web project on the World Wide Web.

3. Edit items on your home page.

To edit any of the items you have already put on your home page, double-click it. An appropriate editing box opens, and you can make the appropriate changes. For instance, if you double-click a line of text, a text editor opens. You can change the text and change the style that it's in. Then click OK to place the revised text back in your Web page.

4. Delete items from your home page.

To delete any of the items you have already put on your home page, click the item to select it. Then press the Delete key, Ctrl+X or the Backspace key; the item is deleted. To undo the deletion, click the Edit menu and then select Undo (Ctrl+Z).

5. Add items to your home page.

To add any item to your home page, click the page to put the insertion point wherever you want the new item. Then click the button that's appropriate for what you want to insert: Headline, Text, Image, and so on. An appropriate editing box appears, and you can enter the text you want, select an image, or whatever, and then you can pick appropriate style options.

6. Continue editing, deleting, and adding items.

Continue working on your home page until it seems ready to publish.

7. Test your home page.

To test your home page in other browsers on your hard disk, click the Test button. Select a browser on your hard disk; it is added to the list of browsers. Then open your page in each browser and see how it looks. Make any changes necessary to have your home page work well in all browsers.

About 90 percent of the browser market today is controlled by recent versions of Netscape Navigator and Microsoft Internet Explorer. You can download these browsers free from the Web and use them to test your Web page. However, this is probably unnecessary; the features in Home Page Wizard don't include anything that is challenging to most browsers out there.

8. Publish.

When you're ready to put your home page on the Web, click the Publish button. The Publishing Wizard starts.

Here are some tips that you can use to create or improve your Web home page:

- ✔ The first forum on CompuServe to go for help with Web page authoring is the NetLauncher Support Forum.

- ✔ If you have switched to another program back while using the Home Page Wizard, the other program may appear after you click Finish. Press Alt+Tab to cycle among programs and return to the Home Page Wizard.

- ✔ To publish the Web page that you created, you must use the Publishing Wizard. This tool works with any HTML-tagged text (not just output from the Home Page Wizard).

Publishing Wizard 101

The Home Page Publishing Wizard publishes any HTML files you have created, either in the Home Page Wizard or elsewhere, and puts them up on CompuServe's servers. These steps describe how to use the Publishing Wizard to get your initial Web site up on the Web.

Before you start the Publishing Wizard, log on to CompuServe. Keep checking that your connection does not drop while entering info in Publishing Wizard. Why do this? At this writing, the Publishing Wizard can't make a connection itself, but needs to have one provided for it — and you must start the connection before Publishing Wizard. If you start Publishing Wizard first, you have to close the program or even reboot before opening a connection, restarting Publishing Wizard and completing the file transfer.

1. **Start the Publishing Wizard.**

   If you came to these steps directly from the previous ones, the Publishing Wizard should be already running. Otherwise, find the Home Page Wizard, start it, and click the Publish button to start the Publishing Wizard.

2. **Click Next.**

3. **Click the Upload Files radio button, then click Next.**

4. **Enter personal information — Name, City, and so on. Then click Next.**

   If you entered this information in the Home Page Wizard, it appears. If not, enter it now; it's only for use by CompuServe, not for display. If Country doesn't appear, choose it from the drop-down list.

   Tips for Americans: America is listed as United States of America and is near the end of the list — a few entries after Tuvalu and a few before Vatican City State (Holy See). You also see a separate entry for United States Minor Outlying, which we assume means U.S. dependencies that are not part of the 50 states.

5. **Enter directory information such as occupation (optional). Then click Next.**

   If you entered this information in the Home Page Wizard, it now appears. If not, you can enter it now so that other Web users can find your Web page more easily.

6. **Check or enter your CompuServe account information. Then click Next.**

7. **Click Next to publish.**

   CompuServe connects to the Publishing Server.

   If you didn't follow the tip above about having CompuServe connected while using the Publishing Wizard, you may get a connection error when connecting to the Publishing Server. I got around this error by restarting my machine, starting CompuServe, and then starting the Publishing Wizard. I then had to go through the steps above, plus identify my Web page files, and then I could upload successfully.

8. **If you have not yet created a CompuServe Personal Address, CompuServe prompts you to create one.**

   A Personal Address is a name that you can use on CompuServe in addition to the numeric user ID that all users get when they sign up. The Suggest button prompts you with some suggested names. Enter a suggested personal address, such as Firstname_Lastname, and then click Next.

   CompuServe registers your personal address.

9. **CompuServe uploads your Web site and then provides you with its URL. Write down the URL, which is in the form:**

```
http://ourworld.compuserve.com/homepages/<personal
address>
```

Share your home page URL with your friends!

10. **Click the View Page button to see your page.**

11. **CompuServe may prompt you for a browser. Choose a browser from the drop-down list; if you have not already used a browser with CompuServe, you have to identify one using the Open dialog box.**

Congratulations — CompuServe opens your home page!

To see other CompuServe members' home pages — over 100,000 of them at this writing — surf over to the CompuServe personal Web pages home page at

```
ourworld.compuserve.com
```

MSN Web publishing "coming soon"

Unlike America Online and CompuServe, The Microsoft Network (MSN) does not — at the time of this writing — offer Web publishing tools or Web server space for user home pages. Microsoft recently came out with a new tool that allows you to use Windows 95 as a personal Web server, so it's not like the company has a blind spot for the Web. It's just taking some time for them to implement this key feature.

MSN users seem to be frequent users of GeoCities and its free personal Web page service, which we describe in Chapter 4. If you use The Microsoft Network, check if things have changed; if not, try GeoCities. If you are not yet a Microsoft Network user, check the Microsoft Web site and the newsgroups described earlier in this chapter to see if personal Web page publishing has yet made it onto MSN.

Part III

Better, Stronger, Faster Sites

The 5th Wave   By Rich Tennant

Well, there's your Web page, Crypto. Designed like you asked. But personally, I think it has too many spinning spirals and blinking lights. It makes...hard reading. Make...tired... look...at...lose...all... con...cen...tra...tion...

Perfect!

CRYPTO THE HYPNOTIST

In this part . . .

After you get your initial Web page up, you'll no doubt want to extend it into a more polished multipage Web site. To do this, you need to know more about linking Web pages, Web graphics, advanced topics like multimedia and push technology, and Web publishing. This part broadens your knowledge and helps to make you a well-rounded Web publisher.

Chapter 6
From Web Page to Web Site

*I*f you followed some of the instructions in previous chapters, you are now a published author of a page on the World Wide Web. Congratulations! If you have not done so, go back and use the instructions in Chapter 4 or Chapter 5 to get a Web page up on GeoCities, America Online, or CompuServe. It's really easy, and it makes the rest of this book "real" to you in a way that nothing else can.

After you get a basic Web page up, the next steps are to improve the original home page and to build the single Web page into an interesting, multipage site. This chapter describes just how to do that. We show how to do things using HTML directly. This takes advantage of the fact that all the easy-to-use Web publishing tools and services described in earlier chapters allow you to enter HTML tags into your Web pages.

However, at this point you also have the option of using one of the Web publishing tools described in Part IV, or something similar. A Web publishing tool either handles the management of the HTML tags for you or hides them completely, which makes carrying out the steps in this chapter that much easier. If you use HTML directly, as described in this chapter, you know more about how Web pages work and have more control; if you switch to a tool, your work will probably be easier (but you should read this chapter anyway as background). Whether you work directly in HTML or use a Web publishing tool, this chapter helps you move up to the next stage of Web publishing.

Getting a Target in Your Sites

As you get beyond your single Web page into a multipage Web site, which may have interactivity, graphics, and multimedia, the amount of time you spend on your site increases dramatically. To get the most value out of your time and create the best site you can within the resources you have available, you should set some goals for your site. Personal sites, topical sites, business sites, and entertainment sites each have different purposes and needs, so you want to set different kinds of goals for each.

Personal sites

For a personal site, your overall goal is likely to be to have fun, both in creating Web pages and in letting the world see them. However, creating Web pages, linking them together, adding graphics and multimedia, and so on, can become tremendously time-consuming activities. The more you work on your Web pages and the more feedback you get, the more you want to create. Yet no matter how much you like working on your personal Web presence, at some point, the rest of your life — job, spouse, kids, bills — is likely to intrude. So setting some simple goals is a good idea.

One way to set your goals is inner-directed. What do you want from your site:

- ✔ To show the world something about your life and interests?
- ✔ To make yourself more employable?
- ✔ To promote some interest or group?

First, figure out what your goal is for the next stage of construction of your Web site, based on what you want from your site. Then, depending on your goal, you can decide how much time and energy to put into your Web site, how many pages to create for your site initially, and if you then want to put the site in maintenance mode or just keep growing it. Write down the answers to these questions and keep the answers in mind while you work on your site.

The other way to set your goals is outer-directed: Find sites that are already out on the Web that you want your site to look like. Finding existing Web sites that have one or more similarities to what you want to accomplish is both fun and educational. You can see how other people have handled (or avoided) the concerns that you face in making your site work well. And you can save dozens of hours by avoiding approaches that haven't worked and borrowing from the best of what works well.

Personal sites that just show the world something about your life and interests, without going too far into any one special topic, are part of what makes the World Wide Web so full of surprises. The Web page creation services mentioned in earlier chapters — GeoCities, America Online, and CompuServe — are home to thousands of such pages. Find several sites that resemble what you would like your site to end up looking like.

Topical sites

Many personal sites, including some of the best ones, aren't just personal. They include topical interests, business interests, or both. Kevin Werbach's home page is a good example. It gives pointers not just to *The Bare Bones Guide to HTML* (see Appendix C), for which Kevin is justly famous, but also to other pages with information about himself and his interests. Figure 6-1 shows the home page to Kevin's personal site, illustrating his wide range of interests while still highlighting *The Bare Bones Guide to HTML*. You can find it at

```
www.werbach.com/home.html
```

Topical sites often grow out of personal sites, as one of a person's many interests crowds out the others and dominates the personal site. Eventually, the topical info may even become its own, separate site. Or the personal side of the site may dwindle or disappear, leaving a purely topical site behind. Other sites continue as interesting mixes of personal and topical.

Figure 6-1: A personal page with a pointer to topical info.

Topical sites need goals, just like personal sites. If one topical part of your site grows, or if you know you want to create a topical site, consider splitting off the topical part from your personal info. Do people who want to know the latest in underwater botany really care about your kids' braces coming off? Then follow the same steps as for a personal site: Decide how much time and energy you can put in; set achievable intermediate goals and then implement them; and continuously look for examples of what works and doesn't work among sites that are similar to yours.

Eventually, a topical site may grow in content and complexity into something very much resembling a business site in terms of organizational concerns caused by the sheer number of pages and the range of subtopics involved. If you find yourself adding things to your site based on other people's requests rather than strictly your own interests, you're probably well on the road to a business-type site. In this case, you need to look at the concerns for business sites and keep those concerns, as well as purely topical concerns, in mind as you grow your site.

One cool topical site is shown in Figure 6-2, a new Internet culture magazine with contributions from people on the Web. You find many more interesting topical sites as you surf the Web. This topical page can be found at

`www.fear.com`

Figure 6-2:
A topical site where there is nothing to fear but fear itself.

Using Web page creation tools

One of the biggest questions you face in creating Web pages is whether to work directly in HTML or use a Web page creation tool like those described in this book. The answer may surprise you.

If you're relatively inexperienced and are working on a single Web page or a small set of pages, consider working directly in HTML. Why? Because HTML is easy to learn and widely understood. (If you use a tool, you have to select, buy, and learn the tool, which may take just as long as learning a little bit of HTML.) You can always see the HTML underlying any Web page and use it as a model for creating similar effects yourself. And you learn a lot about the Web as you work. (These reasons are why this book includes a moderate amount of HTML.)

If you understand the basics of HTML and will be responsible for building or maintaining more than a couple of pages, consider getting a Web page creation tool to help. Why? Because working in HTML is boring and repetitive, and because it's easy to make mistakes. If you do a moderate amount of Web page creation work, a tool saves you time and energy, easily paying off the up-front costs of buying and learning the tool. (These reasons are why this book includes info on the best and most popular Web page creation tools.)

If you're doing advanced Web pages or building or maintaining a lot of pages, use HTML and Web page creation tools — as many as you need. Why? HTML gives you ultimate flexibility and control. Web page creation tools give you speed and ease of use, and they allow you to hand off less demanding tasks to others who can accomplish them using a tool. Combining tools and direct work in HTML can help you create a large, high-tech, interactive Web site (which is the topic of other, more advanced books).

To view the HTML code behind any Web page, use the View Source command in Netscape Navigator, or similar commands in other browsers. Alternatively, use your browser's Save command and save the Web page as "source" into a file on your hard disk. Then open the file in any word processor or text editor to view the HTML source code.

Business sites

Business sites are becoming the main reason most people surf the Web. And big money is involved; Web commerce is estimated to have exceeded the billion-dollar-a-year mark and is more than doubling each year. It's getting to where any business worth its salt must have some kind of Web presence.

The best way to get started on a business site is to shoot for exactly that: a Web presence. You can add and do all kinds of things later, time and money permitting, but people expect a few basic Web-related things of most businesses today:

> ✔ A URL that reflects the name of the business
>
> ✔ A home page
>
> ✔ Additional pages with basic info about the business itself
>
> ✔ Additional pages with basic info about products and services

A business site with just this info is called a *Web presence* site. It allows you to say, without embarrassment, that your business is on the Web. Your Web presence reduces nuisance phone calls and mail to your business by making some basic information available in a place where people who have Web access can easily find it. Your Web presence also increases useful phone calls and mail to your business by letting potential customers know how to reach you. It doesn't cost too much to create or maintain. And yet, despite its low cost and modest goals, it sets the stage for future growth in your business's use of the Web and the Internet.

You can have a lot of different goals for a business site, but this chapter and the information in the rest of this book are suitable for creating a basic Web presence site, with goals such as those above. If you want to go further, you need more advanced information and probably some consulting help as well. (Unless your business goal is to become a Web consultant yourself!) Even if you have bigger goals that require more information than what's in this book, or more time and expertise than you can invest yourself, consider creating a basic personal or business site yourself first; your ability to get where you're going increases immeasurably if you have a little hands-on experience.

Far more than for personal or topical sites, you should create a business site with an eye on existing sites that meet similar goals more or less well. Figure 6-3 shows a Web presence site with a pointer to needed information right on the home page. The Cinebase Web site is at

www.cinebase.com/

Use this and other sites as a model for your own similar site.

Later in this chapter, we show exactly how to create a Web presence site for a small business. This kind of site is the only one that many businesses have, from small storefronts and consultancies right up to major corporations. (The major corporation sites may be fancier and have more pages, but when you look closely you see that they just provide the basic information of a Web presence site, with more pages to reflect their larger number of divisions, products, and services.) This kind of site suits the purposes of many businesses. Creating a Web presence site is all you need to do to turn the Web from being a hole in your business strategy to being an asset to your business.

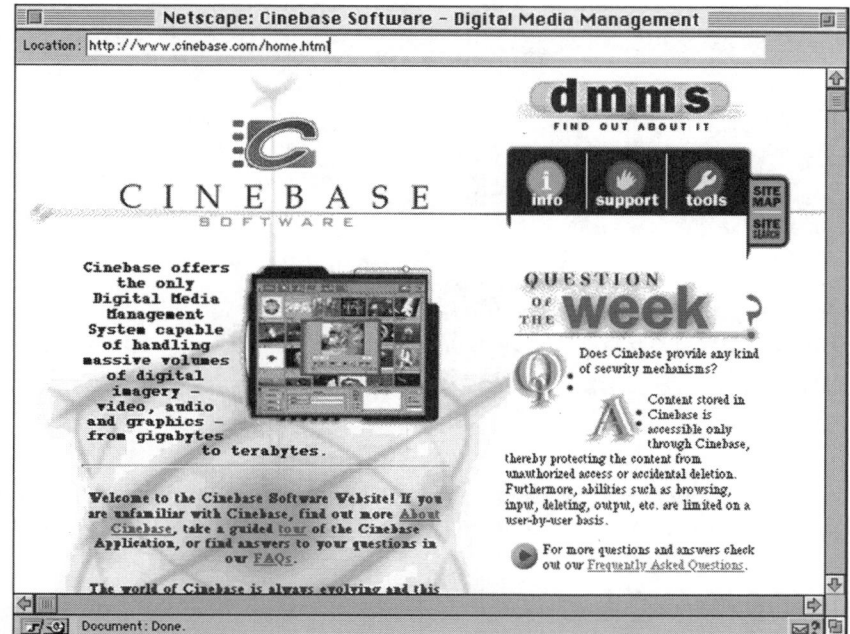

Figure 6-3:
A model
of a Web
presence
site.

Improving Your Site

No, "improving your site" is not an ad for an eyeglass company. (Though spend enough time on the Web and you may need the help of one!) It means, "here are some things you can do to turn your simple, solitary Web page into a robust Web site."

The sections below talk about things you can do with the design, layout, and structure of your site to improve it. This includes links, tables, frames, and more. It does not include graphics and multimedia; those topics have their own chapter — coming up next — Chapter 7.

Adding more pages to your site

The easy-to-use Web page creation tools hosted on the Web, described in earlier chapters, all make it easy to add pages to your Web site. But how do you link one page to another? Luckily, it's pretty easy; just remember a few HTML tags, and you've got it. Here's how to make different kinds of links.

Links to other pages in the site

If you want to link between pages within a site, you need to provide the user some link text to click in one page, and tell the Web browser where to find the other page. You do this with the <A>, or *anchor,* HTML tag.

What's your job?

Getting into Web page creation can be challenging, but getting out can be much harder!

HTML and Web tools are so easy to learn that most people can create a basic site themselves. But growing and maintaining that site is another matter. It's easy to become an "accidental expert" as you try to keep up with the seemingly insatiable demands of a Web site.

So decide up-front how far you want to go in becoming a Web page creation expert. And when the job starts to get too big, be quick to call in a consultant or hire an employee whose sole job is Web site creation and maintenance.

To create links between pages, first create the two pages. Then add an anchor in one page that points to the other. Here's a typical link between pages within a Web site:

```
If you want to give me a job, check out my <A
HREF="myresume.htm">resume</A>.
```

On the screen, this text appears like this:

```
If you want to give me a job, check out my resume.
```

Here's what each part of the HTML code does:

`<A>`	Tells the browser an anchor is coming; displays the text that follows it as underlined.
`HREF="myresume.htm"`	Tells the browser that when the user clicks the underlined text, it should go get file `myresume.htm`, which is the link destination, and display it. Some browsers display the link destination when the user moves the mouse pointer over the underlined text.
`resume`	Because this text is surrounded by the `<A>` and `</A>` tags, it's link text. It is displayed in a different color (usually blue) and underlined to let the user know it's a link. When clicked, it causes the current Web page to be replaced by the page at the link destination.
`</A>`	Tells the browser that the anchor is ending and that it should stop displaying text as underlined.

You can also link to pages that are stored in a different subfolder, but this is complicated and is the source of many, many problems in transferring files and in maintaining links. For sites with relatively few files, keep them all in one subfolder.

Figure 6-4 shows links to other pages within a Web site and other kinds of links in both HTML code and as displayed in a Web browser.

You can try out all this without even firing up a connection to the Internet. Just create a couple of text-only documents with the appropriate HTML tags inside. Use your Web browser to open one of the files. You should be able to link to the other one!

Links within a page

The anchors described in the previous section automatically point to the top of a Web page. You can also create a link to a spot within a page.

To indicate a spot within a page to link to, also known as an anchor, you have to give the spot a name. Here's an example of the HTML code for that:

```
<A NAME="education"></A>
```

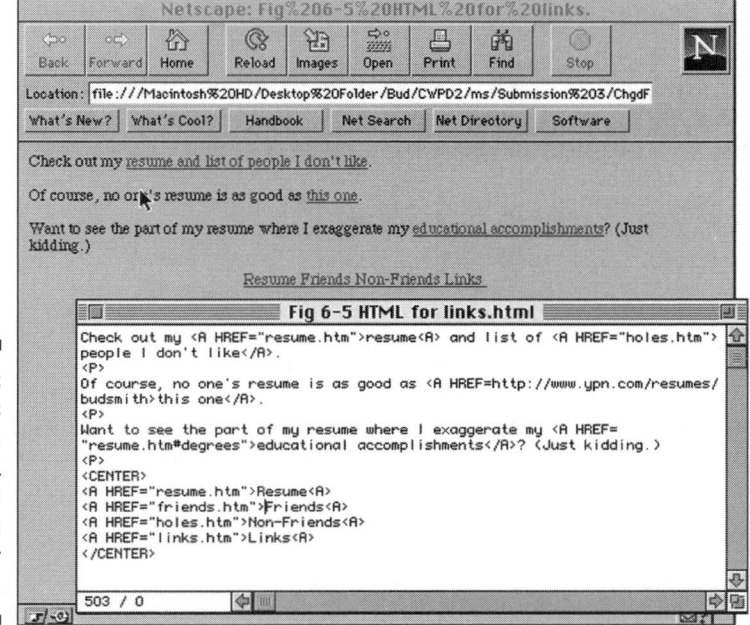

Figure 6-4:
Examples
of linking
in HTML
code and
displayed in
a browser
window.

Here's what each part of the HTML code does:

`<A>, </A>`	Beginning and end of the anchor.
`NAME="linktarget"`	Indicate the name of the target.

To link to the anchor, just add the anchor name to the link tag. If the anchor is in the same page as the link, just give the anchor name:

```
If you want to see my college degrees, check out the <A
HREF="#education">appropriate spot</A> in my resume.
```

Here's what each part of the HTML code does:

`<A>, </A>`	Beginning and end of the anchor.
`HREF="#education"`	Indicate the name of the target.

If the anchor is in a different page than the link, just give the anchor name after the page name:

```
If you want to see my college degrees, check out the <A
HREF="myresume.htm#education">appropriate spot</A> in my
resume.
```

For large documents that you publish on the Web, such as a résumé, it's good to provide lots of anchors in the document and put a list of anchors at the top. But if creating Web pages from scratch, you should avoid creating long pages that need anchors for navigation. The user sees your Web pages one screenful at a time. In the Web pages you create, avoid making the user page down much. If you want to start a new topic, start a new page.

Intra-site navigation

After you have more than four or five Web pages on your site, you should really think hard about navigation within your site. Don't just toss intra-site links into body text, mixed in with links to other sites, graphics, and who knows what else. Provide centralized areas that help the user move around within your site.

A simple solution to the problem of navigating within a site is to always provide a list of all the major areas of your site at the bottom of each page. (For small sites, each "major area" of your site will be a single page; for larger sites, you'll have major areas, subareas within major areas, and more.) Refer to Figure 6-4 for an example of this bottom-of-each-page list, along with other linking examples.

Early in the development of your Web site, create a graphic that provides links to the major areas of your site. Use it at the bottom of each page. Keep the graphic simple, but do provide one; it really upgrades the appearance and usability of your site.

Adding external links to your site

The easiest way to extend the impact of your site is to add links to external sites. However, you should be a little careful with this. After all, you don't want people surfing away immediately; you want them to experience the things you did so much work to create! Yet a site with no external links often comes across as boring and "dead."

So think before you link. Create a useful set of Web pages and links among them; then decide how and where to use external links. Link to the Web sites of specific companies and products that your site's visitors may be interested in. Create tables of links on topics that you know something about. But don't toss in "big-name" links such as Wired just to show that you too are, well, wired: Don't randomly drop in links that don't have a clear purpose.

Adding an external link to your site is easy; it's just like a link within your site, but the destination is a Web URL. All the easy-to-use Web tools described in Chapters 4 and 5 make it easy to include at least some external links; but to have full control over them, you need to know in detail how to create them yourself.

To create an external link, include the prefix `http://` in the destination URL to make it very clear where the link is to. Refer to Figure 6-4 to see the link text in HTML code and displayed in a Web browser. Here's an example of a typical link to another Web site:

```
If you want to give me a job, check out my <A HREF="http://
www.geocities.com/Yosemite/Rapids/7538/resume.htm">resume</
A>, hosted on the GeoCities personal Web page service.
```

On the screen, this text appears like this:

```
If you want to give me a job, check out my resume, hosted on
the GeoCities personal Web page service.
```

Here's what each part of the HTML code does:

`<A>`	Tells the browser an anchor is coming, so display the following text underlined.
`HREF="www.geocities.com/Yosemite/Rapids/7538/resume.htm"`	Tells the browser that, when the user clicks on the underlined text, it should go get file `resume`, in the directory `/Yosemite/Rapids/7538 resumes`, on the Web server `www.geocities.com`.
`resume`	As with other links, because this text is surrounded by the `<A>` and `</A>` tags, it's link text. The browser displays it in a different color (usually blue) and underlined to let the user know it's a link. When clicked, it causes the current Web page to be replaced by the page at the link destination.
`</A>`	Tells the browser that the anchor is ending so it should stop displaying text as underlined.

Note that the example doesn't link to GeoCities, just to the résumé itself. Why? First, it keeps the number of links down. Second, a link to the GeoCities home page is already provided by GeoCities at the bottom of each and every GeoCities home page. Third, any Web surfer worth his salt knows to try to open `www.geocities.com` if he wants more information about a company called GeoCities. If something is important to your Web surfers, make it very easy to get to. But if it's of peripheral interest, don't clutter up your site by trying too hard to provide easy access.

Setting a table in your site

You can use an HTML table in two very different ways. One way is to create a basic table. That's the sense we show you here. The other way is to create a sophisticated page layout; the user doesn't really see that it's a table, just that the page is laid out in an attractive and unusual way. We cover that in Chapter 7.

A simple table is fairly easy to create using HTML. However, as you get into creating more complex tables or using tables to control your overall page layout, the HTML quickly gets complicated and tedious to create and maintain.

Tables are a big reason why the easy-to-use tools profiled in Part IV are so popular. These tools make it much easier to manage tables. So if you start to work much with tables, consider using one of these tools.

How do you create a simple table with, say, headers, two rows, and two columns? Here's an example of how to create such a table in HTML:

```
<TABLE>
<TABLE BORDER=2>
<TH><TD>Production (tons)</TD><TD>% of goal</TD></TH>
<TR><TD>North 40</TD><TD>87</TD><TD>102%</TD></TR>
<TR><TD>South 40</TD><TD>93</TD><TD>110%</TD></TR>
</TABLE>
```

Just add this HTML code to your Web page and you have a simple table.
Figure 6-5 shows how this simple table looks in HTML when viewed in
Netscape Navigator.

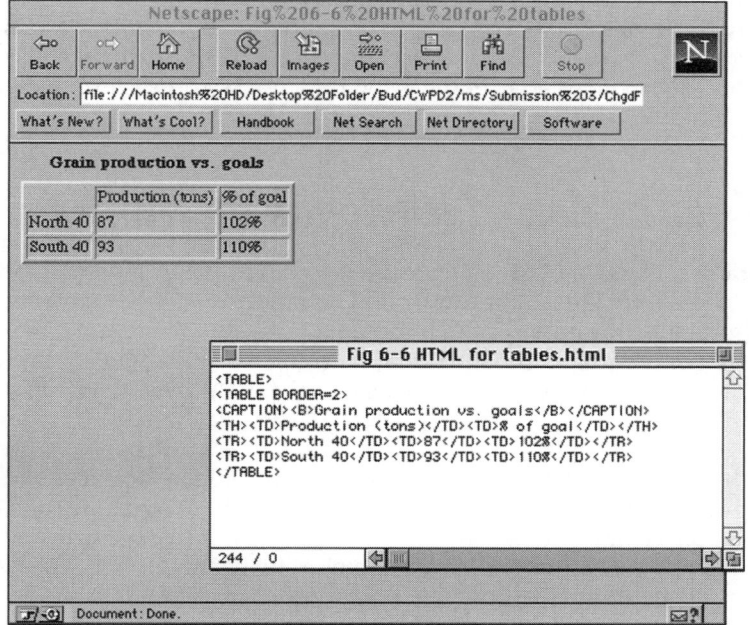

Figure 6-5:
All gather
round the
table . . .

Here's what each part of the HTML code does:

`<TABLE>, </TABLE>`	Begin and end the table.
`<TABLE BORDER=2>`	Create a 2-pixel-wide border around the table. Don't forget this, or else other text and graphics in your Web page will crowd too close to the table.
`<TH>, </TH>`	Begin and end table header. (Automatically leaves first entry blank so rows can contain a column name.)
`<TR>, </TR>`	Begin and end table row.
`<TD>, </TD>`	Begin and end table data item.

So creating a table in HTML is fairly simple, but also fairly tedious. You just create the rows and data items; the columns take care of themselves, if you get the data items right.

Getting the data items right is a lot of the problem, though. To make your table look just right you have to use a lot of alignment and formatting options. It becomes very easy to make mistakes, and very hard to update the appearance of a table. That's why so many people use HTML tools to create and manage tables.

 Tables were first introduced by Netscape Navigator Version 1.1; they were not part of the original HTML standard. So some older browsers don't support tables at all. (Tables are the main reason so many Web pages still say "Best viewed with Netscape Navigator" — for a while it was the only browser with table support.) Also, the official HTML standard and Navigator 1.1 used different versions of the same tags. Luckily, most browsers available today support both.

Friends don't let friends do frames

Frames, like tables, are a Netscape innovation. They separate a Web page into separate areas that can be updated individually. For instance, you can click a link in a frame in the bottom half of a Web page, and it is updated with new content although the other frame stays the same. This seems like a powerful capability. However, frames have not proved nearly as popular as tables.

Why is this? Well, frames are hard to create and manage, just like tables. But advanced Web authors are willing to do just about anything to make their Web pages more attractive and more useful. The trouble with frames comes with the "useful" part; users have a hard time with framed Web pages.

When using a framed page, it's hard to tell where the cursor is. So if you scroll, which frame scrolls? Also, going forward and back in a frame is different than going forward and back in the overall Web page. It's easy for the user to get lost. Finally, there's a functional problem or two. When the user resizes the browser window, framed pages don't always resize correctly. And designing a framed page to work well for various monitor sizes is significantly harder than designing regular pages.

Having said all that, framed pages can be very useful in showing complex sets of data and in supporting navigation. Figure 6-6 shows an example of frames used for an online chat session hosted at

`www.fcg.net/chat/chat.html`

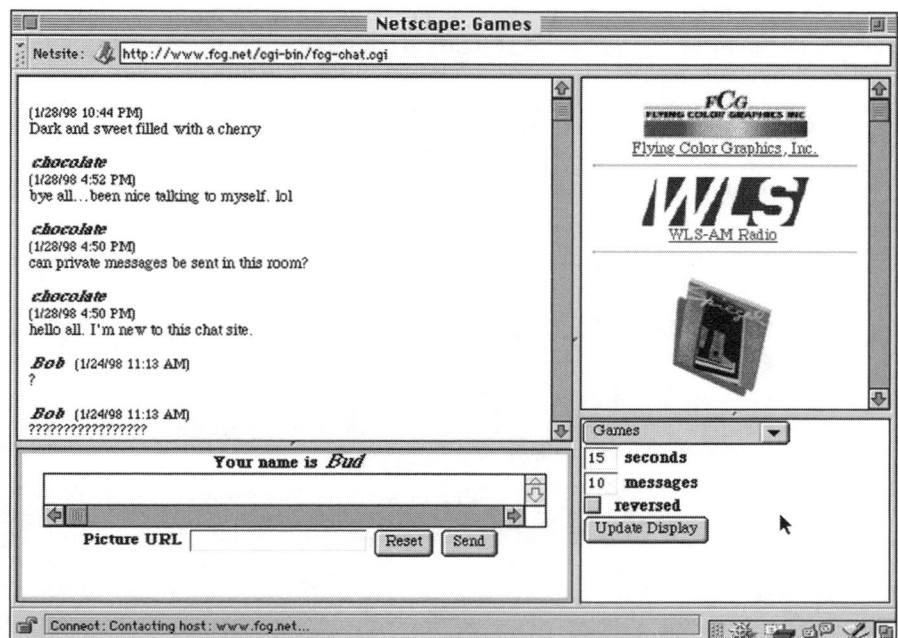

Figure 6-6:
I've been
framed!

Because creating and managing the HTML for frames is even harder than the HTML for tables, we won't show it here; use one of the HTML tools in Part IV if you want to use frames in your pages. (Or look up the appropriate HTML tags in Appendix C and start experimenting!)

Getting good form(s) in your site

Forms are one of the best things in HTML; unlike tables and frames, they're right there in the original HTML definition. That's the good news.

The bad news is that after you put a form in your site, the user is probably going to enter some data in it. So far, so good; but where does the data go? That's the problem: Handling the data from the form requires something called a *CGI (Common Gateway Interface)* script. (No, this is not something a certain South Dakota company uses to sell computers!)

Even worse, it's not enough just to learn how to write CGIs, as CGI scripts are called. You have to get special permission from the Webmaster of your site to run them, or ask the Webmaster to create the script for you. Why? A bad CGI can bring down the entire server. Webmasters can't afford to risk allowing CGIs unless they are notified of them first.

So if you need to use forms, check with the Webmaster of the site your page is on to see what the policies are for CGI support of forms on the server. If necessary, you may even have to move to a different server that offers the CGI support you need. Figure 6-7 shows a forms example from a forms tutorial at the following URL:

```
www.webcom.com/webcom/html/tutor/forms/intro.html
```

See more information about forms in Chapter 7.

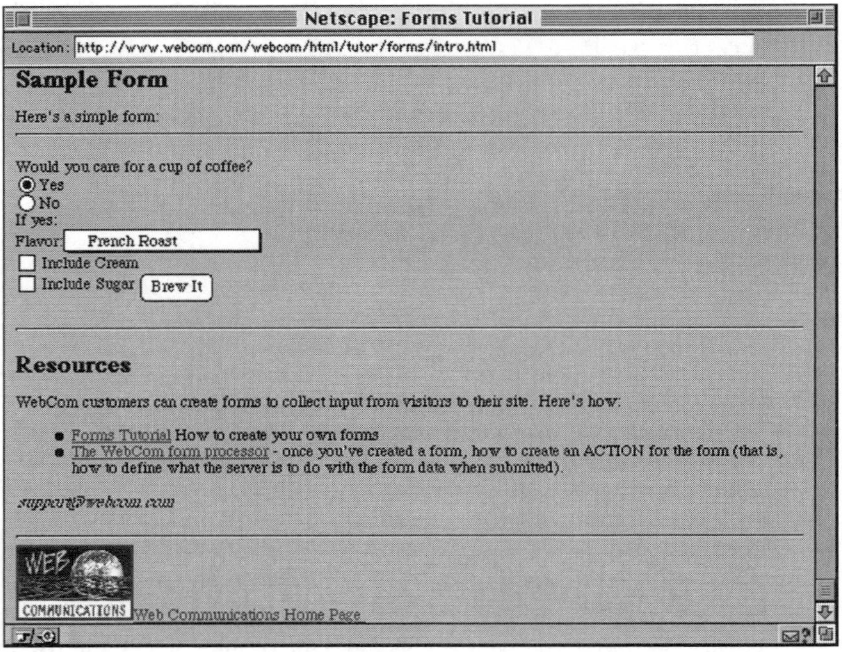

Figure 6-7:
Forms line
up to the
rear.

Making sure your site counts

Counters are one of the best things to have in a Web site. In fact, any serious Web site should have a counter on each page, to make it easy to know what's getting visited and what isn't. The counter doesn't have to display its count to the user, but it should make the count available to you. (You can also see this from the logs produced by the Web server software, but the logs can be hard to read, and you probably don't have access to them unless you run your own Web server. Counters are a nice shortcut.)

However, counters, like forms, require CGI support. Most Webmasters provide counter support. Check with the Web site that your Web page is on to see how to put counters in your Web pages.

A Basic Business Site

Even the smallest businesses can benefit from being on the Web, and any business larger than the smallest *needs* at least a basic Web presence to be taken seriously. But how do you get a basic Web presence without getting in over your head with expensive consultants and Web service providers who might gouge you?

Never fear, *Creating Web Pages For Dummies* is here! In this section, we give you the skeleton of a basic business site. You can edit this site using HTML and then use it with any Web service provider. Literally thousands of other service providers are ready and willing to help you, and you may want to consider them if you have an existing business relationship, need help in specific areas like language, need more CGI support than the biggest services provide, and so on. Whichever way you go, it's not hard to use the template here and a little work and money to get a basic business site up.

 Some of the Web authoring tools covered in Part IV include templates for sites of different kinds, including business sites. Different Web service providers and many Web sites also provide this kind of information, and you can find thousands of books and magazine articles on these topics. Combine ideas from as many resources as you can get your hands on to create a site that suits your needs.

An example business site

The example business site given here is not fancy. Its goal is to provide you with a really basic skeleton that you can add your own information to and put up on the Web, probably with just a few hours' work.

In addition to its simplicity, this site is also put together in such a way as to help you see *why* each Web page in the site exists and how it works with the others. When you start adding to the site, using either your specific business information or resources from other places, keep in mind what you want to accomplish and what each addition can do to help.

 This site is provided, in HTML form, on the CD-ROM that comes with this book. You can copy the site to your hard disk and edit it, using either one of the easy-to-use Web page creation services described in Chapters 4 and 5, using HTML in a text editor, or using one of the Web page creation tools described in Part IV. And don't worry about making mistakes; you can always get a clean copy of the original example site from the CD-ROM.

 The home page in this site is designed as a "panel" — it fills a regular-sized screen without requiring the user to scroll down to see if there's anything more to look at! When you have pages in your site that mostly exist to

provide navigational information, strongly consider designing them as panels, or at least put the key and most used information into the top-most area of the page.

Home page

The home page of the Silicon Valley Publishing Group site, shown in Figure 6-8, is a brief description of the business and a set of pointers to other parts of the site. It serves a few purposes:

✔ To let the Web surfer who doesn't need the information in the site know to "surf on"

✔ To let the Web surfer who does need the information know that he's found the kind of site he's looking for

✔ To provide a positive initial impression of the business

✔ To make it easy for each user to get to the specific information in the site that is needed, or to explore the whole site in a systematic way

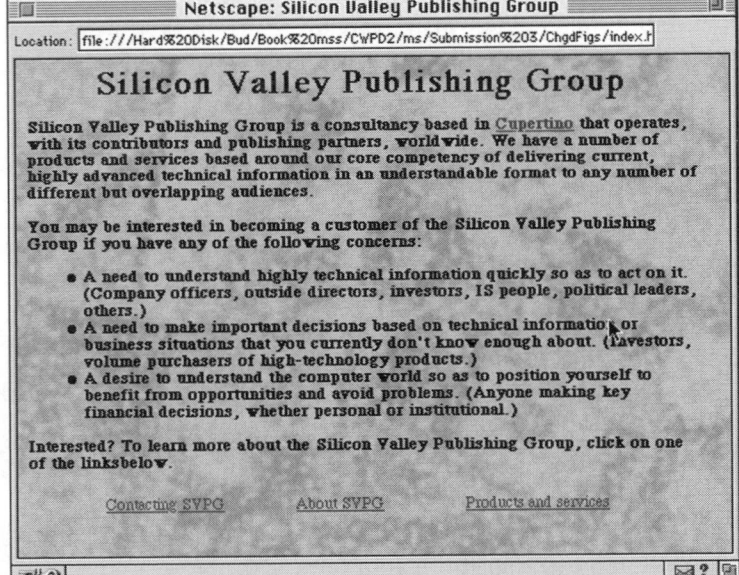

Figure 6-8:
Home page
of the
Silicon
Valley
Publishing
Group.

Contact info

The easiest thing to find in the entire site should be contact info for the business. Remember, people around the world don't have your local phone book! They may only know the name of your business, or a product name, or the name of an employee. With the Web, they can guess your business's URL, or use a search engine to find your site in several different ways. Once at your site, they need to know other ways to reach you. Always make contact information very easy to find in any Web site you create.

Business info

People need to know what you do and why. What are the main impressions you try to leave in the minds of people who do business with you? This is the place to reinforce them. Why do your customers work with you instead of someone else? Use those strengths to communicate a positive and accurate image of your business. In addition to self-description from you, you can use this site to provide information about, and links to, key partners, customers, and suppliers. Each such connection provides another way to make a potential customer feel comfortable about working with you.

Product/service info

Here's where you list the products and services that your business provides. This information alone, backed up by suitable descriptions and photos, is worth its weight in gold to potential customers. (Of course, information doesn't weigh anything, but why let mere facts undermine the point we're trying to make.) Provide a simple, clean list of your products and services, and brief descriptions, illustrations, and photographs to make key points. Then provide a way for the Web surfer to get more information, such as a brochure, the name of a dealer, or a person within your business to talk to.

Going beyond the basics

As a first step, create, test, and publish a simple site like the one previously described. (For details on how to publish your Web site, see Chapter 8.) Then get ready to build it up.

To figure out the right next steps, look both inside your business, and outside it. Within your business, look for resources such as white papers that explain areas of your business or your product line, brochures, advertisements, presentations, even "canned" sales pitches. Figure out how you can get this info onto the Web. In doing so, you save time and money, and you end up with more effective content than you otherwise would likely create.

Add more sophisticated graphics and multimedia. (See Chapter 7 for more information.) Don't try to "wow" the world at first. Just create a simple, clean look to your Web site. Use photographs of products, your facilities, and so on to add interest. Add a few multimedia highlights like a spoken welcome message from the head of the company, or a video clip of a presentation or advertisement.

Also look outside your business. First, look at the Web sites of competitors, partners, and customers. What elements are in their Web sites? Which of these are most needed in yours? Then extend your Web site in the directions indicated.

Finally, look at your overall advertising and marketing budget and then compare it to competitors and other companies like yours. How many of your customers and potential customers are on the Web? What place should the Web play in your plans? Do you want to distinguish yourself on the Web, in print, in broadcast, or in person? This helps you determine whether your Web presence should be just enough to cover your rear end, or something more ambitious. For a great deal more information on using your Web site and other online tools to extend your business's marketing presence into cyberspace, see *Marketing Online For Dummies,* by Frank Catalano and Bud Smith (IDG Books Worldwide, Inc.).

As your site gets more complex, consider hiring out some or all of the work. The knowledge you gain in creating and publishing your own initial Web site makes you a sharp and savvy shopper when looking to hire someone to take over some of the work.

Chapter 7
Graphics, Multimedia, and More

● ●

In This Chapter
▶ Using graphics and multimedia
▶ Making the most of graphics in your Web pages
▶ Using multimedia in your Web pages
▶ Pushing your pages forward
▶ Programming your pages

● ●

*O*ne of the main factors contributing to the success of the Web is the blending of graphics and text in Web pages. This blending makes the Web a dish that can be enjoyed by all who try it. But, long before the Web came into existence, there was substantial and productive online activity in the textual medium. E-mail, Usenet news, and BBS forums were the main vehicles for communication and for online publishing. Gopher was a text-only precursor to the Web. But when the capability to seamlessly combine graphics and text became available in the early Mosaic browser just after 1990, the Web took off.

People like color and people like pictures, so graphics became the seasoning that makes the Web so attractive to people. You can use graphics to convey a thematic "look and feel," to accent certain portions of a Web page, or even to contain the main content of a Web site. Some use of graphics is necessary for any site except the blandest and most utilitarian ones.

Because graphics are so appealing, you can similarly argue for including other types of multimedia content in Web pages. In fact, today's exotic spices will become tomorrow's basic food group. Incorporating audio and even video content in your pages is becoming easier. With a little cooperation from your audience, you can make the presentation of multimedia a seamless process.

In this chapter, we look at the nitty-gritty of using graphics, explain how to create the most common graphic "special effects," describe how to use QuickTime multimedia, and touch briefly on some advanced multimedia topics.

To succeed in the somewhat complex task of adding graphics to your Web page, you need to know some basics of HTML and Web pages in general. Create your basic Web page by using the information in Chapters 4 and 5 before trying to add graphics. And if you aren't yet familiar with HTML tags, review Chapter 3 before reading this chapter.

If you plan to use graphics and/or multimedia in your Web site, you should seriously consider investing some time and money in a Web authoring tool like those described in Part IV. These tools are designed specifically to take the worry out of tedious or complex tasks like placing and sizing graphics, embedding multimedia, and so on.

Dealing with Graphics

The most difficult aspect of including graphics in your Web pages is resolving all the design issues that accompany using graphics. Creating effective graphics and placing them properly in relation to your text is not as easy as boiling water. This book doesn't cover all the complexities of graphic design. However, we can tell you the additional concerns that arise when you use graphics on the Web so that you can effectively apply your own graphics skills, or those of people who work with you, to your Web pages.

Speeding up slow pages

One of the Web's ongoing problems is *download speed* — the amount of time it takes for a Web page to appear on the user's screen. Download times are especially slow for graphics-rich pages, which, although more interesting to view, can be more frustrating because they appear more slowly. And the trade-off is not simple; lots of variables intervene. For example:

- **Access speeds.** Different users access the Web through connections that run at different speeds. And the same server can serve up a Web page at different speeds depending on how busy the server is. When you test your brand-new, graphics-rich page on your local machine, everything may run fast. But when you upload that same page to a server and access it from home over a 28.8 Kbps (kilobits per second) modem at a time when many people are accessing the same server, everything runs much slower.

- **Good and bad graphics.** If you plan to spend your users' time on downloading big graphics, invest some of your own time and money upfront to make sure that the graphics are as good as possible. People don't mind waiting for a good graphic nearly as much as they do for a bad one. A good graphic may be a clickable image with lots of different embedded options. A bad graphic may be a banner that says "HELLO!" in six Day-Glo colors.

> ✔ **Frustration levels.** The same users who enjoy watching your page appear in the morning while drinking a cup of coffee may be tempted to scream at their browser when they try to quickly check out your page just before heading home from work, especially if they had a bad hair day, a bad boss day, or even a bad browser day. The better the job you do with your graphics, the more your page pleases people.

What on earth can you do to address all these factors, especially when they combine to make your page slow and your users grumpy? Be clever! Use compression programs such as WinZip or Stuffit to make your graphics files smaller so that they download quicker. Get expert advice — from someone you know, from a book, or by looking at cool sites online — to help you make the graphics you do use more interesting to look at. You can also sprinkle your page lightly with small graphics rather than burden it with big ones. We explain these tricks and more in this chapter.

Table 7-1 shows the time it takes to download 100K (kilobytes) of data. A text-only page is usually just a few kilobytes, but pages with graphics are much larger. A complex, quarter-screen GIF image, for example, may be about 50K. Compare the total size of all the elements in your planned page to the times shown in Table 7-1 to get an idea of how quickly your page loads for your most speed-deficient user, and then design with that person in mind.

Table 7-1	**Slowest Download Times**	
Access Speed	*Description*	*Time to Download 100K file*
14.4 Kbps	Low-end Internet modem	56 seconds
28.8 Kbps	Fast Internet modem	28 seconds
ISDN	Special phone line, modem	7 seconds
Ethernet	Standard network	<1 second

Graphics formats — GIF and JPEG

Each graphics program saves files in its own *proprietary graphics format* — its own specific arrangement of data that the program uses to save its files. Fortunately, for the purposes of using graphics in HTML, you need to concern yourself with only two formats, GIF and JPEG — and even then you don't really need to know a lot about the gory details of each format to use them.

GIF, or *Graphics Interchange Format,* is the file format used by most people to exchange graphics. Originally made popular on CompuServe, GIF spread to other online services and then to the Internet and the Web. Any browser that supports graphics supports GIF.

Standards for graphics and multimedia

Any up-to-date Web browser is designed to display three types of data: text with HTML tags, GIF graphics, and JPEG graphics. (GIF is pronounced "jiff" by some, "giff" — as in "gift" — by others. We prefer "giff" as in "gift.") A typical Web browser displays HTML-tagged text appropriately, although not all browsers understand all of the same tags. A browser also displays GIF and JPEG graphics *inline* — that is, embedded in the Web page. But for other kinds of graphics and for multimedia, things get a little trickier.

Until 1996, non-GIF graphics and other data types used a *helper application* to display a graphic, play a sound, show a video clip, and so on. The following figure, from a sofa exhibit hosted online by the Ferguson-Taylor group, shows a helper application displaying a JPEG graphic on a Web page. Users had to get the appropriate helper applications for each additional data type. So when a different data type, such as sound, was included in a Web page, users with the right helper application installed could access it — but others couldn't.

Well, helper applications were too hard to download, configure, and use, so the online world, led by Netscape, moved to a *plug-in* model. Plug-ins enable multimedia files to be embedded within a Web page. Netscape Navigator ships with the QuickTime plug-in, which supports animation, sound, and QuickTime VR as well as video clips. Two other very popular plug-ins are the RealAudio plug-in for sound and the ShockWave plug-in for interactive multimedia. The only problem is that if you use these data types in your Web page, you have to give users a way to get the latest plug-in to view them with.

Browsers, led as usual by Netscape Navigator, are being extended to handle more types of data without the need for helper applications. However, the ongoing improvement of the browser base is a gradual process. You can use HTML-tagged text and GIF or JPEG graphics with confidence, but if you use other data types, be ready for some e-mail messages and phone calls from users who can't access everything in your site.

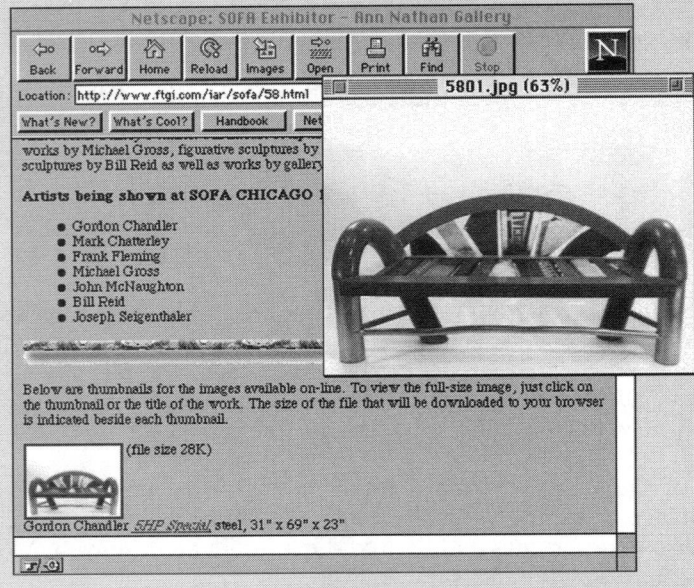

GIF is great for images that have from only a few to a few hundred colors in them, which includes most simple images and most images created on a computer. If an image has more than 256 colors in it, some of the color information is lost when you convert the image to GIF. You have to look at the image before and after converting it to GIF to see if the conversion has much effect on the appearance of the image.

The GIF format was first popularized on CompuServe. A controversy over GIF stems from the fact that Unisys, a patent holder to the GIF format, once tried to force CompuServe and its users and, in fact, the entire online community, to pay royalties for the use of GIF. Unisys seems to have backed off from this issue, but it hasn't licensed its patent freely or done any other things to fully resolve the problem for everyone. For a time, CompuServe was pushing a new, public domain format, *GIF24,* to try to resolve the issue, but GIF24 hasn't caught on and it looks as though the popularity of GIF is continuing despite the controversy.

JPEG, or *Joint Photographic Experts Group* format, is an additional format created to compress complex images. Most browsers now support JPEG in the same way they do GIF, displaying a JPEG image right in the Web page (although sometimes displaying the image in a helper application provides a better looking image). JPEG is a necessity for images with many colors, including photographs and other natural-looking images. (What makes the image look natural is the way that different shades of a color appear as light falls differently on various parts of an object.) These images retain their appearance well when compressed with JPEG.

Controversy abounds about which is the best to use, GIF or JPEG. (Of course, one of your authors can remember a desktop publishing meeting years ago that spent three hours on the merits of another format: gray-scale TIFF!)

JPEG was designed to efficiently compress complex images with many color variations. This design makes JPEG the image format of choice for display-ing photographs on your Web page. Figure 7-1 shows a Web page that uses a photo of Marc Andreesen, founder of Netscape, to graphically illustrate the difference in photo file sizes between GIF and JPEG. The Web page in this figure shows one complete picture of Mark Andreesen and part of a subse-quent one. On the Web page itself, you find several versions of the same picture saved with different types of compression; go to the Web page to see the comparison. The URL for this online comparison is as follows:

```
home.netscape.com/assist/net_sites/impact_docs/e-jpeg.html
```

Use this page, the GIF/JPEG test page, to test the speed of your own Internet connection. The total size of the page and graphics is about 70K.

Figure 7-1:
Marc
Andreesen
served up in
a GIFfy.

GIF files of images with lots of large blocks of solid colors tend to be small and are the preferred choice for banners or images with large areas of solid color, such as bar graphs or icons. In other words, the simple drawings that most of us create work best with GIF. Dense artistic graphics and photos work better with JPEG.

GIF files also give you some graphic design options that you don't get with JPEG files. You can make the colors in GIF images transparent to whatever is in the background of the image, and you can save GIF images in interlaced format. *Interlaced* images are saved in such a way that when your browser starts downloading the image, the browser first displays the image with a very low resolution and then with a progressively clearer resolution until the whole image is displayed. This makes GIF images preferable for quickly displaying a rough-looking graphic that improves with time and for creating fancy special effects. We explain interlaced GIF images in more detail, with pictures, later in this chapter.

Transparent images have a clear area surrounding the object of interest. For instance, in a photo of a watch, you may not want any background color surrounding the watch, just the watch itself sitting directly on the Web page. To achieve this effect you use a transparent GIF, an image where the border area is clear. The background color of the overall Web page shows through the transparent area, and the object of interest appears to "float" over the background. We explain transparent GIF images in more detail, with pictures, along with interlaced images later in this chapter.

Because of these advantages of GIF, a good rule is to use JPEG for photographs and GIF for everything else. When you feel more confident in your design skills, you can play around with both formats and choose the one that's right for you. Read on to find out how to obtain and create graphics for your Web pages and how to save your graphics in either format.

Newer versions of JPEG that support GIF-like features are appearing. However, these new JPEG features are not supported by as many graphics tools or by as many browsers as for GIF. Stick with GIF for these features until your expertise grows.

Obtaining and creating graphics

So you want to put various graphics on your Web page. Great. But how do you create them and get them in the right format (GIF or JPEG)? Fortunately, creating the graphics you want or finding some to use is pretty easy.

The easiest way to obtain graphics is to get access to a clip art collection. Computer stores sell many inexpensive collections of business and recreational graphics on CD-ROM. In addition, you can access a number of royalty-free graphics and icon collections online.

You can spend endless hours looking for art online. In fact, this alone may make you glad to be doing a Web page; you may not get a lot done for a few hours looking for art, but you see a lot of neat stuff!

One great site at which to start your search is the Online Image Archive, at the following URL:

`www.maths.tcd.ie/pub/images/images.html`

Another is the Virtual Image Archive:

`imagiware.com/via.cgi`

And for photographs, try a site with preexisting stock photos, a site with all kinds of graphics, and another that converts your photographs into digital form:

`www.weststock.com`

`www.imageclub.com`

`www.filmworks.com`

More on graphics

The Graphics File Formats FAQ (Frequently Asked Questions) can answer almost any conceivable question about graphics. Visit this Web site for the latest information:

`www.cis.ohio-state.edu/ hypertext/faq/usenet/graphics/ fileformats-faq/top.html`

Links from this site lead to detailed technical information about GIF, JPEG, and other file formats.

For a detailed description of how to use images well, see this site:

`home.netscape.com/assist/ net_sites/impact_docs/index.html`

Many more sites for images and image conversion exist. Start with the sites that we mention and expand your search until you find what you need.

In addition to searching online, another way to get graphics is to whip out any paint program and draw the graphics that you want. Even inexpensive paint programs today enable you to create some stunning graphics; you're limited mostly by your imagination and artistic ability (which for some of us is a pretty restrictive limit!). High-end programs like Adobe Photoshop and Adobe Illustrator are regularly used for big-bucks commercial work and fine art. If you lack talent, you can always ask one of your artistically inclined friends to help you, or you can even recruit a starving art student. Windows includes a free graphics program, Windows Paint, that you can use for your initial graphics work.

The third way to obtain graphics is to head on over to your favorite copy shop and use its scanner. This is a perfect way to put photographs online. Simply scan your graphic or photo, save it in GIF (for graphics) or JPEG (for photographs) format, and slap it on your Web site. Or work with a photo developer, such as Seattle Filmworks (`www.filmworks.com`), that can develop your film right to diskette or PhotoCD.

But how can you make sure that your graphics are in the proper format? That turns out to be easy, too. Many paint programs and most scanning software let you save a graphic in either GIF or JPEG formats. If your program does not save in these formats, it may be for one of two reasons:

- ✔ During installation, you may have chosen not to install converters for GIF and JPEG. Haul out your original install disks and see whether you can reinstall the program with the correct translators.

- ✔ If converters are not the problem, call your program's manufacturer or visit its Web site and see whether it has an update that enables the program to save to GIF and/or JPEG formats. If your software vendor can't sell you a program that handles GIF or JPEG, you can easily find one that does.

What about rights?

A number of great graphics are in books and magazines and online information. Can you just scan or copy those and use them in your Web site?

Yes and no. Yes, you *can*, but no, you *shouldn't*. Publishers either own the images that they use or obtain a license for them. You can't legally use the images without either buying or licensing them.

For many images on the Web, simply sending a note to the publisher gets you a quick okay. But for other Web images and for most images in print, permissions are very hard to get. Creating a new image that serves the same purpose is often easier than negotiating permissions. And then maybe you can make a little money licensing your images out to other people!

No matter what format your graphic came in originally, by using software that you can easily obtain from the Web, you can convert from just about any format to GIF or JPEG. Mac users can run GIFConverter, and Windows users can run the excellent LView program to convert between multiple formats. Save your graphic as a GIF or JPEG file, and you are ready to incorporate it into your Web page. See Appendix D for more information on how to obtain converters and other programs.

Save your image in the program's normal format as well as GIF or JPEG. When you save to GIF or JPEG, you can lose information from the image. If you reopen the GIF or JPEG image, edit the file, and then save it again, you lose even more information. So keep your file in the normal file format for the program that created it and save a separate copy in GIF or JPEG to use on the Web.

Three things to avoid

Don't make these three big mistakes relating to graphics on the Web:

- ✔ **No graphics.** No graphics means boring pages. Because you're reading this chapter, we assume that you're trying not to make this mistake.

- ✔ **Too many graphics.** Using too many graphics may be the biggest "newbie" Web author mistake. (A lot of old hands make this mistake as well.)

- ✔ **No text alternative.** Some users don't have graphical capability at all, and many others run around the Web with graphics turned off, only turning graphics capability on when needed. You need to create your page in a way that supports text-only access as well as graphical access.

Try an experiment: Go into your browser, turn off the graphics display, and load your Web page. If you can't tell what is on the page or what links go where, then you need to redesign your page. (Then, just to blow off steam, try the same experiment on some other people's pages and send them a note if you have problems.)

The usual way to redesign your page for text-only access is to include a textual menu linking to the same places that your graphical menu choices link to. Some sites provide a whole parallel set of Web pages that are purely textual rather than graphical. This lets the user choose whether to go for the attractive, bandwidth-sucking graphical pages, or the fast text-only pages. However, the percentage of users who only use text-only access is dropping, so providing a complete set of text-only pages may be overkill.

Here are the HTML tags for a page that displays an image, MANUGRAPHIC.GIF using the `<IMG>` tag, and then a text menu as an alternative:

```
<IMG SRC="manugraphic.gif" ALT="Menu Graphic"> [ <A
HREF="about.html">About</A> | <A
HREF="home.html">Home page</A> | <A
HREF="links.html">Fun Links</A> | <A
HREF="map.html">Site Map</A> | <A
HREF="search.html">Search Map</A> ]
```

Figure 7-2 shows an example of an image combined with a text menu from Apple's Advanced Technology Group, one of the more interesting sites on the Web, at this URL:

```
www.atg.apple.com
```

These are the most important rules for supporting text and graphical access:

✔ As you design and create your page, think about how your page will look with all graphic access turned off as well as on.

✔ Test your page with graphics turned off.

✔ Test your page in different browsers.

✔ Include ALT tags in all images so that explanatory text appears whenever a graphic is not displayed (see Chapter 3 and Appendix C for details about HTML tags).

✔ Provide text-only menus in addition to icon-based selections and image maps.

✔ If you need to make everyone very happy, consider also creating a text-only version of your site.

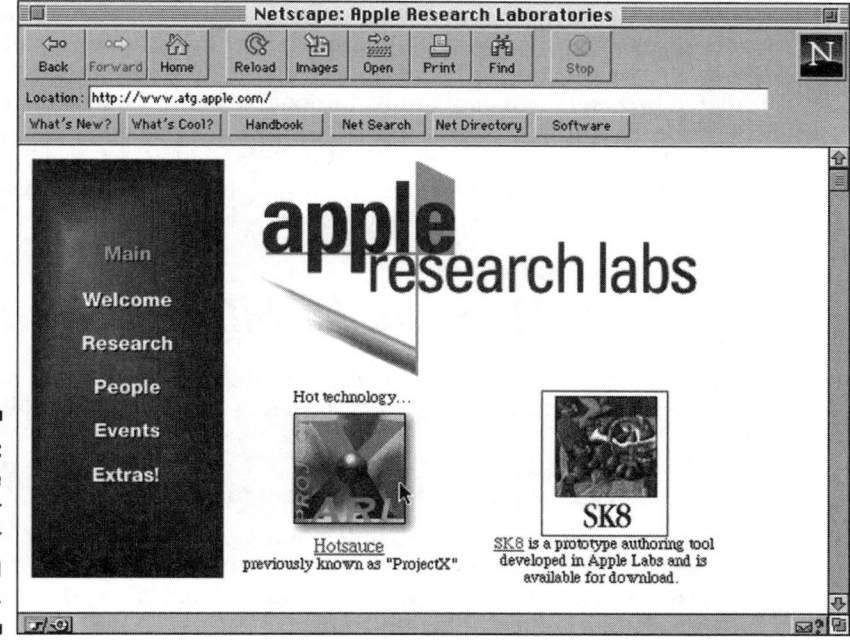

Figure 7-2:
Click the
images, or
the text, or
anything
you want.

Graphics in HTML

Here are three useful graphical effects for your Web pages:

✔ **Accents.** Small graphical images that serve as labels or highlights
("New," "Top 10," and so on).

✔ **Icons.** Small graphical images that serve as links to another page. Click
the icon and you move to a different Web page.

✔ **Thumbnails.** Small graphical images that serve as previews of a larger
image. Clicking the thumbnail downloads the larger image.

Accents use the HTML tag <IMG> (short for "image") to link to a small
graphic — an inline graphic displayed as part of the page, unless graphics
display is turned off.

Icons and thumbnails combine the <IMG> tag, which makes the icon or
thumbnail image appear, with the <A> (or anchor) tag. (Don't start singing
"anchors away" on this one — you need anchors here!) The anchor tag
establishes a link to the Web page or larger graphic that appears when you
click the inline graphic.

The steps in the following sections describe how to use the image tag, the
anchor tag, and the ALT option separately and together. With these tags, you
can combine graphics and navigation to create all kinds of effects.

Review the HTML tag definitions in Appendix C to learn about other options for these tags. Try to achieve the desired effect by using the HTML 2.0 tag definitions first. If you use HTML 3.0 tags, your page may look bad on outdated browsers and may need additional testing. You may also want to look in more advanced books, such as *HTML 4 For Dummies,* by Ed Tittel and Stephen N. James, and *Creating Cool Web Pages with HTML,* 3rd Edition, by Dave Taylor, both from IDG Books Worldwide, Inc., for more details and how-to information on advanced options.

Use the <IMG> tag for inline graphics

To use the <IMG> tag to link to an inline graphic that displays as part of your Web page, along with the ALT option to specify ALTernate text, follow these steps:

1. Create or find a graphic that you want to use.

Inline graphics that are embedded in the page should be small for fast display — about the size of a business card or smaller. Use the sources described in the "Obtaining and creating graphics" section earlier in this chapter to find or create graphics.

2. In your HTML file, add the <IMG> tag with the SRC, or "source," option to specify the image's pathname.

For a graphic that's in the same directory as the HTML file, the <IMG> tag and SRC option are used like this:

```
<IMG SRC="new.gif">
```

For a graphic that's at a different Web site, the <IMG> tag and SRC option are used like this:

```
<IMG SRC="http://www.grafixsite.com/new.gif">
```

3. Add the ALT option to specify text that appears if the graphic can't be viewed — for example, if the user is running a text-only browser or has graphics turned off.

```
<IMG SRC="http://www.grafixsite.com/new.gif" ALT="New!">
```

Don't depend on someone else's site being up at all times and always staying unchanged. If at all possible, copy the graphic that you need into your own site's directory and refer to it there.

Graphics can be a time sink

We spend a lot of time in this chapter discussing how much time the user can spend downloading graphics. But what about the impact of using graphics on your time as a Web page developer?

Creating and editing graphics is fun! But even creating a simple business graphic, such as a bar graph, can consume hours of fooling around with fonts, colors, and image sizes. Getting your images Web-ready and testing them takes up even more time. Working with graphics can easily become the most time-consuming part of creating and updating your Web site.

What to do? Use small graphics and use graphics sparingly while you gain experience. After you have experience, or after you hire someone who does, you can develop and deploy those knockout graphics that distinguish the best Web sites.

Add an A-for-anchor to create a graphical link

As we note in the first part of the section on graphics and HTML, one of the best ways to jazz up a Web page "cheaply" — that is, without slowing down the page for everyone — is to use graphical elements as icons that link to outside information, such as a larger image or a different Web page. This technique is a great way to make your page appear graphically rich without burdening your users with long download times.

To add an anchor to create a graphical link, use the <IMG> tag within beginning and ending anchor tags. If you also embed a word or phrase between the beginning and ending anchor tags, the user has a choice between clicking the image or the phrase. The following steps demonstrate how to create a graphical link:

1. **Within your HTML document, use the <IMG> tag to bring in the inline image that you want to use as a thumbnail image (a small image that represents a larger one) or an icon:**

   ```
   <IMG SRC="minibud.jpg">
   ```

2. **Add an anchor tag to specify the link.**

   To display a larger image when the small image is clicked, specify an anchor with an HREF, or HyperText REFerence, that points to an image file:

   ```
   <A HREF="maxibud.jpg"> <IMG SRC="minibud.jpg"> </A>
   ```

Figure 7-3, from Dave Sag of Australia, shows a thumbnail graphic linked to a larger graphic that's also downloaded. Dave Sag's interesting page can be found at this URL:

```
www.va.com.au/dave/art.html
```

For a link to another page, specify an anchor with an HREF that points to an HTML document:

```
<A HREF="bebakpg.htm"> <IMG SRC="bebak.jpg"> </A>
```

An HTML 3.0/Netscape option not only allows you to resize an image, but it also speeds up page displays. Add the HEIGHT= and WIDTH= options within the <IMG> tag to specify the height and width, in pixels, of your image. Use the image's usual dimensions to tell the browser the height and width. Most browsers use this information to fill in the rest of the page around the image, allowing the user to scroll up and down in the page and read it, and then to fill in the image itself.

One of the most important ways that intermediate and advanced Web authors organize their pages is by using invisible tables to position text and graphics relative to one another. This is tricky! For instance, a table-structured page that looks great at one monitor size can easily look terrible on a larger

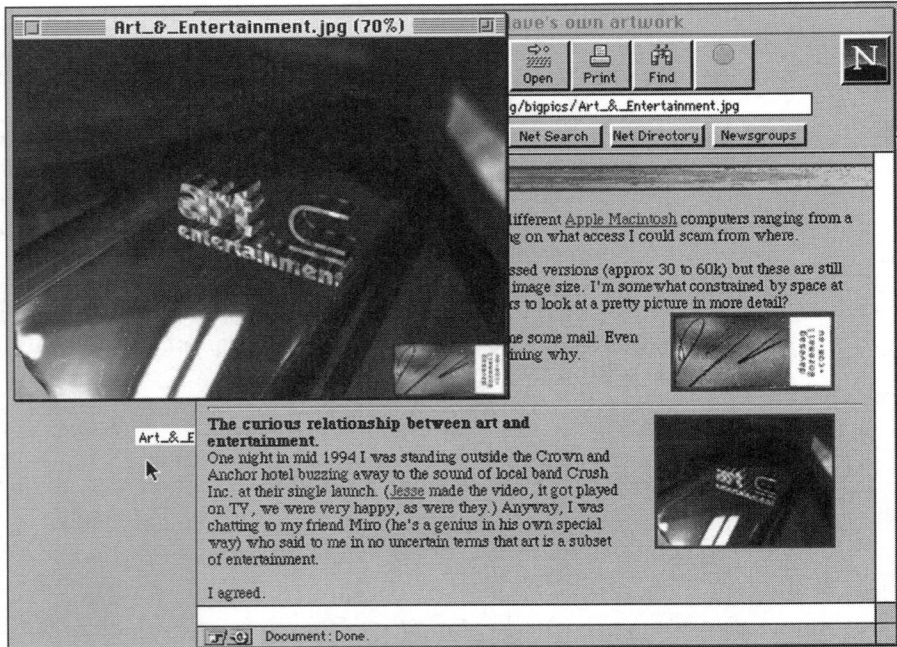

Figure 7-3:
Combining
mini- and
maxi-
graphics.

or smaller screen. Find some well-laid-out Web pages and view the Web pages' HTML source to see how it's done. To see one expert's work, visit Creating Killer Web sites at:

```
www.killersites.com/1-design/jpeg.html
```

Advanced GIFfery

GIFs are widespread on the Web, and download times are important; therefore, four advanced techniques have been developed for doing fancy things with GIFs:

✓ **Transparent GIFs.** Everyone needs to know this one. All GIFs are rectangular, but many of them seem to "float" over the background with no obvious border. Why? Because they're cool! (Beavis, shut up!) Actually, some GIFs are "transparent" — the image's background is invisible — so they blend seamlessly into the browser's background. Figure 7-4 shows a nontransparent and a transparent GIF from the Web 66 Web site, which is part of a cooperative effort between the University of Minnesota College of Education and Development and Hillside Elementary in Minnesota, with support from 3M.

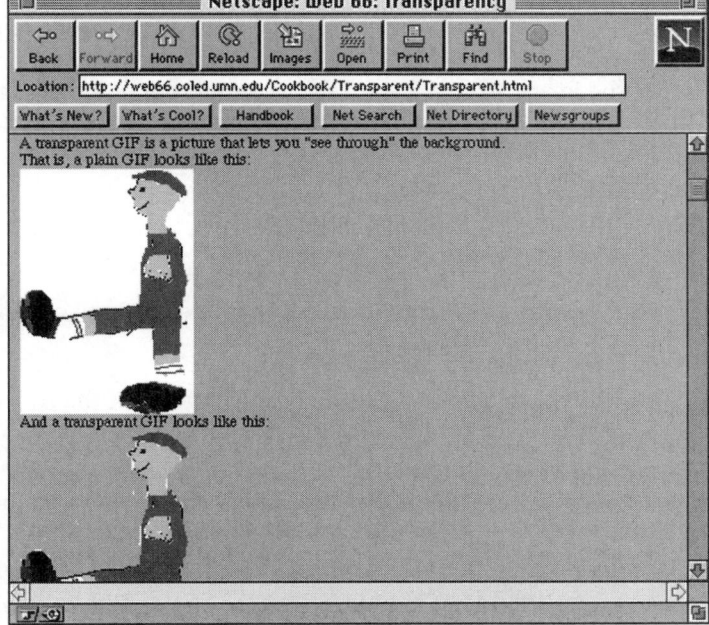

Figure 7-4:
Now you see it (the white rectangle around the graphic), now you don't.

✔ **Interlaced GIFs.** Not everyone needs to know about this one, but we mention it (again!) because if you use complex graphics, interlaced GIFs are worth knowing about. An interlaced GIF depends on an HTML 3.0 feature that paints every fourth line of an image, and then one-fourth of the remaining lines, and so on until the image is complete. The image seems to appear in low resolution and then gradually sharpen until complete.

✔ **Animated GIFs**. To the surprise of many, the basic GIF specification, GIF89a, turns out to support animation as well as static images. All you need to do is create a series of images that, when viewed in sequence, form an animation (like an old-fashioned flip book). Then you package them together as a single GIF, using easily available tools, and include the GIF file in your Web page. Voilà! Instant animation.

✔ **Clickable image maps.** Clickable image maps are very common in big-money sites and even in many smaller ones. A clickable image map is a graphic with different *hot spots* that, when clicked, take you to different Web pages or locations within a Web page. This kind of graphic is cool, but it's YABG (Yet Another Big Graphic) and requires design skill to make a good one.

Here are the steps to create a transparent GIF:

1. **Choose a color in the background to make transparent.**

   Every pixel in your image that's of this color becomes transparent. Choose a color that's used only in the area around the image, not in the image itself, since every pixel of the selected color becomes transparent. You may need to edit the image to make the area surrounding the part of the image that you want to see a different color from the rest. The usual choices for transparency are white, or the light gray background color used by most browsers.

   For details on the procedure for doing this, see the Web 66 Web site, shown in Figure 7-4:

   `web66.coled.umn.edu/Cookbook/Transparent/Transparent.html`

2. **Use your graphics package or a tool to make the image transparent.**

   For the Macintosh, use Transparency.

   For Windows, use LView to get the hex RGB value of the transparent color. Then run giftrans. These tools are all available on the Web.

   For any platform, you can use a Web-based package on the Visioneering page. It will read the image, convert it, and write it back to the same location.

   To use the Visioneering page, you have to move your image to a Web server, as described in Chapter 8. Then go to this URL and follow the instructions:

www.vrl.com/Imaging

This package also makes the GIF interlaced.

3. **Add the image to your page.**

   Add the image to your page as described earlier in this chapter. Use the description that fits the way you want to use the image.

4. **Test to be sure that the image remains transparent with several different backgrounds by bringing up the image in your browser and then changing the browser's default background color.**

Animated GIFs are also supported online. You can learn how to use them and get started with putting them in your Web pages using info out on the Web. To read the true and fascinating story of how animated GIFs were invented, and to link to many supporting examples and resources, go to

www.webreview.com/96/02/09/tech/edge

To create a clickable image map, you must first create the graphic. (See the Apple and SGI sites online for examples of attractive, clickable image maps.) Then you have to create a special file that maps regions of the image to specific URLs. A program that you can download from the Web, Mapedit (see Appendix D), does this for either Macintosh or Windows. Just load the image, click and drag over it to define clickable regions, and then enter the URL you want to link to.

The complication arises during the final part of this process. The original form of image maps, called *server-side image maps,* required that the map file be in a special place where the server can find it. Unfortunately, to use this kind of image map you may need to talk to the server administrator, because no universal standard exists about where this file should be.

Netscape 2.0 and higher, Microsoft Internet Explorer, and other up-to-date browsers support what are known as *client-side image maps* that don't need the server to get involved in any processing when the user clicks an image. Browsers are now smart enough to map the image, click to a URL, and fetch the URL directly without going through the server. See the Netscape 2.0 documentation or the Netscape site for more information.

For much more cool info on Web authoring, see the Web Review home page at

www.webreview.com

Also, see *The Net* magazine online:

www.thenet-usa.com

The Net includes a cool tool called GIFwizard that can shrink the size of GIF graphics and animations by up to 90 percent. Try it!

Making It Multimedia and Beyond

Getting your page right by using the basic Web ingredients of text and graphics is a real challenge but a lot of fun. Get the basics down before you push forward into the realm of multimedia in your own Web pages. However, if you're adventurous, use the information that follows to add exciting multimedia flavorings to your Web pages.

Sound and video

A year ago — about seven Web years — multimedia files were downloaded from the Web, and then played back in a separate application. Now, multimedia files are embedded in Web pages using plug-ins, described in the "Standards for graphics and multimedia" sidebar earlier in this chapter.

Using multimedia yields some of the same problems as using graphics files, only more so. Many users don't have the right plug-ins for viewing graphics and don't know how to get the plug-ins and set them up when needed.

Performance is also a problem. Waiting several minutes to download a small, jerky, brief video clip is frustrating. Many Web sound files don't sound good. And multimedia files can affect the overall performance of the Internet itself. A few hundred people listening to live audio at once may be enough to completely tie up an Internet service provider, limiting access by others as well as causing poor performance for the listeners.

However, when you get multimedia working right, it spices up a Web site like nothing else. Today, only online services such as America Online, CompuServe, and Prodigy (which have greater capacity than ISPs and greater control over factors like the number of logged-in users and event pricing) can use multimedia on a large scale effectively. But multimedia on the wide-open Web is well on its way to becoming as important tomorrow as graphics are today.

The three most important plug-ins for Web multimedia are

> ✔ **RealAudio.** RealAudio is a plug-in for real-time playback of audio files, and it works pretty darn well. The user of a RealAudio-enhanced Web site typically clicks a link to get audio. A reasonably brief pause ensues while an initial part of the file downloads, and then sound starts

playing. The sound is *streamed* in real time, meaning that no big file is stored on the user's hard disk. (This also means that the faster the user's Internet connection, the better the sound quality.)

✔ **QuickTime.** QuickTime is Apple's multimedia technology that has become the industry standard for video editing and playback on computers. QuickTime VR is an offshoot of QuickTime that creates high-resolution virtual reality panoramas and objects. The QuickTime plug-in is the only plug-in bundled with Netscape Navigator. It supports all kinds of multimedia formats including animation, sound, QuickTime VR, and QuickTime video clips. Over half the movie files on the Web are QuickTime files. QuickTime is easy to use in your Web page and there are no licensing or server fees.

✔ **ShockWave.** The ShockWave plug-in allows presentations and experiences created in Macromedia Director to be played back over the Web. Learning Director is no mean feat, but ShockWave is a powerful tool for delivering multimedia experiences over the Web. If you are a Director user, or interested in becoming one, run, don't walk, to the Macromedia Web site to learn more about ShockWave.

To find out more about how to use multimedia on the Web, start by checking out the following URLs:

www.macromedia.com

www.quicktime.apple.com

www.realaudio.com

Putting QuickTime in your Web page

Many different multimedia formats exist, each with its own strengths and weaknesses. But no other multimedia format is as widely accepted, as capable, or supported by as many different multimedia and Web page creation tools as QuickTime. Adding multimedia to your Web page is easy with QuickTime, and using QuickTime-based multimedia is likely to be easy for your users as well. Here are the necessary elements for a successful QuickTime Web authoring experience:

✔ **Multimedia content.** You need a QuickTime multimedia file to put in your page. Dozens of multimedia tools create QuickTime multimedia; for starters, use one someone else has created.

✔ **HTML commands.** A few Web tools, notably PageMill, support embedding of QuickTime content directly. But unless you have such a tool, you need to write HTML commands to embed QuickTime content. Luckily, the commands are simple; an example follows shortly.

✔ **QuickTime and the QuickTime plug-in.** You and your users need the latest version of QuickTime and the QuickTime plug-in. (By the time you read this, QuickTime will include QuickTime VR support as well, adding virtual reality to what you can do with QuickTime.) Many of your users will have this, but many won't; to help your users get updated, provide a link to the QuickTime Web page at

```
quicktime.apple.com
```

QuickTime is big! Users who don't already have QuickTime on their machines have to download it from the Web, and several megabytes is a lot to ask your users to download. However, doing so gets them a lot of capability. Just be aware that you may get some questions and complaints about the download hassle.

Unlike some competing technologies, you don't have to pay fees or sign special licenses before using QuickTime; from a business point of view, it's as easy as putting a GIF or JPEG image in your Web page. Figure 7-5 shows and example of QuickTime content in a Web page. The URL for this page is

```
www.gm.com/about/community/cure/vehicles.html
```

Figure 7-5:
A little QuickTime (and QuickTime VR) can have a lot of impact.

For more information, visit the QuickTime Webmaster's Page, the QuickTime VR home page, and the Berkeley Macintosh User's group QuickTime authoring site at the following Web URLs:

`www.apple.com/quicktime/qtvr`

`www.bmug.org/Services/qt`

Here are the steps to add a QuickTime movie to your Web page:

1. **Install QuickTime and the QuickTime plug-in on your own machine.**

   To download these files, go to the QuickTime software page at
   `quicktime.apple.com/sw/`

2. **Get a QuickTime movie — animation, sound, video, or VR.**

3. **Embed the movie in your Web page.**

   Use the `EMBED` command in HTML. In its basic form, it's very simple:

   ```
   <EMBED SRC="file.mov">
   ```

   You have additional options for the `EMBED` command when used with the QuickTime plug-in; for details, see the QuickTime Web page. But try it with the simple command shown above first to make sure you don't accidentally introduce a problem while adding options.

4. **Test on your own machine.**

   Test the Web page by opening it in Netscape Navigator and seeing if the movie acts properly. Then test in Internet Explorer.

5. **Upload the changed Web page and the multimedia file to the Web and test.**

   Upload the new stuff to the Web and see if it works. When it does, congratulations; you're a multimedia Web publisher!

Page description languages

HTML is not a page description language — that is, a specification for exactly how your text and graphics should look when they're displayed or printed. But Adobe Acrobat *is* a page description language, and so are Envoy from Novell, Inc., and the MiniViewer that's part of Common Ground from Hummingbird Communications, Ltd. (***Note:*** Even though you may overhear at the supermarket: "Give me a pound of premium Java and half a pound of that common ground," Common Ground is not a cheap version of Java, the programming language described later.)

So if you want to put up a formatted page that keeps its look, feel, fonts, and more, use Acrobat, Envoy, or Common Ground. You can put the page up on the Web so that it looks exactly like a printed version. The problem: Users have to download a special viewer for your information, which they're unlikely to bother with unless you have something they really, really want to see. (And expect a few technical support calls from users who can't figure it out.) *The New York Times* is the biggest "name" to adopt Acrobat so far.

To bypass this viewing problem, Acrobat is now supported by a plug-in for Microsoft Internet Explorer and Netscape Navigator. For more information and for a look at *The New York Times* daily online edition that uses Acrobat, see the following URLs:

```
www.adobe.com/prodindex/acrobat/
```

```
www.latimes.com/home/news/pdf
```

```
nytimesfax.com/sample/sample.pdf
```

VRML

VRML, or *Virtual Reality Modeling Language,* is a set of standards for displaying three-dimensional virtual worlds via the World Wide Web. You can think of it as a graphical analog of HTML, specially designed to deal with 3-D graphical objects.

At the time of this writing, VRML is still a rapidly evolving standard. (That means don't touch it with a 10-foot pole, unless you own a fast Web server and have a lot of time to kill!) However, the major points of the VRML standard are now widely agreed on; it's the details of implementation that can still cause problems. Many Web page creators are interested in using VRML to create 3-D front ends and environments for online shopping, information navigation, and games. To learn more, your best bet is to connect to Silicon Graphics' site and an example site to get the latest scoop:

```
www.sgi.com
```

```
www.zdnet.com/products/vrmluser/map/zd3d.html/
```

Pushing Your Pages

Push technology is a new Internet and Web technology that turns traditional use of the Web on its head. Instead of going out and searching for information one Web page at a time, a user of push technology subscribes to a Web page or other Internet information service. At periodic intervals, the user's machine then checks on the Internet for updates and downloads any new information to the user's hard disk. (The download can take a long time, but the machine can be used for other things — even Websurfing — while it's going on, or the download can take place while the machine is otherwise unused.) Once the download is complete, users can look at the information or run any program that was pushed to their machines at very fast hard-disk speeds, not the much slower speeds experienced when accessing information over the Internet.

As a Web page publisher, you can use push technology to have your users access your information without even trying. Using Internet Explorer 4.0 or higher (but not, at this writing, Netscape Navigator), users can subscribe to your Web page. Users are then automatically notified any time your Web page changes. They can then access the Web page in the normal way or download the changed page to their hard disk and view it at high, hard-disk speeds.

You can also create a true push channel using the Channel Definition Format (CDF) from Microsoft and PointCast. This is a relatively simple standard for identifying specific Web pages on which you put new and updated information. The Web pages are then pushed to users. To most easily create this kind of push channel, simply create a "What's New" page in your Web site, if you don't have one already. Then designate that page as the page to push to people.

PointCast offers a wizard called the Connections Builder that makes it easy to set up part of your Web site as a push channel. The Connections Builder is shown in action in Figure 7-6. The Connections Builder is built into the PointCast 2.0 push client software; you can get PointCast 2.0 free from PointCast at www.pointcast.com.

Figure 7-6:
The
Connections
Builder
helps you
get pushy
with users.

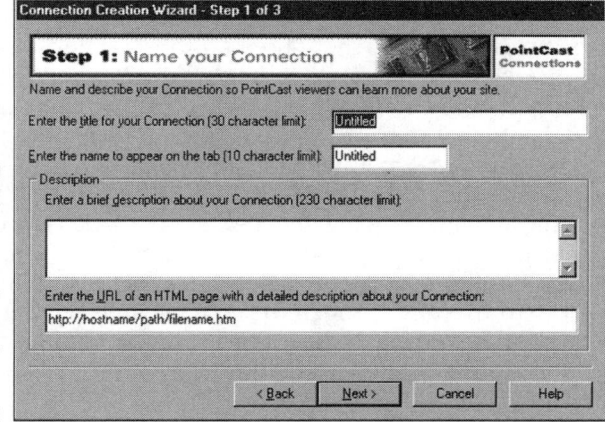

You can also create a complete push channel with Web-like or custom functionality. A complete Web-like push channel is simply a Web site with frequently changing content designed to be pushed to the user, then used at hard-disk speeds. Creating this kind of channel is no harder than creating a Web site, but doing this only makes sense if you update your content frequently. (Otherwise, there's no sense to the user in getting regular updates.) Doing this much updating implies that you'll put in a lot of time creating or finding content for your push channel.

A push channel with custom functionality is an even more specialized beast. To do this, you use a tool like Marimba Castanet or BackWeb that allows you to use programming to create custom applications that incorporate pushed content.

If you are interested in knowing more about using push technology, see *Push Technology For Dummies* by Bud Smith. If you want to create a push channel of your own, see *Web Channel Development For Dummies* by Damon Dean, both from IDG Books Worldwide, Inc.

Programming Your Pages

You can do an awful lot on the Web with only text and graphics, and adding multimedia and push technology extends your powers even further. However, to really "do business on the Web" and support interactivity, you need to consider doing some programming.

Web programming is a complicated topic that is beyond the scope of this book. However, after you get your text and graphics right and then spice up your pages with some multimedia, you may be able to extend your site further by doing some Web programming by using resources that you find on the Web. To go further requires more books, more training, and more work. Want to read *Java For Dummies,* 2nd Edition, by Aaron E. Walsh (IDG Books Worldwide, Inc.), anyone? Check out Web sites that you like to see how they get the effects that they do, and then search your bookstore and the Web to see the different techniques that are available.

For a long time, a big advantage of living in certain areas was the improved access some places have to large and specialty bookstores. For instance, both authors of this book live in Silicon Valley, home of the excellent Computer Literacy bookstores. Now, through the Web, anyone can find nearly any book they need. Start looking at the following URLs:

www.amazon.com

www.barnesandnoble.com

www.clbooks.com

Forms and CGIs

Forms are text boxes and pull-down menus that allow the user to enter information that you request. Forms are actually pretty easy to create. Forms are part of HTML 2.0 and are described in most intermediate Web page creation books. Getting data from the user is pretty easy. What's more complicated is figuring out what to do with the data after you have it.

Processing the data requires a CGI script and an application. A *CGI script,* sometimes simply called "a CGI," is a Common Gateway Interface script — a program that sends the data to an application that you created. The CGI script runs on the server that hosts your Web page. CGI scripts are different on NT, UNIX, and the Macintosh. Many CGI scripts are written in C language and PERL, a cross-platform scripting language.

To run a CGI script, you need the permission of the *sysop* (system operator) responsible for the server that hosts your Web page. Sysops are paid to protect their systems from harm, so getting them to run an unknown program on their precious server may take some doing. Many hosts have prepackaged forms/CGI packages that handle common tasks like counting visitors, allowing users to register, and more. Finding and using one of these prewritten packages is a good intermediate step toward creating your own CGI scripts and applications.

For more information about CGI scripting, see this Web site:

`www.comvista.com/net/www/lessons/START_HERE.html`

Java

Java is the programming language from Sun that makes the creation of interactive Internet applications easier and more flexible. Java promises much more spectacular Web pages, incorporating animation, smart updating, and distributed collaboration applications. Java programs, called *applets,* are downloaded to your computer. This downloading allows for fast execution and interactivity, but the downloading also raises concerns about security. Different models that allow robust interactivity while protecting against virus-type activity are still being implemented in Java. Although Java support is now widespread, some users turn off Java support in their browsers to avoid problems, so not all people with the latest browsers are ready to run Java applications.

Java is a variant of the overly complex computer language C++, and it requires considerable experience and skill to use. (At least, that's what our well-paid programmer friends tell us.) Also, Java is still changing quickly, so learning it at this point means getting on a pretty fast-moving train. As with forms and CGIs, most beginning and intermediate Web page creators are better off plugging in Java applets written by others rather than doing the requisite programming themselves. For more about Java, see Sun's Java Web site and the Gamelan Java directory site, shown in Figure 7-7:

```
java.sun.com/
```

```
www.gamelan.com/
```

ActiveX

ActiveX is technology from Microsoft that allows Microsoft Visual Basic programs to work with the Web. The good news is that it enables you to do some pretty amazing things; the bad news is that it has serious security problems, doesn't work well on the Macintosh, and doesn't work at all on 16-bit Windows (Windows 3.1 and before) or on UNIX. The security holes are so bad that Microsoft is quickly issuing fixes for downloading by worried users, yet appears to be having difficulty catching up with the problems. Microsoft is also working actively with Java, and that may be a stronger future direction for Microsoft as well as for the rest of us. However, if you are willing to do Windows-only Web work and want more information on ActiveX, start at Microsoft's Distributed interNet Applications Architecture site, which includes information on ActiveX:

```
www.microsoft.com/dna/default.asp
```

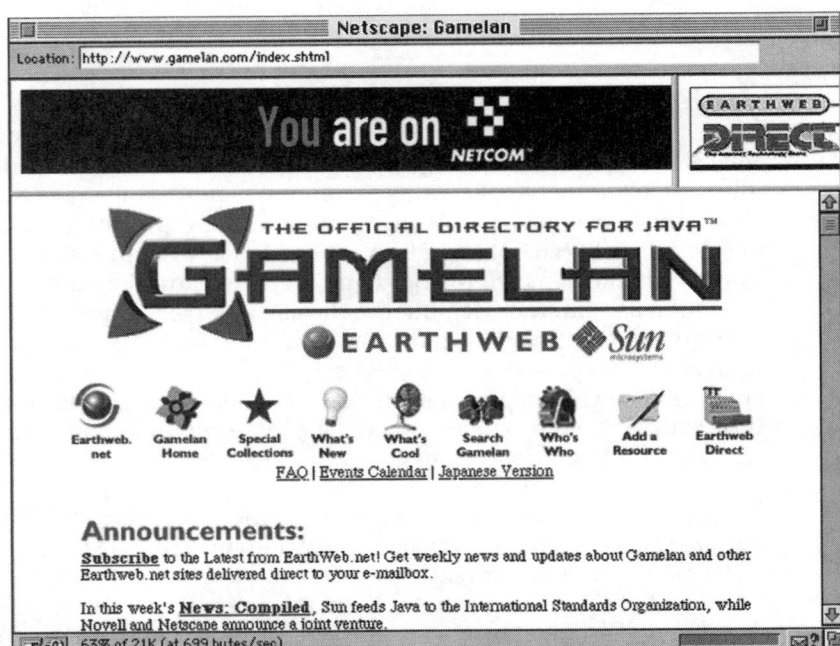

Figure 7-7: Gamelan applies itself to applets.

Also, see Appendix D and the RESOURCE.HTM file on the CD-ROM that comes with this book for more information and pointers.

Beyond HTML

While the simplicity and flexibility of HTML has been the key to the success of the Web, HTML does, of course, have limitations. Two major efforts, Dynamic HTML and XML (eXtended Markup Language), are under way to address those limitations as we write this.

Although any Web author should be aware of new technologies on the horizon, it's best not to implement them in your own Web pages until a majority of the user base has browsers that support the new capabilities. In the case of the new technologies described here, Dynamic HTML and XML, even an optimist would agree that it will be a couple of years before most users are equipped with browsers that support either of them.

HTML gets Dynamic

Dynamic HTML is an extension to HTML that allows multiple layers of information to be sent to the user during a server connection. The user only sees part of the information at first. Additional information can then be unveiled as time passes or as the user undertakes different actions, all without having to connect to the server again.

At this writing, Netscape and Microsoft are considering somewhat different implementations of Dynamic HTML. Netscape will add a LAYER tag to allow some layering to be defined fairly simply. Both will support Style Sheets, a more complex and more capable alternative being defined through the official Web standards process. But Microsoft, which has always followed Netscape's lead on new tags in the past, refuses to support the LAYER tag.

Only the 4.0 versions and above of Netscape Navigator and Microsoft's Internet Explorer support any of this, so other users are left out. If Netscape and Microsoft can agree, and if the Dynamic HTML extensions are enough to help drive millions of users to upgrade to the 4.0 versions of the new browsers, then the majority of Web authors may take the time and trouble to support these new features in their Web pages.

X-ing out HTML with XML

XML, or *eXtensible Markup Language*, is another proposed change to HTML, and probably further out in the future than Dynamic HTML. XML is a superset of HTML, but a subset of the overall *SGML* (Standard Generalized

Markup Language) standard on which HTML is based. It allows complex data structures to be built into a Web page, giving authors the ability to build data-driven applications and deliver them across the Web. Our guess is that XML will be deployed on intranets first because companies will want to develop such applications for internal use and will be able to ensure that all Web authors and users in the company have the ability to use the same version of XML. If you're responsible for intranet-related activity, keep an eye on this one.

And more

Because of its flexible nature, the Web has the theoretical capability to support almost anything that can be done or imagined on a computer. As the connection speed accessible to the average user improves, as more technology is used in advanced Web pages, and as users move up to more capable browsers, more and more will be possible. The trick is not to chase down any of the new pathways before they settle into widely used standards. Develop your skills in the key areas that make the Web useful and productive today. Using the capabilities of today's mainstream Web is the best way to prepare yourself to take advantage of the advanced Web that will be here the day after tomorrow.

Chapter 8

Publishing Your Web Pages

*P*ublishing your Web pages is the most exciting part of the process of creating a Web home page or Web site. After all the fooling around with tools, HTML, GIFs, and other kinds of files, and figuring out what you want to say and how you want to say it, it's time to "go live" and let the world see what you created.

Publishing your Web pages can be straightforward if you're putting up a personal or topical home page that a few friends and/or coworkers see. But if you're creating a site for a business or just need room to grow, publishing involves several steps.

The first step is to get Web server space. You have a lot of options here. Can you get free space? Must you pay for space? Do you want your own domain name so that your site has a simple URL, or are you willing to have your site as a subdirectory in someone else's domain? You need to choose a server space provider that gives you reasonable pricing and support now and room to grow later. Then you need to transfer your files to the site and confirm that you're really online.

But you're not done yet. The whole purpose of getting your Web site online is for people to see it. With all the sites out there, you have to cut through the noise and get people to see your site. After they do see your site, you need to know it. You also need to receive and respond to feedback. Kind of reminds us of those U.S. Army ads — "It's not just a job, it's an adventure."

After your site is up and publicized, you may expect to get a chance to relax. But then, while you cruise the Web, you see something neat that you want to put in your own site. Or looking back at your own pages, you suddenly see a problem in how you described yourself, your company, or your interests. Or maybe you get a blizzard of e-mails asking a question that you thought you already answered on the site — or, worse, you get no feedback at all. Maybe it's time to fire up that HTML editor again. . . .

Sorry to plug my own co-written book here, but if you're in a hurry to create a Web site for a business, you may want to consult *Marketing Online For Dummies* by Frank Catalano and Bud Smith (IDG Books Worldwide, Inc.). *Marketing Online For Dummies* goes into more depth about business-related issues such as how to register the right domain name, how to present your business online, and how to use other Internet services besides the Web as part of your marketing effort.

Getting Web Server Space

A *Web server* is a computer that's connected to the Web and runs special software that allows it to provide information to Web users. Hundreds of thousands of such servers are connected to the Web. Only by creating your own Web server with your files on it, or by placing your site's files on someone else's server, can your site really become part of the Web.

You can easily get space on a Web server. For example, the free Web-based publishing services described in Chapter 4 and the easy-to-use online service Web publishing tools described in Chapter 5 all include free Web server space. You may have a friend or be affiliated with an organization that will lend you Web server space. These are all good options for a single Web home page or a small site.

If real money is involved, though, things get tricky. Whether you create a site for a business or another kind of organization, most of the services mentioned in the preceding paragraph don't give you free space. So if you're going to start paying for something, you want to do some comparison shopping. And to do comparison shopping, you have to know what to compare.

America Online is the one service that continues to allow free Web server space for businesses as well as individuals. See Chapter 5 for details.

Web hosting service features

A number of businesses and organizations offer Web hosting service — that is, space on their Web server for your Web site. Most of these organizations charge for this service, and fees vary. You should look at a number of concerns when choosing a Web hosting provider for your Web pages. Figure 8-1 shows the Web hosting services offered by UUNet, the first company to offer such services. For more information, visit UUNet at

```
www.uu.net/lang.en/products/
```

Focusing on price when choosing a Web hosting provider is understandable. But you should look for many other things that may actually be more important than the immediate cost:

- ✓ **Pricing structure.** Instead of focusing only on what the hosting service provider charges you for your initial, bare-bones site that few people will visit, consider also what they charge you for a somewhat larger site that gets a moderate number of visitors, say a few hundred a month. Some hosting providers charge a very low rate for your initial site, but sock it to you when your needs grow.

- ✓ **Support.** We all need support of one kind or another, but technical support for your Web publishing effort is one of the hardest — and most important — kinds of support to get. You need support for getting your pages onto the server, for answering questions about your site, and for solving problems about speedy access, uptime (how long the service is on the air trouble-free), and so on. Find out what support they offer for each type of Web hosting option that you're considering.

Figure 8-1:
They'll get
you-you on
the net-net.

✔ **Web-related consulting services.** Some Web hosting providers, even the free ones, offer other Web-related services. (See the section on GeoCities in Chapter 4 for an example.) What do the providers charge? How well do they work? Most Web-related services charge by the hour, but some service providers get things done better and faster than others. So a less expensive hourly rate may not mean a lower total bill at the end.

✔ **Site services.** Some Web hosting providers offer sophisticated services, such as counting the number of users who visit your site. Other providers, at least, allow *you* to create and run Computer Gateway Interface (CGI) scripts that perform sophisticated functions. Other Web hosting providers neither provide site services nor allow you to run CGIs. Look for a provider that does the simple stuff for you and supports you in doing the more complex functions yourself.

✔ **Domain name.** The *domain name* is the name of the server that your site is on, but clever providers can put multiple domain names on a single computer. So you can have your own domain name, even for a small site, but the name has to be registered by your Web hosting provider. Registering your name costs your provider $100 initially, plus a $50 per year maintenance charge. Expect your provider to pass this charge on to you, but don't let them charge you a great deal more than what it costs them. Having your own domain name is very desirable because users can find your site easily, and with your own domain name you give the impression that you're serious about your Web site.

Some Web hosting providers offer to register a domain name for you, but then keep ownership of it themselves. This is kind of like those Peanuts cartoons with Lucy setting up the football and then pulling it away when Charlie Brown runs up to kick it. Not owning your domain name free and clear can severely hamper your ability to move your site later.

Find out whether the Web hosting provider that you are considering lets you get your own domain name, either immediately or later. And if so, find out whether the provider will clearly state in writing that you own the domain name and can take your Web site to another host if you want to.

In addition, in considering a Web hosting provider, ask for answers to the following questions:

✔ **Speed.** How fast can users access your Web site? How fast can users download files hosted on the site? You can ask, but you should also test. Try accessing some Web sites hosted by any service that you're considering and see how fast they are, especially at busy times of day. Compare what you find to other Web sites.

What's in a (domain) name?

If you do get your own domain name, your URL is whatever you want, within the rules of how URLs are created, such as

`www.mysite.com`

If you can't get your own domain name, your URL includes the computer's domain name, plus your site's name — something like this:

`members.compuserve.com/mysite`

After you announce your site and its URL, people may put your site in their Web bookmark lists, and you'll put your site's name in press releases, marketing materials, and so on. If that URL includes someone else's business name, you're just providing free publicity for them rather than for yourself. If you want to switch to your own URL later, you have to try to update your materials as well as everyone else's address books. This process is like changing your business address or phone number — not something anyone does easily or quickly.

Consider getting your own URL right up front. If not, limit the degree to which you publicize your Web site and its URL until you do get your own.

- ✔ **Uptime.** Is the Web hosting service that you're considering ever "off the air"? You would think that this is rare but, actually, even entire online services like America Online have downtimes. Find out the track record for uptime of the Web hosting service that you're considering and compare it to your needs.

- ✔ **Switchability.** Having the ability to switch Web hosting providers is crucial. With the right to switch, any other problems can be resolved. Without the right to switch, you may be unhappy with a key element of your Web site for a long time. Two things can keep you "locked in" to a provider: Contractual provisions and control of your domain name. Don't sign a contract that locks you in for more than a few months, and don't let the Web hosting provider register your domain name for you unless the provider states, in writing, that you control your domain name and can take it elsewhere with you.

- ✔ **Price.** All other things being equal, price is the determining factor. But all other things are rarely equal. Consider other factors first, but don't let yourself get ripped off. At this writing, the lowest rate we've seen for Web server space is about $1 per 1MB monthly, or $10 per 1MB annually. The biggest potential "gotcha" is *data transfer fees*.

When users look at a page on your site, all the data on that page is transferred to their machines. If users download files, that's more data transferred. Many Web hosting services offer some free data transfer, but your costs can rise sharply once traffic at your site increases and data transfer rises above a minimal amount. Compare data-transfer pricing carefully.

What makes a Web server fast?

A Web server is usually rated by the number of connections — brief communications sessions between two machines — that it handles in a given period of time. The number of connections that the server handles depends on how quickly the server establishes a connection, deciphers the request, sends the requested file, and terminates the connection. Most people think that the most time-consuming step in this process is the speed with which files are transmitted. Surprise! When small files are transmitted, the bottleneck is usually not how fast the files are transmitted, but how quickly the server's hardware and software establish connections and terminate them.

Here's a really technical tip: Engineers and hangers-on, such as people who write computer-related books, like to call the cause of a bottleneck a *gating factor*. For example, the gating factor in serving simple Web pages is the speed with which the server can connect and disconnect, not the speed with which data can be sent over the wire.

In addition to the speed of connecting and disconnecting to other machines, the speed of the server's connection to the Internet makes a big difference, especially for larger files like big graphics. If you have a direct connection to the Internet (as you find at most large companies and most universities), your client-side connection may be even faster than the server's connection: Lots of personal and small business home pages are sitting on Web servers with nothing but a 28.8 Kbps modem connecting them to the Internet. So don't start cussing at your own modem when that full-color JPEG photograph of the winning Weimaraner takes forever to download; the problem may be at the other end.

The key factors in choosing a Web hosting provider are the freedom to switch when you need to and having control of your domain name.

Options for Web server space

Now that you know what to look for in a host server, where can you find Web server space? Finding the right place to have your Web site hosted is not an easy task. Major Web hosting options include sites that offer free server space, online service Web hosting options, Web hosting services, and creating your own Web server. No matter what choice you make initially, be sure to keep your options open because your needs may change rapidly with the arrival of new players, with your own growing knowledge, and with the increasing role of the Web in business and in daily life.

Using free server space

You can get free server space for relatively small Web sites in several places, as described in Chapters 4 and 5. These sites are great places to create small, initial Web sites to learn about Web page design and construction. However, businesses generally can't use free server space for straightforward business promotion. (But you see lots of not-so-straightforward promotions there!) Also, to get your own domain name, you have to either move to paid server space or create your own Web server.

If you have access to free server space through a friend or work, that's also a good place to get started. Be careful, though, that you don't violate any expectations that the host has about the content of your Web site.

The services described in Chapters 4 and 5 as having free server space are very interested in providing paid-for space as well. GeoCities in particular seems to have a robust and reasonably priced package of services.

Using online-service server space

The major online services — America Online, CompuServe, and The Microsoft Network — are moving quickly to develop business-oriented Web services. (Well, not so quickly in Microsoft's case, but maybe they'll get it going.) Use the free Web services described in Chapter 4 to get started with a personal home page and then check the features and services of each of the online services against your needs. Don't rush in too fast, though. The online services get a lot of Web-related business simply because of their established name, and may charge more or have more restrictive policies than other hosting services.

Using Internet service providers

Internet service providers (ISPs) may be best known for offering Web access, but they also offer a wide range of Web services, from consulting to hosting to programming and more. In fact, as larger players, such as AT&T, move into the Web access business, the ISPs that prosper will be those that move "upstream" into consulting and specialized hosting services.

Some ISPs offer free server space to customers, just like the major online services. They also offer varying levels of paid-for service. Compare major ISPs, such as NetCom, Pipeline USA, TheOnRamp, and UUNet, to see what they offer. If you already have Web access, don't stop checking. Most ISPs offer their add-on services even to those who get their access elsewhere, and some may offer attractive bundles for access plus other services. You still have to be a customer to get that free server space deal, though.

Using paid-for server space

Thousands of Web hosting services exist. The providers vary tremendously in service, price, and competency. Some offer hosting only and charge you per stored or transferred megabyte. Others offer additional services, which may be billed separately or bundled with the "pure" hosting services in an overall fee. This business is changing and growing so rapidly that you need to exercise great care in the selection process to protect yourself. As the Romans figured out, just a few years before the Internet caught on, *caveat emptor* — let the buyer beware!

Creating your own Web server

Like a great many things about the Web, whether you should create your own Web server depends on what you want to accomplish and who you are. If you've set up a Web server before or have a lot of computer and communications experience, setting up your own Web server may work out very well for you. If not, setting up a Web server may turn out to be an expensive nightmare.

Many discussions of doing business on the Web are quick to suggest that you set up your own Web server, but not us. Unless you're an expert, we recommend that you start with a Web hosting provider of some kind. Then consider setting up your own server after you get some experience and get to know some people who can help if problems do arise. If you want details, refer to *Setting Up An Internet Site For Dummies,* 2nd Edition, by Jason Coombs and Ted Coombs, published by IDG Books Worldwide, Inc., for details.

Two things to remember: If you set up your own server for any but the most casual purposes, use a dedicated machine that isn't doing any other work. (If you follow this very good advice, that means you've spent $2,000 or so before you've stored or served a megabyte!) And be ready to devote time and energy to learn about the computer, communications link, and associated Web technologies to do as good a job on your own server as a Web hosting service would.

Finding a Web hosting provider

With the growth of the Web, those wanting to get on the Web will increasingly demand the services of experienced people, yet many such businesses will be part of an influx of new providers that are driven by a gold-rush mentality. This means that finding someone who can really help will be difficult, while paying someone to learn at your expense will be easy. We recommend the following steps to find a good Web hosting provider — someone who can provide the Web hosting services described in the previous section.

Get it all in a cybermall

A *cybermall* is a Web site that hosts a variety of businesses, handling a variety of chores for a moderate price. A cybermall operator may provide any or all of the following:

⮕ Initial goal-setting for your Web site

⮕ Creation of the Web page itself (expect to provide raw materials like product or service descriptions, photographs, and price lists)

⮕ Advertising and publicity

⮕ Support for online sales

Using the right cybermall can be a great way to get started on the Web, especially if you want to go from 0 (no Web presence or expertise) to 60 (robust Web presence with online transaction capabilities) in a few months. Expect to pay several thousand dollars up-front and several hundred dollars in monthly fees. Working with the mall operator also gives you a chance to develop Web expertise so that you can eventually do more of the work yourself. For two popular online cybermalls, see the following sites:

www.netplaza.com

www.industry.net

⮕ **Start small.** Asking the right questions to help you find a Web hosting provider is difficult if you have no Web publishing experience of your own. Start by creating a home page and then a small, special-purpose site of some kind before doing anything more robust. The experience will be valuable even in finding a good hosting provider.

⮕ **Figure out what services you need.** Are you going to create a simple site or a complex one? Do you want to create the site yourself and buy hosting services only, or do you want to contract out most of the work? List your needs and then find someone who's well-suited to fill them.

⮕ **Investigate sites like your own.** Find Web sites that look like the kind you want to create. Ask the Webmasters how they got their sites up and running and what Web hosting provider they use. Ask others in your area about their Web sites and whether they're happy with the services they received. When you consider a specific provider, check into a few of the sites that they host and ask customers whether they're happy.

⮕ **Go local.** You may want to meet occasionally or even regularly with your Web hosting provider, which means choosing someone with a local presence. (Even with all our technological aids, looking someone in the eye can contribute to better and deeper understanding. Unless you find that you really dislike the person!) Though this greatly restricts your choices, it may improve your working relationship significantly.

Is your site too cool?

What if your site is *too* successful? Believe it or not, the success of your site *can* be a problem. Many sites become overloaded when they "catch on," are chosen the Yahoo! Cool Site of the Day, get a Point Top 5% award, or otherwise receive recognition. Be ready to upgrade your Web hosting provisions if your site suddenly gets popular. In particular, if you pay extra for transferred megabytes, make sure that there's a cap on how much you have to pay if usage suddenly shoots up. If not, set up some method by which you're alerted if usage shoots up, or set up some way to track usage frequently. That way you avoid a potentially nasty surprise on your bill.

✔ **Be involved.** No consultant or service provider can do it all. The person or organization that is paying for the site must provide content and guidance throughout the process. You need to be very much involved in the process, so plan on devoting several hours working with your consultant or service provider.

Transferring Your Files

One of the really cool things about Web publishing is that you can set up, test, and modify your Web site on your own machine. The problem is that, at some point, you have to transfer your files to the Web server. Until you become proficient at transferring files, this can lead to some anxious moments. In this section, we try to take some of the worry out of getting your site online.

Arrange your files before transfer

Some of the most difficult things about creating, testing, and transferring your Web pages relate to directory structures. The problem is that a link from, say, your HTML-tagged text to a graphic has to specify what subfolder the graphics file is in. When you transfer your files to a different machine, the subfolders change, which causes the link from your Web page to the graphics file to break. You can take steps to keep your links from breaking when you transfer your Web files from your development machine to the Web server.

For sites with a dozen files or fewer, a simple solution exists. Just put all your files in the same subfolder. That way, your links are simple — you only need to specify the filename, not the directory name — and when transferring your files, you don't need to match up subfolder structures between machines.

For sites with many files, use the simplest directory structure — only one level deep, if possible. Also, create your links by using relative addressing (see Chapter 3 for details). Relative addressing doesn't specify the entire pathname from the root directory downward, just the relative path from the file with the link embedded in it to the file that's being linked in. This makes it possible to move files from one machine to another without having to change all the links between files.

Some people prefer to use a compression program, such as PKZIP, to package files before sending them. Before you do this, make sure that the recipient wants ZIPped files and that they can unZIP them. Also realize that the largest files in a Web site are usually GIF or JPEG graphics files. These files are already compressed, and the additional compression offered by PKZIP doesn't save much space.

As you can see, the underlying theme here is "keep it simple." After you have some initial successes under your belt, you can start taking steps to make things better organized or more convenient.

As simple as FTP

FTP, or File Transfer Protocol, is an Internet service for transferring files between different machines. FTP made the Internet popular even before the World Wide Web caught on. FTP is a relatively easy way to move files from one machine to another. Most Internet users use FTP to download files from an FTP host to their own machine; however, a Web front end to the process protects users from the details of FTP. But to publish your Web pages, you may be asked to use FTP to send files from your own machine to a host. (You will probably be asked to "FTP the files to us.") This is a new operation for most people, but it is not all that complex.

Dozens of FTP programs exist for Macintosh, Windows, and UNIX, each with its own pluses and minuses. (The major online services also have their own facilities for uploading files, described in "Connect to an FTP site" that follows.) Many free FTP clients are available on the Web. The following steps work with most popular FTP programs. However, to upload files you need a "real" FTP program. Many programs with FTP capability can download files from FTP sites but not upload files to an FTP site. So make sure that your FTP program can put (write) as well as get (read) files.

Connect to an FTP site

The following steps are specifically written to work with Fetch, the most popular FTP program for the Macintosh, shown in Figure 8-2. (Notice the little dog, probably a Scottie, running to fetch the file!) But these same steps are generally correct for other FTP programs as well. Use these steps to transfer files to a Web site:

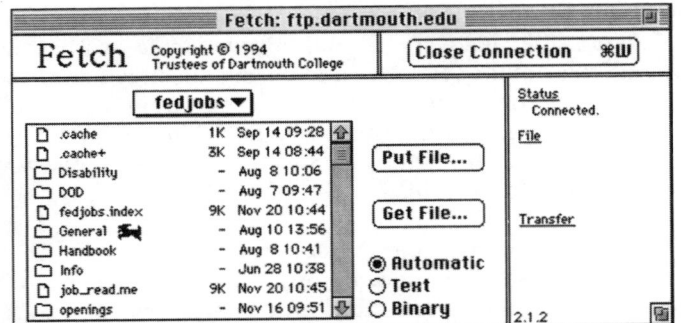

Figure 8-2:
A fetching
Mac FTP
client.

1. **Connect to the Internet.**

2. **Start your FTP program.**

3. **Enter the host name.**

   For a Web site, the FTP host name is often the same as the host name in the Web site's URL, but with ftp in place of www; for example, if the Web site's URL is www.mysite.com, the host name is likely to be ftp.mysite.com.

4. **Enter the user name.**

   Many sites allow you to enter anonymous as the user name and avoid having to enter a specific user name. Other sites give you a user name and password to use when uploading your Web files.

5. **Enter the password.**

   If you entered anonymous as the user name, enter nothing or your e-mail address as your password.

6. **Enter the directory that you want to put files in (that is, to write to).**

   You can also go to the correct directory after you connect, but the process will be more convenient and less error-prone if you enter the correct directory first.

7. **Click OK to connect to the FTP site.**

   If you do everything right and the site is up, you connect. See Figure 8-2 for the Fetch FTP dialog box that appears after you connect. Dartmouth College owns Fetch.

Upload your file(s) and disconnect

Getting connected is half the battle. Writing your files is usually pretty easy.

1. **Click the appropriate option for the file(s) that you want to write: Automatic, Text, or Binary.**

   For HTML files, use Text. For graphics and multimedia files, use Binary. For a combination of both types, either upload the types one at a time with the proper designation, or upload them together and choose Automatic; the server tries to figure out which is which. Until you have experience with a specific server, transfer files one at a time and specify the correct file type before each transfer.

2. Click Put to write your file.

This option may be named something else on some clients and may be selected from a menu rather than initiated by clicking a button.

3. In the dialog box that appears, click the name of the file that you want to write and then click OK.

The file is transferred. Repeat Steps 1 through 3 for each additional file that you need to transfer.

4. Choose Quit from the File menu.

Using online service file transfer

In Chapter 5, we describe how to use the Web publishing programs on the major online services to create and publish a home page. However, the online services' Web facilities are flexible. You can create HTML-tagged text and graphics files with any tools and then upload the files to a server. The online service file transfer tools resemble FTP. Figure 8-3 shows the America Online file transfer program. Other file transfer programs are similar.

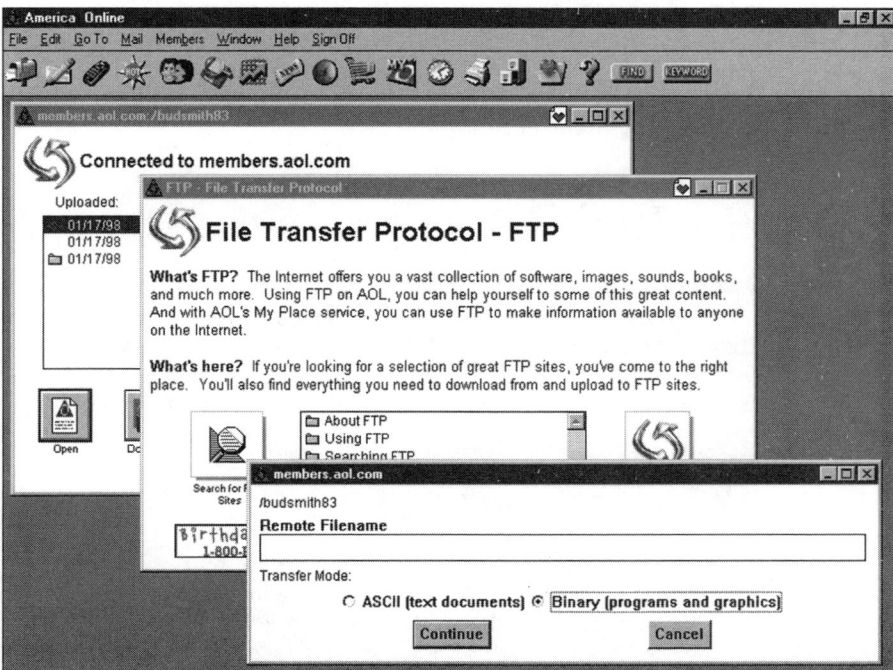

Figure 8-3: File transfer that's not too AOL-ful.

Putting Your Site to Work

After you get your site up on the Web, you'll probably be too relieved and happy to worry about it for a while. But "going live" isn't an ending; it's really just the beginning of a whole new process. The following sections describe some initial steps to make your newly published site really stand out and accomplish your goals.

Test your site

As soon as you get your site up, log on to it like a normal user. See if the site works. Test all links to make sure that they go somewhere. Make sure that you can easily move around between pages. Try accessing your site from a computer with a slow modem connection to see how usable the site is.

Also note your own reactions, as if you were a new user. What does the site look like it's for? Any difficulties or confusion in using it? This kind of open-minded approach to your own site can help you quickly fix subtle problems that otherwise are hard to identify.

Testing your site is a bit frustrating because you find all sorts of things to fix, but if you follow through, you end up with a much better site. Be ready to take notes of your reactions from the moment you first log on to your site until the end of your visit; recapturing first impressions later is difficult.

 Use your browser's Print capability to print out the pages in the Web site, and then put your notes right on the printout. A printout makes it much easier to keep track of your ideas as you go along and to make the right changes the first time.

Get feedback on your site

Ask for feedback! You can put the request for feedback right in your Web site. You can also ask friends and colleagues to try the site and give you their honest opinions. Ask them some leading questions, such as "What do you think the site is for? How does it compare to other sites you've seen? What's the one thing you'd change about the site if you could?"

Publicize your site

After your site is up and tested, publicize your site. The amount of work you should put in depends on your goals for your site. If you are trying to impress press and analysts, do a press release. If it's simply a personal site, telling friends and family about it may be sufficient. If you are trying to let customers know another avenue for communicating with you, put your URL on stationery, business cards, and advertisements. If you are trying to sell on the Web, put ads on other Web sites that attract your prospective customers. Tailor your publicity strategy to your goals.

The first and most important place to publicize your site is on the Web itself. Your basic goal is to get as many "pointers" to your site as possible from What's New lists, What's Cool lists, and especially directories or pages that are specific to the interests addressed by your site. Find pages with a similar purpose and trade pointers from their site to yours, and from your site to theirs.

The Web publicity picture is changing all the time, so the best place to go for information is any of several Web sites with information and pointers:

```
webmagnet.com/howtodoit.html
```

```
www.cyberwave.com/ppoint2.html
```

```
www.submit-it.com
```

These sites give you information on how to get your pages publicized on popular sites like the Yahoo! What's New page. (See Figure 8-4 for an example.) You can find this page at

```
www.yahoo.com/new/
```

You can also use non-Web means of publicizing your site. Put out a press release — but be sure and wait until your site's really ready, not full of Under Construction signs. Many companies proudly include their Web site URLs on business cards, stationery, print ads, and even television ads. You've invested a lot in your Web site; now's the time to benefit from your efforts.

Count and keep users

For Web pages in general and for business Web pages in particular, knowing how many users you have is important. For a business site you should have goals for the number of users who visit your site and for the number who take specified actions, whether downloading software, visiting specific parts of the site, or buying products. Set goals and then measure against them.

Among the things you can track are the number of e-mails you receive from users and the number of people who register on your site (if you support that option). But the most widely accepted measurement of success is a *hit*

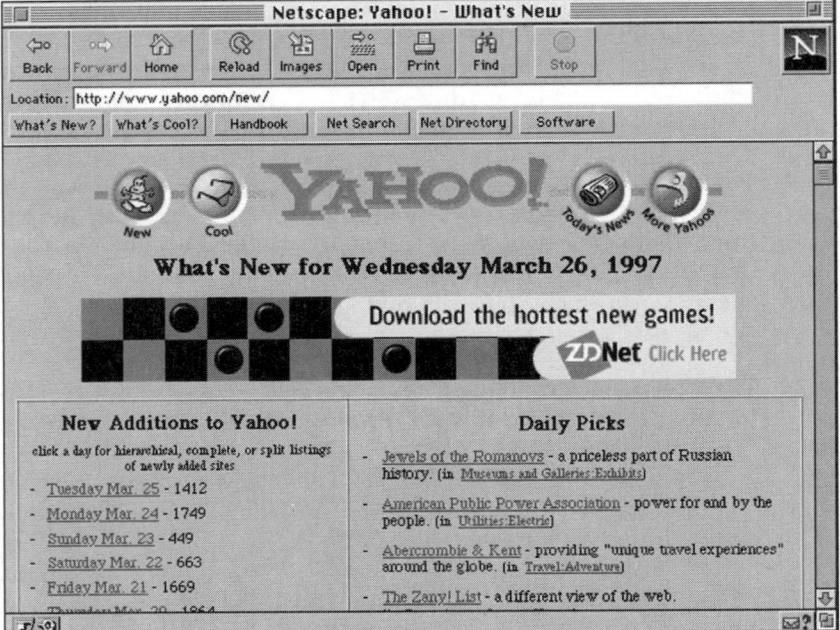

Figure 8-4:
Yahoo! for
new stuff.

counter, which tracks each file downloaded from your Web site. (Each Web page or graphic displayed counts as a separate hit.) Not a great measurement, but it's a start. Set up a hit counter (as described in Chapter 6) and then consider more sophisticated ways to track usage, such as various Web server log analysis tools. Those tools look at logs generated by Web servers and give you statistics on the number of hits on your pages and the number of separate visitors. Many Web hosting providers give you a monthly report or at least let you access the log files from your site for your own review and analysis.

Part IV
Web Publishing Tools

The 5th Wave — By Rich Tennant

"ISN'T THAT OUR WEBMASTER? THESE PEOPLE ALWAYS FIND A CREATIVE WAY TO INTERFACE."

In this part . . .

Web publishing tools are programs that help you create Web pages and manage a Web site. Some help by making it easier for you to remember and manage HTML tags; some tools hide the tags from you by using a graphical interface that is much like a word processor. Other tools work within your existing word processor or convert files from word-processor format to HTML-tagged text. Many very good tools are free; others cost under $100. This part introduces you to many of the best Web publishing tools and tells you how to use them to create your own Web pages.

Chapter 9

Be True to Your Web Authoring Tools

● ●

In This Chapter

▶ What's in a tool?

▶ How do you evaluate tools?

● ●

*L*iterally dozens of Web authoring tools appeared quickly in the early stages of the Web's growth. These tools continue to find users; some are *shareware* — copyrighted computer programs available on a trial basis, with payment expected after some period of use — and others are *freeware* — copyrighted programs available without any charge. Two of the leading freeware tools for Web authoring are Microsoft's FrontPage Express, described in Chapter 10, and Netscape Composer, covered in Chapter 11.

However, major software companies are now the major players in Web publishing. Many *retail software products* — boxed products with documentation and technical support, sold in retail channels such as computer superstores, printed catalogs, and online catalogs — are available and meet many needs. One of the very best finished software products is Adobe PageMill, described in Chapter 12, which we believe is the easiest to use of all the complete Web authoring solutions. If you want to work directly in HTML and want a tool that helps you do that, HotDog Professional (also known as HotDog Pro), which we introduce in Chapter 13, makes the process easier — and yet is powerful enough that many leading Web page authors have used it to create their pages.

Another option for Web publishing is the new "save as HTML" capability in many word processors, which allows you to create and edit a document using the normal word processing commands that you're used to, and then save it in a ready-to-publish HTML form. If you have a word processor with this capability, you should try this — that way, you don't have to fiddle with learning all that HTML or how to use another program. However, you may find it frustrating that not all the capabilities supported by your word processor, such as text that wraps around graphics or many font and font size formatting options, are translated to your Web pages when you use the "save as HTML" capability. Also, you may find yourself plunging into the HTML file that the "save as HTML" function saves in order to fix problems. We discuss "save as HTML" capability in Chapter 14.

The *Creating Web Pages For Dummies* CD-ROM has, we think, the best collection of Web authoring tools yet committed to optical media. In this chapter, we describe the different characteristics that you may want in a Web authoring tool and how the tools on the CD-ROM and elsewhere fit those characteristics.

We also tell you how to find out what others say about Web authoring tools and how to track down tools that aren't on the CD-ROM. All this information may help guide you to the right kind of tool for your needs. But if you're more of a hands-on person than a planner, go right ahead — try all the tools on the CD-ROM until you find the one that meets your needs. Then come back, read this chapter, and send us e-mail about what we got right and what we got wrong. The e-mail address to use is

Bud_Smith@compuserve.com

What's in a Web Authoring Tool?

A Web authoring tool helps you create and edit the HTML-tagged text files that, when viewed from a Web browser, appear as Web pages. (If the phrase *HTML-tagged text file* means nothing to you, please go back and read Chapter 3.) If you sort of understand HTML's purpose but want to refresh yourself on what specific tags do, see the Cheat Sheet or Appendix C.

Use these five questions to determine the best Web authoring tool for you:

- ✔ **Learning curve.** How much effort does it take to learn the tool? How much effort to use it? (Ease of learning and ease of use can be different: For instance, using the "save as HTML" capability in your word processor is very easy to learn; if you try to do advanced work such as complex Web text and graphics layouts in it, however, you may find it hard to use.)

- ✔ **Platform.** Does the tool run on your system — Windows 3.*x*, Windows 95 and NT, the Mac, your version of UNIX?

- ✔ **Add-on versus stand-alone.** Does the tool run on top of or within some other program, or is it a stand-alone application? We prefer stand-alone tools.

✔ **HTML focus versus WYSIWYG focus.** Does the tool help you work directly with HTML tags in text? Or does it hide HTML tags and present you with a more intuitive WYSIWYG (What You See Is What You Get) interface so that you can see what the page looks like, as in a word processor?

✔ **Free versus paid for.** Does the program cost money? If so, does its owner let you try before you buy?

You are going to find a rough correlation between increasing effort to learn a tool, increasing capabilities of the tool, and increasing purchase price of the tool. Free tools, such as FrontPage Express, Netscape Composer, and the "save as HTML" capabilities in your word processor, are easy to learn, but not particularly capable. Mid-priced tools under $100, such as PageMill, are a little harder to learn, but more capable. And more expensive tools, such as HotDog Pro, Microsoft FrontPage 98, and NetObjects Fusion, all of which cost over $100, are noticeably harder to learn but significantly more capable; for instance, these tools can manage a large Web site as well as create individual Web pages. Figure 9-1 summarizes the tools covered in Part IV in terms of the preceding criteria.

Web Wizard, an excellent tool for creating an initial page, isn't listed in Figure 9-1 because it doesn't allow you to edit a page after you create it.

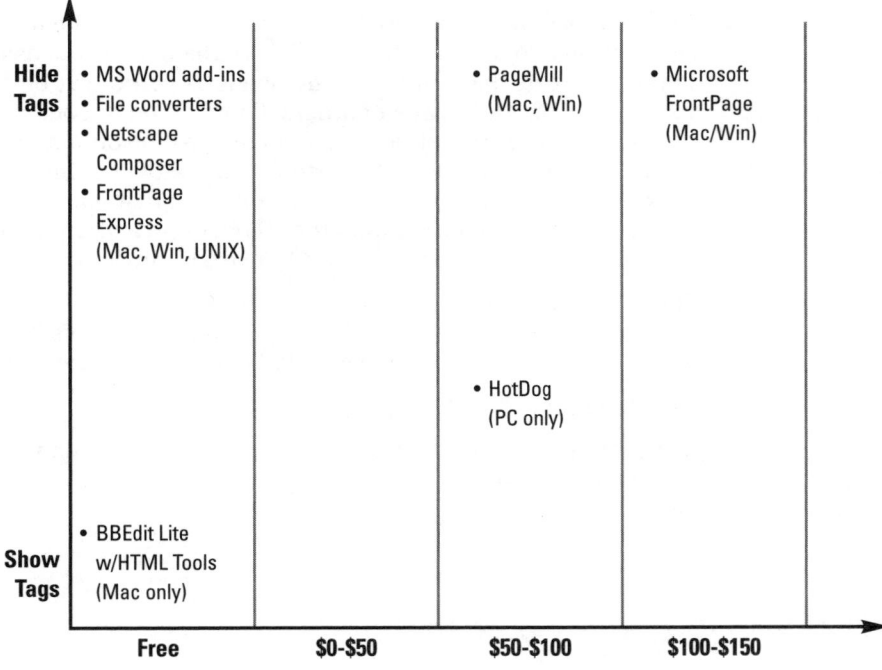

Figure 9-1: Comparison of popular Web authoring tools.

How Do You Evaluate Tools?

Use the following techniques to evaluate HTML tools. Each technique is valuable, and by combining them, you can get a pretty good idea of which tool is right for you:

- ✔ **Read this book.** Just reading the tool descriptions and "how-to" information in the next few chapters, plus looking at the pretty pictures, gives you a good idea of which tool may be right for you. As Obi-Wan Kenobi said in the *Star Wars* movies, "Trust your feelings."

- ✔ **Try the tools.** The CD-ROM that comes with this book has trial versions of many of the HTML authoring tools discussed in this book. These versions are often time-limited or save-disabled, but they're fine for trying the program to get a feel for it. You can quickly install them and do your own "taste test." Then check to see if any similar tools are also worth a try.

- ✔ **Think about where you're going.** Decide whether you want a tool that makes it easy to get started or one that can do a lot. If the most you can see yourself doing in the near future is creating and editing a small personal Web site, go for ease of use and a low or no price. If you want to build a big, frequently updated site, or if you seek to make Web authoring a saleable skill in your personal toolkit, learn a more powerful tool or do some work in several tools.

- ✔ **Ask friends and colleagues.** Word of mouth is often the best source of information about products, especially if the people you ask have similar interests, backgrounds, and needs as yours. But be careful about following the advice of others. People tend to commit early, so the tool that your friend raves about may now be outdated or just no longer the best of its type. And people vary widely in their tolerance for working with straight HTML, so the same tool that you find attractive and easy to use because it puts the HTML tags right up-front may drive another person, who doesn't want to learn HTML, crazy.

- ✔ **Check newsgroups and online sources.** Use the Web to check online sources for specific tools and for comments about tools. One good search engine that you can use to find a tool is OpenText, at this URL:

`index.opentext.net`

Just search for the tool by name, and you're sure to find where to download the tool and find Web pages that were developed by using the tool.

Deja News is a fast tool for finding comments from real people on Web authoring and other topics. You can use it to search a large archive of comments on Usenet, the Internet's bulletin board system for people commenting on any number of issues. The URL for Deja News is

`www.dejanews.com`

Just search for the tool that interests you by its name. You see lots of comments that may alert you to features and benefits, as well as problems, that you may not otherwise know about.

Tool reviews and more

One of the best online sources for Windows Web tool reviews is Stroud's Consummate Winsock Apps List by Carl Stroud (see the figure), a Web site that moves around the Net as the list and demands for it grow.

You can find the site at this URL:

`www.stroud.com/`

Go to the list and look for quick ratings and full reviews of all the tools that interest you.

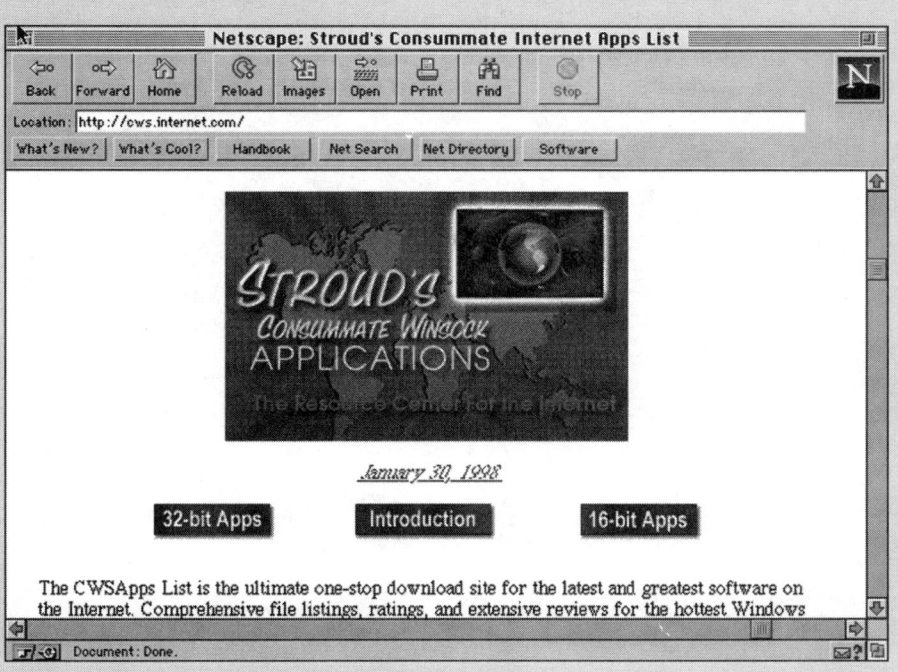

Don't get too caught up in the process of choosing the right tool, though. As Yoda said in a later Star Wars movie, "There is no try, only do." Your goal is to create Web pages, not to become an expert in tools to create Web pages. So spend a little time researching, and then plunge in. With all the free demos of the best and easiest-to-use Web authoring software on the CD-ROM that comes with this book, you can create a few Web pages in one tool and then try another one if necessary until you find the tool that suits you best.

Chapter 10

Tool Along with FrontPage Express

● ●

In This Chapter

▶ Understanding the basics

▶ Getting FrontPage Express

▶ Using FrontPage Express

▶ Going beyond FrontPage Express

● ●

Microsoft, the acknowledged leader of the personal computer industry, is rapidly moving into a position of Internet leadership as well. Although its sales of around $10 billion a year are less than some other computer companies — such as Compaq, IBM, and Intel — its profits outdistance any other computer company.

More importantly, Microsoft software runs on more than 90 percent of all computers, and the company sets technical standards that affect how the PCs of today and tomorrow work. And it has a large and growing share of the browser market (Internet Explorer), the leading Web authoring tool (Microsoft FrontPage 98), and two Top Ten Web sites (www.microsoft.com and www.msn.com). Microsoft has also acquired WebTV and many other exciting Internet-related companies. And Microsoft plays a leading role in the Internet standards-setting process, having recently developed strong alliances in areas such as push technology (see Chapter 8) and new versions of HTML.

Microsoft supports the efforts of Web page creators with its SiteBuilder Network. As its name suggests, the SiteBuilder Network is for professionals who create complete Web sites, rather than those who simply create individual Web pages, which we describe in this book. However, the SiteBuilder Network is worth visiting, if only to whet your appetite for moving further into Web publishing. You can visit SiteBuilder at

www.microsoft.com/sitebuilder/

From this site, you can access information about and download the latest versions of Internet Explorer and FrontPage Express, a stripped-down version of Microsoft's excellent FrontPage Web authoring product.

About FrontPage Express

Though much less functional than FrontPage 98, FrontPage Express has drag-and-drop WYSIWYG (What You See Is What You Get) Web page authoring and even advanced features, such as support for Java, ActiveX, and Dynamic HTML — all advanced programming and page-design standards that many commercial programs don't support.

FrontPage Express or Netscape Composer?

As an aspiring Web publisher you have a choice between two excellent free programs, Microsoft FrontPage Express and Netscape Composer, which come from the companies that make the two leading browsers. In this sidebar, we discuss the best features of FrontPage Express over Netscape Communicator; in a similar sidebar in Chapter 11 we discuss the best features of Netscape Composer over FrontPage Express. May the best free Web authoring tool win! Superior features of FrontPage Express include:

✔ **Truly free.** FrontPage Express is truly free. The Netscape Communicator suite with Netscape Composer is truly free, as well. (Netscape used to ask users to pay for the Netscape Communicator suite within 90 days, but now makes it available for free.)

✔ **Upgrade path.** If you outgrow FrontPage Express, you can smoothly move up to its big brother, the powerful, popular, and not-free FrontPage 98, and you'll already know how to use FrontPage 98's basic functions. Netscape Composer has no such upgrade path. But, then, it doesn't need one.

✔ **Programming controls.** You can insert Java applets or ActiveX controls — Web-friendly computer programs — in a FrontPage Express Web page. If you don't write code yourself, you can get these programs from others and then integrate them into your Web page.

✔ **IE-style Dynamic HTML.** A new version of the HTML language that underlies the Web, called Dynamic HTML, works differently in Microsoft's Internet Explorer 4.0 browser and Netscape's Navigator 4.0 browser. If you use Dynamic HTML, FrontPage Express will get you the Microsoft-supported style until the two companies agree on a unified format.

Both FrontPage Express and Netscape Composer are good products, but if you are a Windows 95 and Windows NT user, want a Web authoring tool that's capable, free, and has an upgrade path to a powerful Web page creation and Web site management tool (FrontPage 98) then FrontPage Express is the way to go.

FrontPage Express currently runs only on Windows 95 and Windows NT. Unfortunately, if you use Windows 3.1, the Macintosh, or UNIX, you can't run FrontPage Express. However, you have an excellent alternative in Netscape Composer, which does run on all these computing platforms; see Chapter 11 for details.

If you do become a FrontPage Express user and your Web authoring needs grow, you can buy a copy of FrontPage 98 and move smoothly to its very similar interface and more powerful capabilities. FrontPage 98 allows you to manage entire Web sites as well as create stand-alone Web pages. It includes the ability to automatically verify HTML links, supports finding and replacing text across multiple pages, supports HTML frames, and has a set of design capabilities called Themes, which you can program as well as modifiy.

FrontPage Express hides HTML formatting tags, but allows you to view them at any time during the editing process with a simple menu choice. This enables you to have the direct control you sometimes need to fix problems or add features. For an introduction to HTML, see Chapter 3.

Understanding the basics

Feel free to use the version of FrontPage Express on the CD-ROM that accompanies this book, or you may want to download it from the Microsoft Web site (www.microsoft.com) as part of the Internet Explorer 4.0 browser suite. And the best thing about it is that you don't have to pay for it!

The system requirements for FrontPage Express are the same as those for the overall Internet Explorer 4.0 browser suite: a PC-compatible computer running Windows 95 or Windows NT 4.0 or higher, 16MB RAM, and at least 30MB of available hard-disk space. If you want to browse the Web while running FrontPage Express to find links, to look at HTML authoring information, or for other reasons, you need more RAM (we recommend 32MB) and more free hard-disk space (about 50MB free should do it).

For a free tool, FrontPage Express has all the important basic features you need to build basic Web pages:

- Creating and editing Web pages without seeing HTML tags
- Dragging and dropping links to other Web locations without typing the URL or pathname
- Cutting and pasting graphics into your Web page, resizing graphics, and adding alternate text
- Creating and editing tables
- Creating and editing *forms* — interactive data entry fields commonly found on Web pages

You can also insert multimedia files and computer programs into your Web page. However, not all users can play back those files or run those programs, because they may not have the appropriate browser or the right plug-ins installed. If you add advanced elements, such as multimedia files or computer programs, into your Web page, be prepared to test your pages with several different browsers and tell your Web visitors what to expect.

FrontPage Express supports forms, but it can't give you the *CGI scripts* — short for Common Gateway Interface scripts — that need to go along with the forms. These scripts process form data; if you can create CGI scripts, you're probably ready for a more advanced tool than FrontPage Express. However, if you don't want to mess with creating these scripts, you can get CGIs that you can use in your Web pages from others on the Web.

FrontPage Express does not support *frames* — advanced HTML elements that split a Web page up into separate, scrollable pieces. Designing Web pages that work well with frames isn't easy, so it makes some sense that FrontPage Express, a free tool, doesn't support frames.

Though FrontPage Express doesn't support frames, it does enable you to add any HTML tags you want directly into your Web page. However, the whole point of using a tool is to reduce the amount of HTML coding you have to do; if you find yourself coding directly in HTML to avoid the limitations of FrontPage Express, consider buying a more capable tool, such as FrontPage 98 or Adobe PageMill (see Chapter 12).

The bottom line

Like Netscape Composer, which we describe in Chapter 11, FrontPage Express is a very good tool for getting started with Web page authoring. If you use Windows 95 or Windows NT and use the Internet Explorer browser, FrontPage Express is probably the best choice for you. (If you use a different computing platform or use Netscape Navigator, try Netscape Composer first.) Getting started with FrontPage Express is easy and fun: The program is very simple, yet surprisingly powerful when considering its support for multimedia and computer programs. And it has a more capable big brother, FrontPage 98, for you to buy when you need more power.

Getting FrontPage Express

You can copy FrontPage Express and the Internet Explorer 4.0 browser for Windows 95 and Windows NT from the CD-ROM that comes with this book. You can also check for newer versions at the Microsoft Web site and download them (described later in the chapter). To buy the full version of FrontPage 98 on CD-ROM, see the up-to-date instructions on the Microsoft Web site.

 If you already have Internet Explorer installed, and just want FrontPage Express, follow the steps in the next section for downloading the online version. The Internet Explorer Setup program will detect your existing files and only install new Internet Explorer files plus FrontPage, if that's the only additional software you request.

Downloading the online version

You may want to download FrontPage Express and Internet Explorer 4.0 from the Web instead of using the CD-ROM version to make sure that you have the most up-to-date version. Follow these steps to download FrontPage Express and Internet Explorer 4.0 from the Web:

1. **Go to the Internet Explorer 4.0 product page on the Microsoft Web site:**

   www.microsoft.com/ie/ie40

   The Microsoft Web site is consistently among the most-visited sites on the Internet and is well-organized and easy to use.

2. **Go to the bottom of the Web page and click the link, Download Internet Explorer 4.0 today!**

   The Internet Explorer 4.0 download page appears, as shown in Figure 10-1.

3. **Click the Download Now! button.**

4. **A series of frames appears within the Web page with options for you to choose from:**

   - **Choose the appropriate version of Internet Explorer from the pull-down list. Click Next.**

   - **Choose your language from the pull-down list. Click Next.**

   - **Choose the download site nearest you. Click the Install setup link.**

   The File Download dialog box appears.

5. **Choose the option, Save this program to disk, and then click OK.**

   The Save As dialog box appears.

6. **Choose a folder to save the Internet Explorer 4.0 setup file to. (Consider saving it on the Windows Desktop to make it easier to find.) Click Save.**

   The file downloads to your hard disk. The download takes about 3 minutes over a 28.8 Kbps modem. At the end, an alert box tells you the download is complete.

7. **Click OK.**

   You return to the browser window.

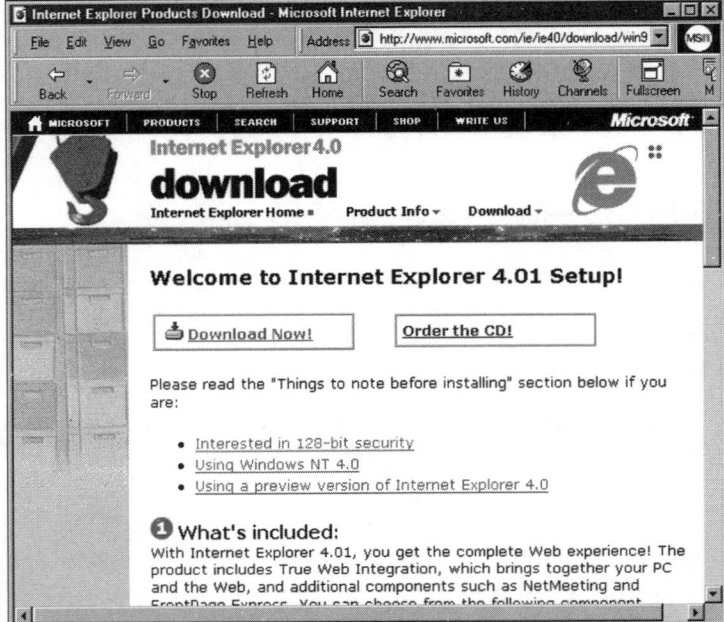

Installing the online version

Installing the online version of Internet Explorer 4.0 is a bit tricky; if you make the wrong choices, you not only don't get FrontPage Express, but you install the Internet Explorer 4.0 Desktop Update, which makes significant changes in the way Windows works. So follow these steps carefully to install Internet Explorer 4.0 and FrontPage Express:

1. **Quit your browser and all other programs.**

2. **Find the Internet Explorer installer file called** ie4setup**, on your hard disk. Double-click it.**

   The Internet Explorer 4.0 Setup panel appears.

3. **In the Internet Explorer 4.0 Setup panel, click Next.**

   The License Agreement panel appears.

4. **In the License Agreement panel, click I accept the agreement. Then click Next.**

   The Download Options panel appears.

5. **In the Download Options panel, click Install. Then click Next.**

   The Installation Option panel appears.

6. In the Installation Option panel, choose Full Installation from the pull-down menu. Then click Next.

If you don't choose the Full Installation option, you won't get FrontPage Express.

After you click Next, the Windows Desktop Update window appears, as shown in Figure 10-2.

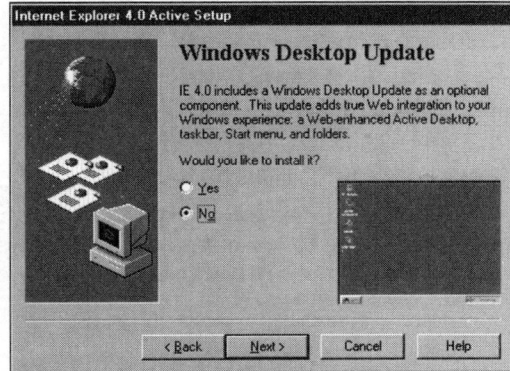

Figure 10-2:
Just say no to Windows Desktop Update.

7. In the Windows Desktop Update panel, click No to retain your normal Windows desktop. Click Yes only if you want to use Windows Desktop Update, which Web-enables your Windows desktop and changes many things about the way Windows works. Once you have made your choice, click Next.

When you see the Windows Desktop Update panel, the Yes option is chosen for you, which installs Windows Desktop Update. To retain your normal Windows desktop, you must click to change to the No option.

After you click Next, the Active Channel Selection panel appears.

8. In the Active Channel Selection panel, choose the region that matches your country and language. Then click Next.

The Destination Folder panel appears.

9. In the Destination Folder panel, change the destination folder that you want to install Internet Explorer into, if you wish. Then click Next.

If you're not already connected to the Internet, the setup program connects you and retrieves site information for you so that you can download the Internet Explorer 4.0 full installation, which includes FrontPage Express. The Download Sites panel appears.

10. **In the Download Sites panel, choose your region and the download site nearest you. Then click <u>N</u>ext.**

   The setup program downloads Internet Explorer 4.0 and the full set of related programs, including FrontPage Express, to your computer — it's about a 30MB download. The download takes about four hours over a 28.8 Kbps modem.

   After the download, the Internet Explorer 4.0 Active Setup panel appears. Active Setup installs onto your computer Internet Explorer 4.0 and all the programs that come with the full installation option. (Web authoring components, meaning FrontPage Express, are the final items installed.)

   After you install all the components, if your computer is connected to the Internet via a dial-up connection, the setup program displays an alert box asking you to disconnect from the Internet.

11. **If your computer is connected to the Internet, find the icon showing two computers connected in the lower-right corner of your screen. Right-click it to see options for the connection. Choose <u>D</u>isconnect. Then close all other running programs.**

   Your computer disconnects from the Internet.

12. **In the Active Setup alert box, click OK.**

   The Internet Explorer 4.0 setup program configures the new software. The setup program then tells you it needs to restart your computer.

13. **Click OK to restart your computer.**

   After your computer restarts, you're ready to use Internet Explorer 4.0 and FrontPage Express.

Using FrontPage Express

Creating an initial Web page with FrontPage Express is fun because you can easily do most things that you'd want to do with a Web page, though it doesn't let you to do anything extra. As you experiment with FrontPage Express, you find that you can recreate many features you have seen on existing Web pages, such as headers, links, and embedded GIF and JPEG graphics. You can learn an awful lot about the program just by fooling around with menu choices and clicking buttons; you can learn more by creating your own initial Web page.

Use FrontPage Express to accomplish some simple Web authoring tasks and create an initial Web page:

  ✔ Create a title for your page.

  ✔ Enter some text and format it.

✔ Add a link.

✔ Add an image.

✔ Look at the underlying HTML-tagged text.

✔ Publish the Web page.

The rest of this chapter shows you how to accomplish these tasks with FrontPage Express; in Chapters 11 through 13, we detail how to accomplish the same tasks with other Web authoring tools. This gives you the opportunity to compare tools just by reading the descriptions, and to learn much more about the tools that seem attractive to you by actually trying the same steps with each tool.

Granting yourself a title

The title of your Web page is not visible to users in your Web page — instead, it shows up in the title bar of the browser window that displays the Web page. In addition to this usage, it's still an important part of the Web page, because search engines use the title to help people find your Web page. You can make the title the same as the document name, and the same as the first visible heading in your document, or it can be different. Take these steps to open a document, save the document, and give it a title:

1. **Choose Start⇨Programs⇨Internet Explorer⇨FrontPage Express.**

   The program starts, and a window named "Untitled Normal Page" appears.

   Tour the program by trying several options. Rest the cursor over different buttons to see the Tool Tips that show what the buttons do. Pull down all the menus to see what options appear.

2. **Choose File⇨Save.**

   The Save As dialog box appears, as shown in Figure 10-3.

3. **In the Page Title text box in the Save As dialog box, enter the title of your document.**

   In the document we created for this chapter, we entered "Sierra Soccer Club California U.S.A."

4. **Click the button, As File.**

   The Save As File dialog box appears.

5. **Save your Web page into a folder on your hard disk.**

   FrontPage Express should save the Web page in its own folder. You can also save the Web page's graphics, any additional Web pages, and other files that become part of a larger Web site in this folder.

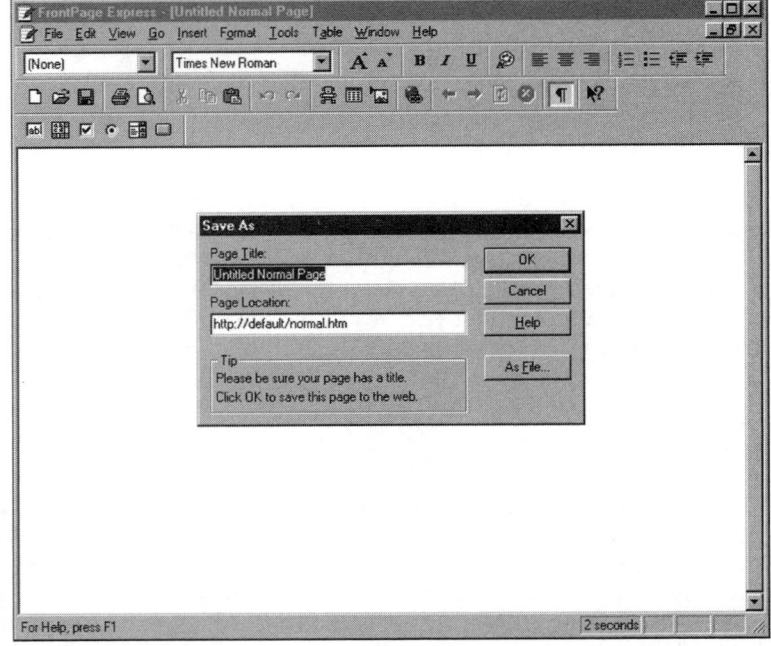

Figure 10-3:
The
FrontPage
Express
main
program
window
with the
Save As
dialog box.

Entering and formatting text

Editing text for Web pages using FrontPage Express and other Web authoring tools is easy and fun because you can use the options that are allowed on Web pages — and only those options. Follow these steps to type and format some text.

1. **Type in the heading that you want at the top of your Web page.**

   In the document we created for this chapter, we entered "Sierra Soccer Club."

2. **Move the cursor to the same line as the heading text.**

   The entire paragraph of text in which the cursor rests is affected by any HTML *styles* — paragraph-level formatting commands — that you choose.

3. **From the left-most pull-down menu, choose Heading 1.**

   The heading text is reformatted in Heading 1 style.

4. **Move the cursor to a new line.**

5. **Type some text introducing your Web page.**

When someone searches for your Web page using a search engine, the search engine may display the Web page title and the first few words that appear in the document after that. So make the first few sentences of text that appear in your Web page an introduction to the entire page or Web site.

In the document we created for this chapter, we typed:

Sierra Soccer Club is a boys' soccer club that practices and plays at the highest altitude of any in the United States. If you meet the following qualifications, you may be eligible to become a member of Sierra Soccer Club: Born in 1988 or 1989. Sierra Soccer Club has played together since its founding members were 5 and 6 years old, and will stick together as they grow up. All our club members must be born in 1988 and 1989. Some soccer experience. If you have played in organized leagues before, or if you're a skilled recreational player, we may be able to help take your game to new levels. Good academic record. We are proud that our club members maintain good standing in school as well as in soccer.

6. **Highlight any text that you want to format.**

   In our document we highlighted the words *Sierra Soccer Club* at the beginning of the first sentence.

7. **Click the button for the formatting style you want: the B button for Bold, the *I* button for Italic, or the U̲ button for Underline.**

   The highlighted text takes on the formatting you choose.

Formatting items into a list works in much the same way as applying paragraph formats, such as Heading 1. Just select the lines of text and then pick the effect that you want:

1. **Highlight the lines that you want to make into a list.**

   In our document we highlighted the lines beginning "Born in 1988 or 1989," "Some soccer experience," and "Good academic record."

2. **From the pull-down menu, choose the list style you want: Bulleted List or Numbered List.**

   The text instantly reformats into a list of the desired style, as shown in Figure 10-4.

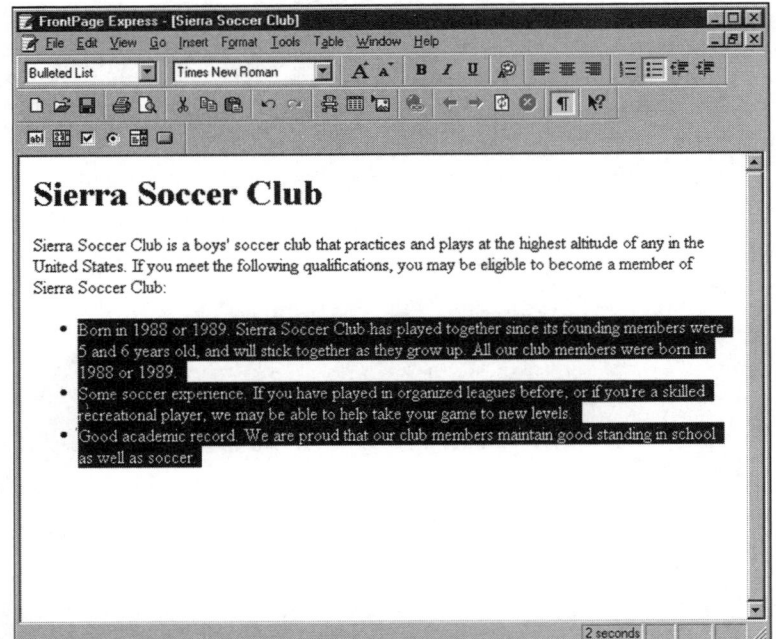

Figure 10-4:
A FrontPage
Express
front page.

If you already know some HTML, terms such as *bulleted list* and *numbered list* should make sense to you. If not, you may want to experiment or read the sections on HTML in Chapter 3 to learn what the choices mean and how best to use them.

Anchoring down a link

Creating and maintaining links is hard work, and this is one area where FrontPage Express can only help to a certain extent. No matter what tool you use, you have to learn the different types of links and then carefully maintain them as you make changes to your Web site. (More advanced tools like FrontPage 98 and NetObjects Fusion can help you maintain links across a site, but that capability isn't available in the free or inexpensive tools we describe in this book.) See Chapter 3 for much more information on the different kinds of links available in HTML. Here's how to use FrontPage Express to add a link from your Web page to a Web URL.

1. Insert some text that you intend to add a link to.

For our example, we added the following text:

```
This page was created with FrontPage Express. For infor-
mation about FrontPage Express and FrontPage 98, see the
FrontPage Frequently Asked Questions document.
```

2. Highlight the text that you want to serve as a link.

In our example, we highlighted the words *Frequently Asked Questions*.

3. Choose Edit⇨Hyperlink (Ctrl+K).

The Create Hyperlink dialog box appears.

4. Select the Hyperlink Type (http:** for a Web page) and enter the URL of the Web page. Click OK.**

For our example, we chose http: as the Hyperlink Type and entered the URL www.microsoft.com/frontpage/productinfo/ faqs.htm#express.

When you click OK, the text that you highlighted turns into a link and displays in blue with an underline. Figure 10-5 shows how the screen looks with the link and the Create Hyperlink dialog box open.

If you surf a Web page in Internet Explorer, and then add a link to the Web page you create in FrontPage Express, the URL of the Web page you have open in Internet Explorer appears as the initial value for the URL in the Create Hyperlink dialog box. (You can edit or type over the URL if it's not what you want.)

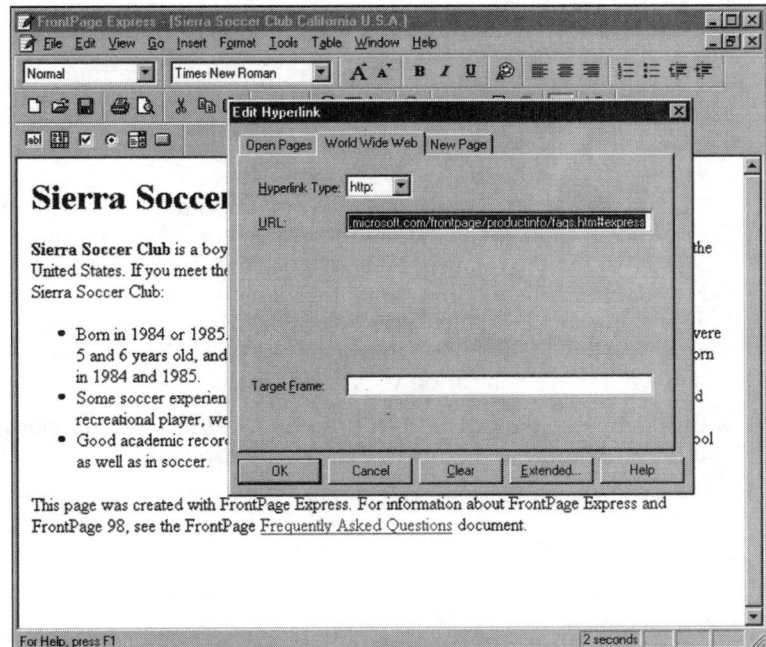

Figure 10-5:
A link that gets people just the FAQs, ma'am.

Adding an image to your image

In FrontPage Express, you can easily add an image to your Web page and, optionally, use that image as an icon to load other documents. Inserting an image in FrontPage Express is a lot like adding a link. From the Insert menu (guess that makes sense!), you choose the Image command. Then use a dialog box to find the image on your hard disk, specify alternative text and other options if you want to, and then click Insert — as we detail in the following steps:

1. **Create or obtain an image to include in your document.**

   The image should be in GIF or JPEG format. The Web contains a number of sources for free clip art. See Chapter 7 for more information. In this example, we use a JPEG file.

   FrontPage Express doesn't include a preview mode for graphics. Use a program that can view graphics, such as the Windows Paint program that comes with Windows 95, to search through the resources available and find the image you need. Note the filename and pathname of the image so that you can quickly find it to put into your Web page.

2. **Open a Web page in FrontPage Express and position the cursor where you want to place the image.**

3. **Choose Insert⇨Image.**

   The Image dialog box appears with the Other Location tab chosen.

4. **Click the Browse button.**

   The Image file open dialog box appears.

   The Image file open dialog box shows you only Web-ready GIF and JPEG graphics files, but you can import other graphics files, including Windows bitmap images, TIFF images, and PostScript images. FrontPage Express converts a file from any of these formats to GIF or JPEG. To see all the file types FrontPage Express handles, pull down the scrolling list, Files of type, in the Image dialog box. Choose the file type you want to search for on your hard disk.

5. **Browse your hard disk to find the image file that you want to include in your document. Double-click on the file icon.**

   For our example, we chose the SOCCERP.JPG file from the Sierra folder.

   The image appears on the Web page.

6. **To set graphics options, double-click on the graphic.**

   The Image Properties dialog box appears, as shown in Figure 10-6.

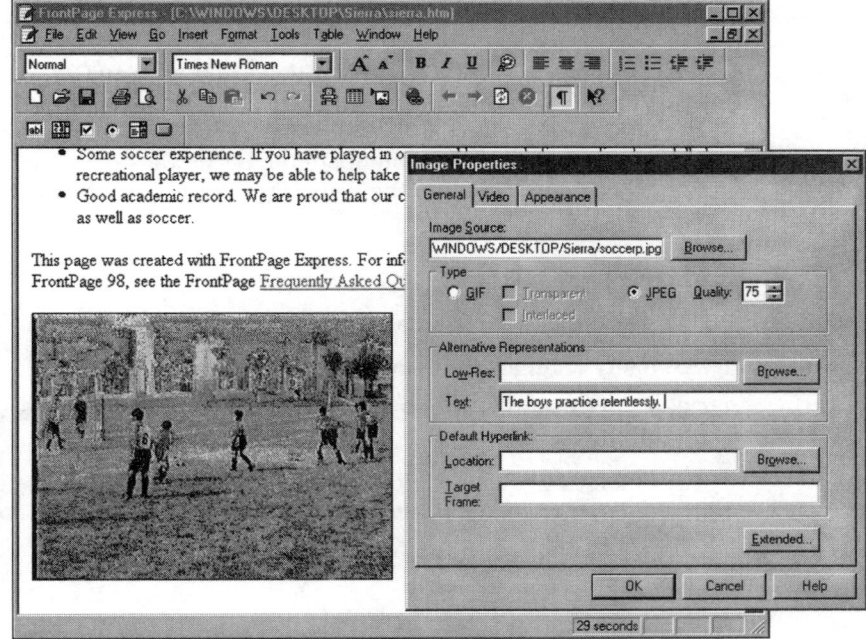

Figure 10-6:
Use Image
Properties
to get your
graphics
right.

7. **In the Image Properties dialog box, set options for the graphic, including**

   - **Alternate text:** To display alternative text when the graphic doesn't display, enter text in the Text: prompt in the Alternative Representations area of the General tab. (Recommended!)

   - **Graphical link:** To make the graphic a clickable hyperlink, select or type in a location next to the Location: prompt in the Default Hyperlink area.

   - **Display options:** To set display options, click the Appearance tab, then enter alignment, spacing around the graphic or a border, and size parameters. If you want to display a text message in browsers that don't display graphics or have graphics turned off, enter the message next to the Alt prompt.

8. **After specifying options in the Image Properties dialog box, click OK.**

   The image updates with the new properties that you entered.

Looking at the HTML

When working in a WYSIWYG (What You See Is What You Get) tool like FrontPage Express, which shows you what the Web page is going to look like, you often want to look at the underlying HTML code to find out how HTML works or to make adjustments in the HTML tags that affect the way your page looks and works on the Web. Here's how to do this in FrontPage Express:

1. **Choose View⇨HTML.**

   The View or Edit HTML dialog box appears.

2. **Make any changes that you want in the HTML.**

3. **Click the Close box in the upper-right corner of the window to close the dialog box.**

   Any changes you made in the HTML code that cause visible differences in your Web page appear in the Web page displayed in the FrontPage Express window.

Publishing your Web page

Like most other HTML editing tools, FrontPage Express creates HTML-tagged text files that you can publish on any Web server. FrontPage Express offers a special Web publishing service for transferring your site to an FTP site or the Web — you simply choose File⇨Save As, click OK to save the page to the Web, and follow the on-screen instructions. However, the Web saving capability doesn't come with detailed instructions, and FrontPage Express doesn't come with technical support, so you may have trouble figuring out what to do; we did. You can try these built-in Web publishing capabilities if you want to, but we suggest you use FTP to transfer your files instead, as we describe in Chapter 8. Your ISP or other service that's hosting your Web site can probably give you more detailed information on how to use FTP than on how to use the built-in Web publishing capabilities of FrontPage Express.

Beyond FrontPage Express

To go beyond an initial Web page and create a full Web site, you need to create a series of linked Web pages that work together. After your Web site grows beyond five or ten linked files, you may find it very difficult to manage the Web pages as they change — and especially links between files as you add and remove material. You may need to consider a more powerful tool than FrontPage Express to manage your site.

If you like the approach taken by FrontPage Express, you may love the full program. To get it, go to just about any software retailer, including online sources like PC Connection at www.pcconnection.com, or the Microsoft FrontPage Web site at www.microsoft.com/frontpage. FrontPage 98 is described in many reviews as the highest-rated and most popular full-featured Web authoring program available today.

Chapter 11

Make Your Web Pages Sing with Netscape Composer

*N*etscape is the company that ignited the spread of the World Wide Web. Started by Marc Andreesen and fellow refugees from the University of Illinois as Mosaic Communications in Silicon Valley and then renamed Netscape Communications, Netscape became a classic Silicon Valley success story. The Netscape Navigator browser was *the* ground-breaking application of 1995 and 1996 and made surfing the Web easy, fun, and cool.

From its start in ground-breaking, trend-setting browser software, Netscape has expanded into other areas, especially server software. Netscape now calls itself an intranet company and focuses on helping create Internet and intranet sites that solve problems within and between businesses. That's understandable; when someone once asked famous criminal Willie Sutton why he robbed banks, he said, "Because that's where the money is." The same is true for intranets — that's where the money is. (Though in the long run, the Internet will probably catch up in terms of financial rewards.)

But Netscape's new focus has not seemed to hurt the usability and excellence of its products for the World Wide Web very much; in fact, one seems to help the other. To fill a gap between its Web browsers and its Web server products, Netscape introduced Netscape Navigator Gold in 1996. When Netscape introduced its Communicator suite of office products in 1997, it upgraded Netscape Navigator Gold to Netscape Composer. Netscape Composer has much of the appeal of the Netscape Navigator browsers, but it adds power to facilitate Web authoring as well as Web surfing.

Netscape Composer or FrontPage Express?

The companies that make the leading Web browsers offer beginning Web publishers a choice between two excellent free Web authoring programs, Netscape Composer and Microsoft FrontPage Express. This sidebar describes the best features of Netscape Composer over Microsoft FrontPage Express; in a similar sidebar in Chapter 10 we discuss the best features of FrontPage Express over Netscape Composer. Both tools are excellent; you can try both and choose the one that works best for you! Outstanding features of Netscape Composer include:

- ✔ **Truly free.** Anyone can now download and use the Netscape Communicator suite, including Composer, for free. (Netscape used to charge a fee for its browser and associated programs such as Composer after 90 days of use, but recently began offering them for free.)

- ✔ **Support for more computer platforms.** Composer supports all the platforms that the Communicator suite supports, including Windows 3.1, the Macintosh, and many flavors of UNIX — all of which lack support from FrontPage Express.

- ✔ **Well-integrated with Communicator.** Composer is well-integrated with Netscape Navigator, Netscape e-mail and groupware software, and other parts of the Netscape Communicator suite. It's easy to use Composer, for instance, to send HTML e-mail with all the graphics and formatting options of a Web page. FrontPage Express doesn't work nearly as well with the Communicator suite.

- ✔ **Free Design Assistant and templates.** Netscape Composer is accompanied by another free program, Design Assistant, and templates for creating your Web page. Training on CD-ROM is available for a fee (see http://learning.netscape.com/courses/desc/composer.htm for details). These additions make Netscape Composer more complete than FrontPage Express and competitive with more expensive stand-alone packages like Adobe PageMill.

- ✔ **More capable than FrontPage Express.** Netscape Composer is a somewhat better tool than FrontPage Express; it includes a spellchecker and access to the add-on software previously described. Computer magazine reviews rate it as more capable and better-integrated. Also, FrontPage Express is considered simply an introduction to FrontPage 98, while Netscape Composer is Netscape's only Web authoring tool. Netscape puts more energy into supporting it than Microsoft does with FrontPage Express.

While Netscape Composer and FrontPage Express are both amazingly good products for the price, many people don't have a choice: Composer is the only game in town if you run Windows 3.1, a Macintosh, or UNIX. Even if you use Windows 95 or Windows NT 4.0, the only platforms that FrontPage Express supports, Composer is probably still a better bet if you use the most popular browser, Netscape Navigator. Only if you're a Windows 95 or Windows NT user who runs the Internet Explorer browser do you really need to consider FrontPage Express; if that describes you, read about both programs in Chapter 10 and this chapter, and choose the one that seems to better fit your needs.

Netscape has a large site devoted to Web authoring and Netscape Composer that is very much worth some serious surfing time. This site is shown in Figure 11-1. See it yourself at:

```
www.netscape.com/assist/net_sites/starter/index.html
```

From this Web site, you can link to the Netscape Composer download site, a very useful demo, general information about Web authoring, and more.

About Netscape Composer

Netscape Composer is tightly integrated with Netscape Navigator but, unlike previous Web authoring tools from Netscape, it's a significantly different-looking program. This makes the learning curve for Netscape Composer a little higher than was the case with previous Netscape Web authoring tools.

Like the Netscape Navigator browser, Netscape Composer is amazing in the breadth of platforms and languages it supports. For those of us accustomed to waiting many months for each new "port" of a software product to a new computer system or a new language, Netscape's ability to hit so many

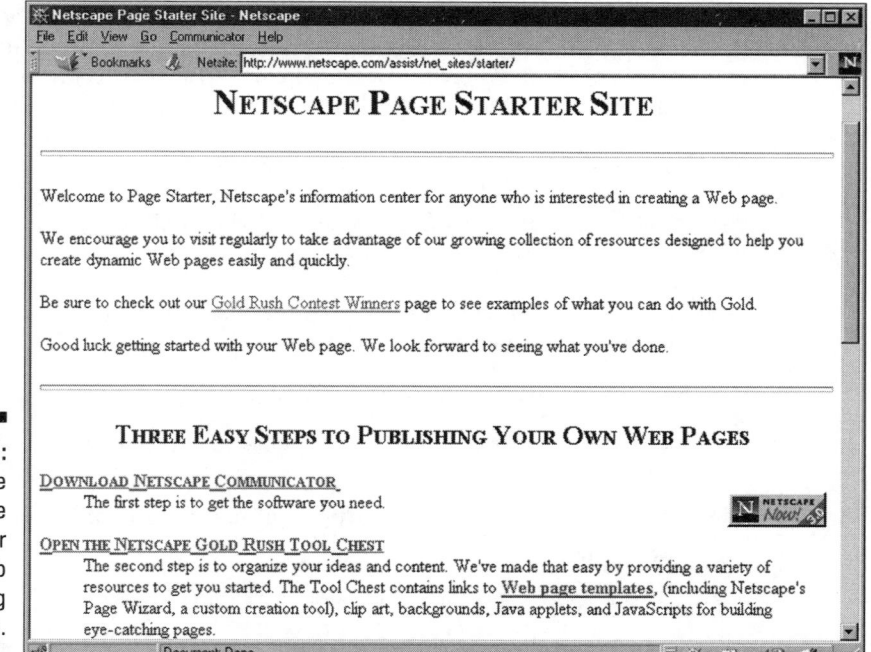

Figure 11-1:
The
Netscape
Navigator
Web
authoring
site.

targets at once is breathtaking. Like the overall Netscape Communicator suite that it's a part of, Netscape Composer runs on 32-bit Windows, Windows 3.1, Macintosh, and ten versions of UNIX. It is available in Brazilian Portuguese, Danish, Dutch, English, French, German, Italian, Japanese, Korean, Spanish, and Swedish.

Netscape Composer is a great starting point for Navigator users who want to get started in Web authoring. You can easily drag and drop hypertext links and graphics from the Navigator browser window to the Composer window. And Composer hides HTML formatting tags from you, but provides a way for you to get at them if you need to.

Netscape Composer hides HTML formatting tags, but you'll be a much better Web author if you have a basic understanding of HTML before beginning. For a solid and well-written introduction, see Chapter 3.

Understanding the basics

You can download the Netscape Communicator suite, including Composer, for free. (Netscape used to offer the Communicator suite free for 90 days, and then ask for a $49 subscription fee, but now offers it completely free.) So Netscape Communicator, like Microsoft's Internet Explorer 4.0, is free.

Netscape doesn't really specify the system requirements for Composer anywhere we could find, but you should have a reasonably powerful machine with lots of RAM. For Windows, a 486 or better with 16MB of RAM should suffice; for the Macintosh, a 68040 or PowerPC-based machine with 24MB of RAM is necessary. You may want 8MB more RAM than the requirements to accommodate running the Netscape Navigator 4.0 browser, which uses several megabytes of memory as well. For UNIX, almost any reasonably current machine should work because most UNIX workstations are set up to do heavier work than mere Web authoring.

Netscape Composer is reasonably full-featured, considering that it's free. Using Composer's key features, you can

- ✔ Create and edit Web pages without seeing HTML tags.
- ✔ Create links to other pages on your Web site without typing the URL or pathname.
- ✔ Insert images by dragging and dropping them into your Web page.
- ✔ Resize graphics.
- ✔ Create and edit tables with a very flexible table editor.

Netscape Composer lacks some features other tools have and some you would expect a tool from Netscape to support:

✔ Composer does not allow direct editing of HTML source code; you have to link to an external program to view and edit source code. (This can be a simple text editor such as SimpleText on the Macintosh or Notepad on Windows, or a more powerful tool such as HotDog Pro on Windows or BBEdit on the Mac.)

✔ Composer does not support frames, a controversial but powerful Web innovation pioneered by Netscape; nor does it support forms, a very basic HTML capability supported by all other serious tools.

Netscape Composer creates Netscape-specific pages, using HTML tags created by Netscape over more standard HTML versions. This is pretty much true of many other tools as well, though. Because about 90 percent of users have either Navigator itself or Microsoft Internet Explorer, which supports both Netscape and standard HTML tags, the Netscape-specific nature of Composer should not be a big problem for you or for your pages' users.

The bottom line

Netscape Composer is a great way to get started with Web page authoring. There isn't much of a learning curve for most people because Composer is so Navigator-like and because the authoring-specific functions are presented in a way that is very easy to learn. The fact that the program is missing a few features is actually a help when it comes to learning it because having fewer features contributes to the program's initial simplicity.

If you do get serious about Web authoring, you may need another, more powerful program. But you can expect Netscape to continue to improve and enhance Composer; in the future, it may become more capable and eventually may be competitive with more highly rated tools such as Microsoft FrontPage 98 and NetObjects Fusion, described in Chapter 13. For now, Netscape Composer is a great way to get started with Web authoring.

Getting Netscape Composer

Netscape Composer is available for free download from the Netscape Web site. You can download it, or tell your friends where to get it, from:

www.netscape.com/

You say Communicator, I say Composer

It can be hard to remember all of the names associated with Netscape's products, especially since the names of the authoring program, Composer, and the name of the overall browser suite that includes the authoring program, Communicator, are so similar. Here's a quick guide to naming the parts:

✓ **"I use Netscape."** Many people refer to the Netscape Navigator browser as simply "Netscape." This is understandable, since the company is best-known for the browser. But now that Netscape offers many products, it's time for people to start saying "Netscape" for the company and the right product name for each product.

✓ **Communicator.** Communicator is the relatively new name for the suite of products that you can get with Navigator, including e-mail, collaboration tools, and Web authoring software.

✓ **Navigator.** This is the name of the most-used browser in the world, Netscape's Navigator browser. You can download Navigator as part of the Communicator suite, or by itself. (But if you download the software by itself, you don't get any Web authoring software.)

✓ **Composer.** Composer is the free Web authoring program from Netscape that we describe extensively in this chapter. You can only get Composer by downloading the entire Communicator suite.

Follow these steps to download the demo version from the Web.

1. Go to the Netscape Web site, shown in Figure 11-2:

```
www.netscape.com
```

2. Look for the Software area. Under the bullet, Netscape Download, click the link Browsers.

The Netscape Download Web page appears.

3. Under the header Communicator/Navigator and Accessories, click on the Communicator Standard Edition link.

The Netscape Download Web page updates to display information about Communicator Standard Edition.

4. Click on the Download button.

The Netscape Download Web page updates to display choices for the version of Communicator that you want.

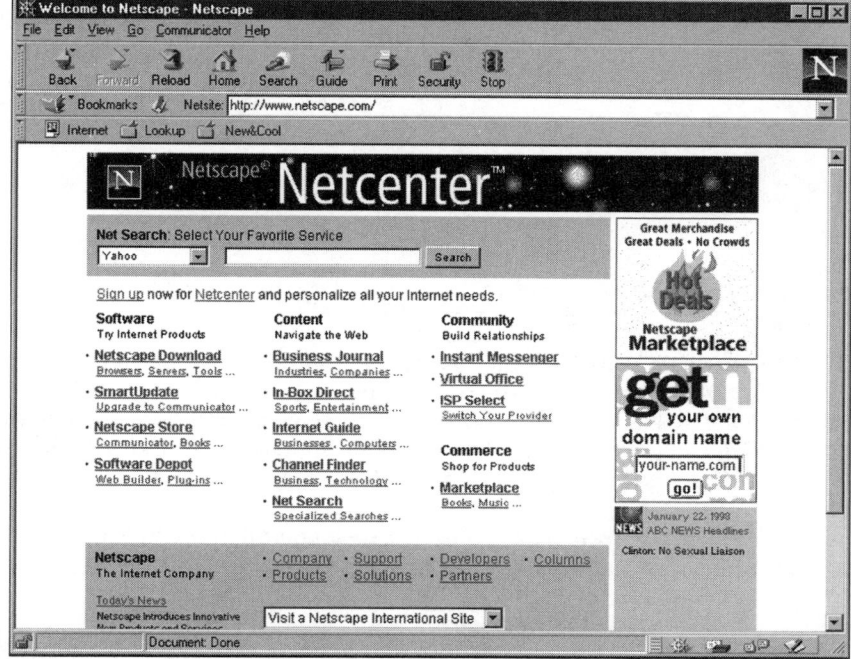

Figure 11-2:
Download
Netscape
products,
including
Netscape
Composer.

5. **Use the pull-down menus to choose your operating system and language. For the version, choose Communicator Standard Latest Version.**

   If you choose the version Navigator Stand Alone Latest Version, you won't get Composer.

6. **Scroll to the bottom of the page and click the Download for Free! button for your region.**

   A Save As dialog box appears.

7. **Browse to the location you want the installer file to be saved to. Click on Save when you've selected the location.**

   The installer for the software downloads. It's about 10MB in size and takes about 2 hours to download over a 28.8 Kbps modem.

8. **Find and double-click the installer to start it.**

   The version we downloaded was called `cc32e404.exe`. Follow the instructions on-screen to install the Netscape Communicator suite, including Composer.

You can buy the Netscape Communicator suite, including Netscape Composer, in a boxed version from many computer software sales outlets. You can get a version that includes Internet access software and other extras. For both Macintosh and Windows versions of the software try the PC Connection Online SuperStore at:

```
www.pcconnection.com
```

Using Netscape Composer

Creating a Web page with Netscape Composer is a pleasant surprise because you're looking at a Web surfing-type tool while actually creating a Web page. Because Netscape Composer combines word processing-like features with a Web surfing environment, you aren't limited by your knowledge (or lack) of HTML. Just keep trying things until something works.

You can use Netscape Composer to accomplish the following and create an initial Web page:

- ✔ Put a title on the page.
- ✔ Enter and format text.
- ✔ Add a link.
- ✔ Add an image.
- ✔ Look at the underlying HTML-tagged text.
- ✔ Publish the Web page.

These steps are covered for each of the Web authoring tools in this part of the book so that you can compare the tools. With any of the tools, these steps are much easier than using HTML directly to do the same thing.

Granting yourself a title

Begin by starting a new Netscape Composer document and titling the document.

1. **Choose Start➪Programs➪Netscape Communicator➪Netscape Composer.**

   Netscape Composer starts, and a window called Untitled appears. Then the editing screen appears, as in Figure 11-3. You can turn off toolbars later to save screen space and access the same functions using the program's menus.

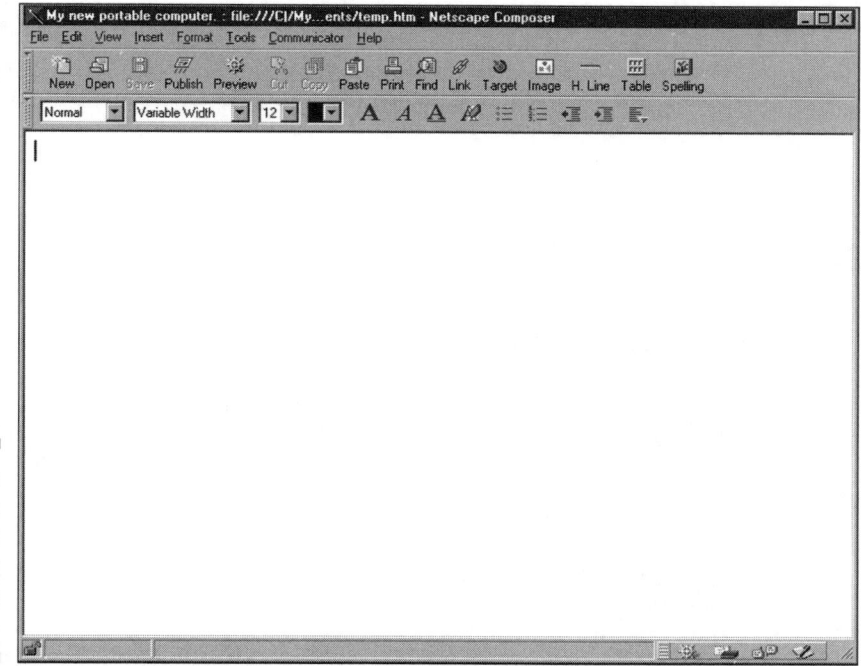

Figure 11-3:
The
Netscape
Composer
editing
window.

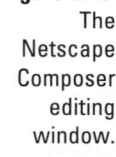

For Composer buttons that don't already have a label, rest the cursor on each button to see what it does. A brief description of the button's function appears underneath the button. Buttons that are not available at any given point are grayed out and don't respond when clicked. For instance, the Cut and Copy buttons are grayed out when nothing has been selected because, until a selection has been made, there is nothing to copy.

2. Choose Format⇔Page Colors and Properties.

The Page Properties dialog box appears.

3. Next to the Title prompt, type your document's title.

In the document we created as an example, shown in the figure, we have typed **My new portable computer**.

4. Next to the Keywords prompt, type keywords for your document.

In our document we typed **Pentium, laptop, Windows 95**.

Both the page title and keywords are used by search engines to help people find your Web page.

5. Click OK.

The title appears in the title bar of the editing window. The document title and keywords will be saved as a property of the document, but they don't appear on-screen.

In the General tab of the Page Properties dialog box, you can also enter other descriptive information about the document such as the author's name (that would be you!) and a document description. You can use the Colors and Background tab to set options such as page background, text color, and link color.

Don't worry about required HTML tag pairs such as <HTML></HTML>, <HEAD></HEAD>, and <BODY></BODY>; Netscape Composer automatically embeds them in your document.

Entering and formatting some text

You may have your most fun with Netscape Composer when you apply formatting to your document, as in a word processing program, and see your document instantly reflect the changes —no worrying about remembering to put a slash in the end HTML tag. In this part of the example, you type and format text.

1. **From the File menu, choose Save. Save the document to your hard disk.**

2. **In the Netscape Composer document window, type some text, including a list.**

   The example shown in this chapter's figures includes the following text:

   `I just got a new portable computer. I'm extremely happy with it. My favorite things about it are:`

   `133 MHz Pentium MMX processor`

   `2GB hard disk`

   `16MB of RAM (I wish it had 32MB though)`

   `It's much faster than my old portable computer. It helps me run Netscape Composer much faster.`

3. **Highlight the text you want to format.**

   In the example text, highlight "extremely" in the phrase "extremely happy."

4. **Click the button that corresponds to the text formatting effect that you want.**

   The text is immediately displayed with the formatting you choose.

   For the example, we clicked the button with a bold **A** on it to select Bold. When we released the mouse button, the word "extremely" was automatically displayed as **extremely**.

If your text has an unwanted style, such as bolding, first highlight the text. Then click the Clear All Styles button in the middle of the Character Formatting toolbar (the one with all the A's in it). The text reverts to normal style.

5. **Highlight the lines that you want to make into a list.**

In the example text, highlight the lines about processor, disk, and RAM.

6. **Click the Bullet List or Numbered List button to create the list.**

The text is immediately displayed as a list.

See Figure 11-4 to see how the screen appears at this point in the example.

If you already know some HTML, you are aware of the types of lists supported by it. For instance, in Figure 11-4, we chose a numbered list. (The numbers don't appear until the page is displayed by a Web browser.) If you're not familiar with HTML lists, then experiment, or learn some more HTML, or read Chapter 3 or the Netscape Composer Help files to understand what the choices mean and how to use them.

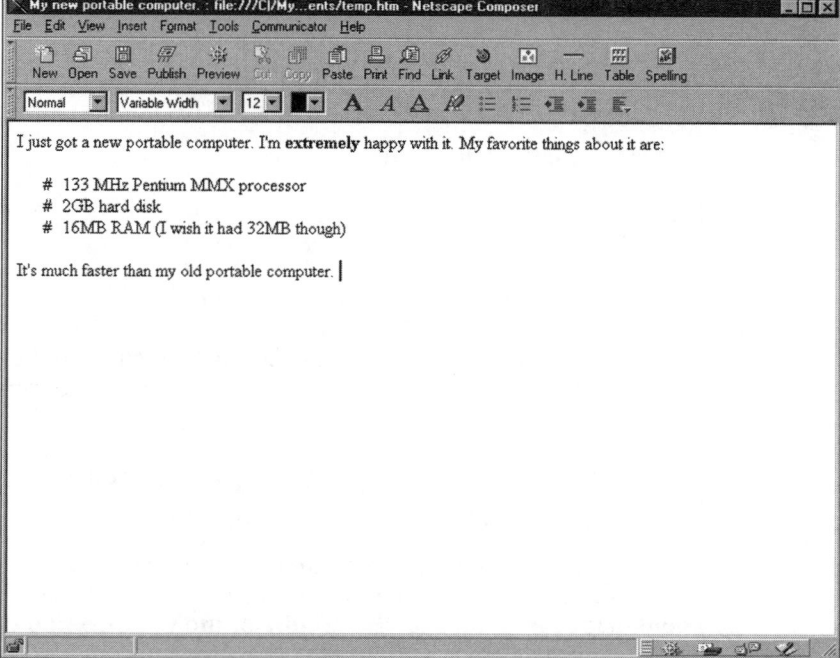

Figure 11-4: In the Netscape Composer editing window, you see the beginnings of a beautiful Netscape Composer Web Page.

Adding a link

One of the biggest problems in creating Web pages is accurately creating links. Netscape Composer eases this task considerably. This example shows how to add a link to a Web page:

1. **Highlight the text that you want to serve as a link.**

   In the example, highlight the words "Pentium MMX."

   If your text comes out with an unwanted paragraph format, such as being part of a bulleted list, highlight the text. Then choose the Normal paragraph format from the pull-down menu in the Paragraph Format toolbar. The text reverts to normal paragraph format.

2. **Click the Link button (the button that looks like a link in a chain in the middle of the Composition toolbar, the one with all the icons and words on it).**

   The Character Properties dialog box appears with the Link tab front-most.

3. **Enter the URL of the address you want to link to under the prompt, Link to a page location or local file.**

   In the example Web page, we entered `www.intel.com/mmx/index.htm`.

   You can copy and paste a link or URL from Netscape Navigator into the text entry area for the link.

4. **Click OK to complete the link.**

Adding an image

To add an image in Netscape Navigator, drag and drop from a Navigator browser window or open a file. The file must be in GIF, JPEG, or Windows BMP format. You can get free graphics from the Web and use them in your documents. Follow these steps to put a graphic stored on your hard disk into your Web page:

1. **Create or obtain an image to include in your document.**

   The image should be in GIF or JPEG format.

2. **Position your cursor in your document at the point where you want to put the image. Then click the Image button (the button with the geometric objects on it in the middle of the Composition toolbar).**

   The Image Properties dialog box appears with the Image tab up front.

3. **Click the Choose File button.**

   The Choose Image File dialog box appears.

4. Select the image file you want. Click Open.

The pathname of the file is displayed in the Image Properties dialog box.

5. Click the button, Alt.Text/Lo̲wRes.

The Alternate Image Properties dialog box appears.

6. Under the prompt Alternate text, enter text describing the image.

For the example shown in Figure 11-5 we entered: Netscape Composer window.

7. Click OK.

The Image Properties dialog box appears again.

8. Click OK.

- If the Image Conversion dialog box appears, click OK.
- If the image is in JPEG format, the JPEG Image Quality dialog box appears.
- If the JPEG Image Quality dialog box appears, choose a quality setting (we recommend Medium for most images) and then click OK.

The image appears in your Web page.

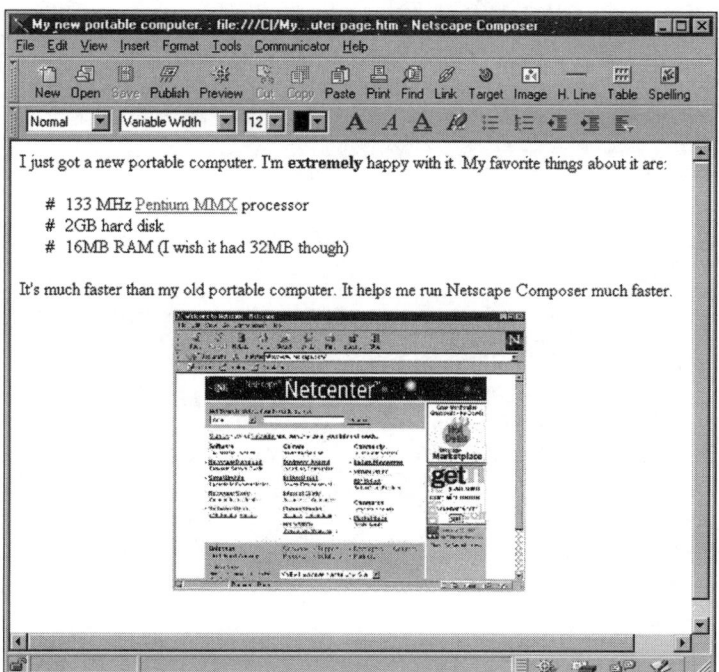

Figure 11-5:
The completed first Web page.

9. Resize or reposition the image if needed.

To resize the image, double-click on it. The Image Properties dialog box will appear again. In the Image Properties dialog box you can change the size of the image, create a border around it, and set other options. For the Web page shown in Figure 11-5, we made the image smaller and then used the Alignment button to center it.

Don't publish a Web page with a "borrowed" graphic in it anywhere but on your own machine without first getting permission from the image's owner.

Looking at the HTML

To view the HTML source of a document in Composer, use the same menu command as in Netscape Navigator:

1. Choose View⇨Page Source.

The HTML-tagged text underlying the Web page appears. You cannot edit the document in this window.

Figure 11-6 shows the HTML-tagged text for the Web page shown in the preceding figure.

```
Netscape                                                                    _□X

<HTML>
<HEAD>
    <META HTTP-EQUIV="Content-Type" CONTENT="text/html; charset=iso-8859-1">
    <META NAME="Author" CONTENT="Bud Smith">
    <META NAME="GENERATOR" CONTENT="Mozilla/4.02 [en] (Win95; I) [Netscape]">
    <META NAME="KeyWords" CONTENT="Pentium, laptop, Window 95">
    <TITLE>My new portable computer.</TITLE>
</HEAD>
<BODY>
I just got a new portable computer. I'm <B>extremely</B>
happy with it. My favorite things about it are:
<OL>
<LI>
133 MHz <A HREF="http://www.intel.com/mmx/index.htm">Pentium MMX</A> processor</LI>

<LI>
2GB hard disk</LI>

<LI>
16MB RAM (I wish it had 32MB though)</LI>
</OL>
It's much faster than my old portable computer. It helps me run Netscape
Composer much faster.
<CENTER><IMG SRC="../WINDOWS/DESKTOP/Online Services/CWP new figures/CW1102.JPG" ALT="Netsc

</BODY>
</HTML>
```

Figure 11-6:
HTML-tagged text for the Web page shown in Figure 11-5.

2. **To edit the document source in HTML, go back to the main Composer window and choose Edit⇨HTML Source.**

   You are asked to choose an HTML editor.

3. **Choose an editor to use for the HTML-tagged text.**

   You can use a text editor such as Windows WordPad, a word processor, or an HTML editor such as HotDog Pro or BBEdit. If you use a word processor, be sure to always save your HTML files in plain text format. If you don't, the word processor adds formatting commands to the document that Netscape Composer won't understand.

4. **Edit the document's HTML-tagged text.**

5. **Save the document and exit the editing program.**

   You return to Netscape Composer.

6. **Click Yes when the Reload File dialog box appears and asks if you want to reload the page to see changes.**

Netscape Composer displays the modified page.

Publishing your Web page

Netscape Composer creates HTML-tagged text files that can be published on any Web server. However, Netscape Composer does not offer any special services for Web publishing. As with most other Web authoring tools, you are on your own when it comes to getting an account on a Web server, transferring your Web files to the server, and testing the site after it becomes available on the Web. See Chapter 7 for information on how to publish your Web page.

To publish a Web page or Web site in Netscape Composer, use the program's built-in Publish function.

1. **Click the Publish button.**

   The Publish Files dialog box appears.

2. **Enter the FTP site or http (Web) site to which to upload the files.**

   If you don't already know this information, obtain it from the Web service provider or other party that will be hosting your site.

3. **Enter your user name and password, if any.**

4. **Click OK.**

The files are transferred to the FTP site or Web server. Go surf them!

Netscape Composer and Beyond

Netscape Composer is free, as is the Netscape Communicator suite that it comes in. However, if you need a somewhat more capable product with printed documentation, technical support, and added features such as templates and clip art, you may want to consider moving up to Adobe PageMill (see Chapter 12), a $99 program that has features such as more graphics conversions, drag-and-drop QuickTime multimedia support, and support for both forms and frames. PageMill also has a "bigger brother," SiteMill, which gives you an upgrade path if you need site management capabilities as well.

Netscape Composer is a great choice for getting started with Web page authoring and for use on UNIX, which has few other easy-to-use Web page creation tools. Look at the other tools covered in this part of the book if you want to go further.

Chapter 12

Grinding Out Pages with PageMill

● ●

In This Chapter

▶ Understanding the basics

▶ Getting PageMill

▶ Using PageMill

▶ PageMill and beyond

● ●

*O*ne of the most exciting developments in Web authoring occurred in late 1995 with the initial demonstrations of PageMill, a Macintosh-based Web authoring tool from a small start-up group called Ceneca. Founded by refugees from the floundering Apple/IBM joint venture Taligent, Ceneca had a unique, near-WYSIWYG (What You See Is What You Get) approach to Web page creation and nice extras like automatic conversion of graphics to Web-approved formats. In late 1995, Adobe bought Ceneca and formally introduced Adobe PageMill at the Seybold graphics show, the industry-leading desktop publishing trade show that has expanded to include Web publishing as well. PageMill was a big hit at the show and has since become one of the leading tools for creating Web pages.

For more information about PageMill and other Adobe products on the Web, go to

```
www.adobe.com/
```

About PageMill

Adobe PageMill is praised as the best Web page authoring tool for the Macintosh, and in Spring 1997 it became available for Windows 95 and Windows NT 4.0 as well. Though no tool can meet the needs of everyone, PageMill is especially well-suited to those starting out in Web authoring because it has the same "look and feel" as a word processing program and because it successfully hides HTML formatting tags from the user. With Version 2.0, PageMill also allows access to the HTML source code, so you can work in either HTML or a Web-page preview.

PageMill lets you create robust Web pages quickly, and you can easily experiment with different formatting and content options. Novice Web authors who have posted comments on the Internet say that PageMill made it possible for them to create attractive Web pages without learning HTML. Experienced Web authors say that they work twice as fast as before because PageMill allows them to quickly experiment with the basic layout of their Web pages and then, if needed, work directly in HTML to fine-tune the details.

Though PageMill, like other advanced Web authoring tools, hides the HTML formatting tags, you still need a basic understanding of HTML to use it effectively. If you aren't familiar with HTML, see the overview in Chapter 3 before proceeding.

Understanding the basics

Adobe PageMill 2.0 is available for Macintosh and 32-bit Windows for about $99 (slightly less through some mass software merchants). PageMill can run on a very low-end machine, but on the Macintosh side, Adobe recommends either a 68040- or PowerPC-based Macintosh with 6MB of free RAM. For Windows 95, Adobe recommends a Pentium machine with 16MB of RAM total; add another 8MB if you want to run PageMill 2.0 on Windows NT. Considering that you may well want to run a graphics program and a Web browser while running PageMill, the more RAM, the better; it's great to have a 32MB system for running several applications at once on either Macintosh or Windows. The program requires at least a 16-color monitor, so you can't run it on a monochrome system. To find out more about Adobe PageMill, go to the following site:

`www.adobe.com/prodindex/pagemill/main.html`

PageMill is about as fully featured as any Web authoring package in its price range. Using its key features, you can do the following:

- ✔ Create and edit Web pages without seeing HTML tags.
- ✔ Work directly in HTML if you want to.
- ✔ Create links to other pages on your Web site without typing the URL or pathname.
- ✔ Insert images by dragging and dropping them into your Web page.
- ✔ Use built-in capabilities to handle conversion and resizing of graphics files.

PageMill is one of the few full-featured Web editing tools — indeed, one of the few Web editing tools of any type — that can be fairly described as *fast*. PageMill is nearly unique in that you can describe it as *fun*. The fact that

PageMill has a word processor-like display with the same kind of familiar pull-down menus and commands as other programs is what makes it so much fun. You can easily experiment with a variety of "looks" to your Web page without having to think about the underlying HTML that makes it all happen.

And what about HTML and PageMill? PageMill supports the basic HTML 2.0 tag set that is supported by all Web browsers, and it supports selected extensions from HTML 3.0 and Netscape. (For an explanation of HTML tags and tag levels, see Chapter 3 and Appendix C.) In Version 2.0, PageMill also supports tables.

PageMill's graphics capabilities are excellent. PageMill allows you to drag in images from the desktop, drop them into your Web page, and then resize them. The program directly supports the display of both GIF and JPEG files and automatically converts images in Macintosh PICT format or Windows BMP format to Web-ready GIF format. PageMill also supports the conversion of GIFs to transparent or interlaced format, or both. And PageMill includes tools for creating clickable image maps.

The bottom line

The fact that you have to pay for a functional version of PageMill (as opposed to the save-disabled demo you can get for free) may be a concern. If you're just creating a few pages and are willing to work with HTML even a little bit, you can get by without PageMill. However, if you are creating more than a couple of Web pages, are averse to HTML, or simply value your time, PageMill is a good answer to your problems.

From a beginner's point of view, PageMill is nearly perfect. Its use of a word-processing interface makes Web page authoring possible for people who otherwise may not try it. Advanced users are happy with features like drag-and-drop QuickTime multimedia support and Java applet support.

Where PageMill drops the ball is in site management — and if you're managing more than a dozen or two files, site management becomes a big concern. Competitors like Microsoft FrontPage and NetObjects Fusion, though somewhat harder to learn, do much more. On the Macintosh, PageMill now includes its SiteMill site management product free, which is a very good deal for Macintosh users. On Windows, however, no site management product is available as a companion to PageMill.

Still, PageMill's future is bright. Adobe's ownership of the program means that PageMill is linked to Adobe's graphics creation tools such as Photoshop and Illustrator — among the best anywhere— and that a lot of talented people are available to improve and support it. PageMill has achieved strong

Cheap versus free

Until recently, Adobe PageMill was the only tool that allowed you to create a Web page truly easily, without HTML coding or complicated site management concerns. Now, however, PageMill is challenged by Microsoft FrontPage Express (Chapter 10) and Netscape Composer (Chapter 11), both free. In fact, these programs are to some extent PageMill clones, with a similar mix of features and capabilities. So why pay for PageMill when you can get these similar programs for free?

On both Macintosh and Windows, PageMill is simply a better program than either of the two free tools — though both of the free tools are amazingly good for the price. PageMill supports drag-and-drop insertion of text and graphics and comes with a great deal of bonus content such as Web page templates, clip art, animations, and multimedia.

For Macintosh users, PageMill 2.0 is an excellent choice. It includes the SiteMill site management program, so if your needs grow beyond authoring a few Web pages to managing a multipage Web site, you don't have to buy another program. Unfortunately, the free trial version of PageMill for the Macintosh doesn't allow saving files to the hard disk. You can try the program without buying it, but without the ability to save you can't really do much. You will have to take it somewhat on faith that PageMill 2.0, with SiteMill included, is worth the $99 or so that you pay for it.

For Windows users, PageMill is not quite as good a deal. PageMill 2.0 for Windows doesn't include the SiteMill site management product, so aspiring Web authors who need site management capabilities may be better off with Microsoft FrontPage for about $139 or NetObjects Fusion for about $295. However, PageMill still shines in the ease-of-use category, and the free trial version of PageMill 2.0 for Windows allows you to save files and do anything else the program can do for up to 15 days. This gives you a chance to create your initial Web page or Web pages for free and then decide whether you need the program in the long run.

If you're only creating a few Web pages and want to keep a close eye on your pocketbook, either FrontPage Express or Netscape Composer, as described Chapters 10 and 11, will probably do the job. But you can do more, and have more fun doing it, with Adobe PageMill 2.0.

sales on the Macintosh, though it hasn't been a big winner up against Microsoft's FrontPage and NetObjects Fusion, which are the leading Web authoring products on the Windows platform. The odds are that PageMill will continue as leader in to-die-for ease of use and continue to be gradually improved on the Macintosh platform as well as in a Windows version.

If you are a beginning Web page author and don't anticipate a short-term need to be managing a large site, PageMill is worth the (relatively low) initial purchase price and the (very shallow) learning curve.

Getting PageMill

A demo version of PageMill for Macintosh is on the CD-ROM that comes with this book. You can also check for a more recent version, or the Windows version, or tell your friends where to get it, at:

www.adobe.com/

The demo version included on the CD-ROM and available on the Adobe Web site has all the Web page creation and editing features of the full version except that you can't save or print files (for the Macintosh version) or use the program for more than 15 days (for the Windows version). So you can experiment for free, but you can't do real work until you're willing to pony up $99.

To get PageMill, either install the free demo version from the *Creating Web Pages For Dummies* CD-ROM, download the free demo version from Adobe's Web site, or buy the full version for $99 from Adobe Software.

Downloading the demo version

To make sure that you have the most up-to-date version, you may want to download the demo version of PageMill from the Web rather than use the CD-ROM version. Follow these steps to download the demo version from the Web.

1. **Go to the Adobe PageMill Web site shown in Figure 12-1 at:**

   www.adobe.com/prodindex/pagemill/main.html

2. **Click on the appropriate link for your computer: Get the Adobe PageMill 2.0 Tryout for Macintosh, or Get the Adobe PageMill 2.0 Tryout for Windows 95 and Windows NT 4.0.**

   The Adobe PageMill registration page appears.

3. **Use the pull-down menu to choose the product you want to download and then fill out the registration page. When you're done, click the Submit Registration button.**

   The license agreement page appears.

4. **Read the license agreement. Then click the Accept button.**

   The Download page appears — finally!

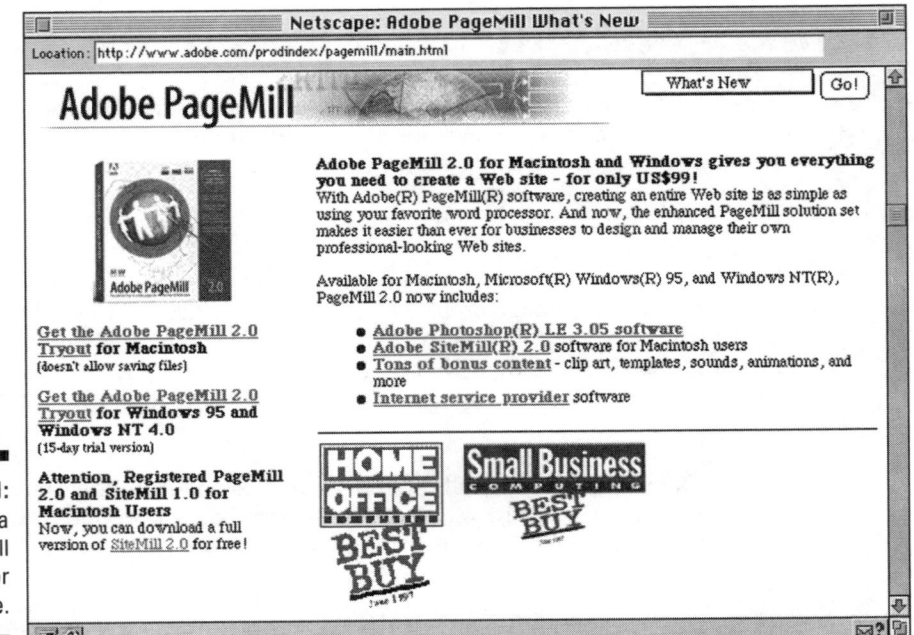

Figure 12-1:
Download a
PageMill
trial for
free.

5. **Click the DOWNLOAD PageMill 2.0 Demo link. (For Macintosh, choose the BinHex version.)**

The file, just over 3MB in size for Macintosh or 5MB in size for Windows, downloads. The Windows version took about 40 minutes to receive over my 28.8 Kbps modem.

6. **Double-click the Install PageMill Demo icon to install the PageMill demo. (For Windows, the demo is called something like PMLW2.EXE.)**

Follow the instructions on-screen to install the PageMill tryout.

Buying the complete version

You can buy Adobe PageMill from most computer software sales outlets or online. To buy the complete version of Adobe PageMill, do either of the following:

✔ Buy PageMill over the Web. Adobe recommends software.net as its preferred supplier. Go to the Web page for orders:

```
www.software.net
```

> ✔ Call Adobe at 800-411-8657 (United States) or 206-628-2749 (other countries) and order by phone.
>
> A cheerful Adobe representative takes your order and sends you the software.

Using PageMill

As we said, creating an initial page with PageMill is easy and fun. Because you work in a word processor-like environment, you aren't limited by your knowledge of HTML. Just try different options and keep using the ones that do what you need.

We show you how to use PageMill to accomplish the following and create an initial Web page:

> ✔ Put a title on the page.
>
> ✔ Enter and format some text.
>
> ✔ Add a link.
>
> ✔ Add an image.
>
> ✔ See the underlying HTML-tagged text.
>
> ✔ Publish the Web page.

These same steps are described for each of the Web authoring tools in this part of this book so that you can compare the tools. With any of the tools, these steps are much easier than using HTML directly to do the same thing.

PageMill includes a tutorial that demonstrates some of the preceding steps as well as steps for intermediate and advanced tasks. Because the tutorial is business-oriented, we wrote the following example to focus on creating a personal Web page. Use the steps shown here to get started and then use PageMill itself to do more with your Web page.

Most of the following steps work equally well with the PageMill demo on the CD-ROM or the full version that you can purchase from Adobe. However, you won't be able to save your work or print it if you use the demo version on your Macintosh.

Granting yourself a title

Begin by starting a new PageMill document and giving it a title. Remember, you won't see the title on-screen, but Web browsers use it when searching for pages.

1. **Double-click the PageMill icon (on your desktop) to start the program (Macintosh) or choose Start⇨Programs⇨Adobe PageMill 2.0 Tryout⇨Adobe PageMill 2.0 Tryout (Windows).**

   The PageMill document window, untitled.html, appears (see Figure 12-2). The inside of the window resembles the inside of a browser window.

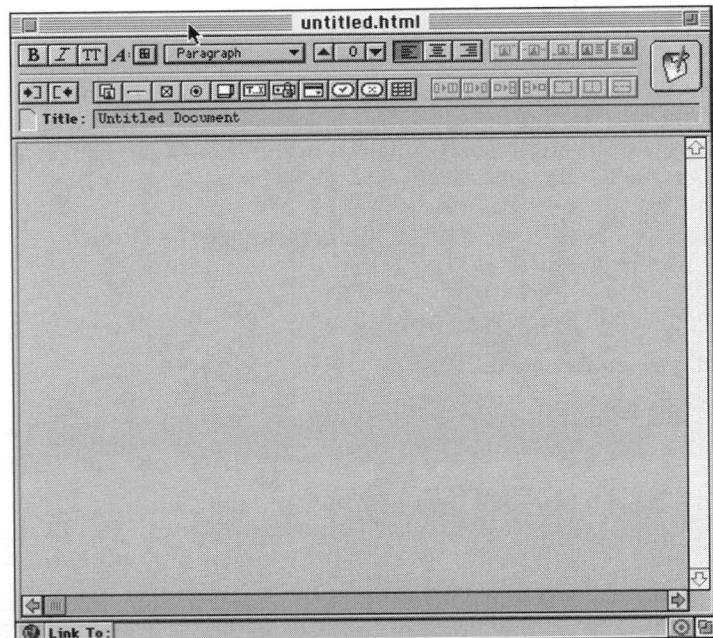

Figure 12-2:
The
PageMill
document
window.

To see what each icon available in PageMill does, rest the cursor on the icon. A brief description of the icon's function appears in the blank area to the right of the icons. Only active icons —— those that are available for use in the program — display a description.

PageMill's display is intended to resemble that of Netscape Navigator; test your PageMill documents in other browsers such as Internet Explorer 4.0 before putting them on the Web.

2. **Type your document's title,** My first Web page, **next to the Title prompt that's just beneath the line of icons. Press Return.**

   When you save your document, PageMill saves it as text with HTML tags. The document title, for example, is automatically stored between the <TITLE> and </TITLE> tags in the HTML-tagged text file.

Don't worry about required HTML tag pairs such as <HTML></HTML>, <HEAD></HEAD>, and <BODY></BODY>; PageMill automatically embeds them in your document.

Entering and formatting some text

Using PageMill is a lot of fun — from quickly formatting text into Web-ready form to dragging and dropping graphics and even multimedia files into your Web page. In this part of the example, we type and format text.

1. In the PageMill document window, type some text, including a list.

The example includes the following text:

```
This is my first Web page. It will contain my hopes,
dreams, and fantasies. Plus a few GIFs and a JPEG or two.
I want to begin with a request for some information. In
my many (too many) hours of searching the Web,
there are a few important topics that I haven't
been able to learn much about in my Web searches
so far. If you can help me find Web sites or
newsgroups that have information about these
topics, please send me e-mail.
Waterskiing.
Dachshunds.
Waterskiing dachshunds.
```

2. Highlight the text you want to format.

In the example text, highlight "too" in the phrase "too many."

3. Click the button that corresponds to the text-formatting effect that you want.

The text is immediately displayed with the formatting you choose.

In the example text, click the B button to select Bold. When you release the mouse button, the word "too" is automatically displayed as **too**.

4. Highlight the lines that you want to make into a list.

In the example text, highlight the lines about waterskiing, dachshunds, and waterskiing dachshunds.

5. Select the Change Format pull-down menu —the one that says Paragraph initially — to see the choices.

The Change Format pull-down menu appears with choices including the list choices Bullet List, Directory List, Menu List, Numbered List, Definition List, and Term List.

If you already know some HTML, these terms should make sense to you. If not, you must experiment, read Chapter 3, Appendix C, or the PageMill documentation to understand what the choices mean and how to use them.

6. **Choose the type of list that you want.**

For a simple list, the best choices are Bullet List and Numbered List.

For the example list, choose Bullet List. The example text will look like the text in Figure 12-3.

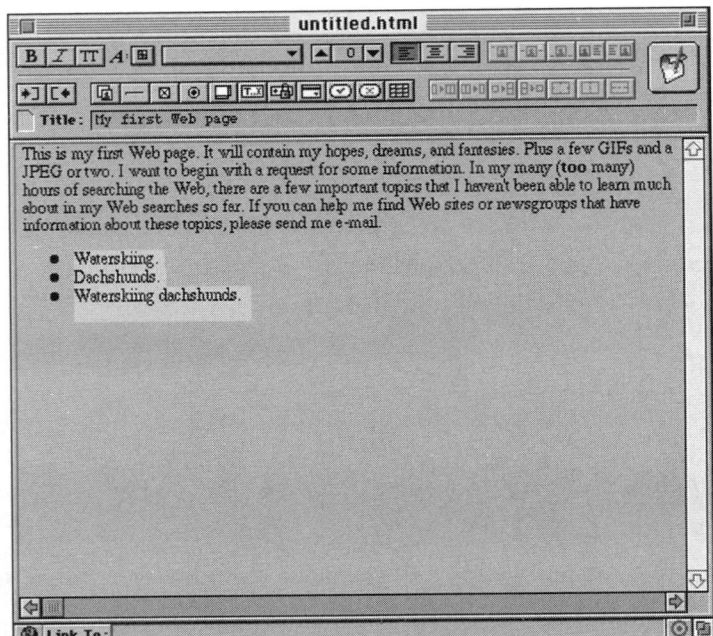

Figure 12-3:
A beginning
PageMill
Web Page.

Adding a link

One of the biggest problems in creating Web pages is accurately creating and maintaining links. PageMill eases this task considerably. The following example shows how to add a link to a local document on your own hard disk (the local document, as well as the HTML document that you're editing, is uploaded later to the server):

1. **Insert some text to which you intend to add a link.**

As an example, add the following text:

```
For more information about PageMill 2.0, see the ReadMe
file.
```

If your text comes out with an unwanted paragraph format, such as being part of a bulleted list, just place the insertion point in the text and then choose Paragraph from the Change Format menu. The text will revert to normal paragraph format — no bullets, numbers, or anything else.

2. **Highlight the text that you want to serve as a link.**

   In the example, highlight the word "ReadMe."

3. **Choose Open from the File menu.**

   The Open file dialog box appears.

4. **Select and open the document that you want to link to.**

   Normally, you open another HTML document at this point.

   For the example, open the ReadMe file, readme.html, in the folder that comes with the PageMill demo.

5. **Drag and resize the document windows so that the spot in your main document where you want to insert the link and the upper-left corner side of the document that you want to link to are both visible.**

6. **From the upper-left corner of the document that you want to link to, next to the Title prompt, grab the page icon (icon looks like a turned-down page).**

7. **Drag the page icon from the document that you want to link to over to the selected text in your main document.**

   The selected text becomes a link to the other document. Figure 12-4 shows how this looks.

Adding an image

Adding an image in PageMill couldn't be easier — just drag and drop.

1. **Create or obtain an image to include in your document.**

   The image should be in Macintosh PICT, Windows BMP, GIF, or JPEG format.

   On the Macintosh, you can quickly create a PICT file by "capturing" your screen: Hold down Cmd+Shift and then press 3. An image of your screen is saved in a file with the name Picture 1 on your start-up hard disk. On Windows, press the Print Screen key to capture the screen, or Alt+Print Screen to capture the front-most window. This copies the screen to the Windows Clipboard. Then paste the Clipboard into the Windows Paint program (choose Start➪ Programs➪Accessories➪Paint).

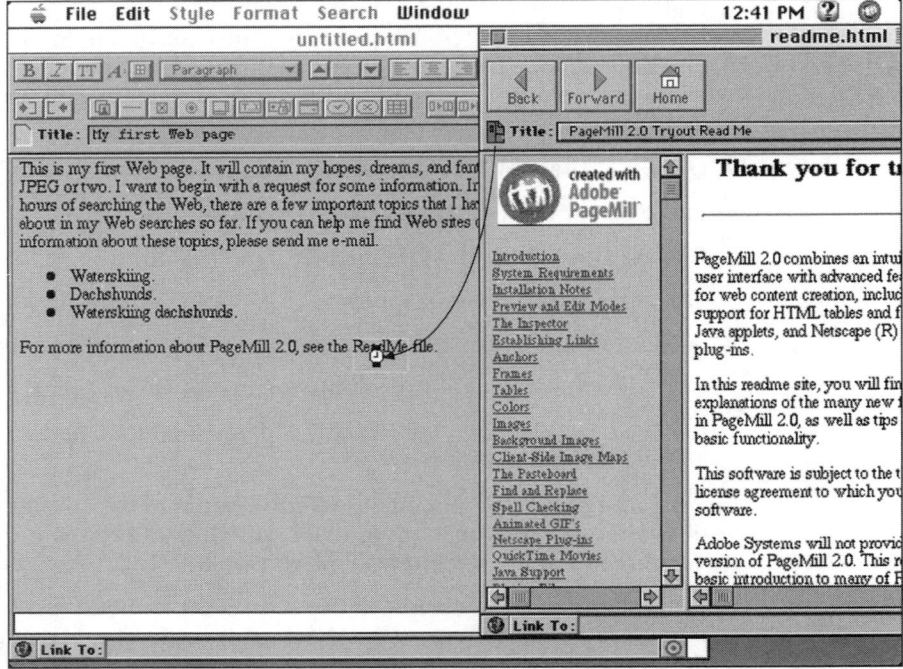

Figure 12-4:
Linking from
one local
page to
another.

2. **Arrange your desktop so that the file with the image you want is visible next to the PageMill window.**

   For this example, open the folder Adobe PageMill 2.0 Tryout and move its window to the far right of your screen so that the image `image4.gif` is visible in the folder.

3. **Click the open PageMill document window to return to PageMill.**

4. **Holding down the mouse button, drag the image's icon from the exposed part of the Finder to the location where you want it to be in your document.**

   For this example, drag the icon for the image `image4.gif` into the editing window.

5. **Release the mouse button to "drop" the image into your document.**

   The image appears in your document. If the image is a Macintosh PICT file or Windows BMP file, it is automatically converted to a GIF file.

6. **Resize or reposition the image if needed.**

   For this example, center the image by clicking the Center button in the middle of the button bar and dragging the image's handles to make it larger. The result is shown in Figure 12-5.

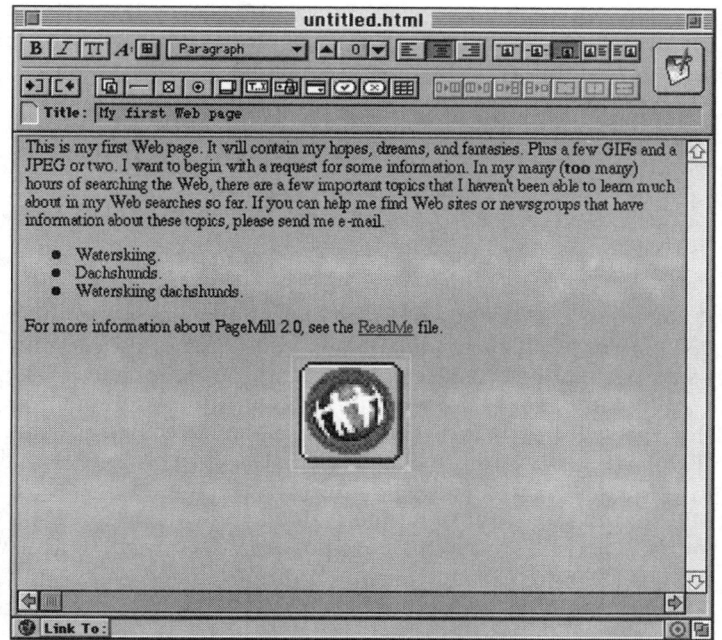

Figure 12-5:
The
completed
first Web
page.

Don't publish a Web page with a "borrowed" graphic in it anywhere but on your own machine without first getting permission from the image's owner.

Looking at the HTML

If you have the full version (not the demo) of PageMill, you can look at the HTML-tagged text by doing the following:

1. **From the Edit menu, choose HTML Source.**

   The HTML-tagged text underlying the Web page appears. You can edit the document in this window as well.

   Figure 12-6 shows the HTML-tagged text for the Web page shown in the preceding figure.

2. **Save the document and exit PageMill.**

Publishing your Web page

PageMill creates HTML-tagged text files that can be published on any Web server. However, PageMill does not offer any special services for Web publishing. As with most other Web authoring tools, you are on your own when it comes to getting an account on a Web server, transferring your Web files to the server, and testing the site after it becomes available on the Web. See Chapter 8 for information on how to publish your Web page.

PageMill and Beyond

To use PageMill for any kind of actual work, you need to move up to the full, paid-for version. The $99 investment for PageMill should be all you need to spend to generate a lot of Web pages. PageMill includes a lot of great extras such as templates, clip art, and animations as part of the package, so it's really worth the price if you're doing any serious amount of Web page creation. And if you ever do need the SiteMill site-management program, Adobe will give it to you for free if you're a Macintosh user. (You can't get SiteMill for Windows.) To buy PageMill, just visit the Adobe Web page.

PageMill should save you both time and money with its complete feature set. You won't need separate tools to convert Macintosh PICT or Windows BMP files to GIF or to create transparent or interlaced GIFs. And you can be very ambitious with graphics and even multimedia. We look forward to seeing your PageMill-created sites on the Web!

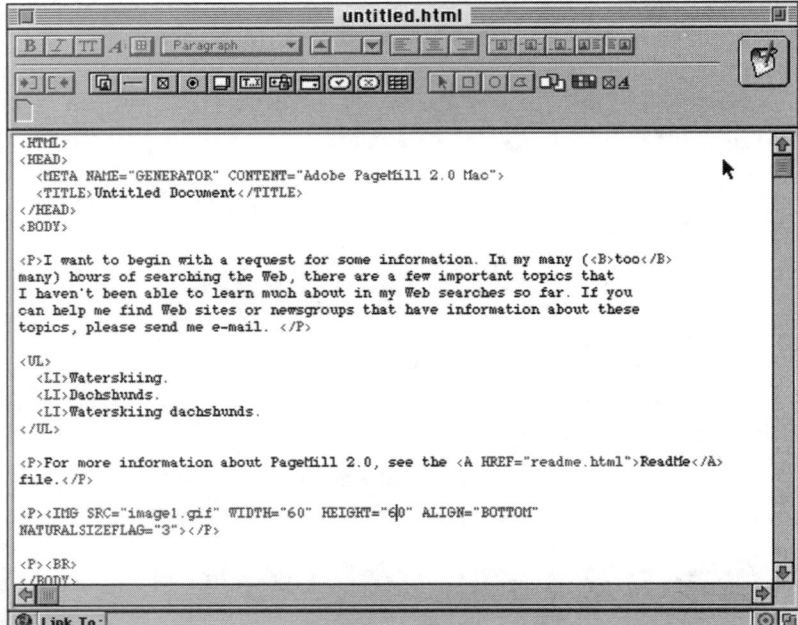

Figure 12-6:
HTML-
tagged text
for the
Web page
shown in
Figure 12-5.

Chapter 13

Heat Up Your HTML with HotDog Pro

*I*n creating Web pages, many people want a tool that insulates them from the details of HTML, the underlying language with which Web pages are made. A brave few of you may like the HTML you learned so far in this book and want to go further with it. You hardy souls may want a tool that allows you to use HTML more quickly and easily, but not hide it away completely. If you are one of this select group, we salute you and offer you this chapter on HotDog Pro from Sausage Software, possibly the best and most popular HTML editor on the market.

Note that we say "HTML editor" and not "Web authoring tool." For most people, the best Web authoring tool is probably something like FrontPage Express (see Chapter 10), Netscape Composer (see Chapter 11), or Adobe PageMill (see Chapter 12) — or even one of the word processor add-ons described in Chapter 14 — anything that keeps the grubby details of HTML at least one step away while you do your work. But if you want an HTML editor that keeps the HTML tags right in your face yet makes it easier to manage them, HotDog Pro may be for you.

You can get started with HotDog Pro even if you don't know much about HTML. Menus and icons in the program enable you to perform tasks like inserting a graphic, creating a link, and formatting text without having to know the HTML tags yourself. However, you still do your work in an HTML view. So the bad news is you will need to learn HTML in order to work most effectively in HotDog Pro. The good news is that HotDog Pro kind of teaches you HTML as you go along, because you always see the HTML tags that are generated when you make a menu choice or select an icon.

HotDog Pro Express

Sausage Software also offers a "lite" version of HotDog Pro called HotDog Pro Express for $49.95. It includes some features of HotDog Pro and boasts ease of use as its most distinguishing feature. However, the free Web-based services offered by GeoCities, AOL, CompuServe, and others described in Chapter 4 and Chapter 5 are just as easy. Although HotDog Pro Express may be a little easier and a little more powerful, it's not enough to warrant the extra price. If you want a version of HotDog, go straight for the "real thing," HotDog Pro (which includes HotDog Pro Express), not the stand-alone HotDog Pro Express program. (But a free demo version is available; if this kind of thing interests you, try it; you might like it.)

To get you started, HotDog Pro includes an HTML tutorial. In this book, see Chapter 3 for a general explanation of HTML and Appendix C for details about HTML. If you are new to HTML and aren't in a hurry to learn more, consider starting your Web authoring efforts with one of the many tools described in this book that hides HTML tags.

The Sausage Software programs only run on Windows machines. A less full-featured version, HotDog 16-bit, is available for Windows 3.*x,* and a more robust version, HotDog Pro, is available for Windows 95 and NT. (This chapter covers HotDog Pro, but most of what it says applies to HotDog 16-bit as well.) Though the company promised a Macintosh version a long time ago, none has shipped yet.

The HotDog Pro demo software for Windows 95 is on the CD-ROM that comes with this book. The demo is free for 30 days, after which it costs $129.95 to register the program. For updated demo versions of HotDog Pro, visit the Sausage Software Web site.

To learn more about HotDog Pro go to

www.sausage.com/

Figure 13-1 shows one part of the Sausage Software Web site. The site is missing some basic marketing information such as the advantages of the product, prominent users, and other stuff book authors as well as customers love to know. But the product itself is really good, so charge on.

Figure 13-1:
Sausage
Software
introduces
their Hot
(green) Dog.

About HotDog Pro

For those who already know something about HTML, HotDog Pro is a
straightforward and powerful tool. The HotDog Pro basic editing window is
just like the editing window of a text editor, which is what many HTML-savvy
folks use to create and edit Web pages. For those of you who have actually
used a text editor to create Web pages, features such as HotDog Pro's access
to HTML tags through icons and the capabilities it provides to preview and
publish your pages make it a dream come true.

Understanding the basics

Sausage Software, a small Australian company, introduced HotDog in June
1995. Since then, HotDog Pro has been introduced and upgraded clear up to
Version 4.5. HotDog Pro runs on Windows 95 and takes advantage of all the
features available to 32-bit Windows programs such as long filenames, faster
execution, and greater crash protection. HotDog Pro takes up only 6MB of
disk space but requires 16MB of RAM. If you want to run HotDog Pro simul-
taneously with an open Internet session, a graphics program, and possibly
other tools as well — and you will, if you're serious— you may need more
RAM; a total of 32MB of RAM should be ample.

When you use HotDog Pro, you definitely want one thing: a large monitor. With all the icons, menu bars, and so on, the editing window is all too small on a regular 13-inch or 14-inch monitor. Plan to buy a larger screen if you get serious about HotDog Pro.

HotDog Pro has a large number of features that make HTML editing easier, including the following:

- **HTML tutorial.** An opportunity to run HotDog Pro's HTML tutorial is one of the first things that you see when you start the program. This tutorial is a good thing to work through even if you don't end up using HotDog Pro.

- **Toolbars and icons.** The most common HTML commands and HotDog Pro functions are available through easy-to-remember icons in toolbars that live in any number of places in the program window.

- **Capability to customize.** You can set more than 50 different options in HotDog Pro. You can change the icon bar, define shortcut keys, create custom templates, and nearly redo the whole program. If there's something you don't like about HotDog Pro, you can probably change it to something you do like.

- **Page Builder.** The Page Builder lets you build up a Web page using predefined building blocks that represent the most common elements of Web pages. Just drag in blocks, fill in the details, edit and rearrange, and you're done.

- **Spellchecker.** Every Web editing tool should be required by law to have a spellchecker because it is one of the biggest time-savers, and embarrassment-savers, that a Web author can have. HotDog Pro has it. (Of course, a spellchecker is no good unless you use it, and the Sausage Software Web site has several misspellings.) In addition to American English (the default), spellchecking dictionaries are available for British English, French, German, and Italian.

- **And more.** Additional HotDog Pro features include drag and drop support, graphics file conversion options, macros, plug-in support, frame support, Dynamic HTML support for both Internet Explorer 4.0 and Netscape Navigator 4.0, push channel support for both Internet Explorer 4.0 and Netscape Navigator 4.0, and much more. Supertoolz, available for extra cost, add additional functionality.

And what about HotDog Pro and the many different versions of HTML? For serious Web authoring, HotDog Pro is superior to more sophisticated tools that "hide" HTML because HotDog Pro always shows the HTML tags, so you quickly learn the exact effects of different HTML tags. HotDog Pro supports both Netscape and HTML 3.0 extensions and allows you to customize your use of different kinds of tags. (For a general explanation of HTML tags and tag levels see Chapter 3 and Appendix C.)

The bottom line

Before you invest the money and (more important in the long term) the time to learn a new software package, you may want to consider the future prospects of both the product and the company that develops it. Sausage Software and HotDog do have a few potential problems. A Web page creation tool that doesn't hide HTML is obviously not going to win over everyone. And starting a software company from scratch is very difficult in this day and age; Sausage Software recently had a $5 million dollar annual loss. The company's Web page claims that it sold 30,000 copies of HotDog in its first two years; nothing to sneeze at, but Adobe sold 30,000 copies of PageMill in its first *month*.

However, Sausage Software seems to be making it. Given the quality of its products and the relatively rugged and independent nature of most people who work directly in HTML, The lean organization of Sausage Software and dependence on word-of-mouth marketing may be sufficient to allow it to grow. The biggest question is whether a larger company will buy the HotDog Pro line, which could bring either better or worse products than has been the case to date.

HotDog Pro is worth your consideration today as an excellent tool for editing HTML-tagged text. Though the future of the product and the company are not entirely predictable, the current version of the product works well enough to make HotDog Pro both a good way to understand HTML while getting real work done, and a powerful tool for many serious Web page authors.

Getting HotDog Pro

A demo version of HotDog Pro for Windows 95 is on the CD-ROM that comes with this book. If you have Windows 95, just install the demo from the CD-ROM. You can download a demo version of HotDog for Windows 3.*x* or check for a newer Windows version at the Sausage Software Web site:

www.sausage.com/

Installing the CD-ROM version

To install the standard demo version of HotDog Pro from the CD-ROM, follow these steps:

1. **Insert the CD-ROM into your CD-ROM drive.**

2. **Click the Start button and then choose the Run command.**

3. **In the box, type** D:\HOTDOG\STANDARD.EXE **(substitute your CD-ROM drive letter if different) and then click the OK button.**

4. **Follow the steps of the HotDog Pro installer program.**

You can download files such as non-American-English spelling dictionaries and a patch program to update the version of HotDog Pro that you install from the CD-ROM to a newer version. Follow the steps in the next section, "Downloading the online version."

Downloading the online version

Windows 3.*x* users will need to download the time-limited version of HotDog 16-bit from the Web. Windows 95 and Windows NT users may want to download the time-limited version of HotDog Pro from the Web, instead of using the version on this book's CD-ROM, in order to be sure to have the most up-to-date version. Follow these steps to download the demo version from the Web:

1. **Go to the Sausage Software Web site at**

   www.sausage.com.

2. **Click the Software link in the graphic on the left side of the page.**

   The downloadable software page appears, as shown in Figure 13-2.

3. **Click the Download HotDog now link (Windows 95 or NT 4.0 users) at the bottom of the page.**

   The HotDog Pro 4.5 download page appears.

4. **Scroll down and click the Download HotDog 4.5 link.**

   The installer program for HotDog Pro 4.5 (6MB) is downloaded to your hard drive. Over a 28.8 Kbps modem, the HotDog Pro 4.5 installer download takes about 30 minutes. The file hotdog45 (HotDog Pro) is saved in the download directory in your browser.

5. **Double-click the installer program icon and follow the steps of the installer program.**

When the HotDog Pro installer asks if you want it to create a shortcut for HotDog Professional 4.5 in the Start menu, click the Yes button to make HotDog Pro appear as a folder in the Programs menu (not as a stand-alone button above other options). If you don't, you may have trouble finding the program to start it up.

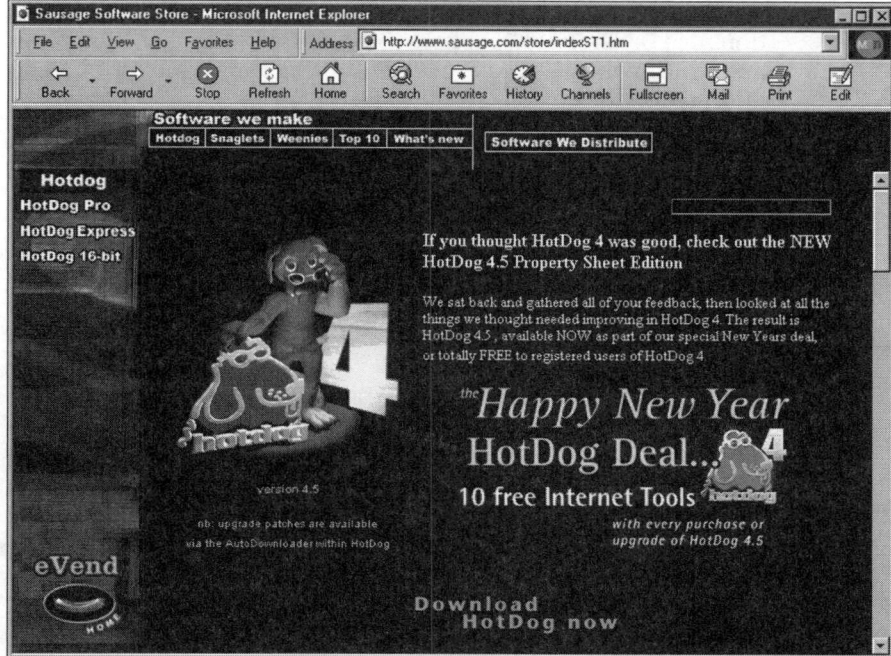

Figure 13-2:
Sausage
Software
download
for HotDog
Pro and
more.

Using HotDog Pro

Creating an initial Web page with HotDog Pro is easy if you know a little HTML. HotDog Pro makes the HTML tags very accessible so you can easily enter them correctly.

Here we show what it takes to use HotDog Pro to accomplish the main steps in creating an initial Web page:

- ✔ Put a title on the page.
- ✔ Enter and format some text.
- ✔ Add a link.
- ✔ Add an image.
- ✔ Look at the Web page produced by the HTML-tagged text.
- ✔ Publish the Web page.

These same steps are covered for each of the Web authoring tools in this book. In this way, you can compare the tools head-to-head on the same tasks. With any of the tools, these steps are much easier than doing the same thing by using HTML directly.

HotDog Pro includes an HTML tutorial as well as HTML reference information. Use the steps shown here to get started and then, if you want to do more with your Web page, use the HotDog Pro HTML tutorial and reference information for help.

Granting yourself a title

Begin by starting a new HotDog Pro document and titling it.

1. **Choose Start⇨Programs⇨HotDog Professional 4⇨HotDog Professional 4.**

   The CISM Wizard transmits your information to Sausage Software and starts HotDog Pro. If you have Internet Explorer installed, the program asks you whether you want to use it instead of the built-in Rover browser. If not, the program starts, and a dialog box appears asking what you want to do.

2. **If HotDog Pro asks you if you want to use Internet Explorer to preview your Web pages instead of the built-in Rover browser, click Yes or No (we suggest No).**

   Using Internet Explorer takes up more screen space than the built-in Rover browser and uses more RAM. We suggest you stick with the Rover browser and preview your Web pages in both Internet Explorer and Netscape Navigator before publication.

   Once you choose an option, the program starts, and a dialog box appears asking what you want to do.

   If you use Internet Explorer as your Web page previewer, HotDog Pro does a good job of showing you what your Web page will look like, just like WYSIWYG programs such as PageMill (see Chapter 12). However, you still have to edit your Web page with HTML tags, and your screen space if very full with both the editing window and Internet Explorer open, so there are still some advantages to WYSIWYG programs.

3. **Click Just Start HotDog.**

   If your computer is sound-capable, you hear the sound of a dog barking. Then HotDog Pro starts and automatically opens to the ReadMe file.

   Do try the other options later; the tutorial is very much worthwhile for understanding the basics of HTML.

4. **Choose File⇨New.**

   The New dialog box appears.

5. **Double-click Normal to open a blank document.**

   A new, untitled window appears, as shown in Figure 13-3.

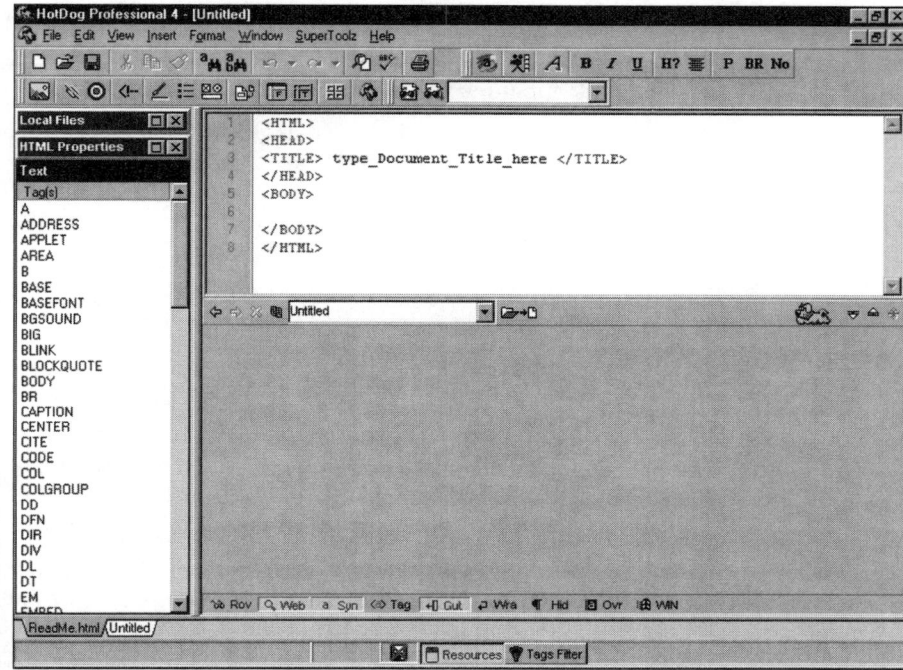

Figure 13-3:
The HotDog
Pro main
program
window.

Don't worry about required HTML tag pairs such as ⟨HTML⟩⟨/HTML⟩,
⟨HEAD⟩⟨/HEAD⟩, and ⟨BODY⟩⟨/BODY⟩; HotDog Professional automatically embeds them in your document.

Later, you can use other HotDog Pro templates such as the default
Web page.

6. Highlight the phrase type_Document_Title_here.

Notice that this text is between the ⟨TITLE⟩ and ⟨/TITLE⟩ HTML tags;
that means this text will be treated as a title and will appear at the top
of the browser window when the finished Web page is displayed.

7. Type the title of your document.

For this example, type **Web Writer Home Page**. You have now titled
your document!

Entering and formatting text

Using HotDog Pro is fun because you can easily and quickly choose the
HTML tags that you want. Though it takes some imagination to figure out
which HTML tags give the effect that you want, you are never surprised at
what's in the actual HTML-tagged text because you create it directly. In the
example included in the following steps, we type and format some text.

1. **In the main part of the HotDog Pro document window, between the** `<BODY>` **and** `</BODY>` **tags, type some text, including a list.**

   The example includes the following text:

   ```
   Web Writer is the exciting new word processing tool for
   the Web. Based on Java, Web Writer saves you the expense
   and hassle of owning a word processing program. Web
   Writer's top 3 features, as told to us by our dozens of
   satisfied beta-test users, are:

   Use it anywhere. Anywhere you can get a Web connection,
   you can use Web Writer.

   No storage hassles. All your data is stored on our secure
   servers here at WebSoft. No need to carry around floppy
   disks or other bulky storage media.

   Automatic backup. Your data is backed up in several
   places on the Internet, which was designed to survive a
   nuclear war! Your data is always safe with Web Writer.
   ```

   Note that your text is displayed twice — once in the Edit View window where you typed it, and once in the Rover View window that displays a preview of your Web page. Use the icons in the upper-right corner of the Rover View window (next to the green dog) to put away and re-trieve (get the pun?) the Rover window as needed.

2. **In the editing window, highlight the text that you want to format.**

   In the example text, highlight "word processing" in the first sentence.

3. **From the button bar, highlight the effect that you want: Bold, Italics, Underline, and so on.**

   The tags for the effect that you choose are inserted around the high-lighted text.

   For this example, choose Bold. In the example, the `<B>` tag is inserted before your highlighted text, and the `</B>` tag is inserted after the highlighted text.

   The idea of having tags automatically inserted around selected text may take a little getting used to, but it's a powerful approach that works well and saves you time.

4. **Highlight the lines that you want to make into a list.**

   In the example text, we highlighted the lines that describe using Web Writer anywhere, with no storage hassles, and automatic backup.

5. **From the Tag(s) menu, double-click UL for Unnumbered List.**

   The text is marked as an unnumbered (bulleted) list.

If you already know some HTML, these terms should make sense to you. If not, read Chapter 3 of this book, experiment, or use the Welcome to HotDog! window's HTML tutorial to understand what the choices mean and how best to use them.

6. For each line in the list, select the line, then double-click the LI tag in the Tag(s) menu (LI means List Item).

Each item is marked as a list item. As each item is marked, the Rover View window updates to reflect the change.

For the example, we highlighted the three features of Web Writer. When we were done, the HotDog Pro screen looked like Figure 13-4.

Window management is an important issue in a complicated program like HotDog Pro. Note that the screen in the example is crowded; you may find yourself frequently resizing windows to see as much of one view or another as you can. Also, note that the user sometimes has to insert carriage returns between tags to make the displayed appearance of the HTML-tagged text cleaner and easier to understand.

Pressing Enter to put a line break in the text as it appears in the HTML editing window does not automatically put a line break in the text that's displayed in a Web page. Insert a Paragraph tag, using the <P> button on the button bar, to force a paragraph break in the text. (A good tip is to put in a <P> tag every place you put in a blank line as a paragraph break.)

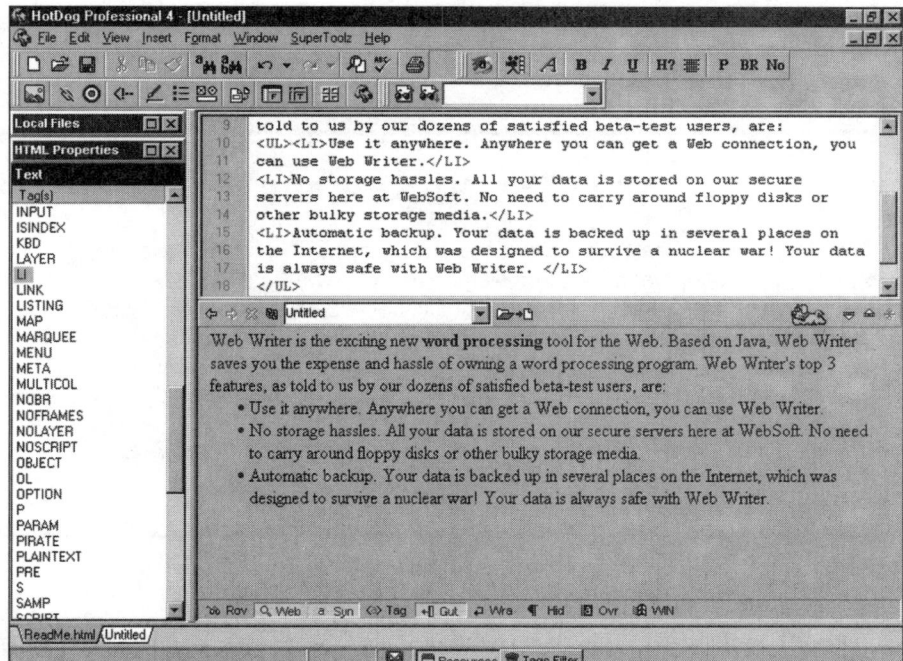

Figure 13-4:
A beginning
HotDog Pro
Web page.

Adding a link

Creating and maintaining links is a tough task, and HotDog Pro doesn't do much to help. You have to understand the different types of links and carefully maintain them as you make changes to your Web site. However, simple linking schemes are fairly easy to implement. Follow these steps to add a link to a local document on your own hard disk:

1. **Insert some text to which you intend to add a link. (Be sure the text is somewhere between the <BODY> and </BODY> tags!)**

   For an example, add the following text:

   ```
   This page was created with HotDog Pro. For more
   information, see the HotDog Pro ReadMe file.
   ```

2. **Highlight the text that you want to serve as a link.**

   In the example, highlight the words "HotDog Pro ReadMe file."

3. **Click the Insert Link button (the one that looks like a link in a chain, second from the left edge of the screen).**

   The Insert Link dialog box appears.

4. **Click the button that looks like an open file folder.**

   The Choose File dialog box appears.

5. **In the scrolling list of files, find the folder HTMLFiles and the file readme. Double-click the readme file to select it.**

   You return to the Insert Link dialog box.

<STRONG> versus <B>

The debate continues over whether to use *physical* HTML tags that tell a browser what to do, such as <B> for bold and <I> for italic, or *logical* tags that let the browser decide for itself, such as <STRONG> (usually displayed as bold) and <EMPHASIZED> (usually displayed as italic). This new version of HotDog Pro leans toward physical tags, as you can see from Figure 13-4. But if you prefer logical tags, which are more in keeping with the spirit of HTML, you can easily change back to logical tags by choosing Options under the Tools menu. Go to the General tab and check the check box, Use Strong and Emphasis, not Bold and Italics. Then pick Save Options to make sure the change is recorded. With the box checked, HotDog Pro uses the logical tags for bold and italics.

6. **Click OK.**

The ⟨A⟩ and ⟨/A⟩ HTML anchor tags surround the text and turn the text into a link. Figure 13-5 shows how the screen looks at this point. The last line near the bottom of the Edit View window, just above the ⟨/BODY⟩ tag, has the link. The Rover View window shows the link text highlighted.

Adding an image

HotDog Pro makes it easy to add an image and, optionally, to use that image as an icon to load other documents. Adding an image in HotDog Pro is a lot like adding a link. Just choose the Insert Image icon, use a dialog box to find the image on your hard disk, specify other documents and a text description if you want, and then click OK. Here are the steps that you follow:

1. **Create or obtain an image to include in your document.**

The image should be in GIF or JPEG format. Free clip art from a number of sources is available on the Web; see Chapter 7 for more information. In this example, we use a GIF file from the HotDog Pro folder.

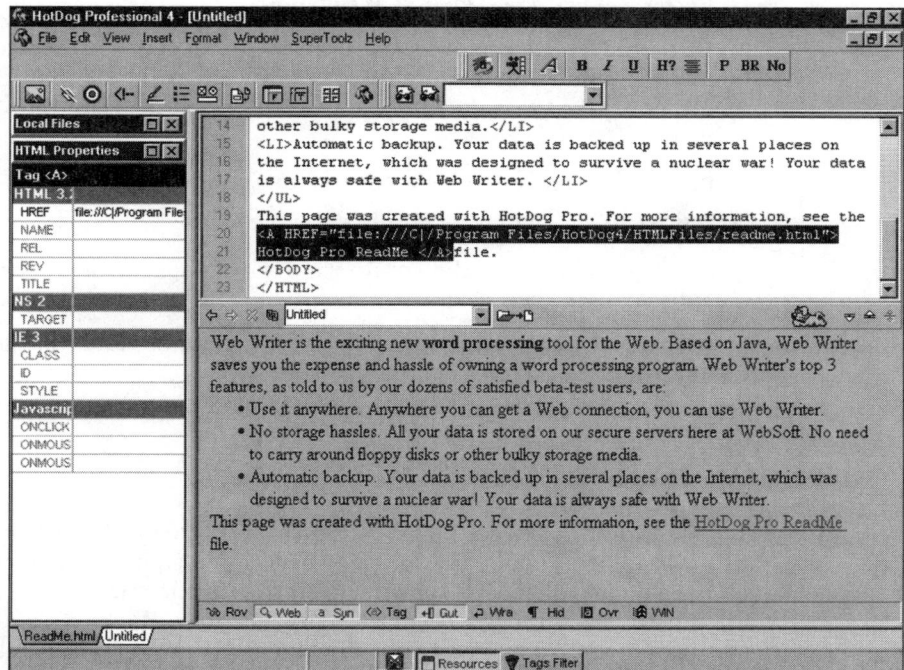

Figure 13-5:
Linking from one local page to another.

HotDog Pro doesn't include a preview mode for graphics. Use a program that can view graphics such as the Paint program that comes with Windows 95 to search through the resources available to you and find the image that you need. Then write down the filename and pathname of the image that you need so that you can quickly enter them in HotDog Pro.

2. **In the Web document that you're creating in HotDog Pro, put the cursor at the location where you want to insert an image.**

3. **Click the Insert Image button (the left-most button in the button bar).**

   The Insert Image dialog box appears.

4. **Under the Filename prompt, click the button that looks like an open button folder.**

   The Open dialog box appears and is already set to the Graphics folder within the HotDog4 folder.

5. **Browse your hard disk to find the image file that you want to include in your document. Double-click the file.**

   In the example, we use an image from the HotDog Pro Graphics folder.

6. *Optional:* **If you want to launch a document when the image that you're adding to your document is clicked, select the document under the prompt, Document to Launch.**

7. *Optional (recommended):* **If you want to display a text message in browsers that either don't display graphics or have graphics turned off, enter the message under the prompt Text description of the image.**

   In this example, enter **This page made with HotDog**.

8. **Click OK.**

   HotDog Pro displays the appropriate HTML tags for the choices you entered.

   Figure 13-6 shows what the HotDog Pro document looks like after following these steps.

Publishing your Web page

Like most other HTML editing tools, HotDog Pro creates HTML-tagged text files that can be published on any Web server. It also has a publishing feature that can consolidate all your Web site documents, update local links, and more in order to make it easier to publish your Web site. Check out the Sausage Software Web site and the documentation that comes with HotDog Pro for more information. Also, see Chapter 8 for a general description of how to get an account on a Web server, transfer your files to the server, and test the site after it's up on the Web.

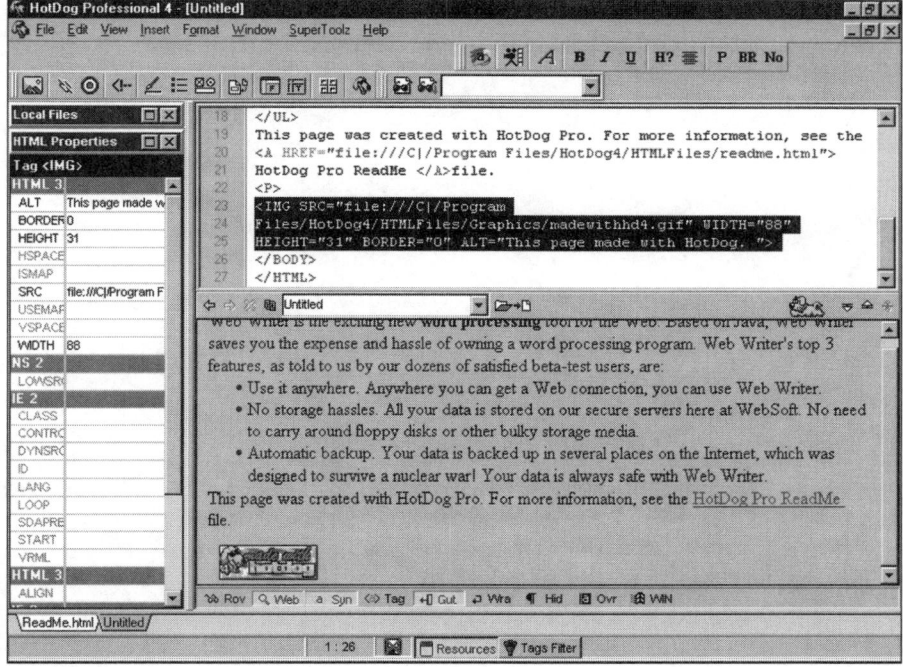

Figure 13-6:
Web Writer
ready to
write off
into the
sunset.

HotDog Pro and Beyond

The previous set of steps gave you a feel for the power — and some of the
problems — of HotDog Pro. If the program feels like a good fit for your
needs, spend some additional time exploring and using it. (Especially check
out the customization options; you can make the program work nearly any
way you want to.) If you decide to buy the program, you can do so at any
time from the Sausage Software Web site.

You may be able to get a better deal than the $129.95 price available on the
Sausage Software Web site. Several years ago we were able to get a boxed
copy of HotDog Pro 2.0 at CompUSA for $49, with a sticker on the box
promising a free upgrade to the then-new Version 3.0. That deal would get
you not only more than half off the sticker price, but printed documentation
to boot.

The complete feature set and HTML emphasis of HotDog Pro give you plenty
of room to grow with the program. If you want to become a serious Web
page author who can work flexibly with HTML, use HotDog Pro and its
associated online documentation to really learn the ins and outs of HTML.
You'll gain the ability to create and debug Web sites that work for the widest
possible range of users, while getting the most out of the Web.

Chapter 14

More Authoring Tools

*N*ot all of the top Web authoring tools are full-fledged authoring packages like those covered in detail in Chapters 10 through 13. Many standard office applications now support Web publishing to some degree, and on the Web and elsewhere you can find word processor add-ons, file converters, simple packages to create an initial Web page, and more. We gathered many of the best into this chapter and onto the CD-ROM that comes with this book.

The Web is a fast-changing place, and new tools are appearing all the time. We think the full-fledged authoring packages covered in previous chapters and the additional tools covered here are the best, but you may disagree. Better tools and upgrades to currently available tools are on the way. So use this book and the CD-ROM as starting points, and then check the Web for new tools, new versions, and new ideas.

How to Find Tools

We recommend several sites as excellent sources for information on Web authoring tools. Unfortunately, more complete review information exists for Windows tools than for Macintosh. But Macintosh users, don't despair — good tools are out there. (And you got PageMill before the PC side did.) Also, no matter which platform you use, check out information on all tools. The best and most popular of the tools that are single-platform today may be ported to other platforms tomorrow.

Check out these sites for information and reviews of Web tools:

Forrest Stroud's Consummate Winsock Apps list. For this excellent list of Windows HTML authoring applications with complete reviews, go to

`www.stroud.com`

TUCOWS, The Ultimate Collection of Winsock Software. Here is another great list and also a great Web site (see Figure 14-1); each tool gets a rating in number of cows.

To find it, go to

`www.tucows.com/`

If you compare the information in Stroud's list, TUCOWS, the Davis list described next, and this book, you can get a really good idea of which key applications may meet your needs.

Carl Davis' HTML Editor Reviews. This site is so hot that Carl Davis has to keep moving it to donated space on bigger and bigger servers. To link to the current site, go to

`homepage.interaccess.com/~cdavis/edit_rev.html`

Figure 14-1:
TUCOWS
for the price
of none!

Converters and so on versus Web authoring tools

As an aspiring Web author, you're going to face the question: Should I try to use tools that I already have to create my first World Wide Web page, or should I use specific Web authoring tools? We lean toward using specific Web authoring tools.

Many word processing programs and other office programs such as spreadsheets have "save as HTML" capability that allows you to save your normal office files in Web-ready format. And converters exist that will translate almost any file into Web-ready HTML format. The trouble is, the result rarely comes out looking exactly the way you want it to. This is because your standard office programs were not originally built for the Web, so they allow you to think that you have much more control over the look of your page than the Web allows. When you convert files from your office program to the Web, most of the formatting is thrown away in the conversion to the much simpler Web formatting. Also, the resulting Web page may have formatting errors, or may work well on some browsers but not others.

The natural reaction that you may have when you see problems in your converted Web page is to go in and fix them up — but to do so requires detailed knowledge of HTML and lots of time, neither of which you are likely to have.

(If you knew HTML well, you would have just written the Web page in HTML in the first place! And who has lots of time these days?) The better course is to create your Web pages using one of the full-featured Web-specific tools described in Chapters 10 through 13, which only let you create formatting that will work well on the Web.

So why bother with built-in "save as HTML" capabilities or conversion tools at all? Some people love their word processors so much they would rather use them than anything else, which is fine. But the major purpose of such tools is to convert large numbers of existing "legacy" documents to the Web. (Legacy documents are earlier documents saved in a format no longer commonly used on computers.) Another purpose is to create a large number of least-common-denominator documents that don't look great in print and on the Web, but don't look bad on either. To perform either of these functions, you need to become somewhat expert in using your word processor and somewhat expert in HTML. If you need to convert or create large numbers of Web-ready documents, use this chapter to get started; then use your word processor documentation and the HTML information in Chapter 3 and Appendix C to understand enough HTML to get good at converting files.

Davis has a big table that compares the basics of each package — perfect for matching your specific needs with the current state of the art in editing packages.

Deja News Research Service. This is not a set of reviews but rather a search engine for searching Usenet newsgroups, in which people comment on almost anything, including HTML authoring tools. Start your search at:

www.dejanews.com/

When you search the newsgroups by using Deja News, just use the name of the application that you're interested in. This is the best way to find out the "dirt" on the latest version of the great tool that you heard about — which may turn out to be not so great after all.

Newsgroups. The main newsgroup for Web authoring is

```
comp.infosystems.www.authoring.html
```

Join this newsgroup to keep up with ongoing comments and to contribute your own insights. But before you ask a question, check the Frequently Asked Questions (FAQ) list and use Deja News to see whether the answer is already online. If not, ask away.

Cross-Platform Authoring Tools

As Web page creation tools become more powerful and more popular, the importance of their being cross-platform increases as well. Being cross-platform helps the product gain market share and makes it possible for large shops that have several different kinds of computers to standardize on one tool.

Increasingly, the computer world may seem to be Windows 95 (or 98) and NT-centric. However, this impression is less true of the Web than elsewhere. The Macintosh has a significant share of the Web page creation market and of Web servers; and UNIX is also widely used for Web servers. Even Windows 3.1 is well-represented on the Web; one recent survey of a popular site showed that almost as many hits came from Windows 3.1 as from Windows 95. So no computer platform can be ignored in the quest for the best tools.

The ultimate cross-platform tool is HTML itself. Editable from any text editor or word processor, HTML-tagged text is extremely portable. A basic knowledge of HTML will serve you well whatever kind of computer you use.

Right behind HTML is Netscape Composer, described in detail in Chapter 10. Netscape Composer runs on 32-bit Windows, 16-bit Windows, the Macintosh, and 10 different kinds of UNIX. Netscape Composer is also very easy to use, if a bit behind in the features race.

Mixed shops would do well to standardize on Netscape Composer and then let experts use other tools as well.

Other cross-platform tools run on Windows and Macintosh only, and even that can be sliced more thinly: some tools don't run on Windows 3.1, others don't run on 680 x 0-based Macintoshes (that is, most Macs sold before

1996). Add-ons that work with a specific word processor may run only on more recent versions of the word processor package. So check the system requirements carefully before you buy a tool, or you may end up having to return it and try again.

High-end authoring tools

This book is written for users who are just getting into Web authoring, and it includes tools that meet the needs of beginning and intermediate users. Because of this focus, we don't include tools that are best-suited for intermediate users and above, such as tools that include built-in site management features and that, not coincidentally, tend to have a street price of more than $100. Two excellent tools that fit this description are Microsoft FrontPage and NetObjects Fusion.

Microsoft FrontPage

Microsoft FrontPage is a very powerful Web authoring and site-management tool that retails for about $140. It allows drag-and-drop Web site management as well as drag-and-drop Web authoring. FrontPage is available as FrontPage 98 for Windows 95 and as FrontPage 1.0 for the Macintosh. It's the "big brother" of FrontPage Express, the free Web authoring tool we describe at length in Chapter 10.

Among its many very powerful features, FrontPage has an outstanding image editor for creating Web-based graphics. It also leads in support for ActiveX, described in Chapter 8; however, Netscape Navigator, still the browser used by most people, does not support ActiveX. You will have to get all your site's users to move to Internet Explorer to take advantage of ActiveX if you use this feature.

If you are a heavy user of Microsoft Office, or just need a full-featured Web authoring and site management tool at a reasonable price, consider Microsoft FrontPage.

NetObjects Fusion 3.0

NetObjects Fusion is a site-oriented tool for Web page creation and site management, available for both Windows and Macintosh. Two outstanding features of this tool are its use of a site view as the starting point for your Web work, and its support for precision layout of Web pages — something normally not possible in HTML.

Fusion also has outstanding support for Java-based interactivity. As with ActiveX, not all Web browsers support Java, or support it the same way. However, Java is the wave of the future, and its capabilities make using it worth serious consideration.

NetObjects Fusion 2.0 has been called "the king of Web authoring tools" by no less an authority than C|NET, and its power and breakthrough features support that description for the 3.0 version as well. However, like other kings, the program may seem somewhat unapproachable at first. But if you want to jump into the deep end of the pool, or shoot for the stars, consider NetObjects Fusion 3.0.

The Ant

The Ant is a set of tools for converting Word 6.0 and above files to HTML files and displaying HTML files in a WYSIWYG (What You See Is What You Get) graphical preview, plus other functions. These tools work from within Word 6.0 and provide a great deal of flexibility. They are available for Windows 3.*x*, Windows 95, Windows NT, and the Macintosh. The Ant tools are flexible and customizable as well.

What it's like

The Ant tools work from within Word, giving you flexibility and variety (except that you can't open a Web page from within Word, which is not a big loss). Oops — the tools also don't currently support Microsoft-specific HTML extensions, such as watermarks. But this just means that your pages will be readable by more people.

Using The Ant template is easy and intuitive. The buttons are colorful and intuitive as well. Using the other tools is a bit more work because you have to learn what the tools do and remember when to use them. However, if you need to, for example, convert among HTML and Word, ASCII, and RTF files, The Ant may be invaluable.

Where to get it

For a demonstration version of The Ant tools, check the *Creating Web Pages For Dummies,* CD-ROM. To check for the latest version of the demo, to buy the product, or to get more information, go to The Ant's Web site at:

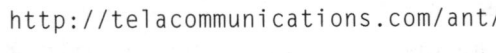

```
http://telacommunications.com/ant/
```

In the URL for The Ant tools, that really is "telacommunications," not "telecommunications."

When to use it

If you're a Macintosh Word 6.0 user, you will find that The Ant is definitely worth trying as a way to use Word for Web-page editing. If you're a user of

Windows Word 6.0 or above, you can try both the Microsoft Internet Assistant for Word and The Ant to see which one fits your needs or to see whether both are useful for different purposes.

What's the buzz?

Comments on the Web call The Ant the best Word template for Web authoring, which is saying something — a lot of Word templates are out there.

The bottom line

If you're a Word user, try The Ant tools first, even if you have access to Internet Assistant for Word. The Ant tools have more HTML functionality, and you may find them to be faster and less buggy.

Windows-Only Authoring Tools

You can find more full HTML authoring tools — as well as other types of tools — for Windows than we are able to cover in this book, although we think we've got the best of them:

- ✔ **Full-authoring tools.** Numerous full authoring tools exist besides the cross-platform Netscape Composer and Adobe PageMill, the Windows-only FrontPage Express and HotDog Pro, and the Windows-compatible full authoring tools covered in previous chapters. One good tool is InContext Spider, covered later in this chapter. Others include HoTMetaL and HoTMetaL Pro, very popular text-based packages somewhat like (but recently less celebrated than) HotDog.

- ✔ **Application extensions and add-ins.** Most major word processing and desktop publishing programs now have updated versions or add-ins that provide varying levels of HTML authoring capability. Check Deja News, described earlier, or check with the manufacturer of your favorite word processor or desktop publishing package to see what's available for your application. In this chapter, Ant Tools is an example of an application add-in.

- ✔ **Limited-function authoring tools.** A number of authoring tools have limited functionality because they're designed to be easy to use for a specific purpose. One such tool that's received lots of applause is WEB Wizard, a tool for creating an initial Web page.

- ✔ **Other tools.** Dozens of PC tools are for other Internet functions such as Web graphics, Common Gateway Interface (CGI) scripting, Web site management, and many, many other purposes. Another book would be required to (start to!) cover it all. After you master the basics of HTML authoring, use the sites listed earlier in this chapter to investigate these additional kinds of tools.

InContext Spider

InContext Spider is a full-fledged HTML authoring tool from the hot Internet company InContext. InContext is a leader in tools for Standard Generalized Markup Language (SGML), the document markup language from which HTML was derived. InContext is in touch with the most advanced and complex issues that relate to Web authoring.

As you might expect, therefore, Spider has several advanced features, such as the Logical Editor that provides a tree-like view of your document. But these features are matched to an interface that is confusing to novices, in some ways because of the program's very power.

What it's like

The demo version of InContext Spider is certainly the most robust demo that you're likely to see. The file that we downloaded for testing was 9MB, and the installation took several minutes. The demo version's time limit runs out quickly — 30 days after you get it — and it's plain that InContext intends for anyone who uses the program to buy it.

When you start InContext Spider, you get a choice of templates to use. After you choose a template (and you should preview them all at some point to see what's available), the program really starts. The editing window is split between a tree-and-leaf representation of your document and a more typical editing window (see Figure 14-2). You have to figure out the tree-and-leaf thing to feel comfortable working, and that requires a look at the documentation provided with the demo. The documentation is in Microsoft Help File format and is easy to access through the program's Help menu, but expect to click around and read for a while.

After you get over the initial learning curve, you will find that Spider is a powerful tool for use with larger Web sites. The Logical Editor works like an outliner that can enable you to quickly move through your document. When you get the full version of the program, the integration with the built-in Spider Mosaic browser can also be helpful.

Where to get it

On the *Creating Web Pages For Dummies* CD-ROM, we've included a multimedia movie that demonstrates some of InContext Spider's features. To check for the latest version of the demo, to buy the product, or to get more information, go to InContext's Web site at

www.incontext.ca/

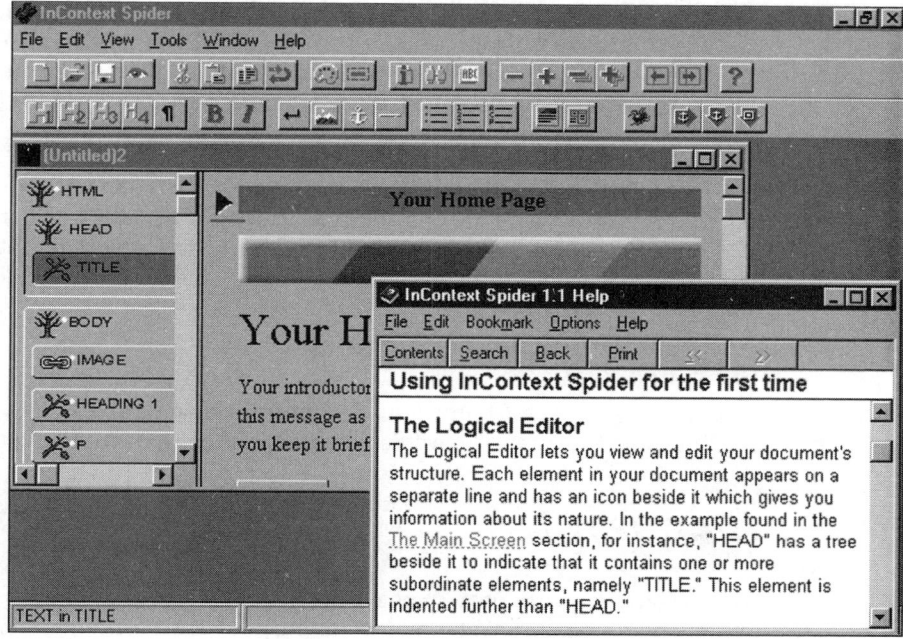

Figure 14-2:
Spin a
Web with
InContext
Spider.

The InContext Web site also has information on InContext's other tools, including authoring tools for SGML. SGML is used in many large shops as a standard way of saving and exchanging documents.

When to use it

If you're using SGML or working in an environment that does, take a hard look at Spider and other tools from InContext. And if you really like using an outlining program or the outlining features of your word processor or spreadsheet, you may feel very comfortable with InContext Spider. Otherwise, take a look at the program and its documentation and see whether the look and feel of the program appeal to you. If so, consider plunging further and using Spider as your main Web authoring tool. If not, keep Spider in mind. As you grow in your Web authoring skills and create more complex Web pages, you may want to revisit this tool.

What's the buzz?

The main newsgroup comments about InContext are how hot its stock was just after the company went public, not the merits of Spider or other InContext products. Oh well.

Online reviews are mixed. People aren't sure how to use the product, and they think it takes too long to figure out the product compared to most of the other Web authoring tools out there. True enough. But Spider is a deeper program than most, and it rewards the serious efforts of those who learn to use it.

InContext and Microsoft just announced plans to integrate Microsoft Internet Explorer into the Spider package and support Microsoft Internet Explorer extensions in Spider. This is a good thing if you want to depend on Microsoft products, but may not be so good if you want your pages to be readable by users of non-Microsoft browsers.

The bottom line

InContext Spider is probably a bit much if you're a novice, unless you really like outlining tools. But keep this program in mind for more advanced work.

WEB Wizard

WEB Wizard is a very easy-to-use tool with a specific purpose: to create an initial, uncomplicated Web page. In its purpose and workings, WEB Wizard is not unlike the Web-based Web-page-creation tools described in Chapter 4 and the online-service Web-page-creation tools described in Chapter 5. However, WEB Wizard is just as easy — or maybe even easier — to use. And you have the HTML file right there on your hard disk in case you need to do more editing with a text editor (if you want to mess with HTML tags yourself) or with one of the other tools described here or included on the CD-ROM that came with this book. The bad news is that you have the HTML file right there on your hard disk, not on a Web server (yet). You need to find space on a Web server and upload the HTML file to it when you're ready.

Where to get it

You'll find the Windows version of WEB Wizard on this book's CD-ROM. To check for an update or download the promised Macintosh version go to

www.halcyon.com/artamedia/webwizard/

If you search for WEB Wizard information on the Web, be sure to search for "WEB Wizard" with a space between the words. If you don't, you'll get lots of hits. (Even if you're careful and include the space, you'll still get lots of hits because so many people describe themselves as Web wizards.)

What it's like

It's, as we keep saying, easy. WEB Wizard puts up eight screens covering the following topics:

- ✔ Title
- ✔ Background color
- ✔ Image
- ✔ Text
- ✔ List
- ✔ Links
- ✔ E-mail address
- ✔ Filename

Simply provide the requested information in each screen. Figure 14-3 shows a sample screen from WEB Wizard. To go into more detail here would probably take more of your time than it will for you if you try it yourself.

When to use it

Use WEB Wizard for two purposes:

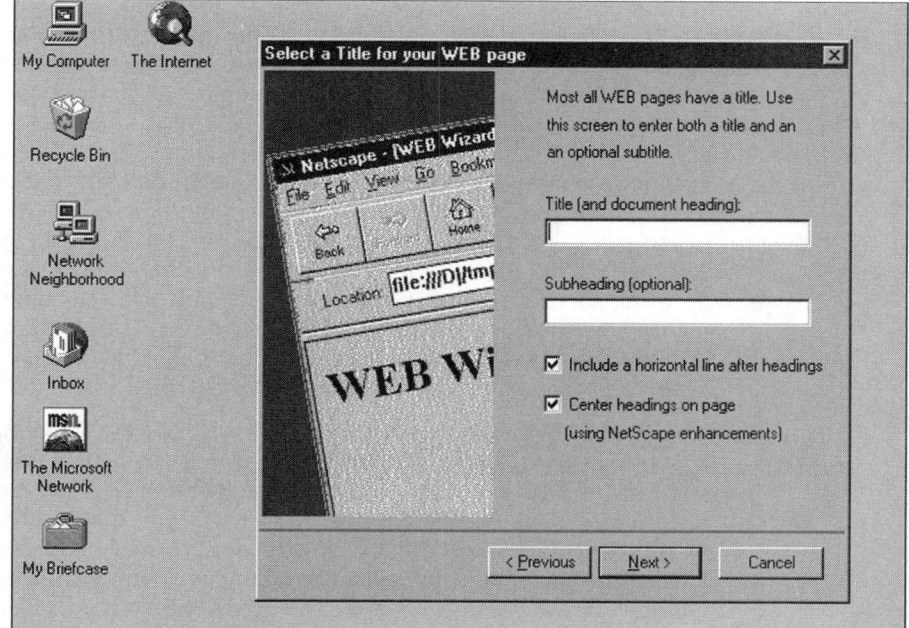

Figure 14-3: Whiz onto the Web with WEB Wizard.

> ✔ To create your own first Web page
>
> ✔ To give to your friends who bug you about how to create a Web page

What's the buzz?

The good news: Artamedia says that a Mac version of WEB Wizard is coming soon.

The bad news: They've been saying that since late 1995, and we still haven't seen it yet.

More good news: The tool does what it says it's going to do — and does it well. (And no bad news with this one!)

You won't need WEB Wizard much after you learn some HTML or how to use another Web authoring tool. But you'll still have WEB Wizard for fending off your friends who are *home-page-deprived*.

The bottom line

Try this just for fun and spread it around. This tool is a good one.

Macintosh-Only Authoring Tools

You can find somewhat fewer full HTML authoring tools for the Macintosh than for the PC, and we've covered the best of the easy-to-use offerings thoroughly in this book. But look for upcoming developments and check out some of the other HTML-related tools.

✔ **Full authoring tools.** The most popular Macintosh Web authoring tools are the ones that have their own chapters in this book: Netscape Composer (also a Windows and UNIX tool — see Chapter 11), and Adobe PageMill (also a Windows tool — see Chapter 12). Also worth knowing about are NetObjects Fusion 3.0, which will become available on the Macintosh shortly after its debut on the PC, and Microsoft FrontPage 1.0, which is available on Macintosh. (Later versions of FrontPage such as FrontPage 98 are not available for Macintosh.)

✔ **Application extensions and add-ins.** As with the PC, most major word processing and desktop publishing programs now have updated versions or add-ins that provide varying levels of HTML authoring capability. Check Deja News, described earlier in this chapter, or check with the manufacturer of your favorite word processor or desktop publishing package to see what's available for your application. In this chapter, The Ant is an example of an application add-in.

✔ **Limited-function authoring tools.** A number of authoring tools have limited functionality because they're designed to be very easy to use for a specific purpose, including several easy-to-use HyperCard stacks for Web authoring. Check the Macintosh-related areas of the Web information sources described at the start of the chapter — the ones that aren't Windows-specific, anyway — for such tools.

✔ **Other tools.** Dozens of Macintosh tools exist for other Internet functions like Web graphics, Common Gateway Interface (CGI) scripting, Web site management, and many, many other purposes. After you've mastered the basics of HTML authoring, use the sites listed at the start of this chapter to investigate these additional kinds of tools.

Other Macintosh tools on the CD-ROM that comes with this book include two tools for converting files to HTML format and a tool for easily creating tables, which is especially valuable for use with the freeware version of BBEdit or any other tool that doesn't support table creation.

BBEdit and HTML Tools

BBEdit is a very popular shareware text editor for the Macintosh, and its popularity has greatly increased due to the availability of two excellent sets of BBEdit extensions for Web authoring: Lindsay Davies' BBEdit HTML tools, and Carle Bellver's HTML Extensions. Lindsay Davies' BBEdit HTML Tools are now included as part of BBEdit, so they're the ones you're more likely to end up using.

BBEdit is very popular; it's won awards for its capabilities as a Web authoring tool. If you start using BBEdit for HTML authoring, you'll be joining a distinguished group of Web authors who work on the Macintosh and who do much of their work directly with HTML.

Learning BBEdit and the BBEdit HTML tools takes some doing. You work directly with text and HTML tags; no built-in preview mode is available, although you can always look at the HTML-tagged text in a browser to see how the Web page is coming along. Many people use other programs to create their initial Web pages and then use BBEdit to fine-tune the HTML tags directly.

If you are a Macintosh user and need easy-to-learn tools for editing the HTML text of your Web pages, BBEdit with HTML Extensions is the tool of choice.

BBEdit Lite, a freeware version of BBEdit, and Lindsay Davies' BBEdit HTML Tools are on the CD-ROM that comes with this book. For an updated version and further information about the program, go to

www.barebones.com

TextToHTML

TextToHTML converts text and RTF (Rich Text Format) documents to HTML format. Any word processor or text editor can save its documents to text or RTF, which makes TextToHTML a flexible tool indeed.

To set up TextToHTML, run the Setup TextToHTML application. Then create or locate a text or RTF document that you want to convert. (If you have a choice of how to save a document from a word processor, for example, choose RTF format instead of text. Much more formatting should be preserved.) Now for the fun part. Just drag your text or RTF document over the TextToHTML icon, and it automatically is converted.

You will find that TextToHTML is really easy to use and flexible. However, it's very much freeware; if the program doesn't work, you shouldn't expect any recourse or fixes.

TextToHTML is on this book's CD-ROM. For the latest version and more info, go to:

```
http://ourworld.compuserve.com/homepages/kristiaan/
          software.htm
```

This URL takes you to an archive file that decompresses automatically to a readme file, which explains more about the program and how to use it.

HTML TableTool

HTML TableTool, shown in Figure 14-4, is a small, special-purpose HyperCard stack that has a valuable role: It creates HTML tables. To get the tool, go to this URL:

```
www.ncl.ac.uk/wwwtools/htmltabletool.html
```

The archive file you find at this URL decompresses automatically to a readme file that explains more about the program and how to use it.

To use HTML TableTool, follow this process:

1. **Create your table in a spreadsheet or database.**

2. **Save the table as a tab-delimited text file.**

3. **Open TableTool by double-clicking on it.**

4. **Click the Open button to open the text file.**

   The text file is automatically converted to a table and displayed in a scrollable, editable window inside the program.

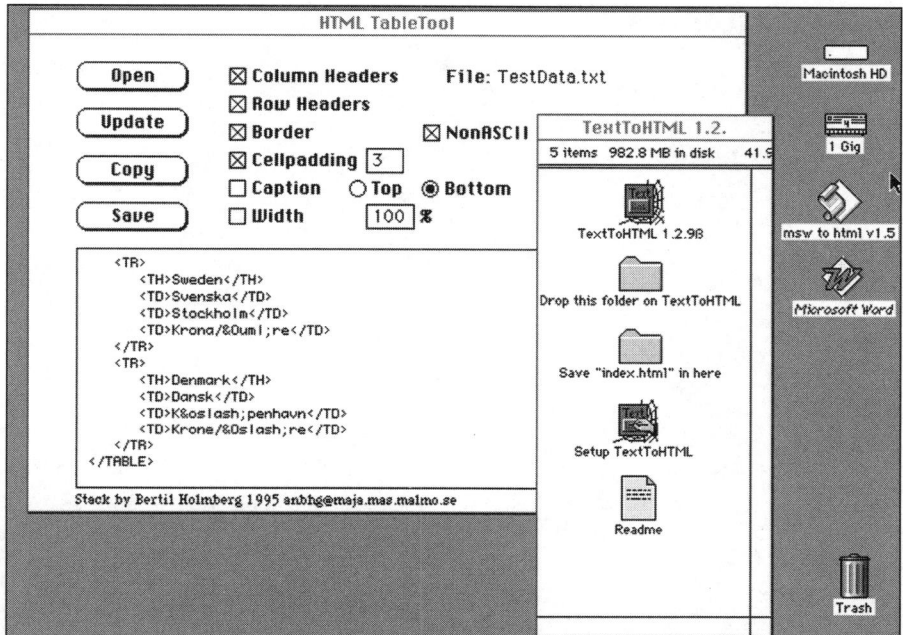

The bottom line

These tools are just a few of the best of the hundreds of Windows, Macintosh, and UNIX shareware and freeware utilities available on the World Wide Web. Use the resources at the start of this chapter to search for additional tools that meet your needs.

Part V
The Part of Tens

The 5th Wave   By Rich Tennant

"Can someone please tell me how long 'Larry's Lunch Truck' has been co-authoring our new corporate Web page?"

In this part . . .

Our Top Tens tell you the DO's and DON'Ts of creating Web pages so you can look like a pro your first time out on the Web.

Chapter 15
Ten Web Publishing DO's

In This Chapter

▶ Do think about your target audience

▶ Do use good sites as models

▶ Do get permissions for content

▶ Do use links to outside sites

▶ Do use graphics and multimedia

▶ Do think before you create

▶ Do ask for feedback

▶ Do test your pages

▶ Do publicize your site

▶ Do update your site

Anyone else remember Mr. Do-Bee from the *Romper Room* TV show of the 1960s? He was famous for words of wisdom that always began, "Mr. Do-Bee says. . . . " Well, if Mr. Do-Bee were a Web author, here are ten things he would definitely do.

DO think about your target audience

Who is your Web site targeting? A little thought along those lines can make your pages much more appealing to your visitors. Before you begin creating your Web site, choose the right look and feel and style of presentation that is appropriate for your audience. Include links that your visitors find interesting, not just the ones that you find interesting — unless that's the point of your page, of course. In addition to using good sites as models (see the next "DO"), research other media, such as newspapers and magazines — the articles and the ads — that have a similar audience as yours to find good and bad examples.

DO use good sites as models

Many good sites are out there. Ignoring those good examples when designing your own site is not the best idea. Take a look around and find the designs that work. Think about why each design you like works well for you. Is it the use of color and layout of the Web page? The fact that the site loads quickly? Well-organized content? Note what works and why, and then strive to duplicate that effect in your own Web pages. Look for conventions in presenting information that Web users have grown accustomed to, neat design ideas, and various types of content. You'll be surprised how many ideas you get from this huge reservoir of Web expertise.

DO get permissions for content

You can easily peek at the HTML source of any Web page, and that's a good way to learn new design techniques. But you can also easily grab any content that exists on the Web, even privately owned content that belongs to others. However, the fact that grabbing others' content is easy does not make it right or legal. It's also not necessary.

A great deal of public domain content is out there, and getting permission to use private content is not hard. If a Web page does not explicitly say that its content can be freely borrowed, assume that it's copyrighted or otherwise protected — which means you should ask before borrowing any of it. Many people are happy to let you use their content in order to gain exposure on your pages, as long as you provide proper attribution and reciprocal links. In the process, you may just gain new friends or business contacts, as well as avoid legal problems down the road. (And in case you get tempted to borrow quietly, keep in mind that word of unethical practices gets around quickly on this amazing global network.)

DO use links to outside sites

No matter how great your content is, you'd be wasting the most important feature of the Web if you did not include links to sites outside your own. No matter what your topic, you can find complementary sites out there on the Web. Giving your visitors links to those sites is only courteous. If you research your links carefully and organize them well, your links can be a valuable resource to others. In your own Web surfing, you've probably found it to be true that one of the best experiences on the Web is the serendipity of stumbling upon some cool link that you had no idea existed; give your visitors that experience. Point them to the outside world. That's why it's the Web and not the Thread.

DO use graphics and multimedia

A prime attraction of the Web is that it is designed to present graphical information, yet there are still many beginning Web authors who are intimidated by graphics and shy away from using them. Include a picture, icons, bars, and graphical menus in your Web page. Go ahead, try out transparent and interlaced GIFs. Multimedia is a great addition too; one or two sound files, a QuickTime movie, even a simple animated GIF can really liven up a site. The bottom line is that sites rich with graphics and multimedia are much more interesting than purely text-oriented ones. Give it a go. (But be prudent; see Chapter 16 for a matching DON'T.)

DO think before you create

It may sound basic, but a surprising number of people just jump in and start throwing around text and HTML tags with no clue about where they're going or what they want to accomplish. That approach is fine if you just want to play around —in fact, that approach can be a lot of fun. But if you want to make a good impression on the Web, sitting down and thinking about a few things ahead of time really pays off. Sketch your ideas on paper. Then describe them to someone else and ask for feedback. This prep work forces you to consider things that you may not think about otherwise: Page layout, graphic design, relationship between pages, target audience, content structure, link grouping, and other issues that, when properly integrated, can make your site a first-class Net surfing experience.

DO ask for feedback

You'll be amazed by what people say about your pages. (Some of the comments may even be complimentary!) Put your e-mail address on your home page and ask for comments. People who have never before seen your site will have a good, fresh perspective and can give you feedback on things that you may not have thought about. Everyone can benefit from outside input. Criticism by your prospective audience is not only useful, it's also educational. You can learn a lot about what people expect and want. Criticism can't hurt anything but your pride, and it almost always improves your site.

DO test your pages

Testing your pages is easy. You probably don't send e-mail without spell-checking it. Similarly, you should not put up your Web pages without testing them. That means looking at your pages on your own machine before testing them on the Web — follow links, see how graphics and text fit together, and so on. Also, looking at your pages in different browsers doesn't hurt. If you can't do it, ask a friend or even a stranger to help. Oh, again, don't forget to spellcheck your pages.

DO publicize your site

Nothing is more frustrating than putting up a site that no one visits. Fortunately, publicizing your site is not hard. Add your site to the popular indexes, for example, through the excellent Submit–It site:

```
www.submit-it.com/
```

You can also post to appropriate Usenet newsgroups, put out a press release, or shout it from the rooftops. Just building a site doesn't necessarily mean people will come to it. You still have to get the word out.

DO update your site

A static site is a boring site. True, it works for some purposes, but in general, if you want people to continually revisit your site, you must keep it updated. The best sites are those that continually provide new and interesting content. Include pointers to information that's frequently updated, like "Thought for the day" or "Links to new, cool sites." Let users know how often to expect updates and be sure to showcase new content. A "New" icon next to recently added or updated content can work wonders.

Chapter 16
Ten Web Publishing DON'Ts

So, does Mr. Do-Bee, mentioned in Chapter 15, have an evil twin, Mr. Don't-Be? Well, don't be repeating others' mistakes. Avoid these Web publishing don'ts.

DON'T inadvertently limit your audience

Be careful when designing your pages not to inadvertently limit your audience by using some oddball feature that can't be read by large numbers of people who use different Web browsers. Stick to basic HTML and Netscape additions through Netscape Navigator Version 2.0. Think twice before using HTML frames, Java programs, or ActiveX programs; many people won't be able to access them. Warn people if you use nonstandard features. Often providing alternative pages, such as text-only versions of your pages, is worthwhile. And including links to the software that works with your pages often pays off — a link to Netscape if you use Navigator-specific tags, or a link to the RealAudio site if you include RealAudio sound, are two good examples.

DON'T abuse netiquette

Abusing the etiquette of the Internet is easy to do and can bring you a lot of negative attention. If you make any serious offenses, your Web service provider's server may remove your pages. And you can even get into legal problems. Avoid dubious practices such as *spamming*, sending unwanted e-mail to publicize your site; *flaming*, being fervently disparaging of other people or other Web pages; or putting up offensive material without some kind of warning label. Netiquette is an amorphous and evolving area of online behavior, so you may want to join a Web-oriented newsgroup where you can ask questions before publishing. Also, check out this site for more info: www.fau.edu/rinaldi/netiquette.html.

DON'T "borrow" content without asking

Make sure that content you get from the Web to use on your own Web page is labeled as being freely available for reuse, or else get permission to reuse it. Most people are quite happy to help if you ask nicely and credit their work. The best part is that you make some good contacts with other interesting people. You also keep the law on your side.

DON'T make your site hard to navigate

Beginners often organize their pages so that their sites are hard to navigate. If your site has more than two levels, you should give some thought as to how your visitors will navigate it. Nobody likes wandering from link to link with no idea what is where or having to follow ten links to find one piece of information. Keep the relationship between your pages simple. Make it clear which links are internal to your own site and which go out to other sites. Provide an index page or a common menu. And make navigation work consistently throughout the site.

DON'T abuse graphics and multimedia

The biggest mistake beginning Web authors — and some experts — make is overusing graphics on a page. Keep in mind that not everyone has fast, expensive T1 lines (special high-bandwidth phone lines) wired directly to their home PCs; by far, the greatest majority of folks receive your Web pages via a more limited 28.8 Kbps modem. Keep your page size, including text and graphics, under 100K. Here are ways that you can do this without sacrificing design flexibility:

  ✔ Convert all photos to JPEG format.
  ✔ Use simple icons and banners — images without very many colors or complex textures —in GIF format.

✔ Lay out your site to limit the amount of graphics on any one page, adding pages if you need to display more graphics.

✔ Use thumbnail icons to give access to larger images.

All those strategies make your pages smaller and faster for others to download. Your Net surfers will thank you.

DON'T forget ALT tags and text-equivalent menus

Another basic mistake is not using text-equivalent menus forgetting that many people surf the Net without graphics turned on. Who would turn off graphics, you ask?

Many home users turn off graphics to speed things along, downloading only the graphics that they really need. Some people pay a high hourly rate for their Internet access, especially in much of the non-Western world, and turn off graphics to save money on their connection time. Others receive Web pages via e-mail because they don't have a direct Internet connection. And some people who are visually impaired use the Web with software that translates text — but not graphics — into spoken words. Always use the ALT tag to provide text equivalents to your graphics, as described in Chapter 7. Using the ALT tag is easy to do and will make it possible and easier for all these people to access your content.

DON'T forget the basics

Your site may be the greatest thing since sliced bread, but if you forget to include contact information for yourself in the site, how will you find out that you misspelled "bureaucracy" all over the place? Similarly, you won't get many orders for your spiffy new widget if you put the ordering information five levels down in a Web page called "Fruitbat guano statistics – 1876." More basics:

✔ Use mailto: tags (HTML tags used to specify your e-mail address; for example, `<A HRES="MAILTO:comments@mysite.com>`).

✔ Include a copyright notice.

✔ Add an index.

✔ Give credit where credit is due.

✔ Make the important info prominent. Be ready to revise, based on user feedback.

DON'T start by setting up your own Web server

There are several "easy-to-use" Web server packages on the market, and Web server capability is even being built into Macs and PCs. But even with these efforts, buying, setting up, and maintaining a Web server can become the most expensive, most complicated, and most frustrating part of Web publishing. Luckily, you can use the free services described in this book, or paid services, to put your content on someone else's Web server while you learn the other tricks of the trade. Then, as your knowledge and experience grow, consider setting up your own Web server.

DON'T forget the "World" in World Wide Web

Remember that your Web pages are available and accessible to the whole world. Think a bit about that foreign audience. Is it worthwhile to include some foreign language content? Do you use colloquialisms that may not be understood by your foreign Net surfers? How do your pages look to your overseas colleagues who view them through the slow transoceanic Net link? Will your humorous or risqué content offend someone in another country or culture?

When you become a Web publisher, you also become a global citizen, and your Web pages play on a global stage. Think through the meaning of your page in advance.

DON'T be afraid to learn more

Web publishing is not rocket science. It *is* computer science, but it's relatively easy computer science. You're not trying to land the space shuttle here —and chances are, lives are not at stake. Experiment, try weird things. Ask for feedback. Never be afraid to learn complex and hard stuff. (It's only complex and hard because you don't understand it yet!) Neat stuff is being developed (and some cool stuff is already out there) that will make Web publishing even more exciting — VRML, Java, new browsers and publishing tools, groupware, Net-based games, and online business infrastructure. All this new stuff is understandable and usable by normal folks like you. Don't be intimidated. You can use all of them. (If you've come this far, you've got what it takes!)

Part VI
Appendixes

The 5th Wave   By Rich Tennant

"I heard you say you needed a new Web dowser, Andy, and I thought old gramps could help out, but dang if I can find one that'll work!"

In this part . . .

This part includes appendixes that are a bridge to a wide range of different kinds of resources, including Web publishing definitions, Web service providers, HTML tag definitions, and developer resources that are online.

Appendix A
Web Words Worth Knowing

This glossary defines important terms used in this book. To see where a term is used in the book, check the index.

Absolute address. A description of a file's location that starts with the machine name or disk name on which the file is located. See also *Pathname,* and *Relative address.*

Anchor. One end of a link between two files. When you look at a Web page, the underlined, colored text that you see is an anchor at one end of a hypertext link. Clicking the text brings up another Web page, which is the anchor at the other end of the link.

Animated GIF. A GIF graphic that includes several slightly different images in sequence. Up-to-date browsers that support animated GIFs display the graphics one at a time to create an animation.

Attribute. In HTML, an attribute is a set of characters after the first set within an HTML tag. It modifies the tag's (see *Tag*) purpose. Example: In the tag `<IMG SRC="budpic.jpg">`, the attribute is `SRC`.

Browser. A program used to look at World Wide Web documents. Mosaic was the first popular browser, and Netscape Navigator is currently the market leader, with Microsoft Internet Explorer gaining momentum.

Clickable image map. A graphic that includes areas called "hot spots," which, when clicked, take you to different Web pages or locations within a Web page. Many large Web sites use clickable image maps on their home pages to entice the user to move farther into the site.

Common Gateway Interface script (CGI script). A program used to transfer data from an HTML form (see *Form*) to an application. The CGI script runs on the server that hosts the Web page that has the form.

Definition list. A type of HTML list in which terms occupy a column on the left side of the screen and definitions occupy a wider column on the right side.

Domain name. A domain name represents a Web site to the outside world. In the United States the domain name can end in `.com` (for businesses), `.edu` (for educational institutions), `.org` (for non-profit organizations), or the prestigious `.net` (for organizations that are part of the structure of the Web itself). Other countries can use different suffixes. Additionally, a country code such as `.uk`, for United Kingdom, can be added to represent a country or region. The part before the suffix, such as "`stanford`" in "`stanford.edu`", is either the name of the group that puts up the Web site, or something that attracts people to the site. Domain names can start with "`www`" if desired, but it's not necessary.

Downloadable image. An image that's associated with a Web page but not displayed unless the user clicks a graphic to display it.

Electronic mail (e-mail). A message sent from one computer user over a network to another computer user. The most popular service on the Internet. Used as a noun ("I just got an e-mail.") and a verb ("E-mail me on that, will you?"). Also used as singular ("I just deleted an e-mail.") and plural ("I just deleted all my e-mail.").

Element. In HTML, an element is the first character or set of characters within a tag that specifies the tag's purpose. Example: In the tag `<IMG SRC="budpic.jpg">`, the element is `IMG`.

File Transfer Protocol (FTP). An Internet service for transferring files between different machines, including those that run different operating systems.

Finished software product. No, this is not software that has all the bugs out of it. It's software from the country between Russia and Sweden. . . . Actually, a finished software product is just software that is sold as a product, with the user paying up-front before taking possession of the software. See *Freeware* and *Shareware*.

Firewall. Hardware, software, or a combination that protects a network from unauthorized access while allowing authorized access.

Form. An HTML-defined way to specify text boxes and pull-down menus to enable users of a Web page to enter data. The data from the form must be processed on the Web server by a CGI script.

Freeware. Software that can be used for free, without payment, though often with a license that contains some restrictions on its use. See *Finished software product* and *Shareware*.

Graphic Interchange Format (GIF). Can be pronounced "jiff" or "gif" (sounds like "gift"). A format for encoding images, including computer-generated art and photographs, for transfer among machines. GIF format is the most popular means for storing images for transfer over the Internet and is supported by all graphical Web browsers. An image stored in GIF format is often referred to as "a GIF." See also *Interlaced GIF,* and *Transparent GIF.*

Graphical User Interface (GUI). Software that allows you to interact with a computer by using a mouse and keyboard to manipulate images and menus on the computer's screen. The Windows and Macintosh user interfaces are both examples of GUIs.

Helper application. An application used to view data associated with a Web page but not supported directly by the browser. Originally, a helper application was needed to view any data not in HTML or GIF format, but browsers are expanding to handle different types of data directly. Users specify which helper applications to use for different data types in the user preferences options of their Web browser.

Hexadecimal. What the witch did to her accountant so that her tax bill would be more favorable. More commonly, a way of counting that uses 16 "digits," 0–9 plus A–F, instead of the 10 digits that common decimal numbering uses. Hexadecimal numbers are often used to describe values stored inside a computer.

In hexadecimal numbering, 0–9 have their normal values, but A represents 10, B represents 11, and so on through F, which represents 15. Place values are also different; each successive place represents the next greater power of 16. Example: 2F in hexadecimal translates to 47 in decimal; the 2 represents two 16s, and the F represents fifteen 1s.

Hit. This is what would happen to people who used the Netscape BLINK tag too much if the Mob ran the Net. Also: A successful connection, file transfer, and disconnection between a Web client and a Web server (see also *Web client* and *Web server*). Accessing a single, text-only page generates one hit; accessing a single page with three graphics on it generates four hits. Hits can be counted fairly easily and are a crude measure of the popularity of a Web site. When you see a site that advertises "a million hits a week," remember that the number of hits may be 10 times or more greater than the number of different people who visited.

Home page. A Web page that you intend users to come to directly. If a Web site has multiple pages, the home page usually serves as a guide to all the pages.

HTML 2.0. The most broadly used version of HyperText Markup Language. All browsers available today support this basic version of HTML, though different browsers may interpret some tags differently. See also *Netscape Navigator.*

HTML 3.2. The newest version of HyperText Markup Language at the time of this writing, though HTML 4 is hot on the horizon. See also *Netscape Navigator.*

HyperText Markup Language (HTML). The language used to "mark up" text documents so that they can be formatted appropriately and linked to other documents for use on the World Wide Web.

HyperText Transfer Protocol (HTTP). The agreed-upon format for exchanging messages among World Wide Web servers and between Web servers and clients.

Image map. See *Clickable image map.*

Inline image (also spelled **in-line image).** An image displayed embedded within a Web page.

Integrated Services Digital Network (ISDN). A special type of phone line now becoming available to many businesses and homes. ISDN supports faster transmission of data than standard phone lines.

Interlaced GIF. A GIF graphic displayed gradually by showing every fourth line, then showing the next one-fourth of the lines, and so on, until the entire image is displayed. This process quickly displays a blurry version of the graphic that sharpens as time passes and the missing lines are filled in. Interlaced GIFs save users time by allowing them to quickly see the initial, blurry version and, if desired, move on before it is entirely displayed.

Internet. The hardware and software that together support the interconnection of most existing computer networks, allowing a computer anywhere in the world to communicate with any other computer that's also connected to the Internet. The Internet supports a variety of services including the World Wide Web.

Internet Protocol (IP). The networking specification that underlies the Internet. IP's most important feature is its support for routing of the packets — small chunks of information that make up a communication — across multiple connections to its final destination.

Internet Service Provider (ISP). An Internet Service Provider offers connections to the Internet and support for Internet services such as the World Wide Web.

Intranet. An internal network used for distributing information broadly within an organization but not to the general public. Many intranets work just like the Internet and World Wide Web, only on a smaller scale.

Java. A programming language that supports the creation of distributed programs, called applets, whose functionality can be easily and flexibly split between a client computer and the server that it's connected to. Java provides a way for the Web to support easy sharing of programs as well as data.

Joint Photographic Experts Group (JPEG). A format for storing compressed images. JPEG images were once supported by helper applications but are now directly supported by many browsers. JPEG is the best format for most photographs.

Link. A connection between two documents on the Web, usually specified by an anchor in an HTML document.

Mirroring. Keeping a copy of data on additional servers to make data available more quickly and to a greater number of simultaneous users.

Multimedia. Literally means "many media," and in this sense, a Web page with graphics is multimedia. However, multimedia is usually understood to mean either more than two types of media; or alternatively, to mean time-based media such as animation, sound, or video, and space-based media such as 3-D and virtual reality. On the Web, multimedia is also used to mean any extension of the Web beyond the basics of text, hyperlinks, GIF graphics, and JPEG graphics.

Netscape Navigator 1.0, 1.1. Early versions of the Netscape Navigator browser that introduced new HTML tags supported, at first, only by Navigator browsers. These tags are referred to collectively as the Netscape 1.0 and 1.1 extensions to HTML. Many of these features, most importantly tables, are now supported by other browsers.

Netscape Navigator 2.0. A recent version of the Netscape Navigator browser that introduced new HTML tags supported, at first, only by the Navigator 2.0 browser. These tags are referred to collectively as the Netscape 2.0 extensions to HTML. The most important such feature, frames, is now supported by most other browsers as well.

Newsgroup. An ongoing exchange of electronic messages about a specific topic, such as pets, restaurants, or Web authoring. To access newsgroups, use news reader software, which you can find on the Web or included as a feature of some browsers, such as Netscape 2.0 and later versions.

Numbered list. A type of HTML list in which each item is given a number, in sequence, when the list displays. The author of the list can rearrange it as needed, and the numbers adjust accordingly because the numbers are assigned only when the list displays.

Online service. Also referred to as a "traditional" or "proprietary" online service to differentiate from the Internet, which is seen as an "open" online service. Traditional online services, such as America Online, CompuServe, and The Microsoft Network, package access and content into a single branded product. The Internet and the Web are eroding the boundaries between online services by allowing cross-service functionality, such as e-mail between subscribers of different online services. The online service providers are further eroding these boundaries by offering Internet access, Web access, and even Web authoring support.

Ordered list. See *Numbered list.*

Page description language. A defined format for specifying the appearance of a document when displayed or printed. Adobe's PostScript, used by many programs and in many laser printers, is a page description language, not a structural markup language like HTML or SGML.

Pathname. A description of the location of a file. Pathnames can be specified by absolute addressing or relative addressing.

Plug-in. A small program that works with a Web browser to allow multimedia files to be displayed in a Web page, or that otherwise extends the capabilities of the browser.

PointCast. A company that introduced the first widely used software program and content for *push technology.*

Protocol. A format for exchanging data.

Push technology. A new use of the Internet in which your computer automatically checks in with Web sites for any new data; if new information exists, you are notified, and in some cases the new data is automatically sent (pushed) to your computer.

QuickTime. A multiplatform standard from Apple Computer, Inc., for multimedia. See also *Multimedia, QuickTime VR,* and *QuickTime plug-in.*

QuickTime plug-in. A plug-in for Netscape Navigator and Microsoft Internet Explorer that supports user interaction with QuickTime and QuickTime VR content embedded in a Web page. See also *QuickTime,* and *QuickTime VR.*

QuickTime VR. A multi-platform standard for image-based virtual reality. See *QuickTime,* and *QuickTime plug-in.*

Relative address. The path from a base document, such as an HTML document, to another document on the same computer, such as another Web page on the same site. See also *Pathname,* and *Absolute address.*

Service. In general, a service is a method for providing people with the use of something. Specifically, an online service is a method for providing computer users with the ability to exchange information and computer programs via a computer modem; a Web-based service is a method for providing Web users with the ability to exchange information and computer programs via the Web.

Shareware. Software that can be used for free for a limited period of time, after which the user is requested (though usually not forced) to pay a fee for continued use. See *Finished software product* and *Freeware.*

Standard. An agreed-upon way to do something, such as building a computer system (for example, the IBM-compatible standard) or exchanging data (for example, the ASCII standard). Several different standards exist, ranging from those created by a single manufacturer for its own purposes (the DOS standard) to those created by internationally recognized standards bodies such as ISO (the International Standards Organization). In other words, in computing, the definition of standard is not very standard.

Standard Generalized Markup Language (SGML). A full-featured specification for describing the content and structure of documents but not the exact appearance with which they appear. HTML is a subset of SGML.

Syntax. A fee paid for moral or legal violations — no, wait, that's a "sin tax." A syntax is the ordering of the elements in a language or protocol.

System operator (sysop). A person responsible for some part of the operations of a computer system, including online services. A sysop's responsibilities can vary from the technical, such as backing up a computer hard drive, to the nontechnical, such as monitoring a newsgroup for inappropriate or irrelevant content and removing it if found.

Tag. An HTML element that contains information besides the actual document content, such as formatting information or an anchor. Example: The `<B>` tag starts bolding of the characters that follow it, and the `</B>` tag ends bolding. So to make a word or phrase bold, surround it with the `<B>` and `</B>` tags.

Text editor. A program that allows text to be entered and edited but not formatted for display. Text editors save their files without proprietary formatting information, so the files are portable across different application programs and different computer systems. Examples are Notepad (Windows), BBEdit (Macintosh), and vi (UNIX).

Thumbnail. A small graphical image that serves as a preview of a larger image.

Tool. In computing, a tool is similar to a program but more narrowly focused on a single task or set of tasks. It's capable of being used more flexibly with other tools, and it's more likely to be provided from an online source or even used directly online, rather than run on the user's computer.

Transmission Control Protocol/Internet Protocol (TCP/IP). A communications protocol developed under contract from the U.S. Department of Defense in the 1970s to connect different systems and different networks. TCP/IP is the protocol on which the Internet is based.

Transparent GIF. A file stored in Graphic Interchange Format and modified so that the area around the objects of interest is assigned the color "transparent." This capability makes the rectangular frame around the objects seem to disappear so that the graphic appears to "float" over the page on which it appears.

Uniform Resource Locator (URL). A specification for identifying any file on the Internet. The URL is made up of the name of the protocol by which the file should be accessed, the name of the server that the file is stored on, and the pathname of the file on the server. Here is an example URL for an HTML file named MyCruise, to be accessed by using the Web protocol `http`, which is stored on a server called `www.bigweb.com` in the `Travel` subdirectory:

```
http://www.bigweb.com/Travel/
MyCruise.html
```

If no filename is given at the end of the path, a default file, typically index.html for Web servers, is returned.

Unnumbered list. A type of HTML list in which each item is displayed next to a symbol such as a bullet.

Virtual Reality Modeling Language (VRML). A set of standards for displaying 3-D data on the Web.

Web authoring. Creating documents for use on the World Wide Web. Web authoring includes creating text documents with HTML tags, as well as creating or obtaining suitable graphics and, in many cases, multimedia files.

Web-based service. See *Service.*

Web browser. See *Browser.*

Web client. A computer that connects to the World Wide Web and downloads Web pages and other data from it.

Web page. A text document with HTML tags to specify formatting and links from the document to other documents and to graphics and multimedia files.

Web publishing. The entire process of creating and maintaining a Web site, from creating text documents with HTML tags and graphics, to putting the documents on a server, to revising the documents over time.

Web server. A computer that connects to the World Wide Web and hosts HTML-tagged text documents, graphics, and multimedia files to be downloaded by Web clients.

Web site. One or more linked Web pages accessed through a home page. The URL of the home page is made available to users on the Web, and often through other advertising and marketing means as well.

Word processor. A program for creating and editing text files with formatting. Files created by a word processor contain formatting codes and cannot be used on the Web unless specifically saved in "text-only" or "plain-text" format, without the proprietary codes that word processors embed in the file to indicate formatting.

World Wide Web (also known as **the Web** or **W3).** An Internet service that provides files linked by HyperText Transfer Protocol. The Web specification allows formatted text and graphics to be viewed directly by a Web browser and allows other kinds of files to be opened separately by helper applications specified in the Web browser's setup. The Web is the most popular Internet service, partly because it can also be used to access other Internet services, such as newsgroups and FTP.

Appendix B
Web Service Providers

● ●

*O*ne of the best resources for Web service providers is on the Web itself at

`www.boardwatch.com`

You can log on to Boardwatch to get a directory of local Internet service providers (ISPs) in any part of the United States or Canada. Local providers sometimes offer the best access, but of course the level of service you get varies from one provider to another. Boardwatch also offers a list of national service providers.

Another great source for Internet access providers is Yahoo!; check out:

`www.yahoo.com/Business_and_Economy: Companies: Internet_Services:Access_Providers.`

Typing out the long URL is worth it; Yahoo! provides links to regional, national, and international ISPs, as well as links to other ISP directories online.

For your browsing pleasure — in the old-fashioned, analog sense of the word "browsing" — here's a brief list of some of the top national Web service providers. This list is U.S.-centric; if you live elsewhere or travel, check online sources, or check with the providers listed in this appendix to see which can meet your needs.

America Online
Tyson's Corner, VA
800-827-6364

`www.aol.com/`

AT&T
Basking Ridge, NJ
800-309-3349

`www.att.com/`

BBN Planet
Cambridge, MA
800-472-4565

`www.bbnplanet.com/`

CerfNet
San Diego, CA
800-867-2373

`www.cerf.net/`

CompuServe
Columbus, OH
800-848-8990

www.compuserve.com/

The Microsoft Network
Redmond, WA
206-882-8080

www.msn.com/

NetCom On-Line Communication Services
San Jose, CA
800-638-2661

www.netcom.com/

Prodigy
White Plains, NY
800-776-3449

www.prodigy.com/

TheOnRamp
Youngstown, OH
216-759-2103

www.theonramp.net/

UUNet Technologies
Fairfax, VA
800-488-6383

www.uu.net/

Appendix C
A Quick Guide to HTML Tags

● ●

*O*ne of the best resources on the Web is *The Bare Bones Guide to HTML*. At this writing, this excellent reference lists nearly all the tags in the latest version of HTML, Version 3.2, plus Netscape extensions. This site was developed and is maintained by Kevin Werbach, a Harvard Law graduate and FCC attorney in Washington who has invested a lot of time and thought into Web authoring. You can learn an awful lot about Web authoring from the thoughts, resources, and examples listed on Kevin's home page at

www.werbach.com/

The Bare Bones Guide lists tags from the different versions of HTML with notes describing which version of HTML a given tag supports. We thought splitting out the HTML tags into separate tables by the version of HTML they support would help you.

In the version of *The Bare Bones Guide* in this book, only HTML tags from HTML versions up through Version 3.2 are included. This is because these tags are the most used by the broad range of Web pages and Web browsers out there. The online version of *The Bare Bones Guide to HTML* lists tags up to the current version of the HTML standard at the time that you access it.

The original *The Bare Bones Guide to HTML* from which we adapted this version is copyrighted (© 1995, 1997) to Kevin Werbach. For the latest version, see

www.werbach.com/barebones/

Note: *The Bare Bones Guide to HTML* is not affiliated with Bare Bones Software, makers of the BBEdit text editor for the Macintosh (www.barebones.com).

Versions of HTML

The tags in this table are part of the HTML 3.2 standard and are supported by all modern browsers. So if you aren't worried about ancient history — in Web terms, that's anything that happened more than a year ago — and aren't worried about the stubborn few users of your Web pages who may still have old browsers, you can ignore this section and go straight to the tables. But if you really want to know the details, read on.

The versions of HTML described in this appendix are:

- **HTML 2.0.** All browsers available today support this basic version of HTML. However, some tags are interpreted differently by different browsers. For example, a top-level heading, marked by an <H1> tag, may appear very differently in different browsers.

- **Netscape Navigator 1.0, 1.1.** These early versions of Netscape Navigator fueled the first huge surge in the growth of the Web. These were the first browsers to provide support for centered text, floating graphics, and colored text and backgrounds by using new "extensions" to HTML 2.0. Other browsers have adopted many of the features and new tags introduced by Netscape in Netscape Navigator 1.0 and 1.1.

- **HTML 3.2.** This is the new version of the HTML standard. Many of the ideas originally included in the HTML 3.0 proposal, such as tables and paragraph alignment, were first supported by Netscape Navigator 1.0 and 1.1. Although the HTML 3.2 standard is not officially finalized, many tags from of the HTML 3.2 specification are widely implemented in browsers.

- **Netscape Navigator 2.0.** This newer version of Netscape Navigator implements a few minor features, plus a major one: frames, which are specific areas within the browser window that contain different content and can be updated separately.

Over time, browsers are updated and improved to support a wider range of tags. However, some users will still have the old version of the browser. So don't assume that just because the new version of a browser supports specific tags, all users of that browser will upgrade and gain the ability to view those tags correctly.

The Microsoft Internet Explorer browser closely tracks the features and tag set of Netscape Navigator versions through Version 2.0. So Netscape Navigator features, such as tables and frames, are supported in Internet Explorer as well. Because these two browsers account for about 90 percent of the market, and because the browsers that make up the remaining 10 percent of the market try to keep up with them, you're pretty safe in using features that depend on Netscape Navigator 2.0 tags.

How to Use This Appendix

To use this appendix when creating your own pages, start with the first table, a basic list of HTML 2.0-compliant tags that work with almost any browser. If you use only the tags in this list, your pages will be as widely usable as possible. Then you can selectively spice up your pages by using tags from the different sets of HTML extensions listed in the later tables. You can also use this list to create separate versions of your pages: one version for all browsers and another for browsers that support the specific extensions that you use.

This appendix includes HTML tags that have not been discussed in the text of this book. To find out more about a specific tag, experiment with it in your Web text and your browser. If you need more information than you can get by experimenting, buy a more advanced book on HTML, *HTML 4 For Dummies,* by Ed Tittel and Steve James (IDG Books Worldwide, Inc.).

Reading the Tables

Within the tables you will see some tags that are not preceded by a dash, followed by tags preceded by a dash, such as:

Tag Name	Tag	Notes
Preformatted	`<PRE></PRE>`	Display text spacing as-is
- Width	`<PRE WIDTH=?></PRE>`	Width in characters

The tags with descriptions that start with a dash are actually options within other tags. These optional tags modify the effect of the tag that they appear with. You will always see the option listed with the tag that it modifies so that you can see how to use it in your own HTML-tagged text.

The use of the dash symbol to indicate optional tags and other symbols in the tables are described in Table C-1.

Note: In order to align columns correctly, some tags are broken. At the points that these tags break, we placed a downward, left-curving arrow (↩) to indicate the break.

Table C-1	Symbols Used in the Tables
Symbol	*Meaning*
URL	URL of an external file (or just filename if in the same directory)
?	Arbitrary number (for example, <H?> means <H1>, <H2>, <H3>, and so on)
%	Arbitrary percentage (for example, <HR WIDTH=%> means <HR WIDTH=50%>, and so on)
***	Arbitrary text (for example, ALT="***" means fill in with text)
$$$$$$	Arbitrary hexadecimal number* (for example, BGCOLOR="#$$$$$$" means BGCOLOR="#00FF1C", and so on)
|	Alternatives (for example, ALIGN=LEFT|RIGHT|CENTER means pick one of these)
- Option	An option within a tag

For an explanation of hexadecimal numbering, see Appendix A.

HTML 2.0-Compliant Tags

The following tags are in the HTML 2.0 specification and should work in all browsers.

Table C-2	Generally All HTML Documents Should Have These Tags	
Tag Name	*Tag*	*Notes*
Document Type	<HTML></HTML>	Beginning and end of file
Title	<TITLE></TITLE>	Must be in header
Header	<HEAD></HEAD>	Descriptive info, such as title
Body	<BODY></BODY>	Bulk of the page

Table C-3	**Structural Definition: Appearance Controlled by the Browser's Preferences**	
Tag Name	*Tag*	*Notes*
Heading	`<H?></H?>`	The HTML 2.0 specification defines six levels
Block Quote	`<BLOCKQUOTE></BLOCKQUOTE>`	Usually indented
Emphasis	`<EM></EM>`	Usually displayed as italic
Strong Emphasis	`<STRONG></STRONG>`	Usually displayed as bold
Citation	`<CITE></CITE>`	Usually italics
Code	`<CODE></CODE>`	For source code listings
Sample Output	`<SAMP></SAMP>`	
Keyboard Input	`<KBD></KBD>`	
Variable	`<VAR></VAR>`	
Definition	`<DFN></DFN>`	Not widely implemented
Author's Address	`<ADDRESS></ADDRESS>`	

Table C-4	**Presentation Formatting: Author Specifies Text Appearance**	
Tag Name	*Tag*	*Notes*
Bold	`<B></B>`	
Italic	`<I></I>`	
Typewriter	`<TT></TT>`	Displayed in a monospaced font
Preformatted	`<PRE></PRE>`	Displays text spacing as-is
- Width	`<PRE WIDTH=?>` `</PRE>`	Width in characters

Table C-5	**Links and Graphics**	
Tag Name	*Tag*	*Notes*
Link	`<A HREF="URL"></A>`	
Link to Target	`<A HREF="URL#***"></A>`	If in another document

(continued)

Table C-5 *(continued)*

Tag Name	Tag	Notes
	`<A HREF="#***"></A>`	If in current document
Define Target	`<A NAME="***"></A>`	
Display Image	`<IMG SRC="URL">`	
- Alignment	`<IMG SRC="URL" ALIGN ↵` `=TOP|BOTTOM|MIDDLE>`	
- Alternate	`<IMG SRC="URL" ALT="***">`	
- Imagemap	`<IMG SRC="URL" ISMAP>`	Requires a script

Table C-6   Dividers

Tag Name	Tag	Notes
Paragraph	`<P>`	Usually a double return
Line Break	` `	A single carriage return
Horizontal Rule	`<HR>`	

Table C-7   Lists: Can Be Nested

Tag Name	Tag	Notes
Unordered List	`<UL><LI></UL>`	`<LI>` before each list item
Ordered List	`<OL><LI></OL>`	`<LI>` before each list item
Definition List	`<DL><DT><DD></DL>`	`<DT>` = term, `<DD>` = definition
Menu List	`<MENU><LI></MENU>`	`<LI>` before each list item
Directory List	`<DIR><LI></DIR>`	`<LI>` before each list item

Table C-8   Special Characters: Must All Be Lowercase

Tag Name	Tag	Notes
Special Character	`&#?;`	Where ? is the ISO 8859-1 code for the character
`<`	`&lt;`	
`>`	`&gt;`	

Tag Name	Tag	Notes
&	`&amp;`	
"	`&quot;`	
Registered TM	`&#174;`	
Copyright	`&#169;`	

See a complete list of special characters at

`www.bbsinc.com/iso8859.htm`

Table C-9 Forms: Generally Require a CGI Script on Your Server

Tag Name	Tag	Notes
Define Form	`<FORM ACTION=`↩ `"URL" METHOD=GET|`↩ `POST></FORM>`	
Input Field	`<INPUT TYPE="TEXT|`↩ `PASSWORD|CHECKBOX|`↩ `RADIO|IMAGE|HIDDEN|`↩ `SUBMIT|RESET">`	
- Field Name	`<INPUT NAME="***">`	
- Field Value	`<INPUT VALUE="***">`	
- Checked?	`<INPUT CHECKED>`	Check boxes and radio buttons
- Field Size	`<INPUT SIZE=?>`	In characters
- Max Length	`<INPUT MAXLENGTH=?>`	In characters
Selection List	`<SELECT></SELECT>`	
- Name of List	`<SELECT NAME="***">`↩ `</SELECT>`	
- # of Options	`<SELECT SIZE=?>`↩ `</SELECT>`	
- Multiple Choice	`<SELECT MULTIPLE>`	Can select more than one
Option	`<OPTION>`	Items that can be selected

(continued)

Table C-9 *(continued)*

Tag Name	Tag	Notes
- Default Option	`<OPTION SELECTED>`	
Input Box Size	`<TEXTAREA ROWS=? COLS=?>↩` `</TEXTAREA>`	
- Name of Box	`<TEXTAREA NAME="***">` CCC `</TEXTAREA>`	

Frames define and manipulate specific regions of the screen and are implemented only as Netscape Navigator 2.0 enhancements. See later sections of this appendix.

Table C-10   Miscellaneous

Tag Name	Tag	Notes
Comment	`<!- *** ->`	Not displayed by the browser

Prologue	`<!DOCTYPE HTML↩`
	`PUBLIC "-//IETF//↩`
	`DTD HTML 2.0//EN">`	

Searchable	`<ISINDEX>`	Indicates a searchable index
Send Search	`<A HREF="URL?***">↩` `</A>`	Use a real question mark
URL of This File	`<BASE HREF="URL">`	Must be in header
Relationship	`<LINK REV="***"↩` `REL= "***" HREF="URL">`	In header
Meta Information	`<META>`	Must be in header

Other Widely Used Tags

These tags work with nearly all of the browsers currently in use. For a frequently updated list of widely used tags, see *The Bare Bones Guide to HTML* at the URL listed at the beginning of this chapter.

Table C-11 **Structural Definition: Appearance Controlled by the Browser's Preferences**

Tag Name	Tag	Notes
- Align Heading	`<H? ALIGN=LEFT|`↩`CENTER| RIGHT></H?>`	HTML 3.0 Option within the HTML 2.0-compliant Heading tag
Division	`<DIV></DIV>`	HTML 3.0
- Align Division	`<DIV ALIGN=LEFT|`↩`RIGHT|CENTER|`↩`JUSTIFY></DIV>`	HTML 3.0
Large Font Size	`<BIG></BIG>`	HTML 3.0
Small Font Size	`<SMALL></SMALL>`	HTML 3.0

Table C-12 **Presentation Formatting: Author Specifies Text Appearance**

Tag Name	Tag	Notes
Underline	`<U></U>`	HTML 3.0
Strikeout	`<S></S>`	HTML 3.0
Subscript	`<SUB></SUB>`	HTML 3.0
Superscript	`<SUP></SUP>`	HTML 3.0
Center	`<CENTER></CENTER>`	Netscape 1.0. widely implemented; for both text and images

Table C-13 **Links and Graphics**

Tag Name	Tag	Notes
Dimensions	`<IMG SRC="URL"`↩`WIDTH="?" HEIGHT=`↩`"?">`	HTML 3.0. Image width and height in pixels

Table C-14 **Dividers**

Tag Name	Tag	Notes
Paragraph	`<P></P>`	HTML 3.0. Paragraph tag, `<P>`, redefined as a container tag

(continued)

Table C-14 *(continued)*

Tag Name	Tag	Notes
- Align Text	`<P ALIGN=LEFT|`↵`CENTER|RIGHT|`↵`JUSTIFY></P>`	HTML 3.0
- No Line Breaks	`<P NOWRAP></P>`	HTML 3.0

Table C-15   **Backgrounds and Colors**

Tag Name	Tag	Notes
Tiled Bkground	`<BODY BACKGROUND=`↵`"URL">`	HTML 3.0
Background Color	`<BODY BGCOLOR=`↵`"#$$$$$$">`	Navigator 1.1. Color order, red/green/blue
Text Color	`<BODY TEXT=`↵`"#$$$$$$">`	Navigator 1.1. Color order, red/green/blue
Link Color	`<BODY LINK=`↵`"#$$$$$$">`	Navigator 1.1. Color order, red/green/blue
Active Link	`<BODY ALINK=`↵`"#$$$$$$">`	Navigator 1.1. Color order, red/green/blue
Visited Link	`<BODY VLINK=`↵`"#$$$$$$">`	Navigator 1.1. Color order, red/green/blue

You can find more info at

`www.access.digex.net/~werbach/wwwhelp.html#color>`

Table C-16   **Special Characters: Must All Be Lowercase**

Tag Name	Tag	Notes
Registered TM	`&reg;`	Navigator 1.0
Copyright	`&copy;`	Navigator 1.0

For a complete list of special characters, go to

`www.bbsinc.com/iso8859.htm`

HTML 3.0 options are more likely to be widely implemented than are Netscape Navigator-specific options. Where two versions of the same option exist, use the HTML 3.0 option.

Table C-17	Tables	
Tag Name	**Tag**	**Notes**
Define Table	`<TABLE></TABLE>`	HTML 3.0
- Table Border	`<TABLE BORDER>↩</TABLE>`	HTML 3.0. Either on or off
- Table Border	`<TABLE BORDER=?>↩</TABLE>`	Navigator 1.1. Can set the border width in pixels
- Cell Spacing	`<TABLE CELLSPACING=?>`	Navigator 1.1
- Cell Padding	`<TABLE CELLPADDING=?>`	Navigator 1.1
- Desired Width	`<TABLE WIDTH=?>`	Navigator 1.1. In pixels
- Width Percent	`<TABLE WIDTH=%>`	Navigator 1.1. Percentage of page
Table Row	`<TR></TR>`	HTML 3.0
- Alignment	`<TR ALIGN=LEFT|RIGHT|↩CENTER VALIGN=TOP|↩MIDDLE|BOTTOM>`	HTML 3.0
Table Cell	`<TD></TD>`	HTML 3.0. Must appear within table rows
- Alignment	`<TD ALIGN=LEFT|↩RIGHT|CENTER↩VALIGN=TOP|MIDDLE|↩BOTTOM>`	HTML 3.0
- No Line Breaks	`<TD NOWRAP>`	HTML 3.0
- Columns to Span	`<TD COLSPAN=?>`	HTML 3.0
- Rows to Span	`<TD ROWSPAN=?>`	HTML 3.0
- Desired Width	`<TD WIDTH=?>`	Navigator 1.1. In pixels

(continued)

Table C-17 *(continued)*

Tag Name	Tag	Notes
- Width Percent	`<TD WIDTH=%>`	Navigator 1.1. Percentage of table
- Desired Height	`<TD HEIGHT=?>`	Navigator 1.1. In pixels
- Height Percent	`<TD HEIGHT=%>`	Navigator 1.1. Percentage of page
Table Header	`<TH></TH>`	HTML 3.0. Same as data, except bold centered
- Alignment	`<TH ALIGN=LEFT|RIGHT| CENTER VALIGN=TOP| MIDDLE|BOTTOM>`	HTML 3.0
- No Line Breaks	`<TH NOWRAP>`	HTML 3.0
- Columns to Span	`<TH COLSPAN=?>`	HTML 3.0
- Rows to Span	`<TH ROWSPAN=?>`	HTML 3.0
- Desired Width	`<TH WIDTH=?>`	Navigator 1.1. In pixels
- Width Percent	`<TH WIDTH=%>`	Navigator 1.1. Percentage of table
- Desired Height	`<TH HEIGHT=?>`	Navigator 1.1. In pixels
- Height Percent	`<TH HEIGHT=%>`	Navigator 1.1. Percentage of page
Table Caption	`<CAPTION></CAPTION>`	HTML 3.0
- Alignment	`<CAPTION ALIGN=TOP| BOTTOM>`	HTML 3.0. Above/below table

Table C-18   Miscellaneous

Tag Name	Tag	Notes
Java Applet	`<APPLET>`	HTML 3.0
- Applet Name	`<APPLET NAME="***">`	HTML 3.0
- Alternate Text	`<APPLET ALT="***">`	HTML 3.0
- Applet Code Location	`<APPLET CODE="URL">`	HTML 3.0
- Code Base Directory	`<APPLET CODEBASE="URL">`	HTML 3.0

Tag Name	Tag	Notes
- Applet Window Height	`<APPLET HEIGHT=?>`	HTML 3.0. In pixels
- Width	`<APPLET WIDTH=?>`	HTML 3.0. In pixels
- Horizontal Offset	`<APPLET HSPACE=?>`	HTML 3.0. In pixels
- Vertical Offset	`<APPLET VSPACE=?>`	HTML 3.0. In pixels
- Alignment	`<APPLET ALIGN=["left"| "right"|"top"| "middle"|"bottom"]>`	HTML 3.0
Applet Parameter	`<PARAM>`	HTML 3.0
Parameter Name, Value	`<PARAM NAME="applet name", VALUE=" parameter value">`	HTML 3.0
3.0 Prologue	`<!DOCTYPE HTML PUBLIC"-//W3O//DTD W3 HTML3.0//EN">`	HTML 3.0

Less Frequently Used Navigator Tags

Some Netscape Navigator-only tags were slow to be adopted by non-Netscape browsers. However, they can be used with up-to-date browsers.

Table C-19	Presentation Formatting: Author Specifies Text Appearance	
Tag Name	**Tag**	**Notes**
Blinking	`<BLINK></BLINK>`	Navigator 1.0. Most derided tag ever
Font Size	`<FONT SIZE=?></FONT>`	Navigator 1.0. Ranges from 1-7
Change Font Size	`<FONT SIZE=+|-?> </FONT>`	Navigator 1.0
Base Font Size	`<BASEFONT SIZE=?>`	Navigator 1.0. From 1-7; default is 3
Font Color	`<FONT COLOR= "#$$$$$$"></FONT>`	Navigator 2.0

Table C-20	Links and Graphics	
Tag Name	*Tag*	*Notes*
- Target Window	`<A HREF="URL"` `TARGET="***"></A>`	Navigator 2.0. Option within the HTML 2.0-compliant Link tag
- Alignment	`<IMG SRC="URL"` `ALIGN= LEFT|RIGHT|` `TEXTTOP| ABSMIDDLE|` `BASELINE| ABSBOTTOM>`	Navigator 1.0. Option within the HTML 2.0-compliant Display Image tag
- Image Map	`<IMG SRC="URL"` `USEMAP="URL">`	Navigator 2.0. Option within the HTML 2.0-compliant Display Image tag
- Map	`<MAP NAME="***">` `</MAP>`	Navigator 2.0. Describes the map. Option within the HTML 2.0-compliant Display Image tag
- Section	`<AREA SHAPE="RECT"` `COORDS="#,#,#,"HREF=` `"URL"|NOHREF>`	Navigator 2.0. Option within the HTML 2.0-compliant Display Image tag
- Border	`<IMG SRC="URL"` `BORDER=?>`	Navigator 1.0. In pixels. Option within the HTML 3.0-compliant Dimensions tag
Runaround Space	`<IMG SRC="URL"` `HSPACE= ? VSPACE=?>`	Navigator 1.0. In pixels
Low-Res Proxy	`<IMG SRC="URL"` `LOWSRC= "URL">`	
N1.1 Client Pull	`<META HTTP-EQUIV=` `"Refresh" CONTENT=` `"?; URL=URL">`	Navigator 1.1
Embed Object	`<EMBED SRC="URL">`	Navigator 2.0. Insert object into page
- Object Size	`<EMBED SRC="URL"` `WIDTH="?" HEIGHT=` `"?">`	Navigator 2.0

Table C-21	Dividers	
Tag Name	*Tag*	*Notes*
- Clear Text Wrap	`<BR CLEAR=LEFT|` ↵ `RIGHT|ALL>`	Navigator 1.0. Option within the HTML 2.0-compliant Line Break tag
- Alignment	`<HR ALIGN=LEFT|` ↵ `RIGHT|CENTER>`	Navigator 1.0. Option within the HTML 2.0-compliant Horizontal Rule tag
- Thickness	`<HR SIZE=?>`	Navigator 1.0. In pixels. Option within the HTML 2.0-compliant Horizontal Rule tag
- Width	`<HR WIDTH=?%>`	Navigator 1.0. In pixels. Option within the HTML 2.0-compliant Horizontal Rule tag
- Width Percent	`<HR WIDTH=?%>`	Navigator 1.0. As a percentage of page width. Option within the HTML 2.0-compliant Horizontal Rule tag
- Solid Line	`<HR NOSHADE>`	Navigator 1.0. Without the 3-D cutout look. Option within the HTML 2.0-compliant Horizontal Rule tag
No Break	`<NOBR></NOBR>`	Navigator 1.0. Prevents line breaks
Word Break	`<WBR>`	Navigator 1.0. Where to break a line if needed

Table C-22	Lists: Can Be Nested	
Tag Name	*Tag*	*Notes*
- Bullet Type	`<UL TYPE=DISC|` ↵ `CIRCLE| SQUARE>`	Navigator 1.0. For the whole list. Option within the HTML 2.0-compliant Unordered List tag
	`<LI TYPE=DISC|` ↵ `CIRCLE| SQUARE>`	Navigator 1.0. This and subsequent list items. Option within the HTML 2.0-compliant Unordered List tag

(continued)

Table C-22 *(continued)*

Tag Name	Tag	Notes
- Numbering Type	`<OL TYPE=A|a|I|i|1>`	Navigator 1.0. For the whole list. Option within the HTML 2.0-compliant Ordered List tag
	`<LI TYPE=A|a|I|i|1>`	This and subsequent list items; Navigator 1.0. Option within the HTML 2.0-compliant Ordered List tag
- Starting Number	`<OL VALUE=?>`	Navigator 1.0. For the whole list. Option within the HTML 2.0-compliant Ordered List tag

Table C-23 Backgrounds and Colors

Tag Name	Tag	Notes
N1.1 Active Link	`<BODY ALINK=⊃ "#$$$$$$">`	Navigator 1.1

You can find more info at

`werbach.com/web/wwwhelp.html#color`

Table C-24 Forms: Generally Require a CGI Script on Your Server

Tag Name	Tag	Notes
- File Upload	`<FORM ENCTYPE=⊃ "multipart/form-data></FORM>`	Navigator 2.0. Option of the HTML 2.0-compliant Define Form tag
- Wrap Text	`<TEXTAREA WRAP=OFF|⊃ VIRTUAL|PHYSICAL>⊃ </TEXTAREA>`	Navigator 2.0. Option of the HTML 2.0-compliant Input Box Size tag

Table C-25 Frames: Define and Manipulate Specific Regions of the Screen

Tag Name	Tag	Notes
Frame Document	`<FRAMESET></FRAMESET>`	Navigator 2.0. Instead of `<BODY>`
- Row Heights	`<FRAMESET ROWS=⊃ #,#,#,></FRAMESET>`	Navigator 2.0. Pixels or percent

Tag Name	Tag	Notes
- Row Heights	`<FRAMESET ROWS=*>⤵ </FRAMESET>`	Navigator 2.0. * = relative size
- Column Widths	`<FRAMESET COLS=⤵ #,#,#,> </FRAMESET>`	Navigator 2.0. Pixels or percent
- Column Widths	`<FRAMESET COLS=*>⤵ </FRAMESET>`	Navigator 2.0. = relative size
Define Frame	`<FRAME>`	Navigator 2.0. Contents of an individual frame
- Display Document	`<FRAME SRC="URL">`	Navigator 2.0
- Frame Name	`<FRAME NAME="***"|⤵ _blank|_self|⤵ _parent|_top>`	Navigator 2.0
- Margin Width	`<FRAME MARGINWIDTH=?>`	Navigator 2.0. Left and right margins
- Margin Height	`<FRAME⤵ MARGINHEIGHT=?>`	Navigator 2.0. Top and bottom margins
- Scroll bar?	`<FRAME SCROLLING=⤵ "YES|NO|AUTO">`	Navigator 2.0
- Not Resizable	`<FRAME NORESIZE>`	Navigator 2.0
Unframed Content	`<NOFRAMES></NOFRAMES>`	Navigator 2.0. For non-frames browsers

Table C-26	Miscellaneous	
Tag Name	**Tag**	**Notes**
- Prompt	`<ISINDEX PROMPT=⤵ "***">`	Navigator 1.0. option within the HTML 2.0-compliant Searchable tag; text to prompt input
Base Window Name	`<BASE TARGET="***">`	Navigator 2.0. Must be in header

Appendix D

Using Resource.htm

• •

A great many resources are available online for Web developers of all skill levels. On the CD-ROM enclosed with this book, you will find a file called *Resource.htm*. To use this file, start your browser and then use the Open command from the File menu to open the Resource.htm Web page.

In Resource.htm, you find links to numerous sources of Web authoring information and links to sites that support some of the more popular Web software packages. Some of those packages are enclosed on the CD-ROM, but it is always good to check the support sites for the latest upgrades and bug reports. The following is a short description of the key sites and software packages that you can access via this resource page.

General Web Developer Resources

Probably the most useful sources of Web information are the excellent World Wide Web FAQ files by Thomas Boutell. The files are brimming with answers to many questions about the Web and contain numerous links to a variety of sites that provide further information or support for Web and Internet-related software. At the time of publication, Tom was reorganizing his FAQ collection, so we're giving you the URLs for both his new and old FAQ documents, since both are still wonderfully useful.

These files are an excellent starting point for any would-be Web author and netsurfer.

✔ World Wide Web FAQs

```
www.boutell.com/faq/
```

✔ Yahoo! World Wide Web Resources

```
www.yahoo.com/ Computers_and_Internet/Internet/
World Wide Web/
```

The indispensable Yahoo! index has a superb collection of links to just about every Web- and Internet-related topic under the sun. We saved you the trouble of searching and provide a link to the Yahoo! World Wide Web section directly. The topic selection is vast and comprehensive.

For more advanced topics and resources specifically related to Web authoring, check out the following sites:

✔ ZDNet Internet User Page

   www.zdnet.com/products/internetuser.html

✔ The Web Developer's Virtual Library

   www.stars.com/Vlib/

✔ WWW & HTML Developer's Jumpstation

   oneworld.wa.com/htmldev/devpage/dev-page.html

Four special topic resources are always in high demand. The WWW Security FAQ covers various aspects of maintaining secure Web sites and writing secure Web scripts. The CGI Script Archive gives you tons of information about writing programs which run on Web servers. Finally, the GIF-related sites teach you all you need to know about creating transparent, interlaced, and animated GIFs.

✔ The World Wide Web Security FAQ

   www.w3.org/Security/Faq/

✔ Selena Sol's CGI Script Archive

   www.extropia.com/Scripts/

✔ The Transparent/Interlaced GIF Resource Page

   www.best.com/~adamb/GIFpage.html

✔ CNet Feature on GIF89a Animation

   www.cnet.com/Content/Features/Techno/Gif89/

Microsoft Windows Web Resources

In this section, you find a number of sites that deal specifically with Microsoft Windows Internet and Web software. You will find everything from browsers to file viewers to FTP and Telnet clients to helper applications, and even various system administration utilities. If you're looking for just the right Windows netsurfing tool, these sites are the place to start:

✔ Tucows: The Ultimate Collection Of Winsock Software

   `www.tucows.com/`

✔ Stroud's Consummate Winsock Applications

   `cws.iworld.com/`

✔ ZDNet Software Library

   `www.hotfiles.com`

✔ Stardust Technologies' WinSock Software Directory

   `www.stardust.com/wsdir/`

Microsoft Windows Software

The *Resource.htm* Web page on your CD-ROM contains links to support sites for a variety of software programs that make life easier for the Web developer. You can find some of these programs on the enclosed CD-ROM. Others are freely available online either as shareware, freeware, or demo versions.

Your *Resource.htm* Web page offers links to no less then two browsers (Netscape Communicator and Microsoft Explorer) and six HTML editors (Adobe PageMill, InContext Spider, SoftQuad HotMetal, HomeSite, WebWizard, and HotDog). Other goodies include a filter program to translate Microsoft Word documents to HTML (Ant Tools). You can also check out Mapedit, the elegant image map editor, a couple of spiffy graphics programs (Paint Shop Pro, and LView Pro), as well as several other generally useful Web page utilities (SiteCheck, Weblater, and Wusage). Two other sites provide a great source for filter programs that convert just about any word processing or database format to HTML. Finally, if you're ready to play with Java animations on your Web pages, take a look at the Sausage Software SiteFX page.

Macintosh Web Resources

This section contains Macintosh-oriented sites. For general Web authoring resources, nothing beats Jon Wiederspan's Mac Internet Resource Directory. StarNine has an excellent site devoted to tools which work with their very popular WebSTAR Macintosh Web server. NCSA, the birthplace of the Web, and the Internet Interstate's Macintosh Web both have links to a great collection of Mac Internet-related software.

- Mac Internet Resource Directory

  `host.comvista.com/Internet.tfm`

- StarNine Development Services Resource Page

  `www.starnine.com/development/development.html`

- NCSA Mac Helpers FTP directory

  `ftp://ftp.ncsa.uiuc.edu/Mosaic/Mac/Helpers/`

- Internet Interstate's Macintosh Web

  `macweb.intr.net/`

Macintosh Web Software

We include links to both Netscape Communicator and Microsoft Explorer, as well as several Mac Web editors (Adobe PageMill, BBEdit, SoftQuad HotMetal, HTMLPro, and the freeware HTMLEdit). ANT_HTML and TextToHTML should let you translate Microsoft Word and plain text files to HTML instantly. GIFConverter, GifBuilder, and JPEGView can meet your graphics display and conversion needs. Two image-map editing programs, Mapedit and Nisseb mapper, will let you create images with clickable hot spots. SiteCheck and the Nisseb Link Checker will help your visitors avoid the dreaded "404 Not Found" display, while the two sites devoted to translators and filters will meet all your data conversion needs.

Perl

Perl is an immensely powerful and flexible scripting language which has become insanely popular with system administrators and Web developers. If you want to delve into the creation of more sophisticated Web based applications you can take advantage of a huge base of existing programs and tools written in Perl. The key general sites for Perl include the non-profit Perl Institute, and the commercial Perl Language Home pages. The Comprehensive Perl Archive Network lets you tap the power of a worldwide Perl developer community through of thousands of pre-build applications and modules. Essential magazines include the Perl Journal and the ZDNet Perl User. Finally, the Macintosh user can obtain a first-class Macintosh Perl FAQ.

- The Perl Institute

  `www.perl.org/`

- The Perl Language Home Page

  `language.perl.com/`

- CPAN – Comprehensive Perl Archive Network (Mirrors Listing at Yahoo!)

  ```
  www.yahoo.com/Computers_and_Internet Programming_
  Languages/ Perl/CPAN Comprehensive_Perl_Archive_Network/
  ```

- The Perl Journal

  ```
  tpj.com/
  ```

- ZDNet Perl User

  ```
  www.zdnet.com/products/perluser.html
  ```

- Macintosh Perl FAQ

  ```
  www.perl.com/CPAN-local/doc/FAQs/mac/MacPerlFAQ.html
  ```

Java

Java is rapidly emerging as the language of choice in creating interactive Web applications. These sites contain a plethora of information about Java, with both developer resources and numerous example applications.

- Sun Java Site

  ```
  java.sun.com/
  ```

- Gamelan; A Directory and Registry of Java Resources

  ```
  www.gamelan.com/
  ```

- Yahoo! Java Resources

  ```
  www.yahoo.com/Computers_and_Internet/
  Programming_Languages/Java/
  ```

- Java FAQ Archives

  ```
  www-net.com/java/faq/
  ```

ActiveX

ActiveX is Microsoft's answer to Java for Web interactivity, although Microsoft is hedging its bets; the company is very active in the Java world as well. Still, ActiveX is a real force in the 32-bit Windows world, which, after all, dominates the computer industry. ActiveX enables programmers to extend the Web to do a great deal more, with many different kinds of data, than plain old HTML. Some pretty amazing things are already being done with ActiveX. To see more, visit the CNET ActiveX affinity site:

```
www.activex.com/
```

Also, see Microsoft's site: `www.microsoft.com/activex/`

However, ActiveX is a flop so far on the Macintosh, and it's not even on UNIX — two computer platforms that are more important on the Web than they might be in the rest of the computer world.

If you are willing to consider Windows32-only development and deployment, you can't ignore ActiveX. For a set of links to more sites, see Yahoo! at:

`www.yahoo.com/Computers_and_Internet/Operating_Systems/`
`Microsoft_Windows/Windows_95/Technical/ActiveX/`

VRML

Designed explicitly for the description of three-dimensional virtual reality on the Internet, VRML is another exciting technology that holds the promise of revolutionizing the Web. These sites cover the VRML language and provide links to numerous virtual worlds that already exist in cyberspace.

- ✔ The VRML Repository

  `www.sdsc.edu/vrml/`
- ✔ The VRML Consortium

  `www.vrml.org/`
- ✔ The VRML FAQ

  `hiwaay.net/~crispen/vrml/faq.html`
- ✔ Yahoo! VRML Resources

  `www.yahoo.com/Computers_and_Internet/Internet/`
  `World_Wide_Web/Virtual_Reality_Modeling_Language__VRML`

USENET Newsgroups

Whatever your Internet- or Web-related passion, you are sure to find others with the same interests on Usenet. Here is a selection of newsgroups dealing with various aspects of Web page creation.

Here you can ask and answer questions, debate, and participate in standard setting projects. The Resource.htm file has links to a selection newsgroups most useful to Web authors.

Appendix E
About the CD-ROM

*H*ere's some of what you can find on the *Creating Web Pages For Dummies,* 3rd Edition, CD-ROM:

- A Web page with links to numerous useful online Web page creation sites
- Signup software for MindSpring, a popular Internet service provider
- Microsoft Explorer 4.0 Web browser
- PageMill HTML Page Editor, a demo of a full featured professional HTML editor
- HotDog HTML Editor demo and HotDog Express, a simple HTML page creation utility
- Mapedit, a program which lets you easily create image maps for your Web pages
- Paint Shop Pro, a great shareware graphics program for Windows
- BBEdit Lite, a freeware text editor for Mac OS computers that is useful for HTML editing
- Numerous miscellaneous utilities useful for the beginning Web page creator

System Requirements

Make sure your computer meets the minimum system requirements listed below. If your computer doesn't match up to most of these requirements, you may have problems in using the contents of the CD.

- A PC with a 486 or faster processor (Pentium recommended), or a Mac OS computer with a 68030 or faster processor.
- Microsoft Windows 95/NT, or Mac OS system software 7.5 or later.

✔ At least 16MB of total RAM installed on your computer. For best performance, we recommend that Windows 95-equipped PCs and Mac OS computers with PowerPC processors have at least 16MB of RAM installed.

✔ At least 50MB of hard-drive space available to install all the software from this CD. (You'll need less space if you don't install every program.)

✔ A CD-ROM drive — double-speed (2x) or faster.

✔ A monitor capable of displaying at least 256 colors or grayscale.

✔ A modem with a speed of at least 14,400 bps.

If you need more information on the basics, check out *PCs For Dummies,* 4th Edition, by Dan Gookin; *Macs For Dummies,* 4th Edition by David Pogue; *Windows 95 For Dummies* by Andy Rathbone; or *Windows 3.11 For Dummies,* 3rd Edition, by Andy Rathbone (all published by IDG Books Worldwide, Inc.).

How to Use the CD Using Microsoft Windows

To install the items from the CD to your hard drive, follow these steps:

1. **Insert the CD into your computer's CD-ROM drive.**

2. **Click the Start button and click Run.**

3. **In the dialog box that appears, type** D:\SETUP.EXE.

   Most of you probably have your CD-ROM drive listed as drive D under My Computer in Windows 95. Type in the proper drive letter if your CD-ROM drive uses a different letter.

4. **Click OK.**

   A license agreement window appears.

5. **Because I'm sure you'll want to use the CD, read through the license agreement, nod your head, and then click the Accept button. Once you click Accept, you'll never be bothered by the License Agreement window again.**

   From here, the CD interface appears. The CD interface is a little program that shows you what is on the CD and coordinates installing the programs and running the demos. The interface basically lets you click a button or two to make things happen.

6. **The first screen you see is the Welcome screen. Click anywhere on this screen to enter the interface.**

   Now you are getting to the action. This next screen lists categories for the software on the CD.

7. **To view the items within a category, just click the category's name.**

   A list of programs in the category appears.

8. **For more information about a program, click the program's name.**

   Be sure to read the information that appears. Sometimes a program requires you to do a few tricks on your computer first, and this screen tells you where to go for that information, if necessary.

9. **To install the program, click the appropriate Install button. If you don't want to install the program, click the Go Back button to return to the previous screen.**

   You can always return to the previous screen by clicking the Go Back button. This allows you to browse the different categories and products and decide what you want to install.

   Once you click an install button, the CD interface drops to the background while the CD begins installation of the program you chose.

10. **To install other items, repeat Steps 7, 8 and 9.**

11. **When you're done installing programs, click the Quit button to close the interface.**

    You can eject the CD now. Carefully place it back in the plastic jacket of the book for safekeeping.

How to Use the CD Using the Mac OS

To install the items from the CD to your hard drive, follow these steps:

1. **Insert the CD into your computer's CD-ROM drive.**

   In a moment, an icon representing the CD you just inserted appears on your Mac desktop. Chances are, the icon looks like a CD-ROM.

2. **Double-click the CD icon to show the CD's contents.**

3. **Double-click the Read Me First icon.**

   This text file contains information about the CD's programs and any last-minute instructions you need to know about installing the programs on the CD that we don't cover in this appendix.

4. **To install most programs, just drag the program's folder from the CD window and drop it on your hard-drive icon.**

5. **Some programs come with installer programs —with those you simply open the program's folder on the CD and double-click the icon with the words "Install" or "Installer."**

Once you have installed the programs that you want, you can eject the CD. Carefully place it back in the plastic jacket of the book for safekeeping.

What You'll Find

Here's a summary of the software on this CD. If you use Windows, the CD interface helps you install software easily. (If you have no idea what I'm talking about when I say "CD interface," flip back a page or two to find the section, "How to Use the CD Using Microsoft Windows.")

If you use a Mac OS computer, you can enjoy the ease of the Mac interface to quickly install the programs.

A Quick Overview

This book includes a CD-ROM with a variety of PC and Macintosh programs and demos that you will find useful while creating your Web pages. You can use some of these programs for one of the most important tasks in Web authoring: using HTML tags to create the text file that will be seen by users as a Web page. (How HTML tags work with text and with a browser to create a usable Web page is described in Chapter 3.)

The programs on the CD are either free, try before you buy, or demo versions. Several programs are add-ons or file converters that work with specific word-processing packages, while others are stand-alone programs. Some of the programs are HTML focused, and others hide the HTML tags and give you a more intuitive interface to work with.

And while all the programs on the CD-ROM are free in their current form, some require you to pay a fee to get a fully functional version by registering the program. Other programs are functional and ready to go "as is," with no payment required.

The HTML file "Resource.htm" contained on your CD-ROM and described in Appendix D has links to numerous online resources for the budding Web creator.

In this appendix, you find a brief description of the contents of the *Creating Web Pages For Dummies* CD-ROM. Each program listing also includes a pointer to the URL of the program's Web site where you can check for the latest upgrade and support information. Have fun!

Be sure to read the software's Read Me files just in case there are any unusual additional install steps after you use our nifty installer program.

Resource.htm

For Windows and Mac OS, In the Internet Access category. This is probably the most useful file on your CD-ROM. This HTML file contains links to numerous Internet resources of use to the budding Web page creator. To use this file productively, you'll need an Internet connection and a Web browser installed on your computer. You will find links to all sorts of HTML and image editing tools, to sources of information, and to Usenet newsgroups dealing with the Web. Some of these resources are covered in more detail in Appendix D. To use this file, simply open it in your browser using the File⇨Open menu.

Microsoft Explorer 4.0 Web Browser

For Windows and Mac OS. In the Internet Access category. We won't insult your intelligence by telling you what a browser is, and we'd be very surprised if you've never heard of Microsoft Explorer. However, just in case you don't have the latest version (at the time of publication), we include a copy of Microsoft Explorer 4.0 on this CD-ROM. You can always find the latest information about Explorer at the Microsoft support site: www.microsoft.com/ie.

Adobe PageMill 2.0 Tryout

For Windows and Mac OS. In the Web Page Editing Software category. Adobe PageMill is one of the best commercial Web page creation tools available. It is a sophisticated, feature-rich program, useful not only for beginners but also for more sophisticated Web page authors. This demo version introduces you to the power of this software. However, you are not able to save or print your work. Chapter 11 describes how to use PageMill. For more information about Adobe PageMill and ordering information to upgrade the demo version to the full version, go to the Adobe Web site: adobe.com/prodindex/pagemill.

Ant HTML Conversion Tools for Word

For Windows and Mac OS. In the Useful Utilities category. This is a demo of Ant Tools, a set of Microsoft Word macros. The tools are designed to work with Microsoft Word documents to facilitate the creation of hypertext documents. The tools enable you to insert HTML tags into any new or previously prepared Word or plain-text document. You can get more information about Ant tools and obtain the latest version of the tools at the Ant Web site: `telacommunications.com/ant/t/`.

The Ant Web site and the installed files have extensive documentation for these utilities.

BBEdit Lite 4.0.1 and BBEdit 4.5 Demo

For Mac OS. In the Web Page Editing Software category. BBEdit Lite 4.0.1, from Bare Bones Software, Inc., is a Macintosh freeware text editor with powerful features that make creating HTML scripts for your Web pages easy. The commercial version of this program, BBEdit 4.5, has stronger HTML editing features. We include a demo version of BBEdit 4.5 on the CD. This demo is fully featured but cannot save files: `web.barebones.com/products/ bbedit/litevfull.html`.

GraphicConverter 2.9.1

For Mac OS. In the Graphic Tools category. GraphicConverter is Macintosh shareware that converts pictures to various formats. The program also contains features that you can use for image manipulation. If you're using a Mac, GraphicConverter is a goldmine. Visit the support site for more information: `www.goldinc.com/Lemke/gc.html`.

HomeSite 2.5A HTML Editor

For Windows. In the Web Page Editing Software category. Allaire HomeSite is a shareware HTML editor for Windows 95/NT. It is an elegant and easy-to-use Web page creation tool that includes wizards to handle common but complex tasks, such as table or frame creation. For more information about HomeSite, visit its home page: `www.dexnet.com/homesite.html`.

HotDog Pro 4.5 Demo and HotDog Express 1.09

For Windows. In the Web Page Editing Software category. The HotDog HTML Editor from Sausage Software is a fast, flexible, and user friendly HTML editor that has been getting rave reviews on the Net. This is a fully functional demo of the Professional version of the HotDog HTML editor. (Note that the demo expires in 30 days, after which you have an opportunity to register for the Professional version.) Chapter 12 describes how to use HotDog for Web publishing. HotDog Express is a nifty, simple Web page creation utility without the full blown complexity of HotDog Editor — perfect for quick and dirty page creation jobs. For more information about HotDog software, and the latest versions, go to the Sausage Software Web site at: www.sausage.com/.

HTML Pro 1.08 Macintosh HTML Editor

For Mac OS. In the Web Page Editing Software category. HTML Pro is yet another Macintosh Web page editor which lets you work on the graphical view of a page and the source HTML code at the same time. More information is available at the HTML Pro Web site: www.acc.umu.se/~r2d2/files/HTML_Pro_info.html.

InContext Spider Demo 1.2

For Windows. In the Web Page Editing Software category. InContext Spider is an easy-to-use, Windows-based HTML editor. Features include quick-start templates, automatic HTML validation, drag-and-drop links and images, and more. For more information about InContext Spider and the latest version of the InContext Spider evaluation version, go to the InContext Web site: www.incontext.ca/demo/.

Mapedit Image Map Creation Utilities

For Windows and Mac OS. In the Graphic Tools category. Mapedit is an elegant utility for creating image maps for Web pages. An image map is simply a picture which can have clickable image areas linked to other Web pages. You can find out more about Mapedit and image maps by visiting the Mapedit Web site at: www.boutell.com/mapedit/.

MindSpring Internet Service Provider Software

For Windows and Mac OS. In the Internet Access category. In case you don't have an Internet connection, the CD includes sign-on software for MindSpring, an Internet service provider. For more information and updates of MindSpring, visit the MindSpring Web site: www.mindspring.com/.

Paint Shop Pro 4.14, from JASC Inc.

For Windows. In the Graphics Tools category. Paint Shop Pro is a powerful and easy-to-use image viewing, editing, and conversion program, which also happens to include many drawing and painting tools. You can find the latest versions at the JASC Web site. Also, don't overlook the Paint Shop Pro Web Graphics page which has a great deal of information on how to use this program to produce stunning graphics for your Web pages.

JASC Paint Shop Pro: www.jasc.com/

PSP Web Graphics: www.pspro.ml.org/

SiteCheck Link Checking Utility

For Windows and Mac OS. In the Useful Utilities category. SiteCheck is a useful application that provides a fast and convenient way to check all the hypertext links at your Web site to make sure they still point to valid pages.

SiteFX 1.4 Java Graphic Effects Tools

For Windows. In the Graphic Tools category. SiteFX is a set of nifty Java-based utilities that enable you to add cool graphic effects to your Web pages. Some of the things you can do with SiteFX include image animations, clickable buttons, text animations, pulldown lists, and so on. For more information about SiteFX and for the latest upgrades, go to the Sausage Software Web site at: www.sausage.com/sitefx.htm.

TextToHTML Macintosh Filter

For Mac OS. In the Useful Utilities category. TextToHTML enables you to, not surprisingly, translate text files to HTML. Keep an eye on the author's Web site for updates and bug fixes: `www.ourworld.compuserve.com/homepages/kristiaan/Software.htm`.

WebLater 1.3 URL Capture Utility

For Windows. In the Useful Utilities category. WebLater watches your Windows Clipboard. Every time you copy a URL to the Clipboard, WebLater makes a note of it. Later, when you are ready to follow that link, just pop up WebLater and pick it from the list. Pretty cool. `www.boutell.com/weblater/`.

WEB Wizard 1.2 HTML Editor

For Windows. In the Web Page Editing Software category. "WEB Wizard: The Duke of URL" is a Windows shareware program designed to help you very quickly create simple home pages. The WEB Wizard interviews you about what you would like on your home page and spits out an HTML file; it's excellent for quick and dirty Web work. Using WEB Wizard is described in Chapter 14. For more information about WEB Wizard, go to the WEB Wizard Web site at: `www.halcyon.com/artamedia/webwizard`.

If You've Got Problems (Of the CD Kind)

We tried our best to compile programs that work on most computers with the minimum system requirements. Alas, your computer may differ, and some programs may not work properly for some reason.

The two likeliest problems are that you don't have enough memory (RAM) for the programs you want to use, or you have other programs running that are affecting installation or running of a program. If you get error messages like `Not enough memory` or `Setup cannot continue`, try one or more of these methods and then try using the software again:

✔ Turn off any antivirus software that you have on your computer. Installers sometimes mimic virus activity and may make your computer incorrectly believe that it is being infected by a virus.

✔ Close all running programs. The more programs you're running, the less memory is available to other programs. Installers also typically update files and programs. So if you keep other programs running, installation may not work properly.

✔ Have your local computer store add more RAM to your computer. This is, admittedly, a drastic and somewhat expensive step. However, if you have a Windows 95 PC or a Mac OS computer with a PowerPC chip, adding more memory can really help the speed of your computer and enable more programs to run at the same time. This may include closing the CD interface and running a product's installation program from Windows Explorer.

If you still have trouble with installing the items from the CD, please call the IDG Books Worldwide Customer Service phone number: 800-762-2974 (outside the U.S.: 317-596-5430).

Index

(continued)

(continued)

(continued)

(continued)

• X •

• Y •

• Z •

IDG Books Worldwide, Inc., End-User License Agreement

READ THIS. You should carefully read these terms and conditions before opening the software packet(s) included with this book ("Book"). This is a license agreement ("Agreement") between you and IDG Books Worldwide, Inc. ("IDGB"). By opening the accompanying software packet(s), you acknowledge that you have read and accept the following terms and conditions. If you do not agree and do not want to be bound by such terms and conditions, promptly return the Book and the unopened software packet(s) to the place you obtained them for a full refund.

1. **License Grant.** IDGB grants to you (either an individual or entity) a nonexclusive license to use one copy of the enclosed software program(s) (collectively, the "Software") solely for your own personal or business purposes on a single computer (whether a standard computer or a workstation component of a multiuser network). The Software is in use on a computer when it is loaded into temporary memory (RAM) or installed into permanent memory (hard disk, CD-ROM, or other storage device). IDGB reserves all rights not expressly granted herein.

2. **Ownership.** IDGB is the owner of all right, title, and interest, including copyright, in and to the compilation of the Software recorded on the disk(s) or CD-ROM ("Software Media"). Copyright to the individual programs recorded on the Software Media is owned by the author or other authorized copyright owner of each program. Ownership of the Software and all proprietary rights relating thereto remain with IDGB and its licensers.

3. **Restrictions on Use and Transfer.**

   (a) You may only (i) make one copy of the Software for backup or archival purposes, or (ii) transfer the Software to a single hard disk, provided that you keep the original for backup or archival purposes. You may not (i) rent or lease the Software, (ii) copy or reproduce the Software through a LAN or other network system or through any computer subscriber system or bulletin-board system, or (iii) modify, adapt, or create derivative works based on the Software.

   (b) You may not reverse engineer, decompile, or disassemble the Software. You may transfer the Software and user documentation on a permanent basis, provided that the transferee agrees to accept the terms and conditions of this Agreement and you retain no copies. If the Software is an update or has been updated, any transfer must include the most recent update and all prior versions.

4. **Restrictions on Use of Individual Programs.** You must follow the individual requirements and restrictions detailed for each individual program in Appendix E of this Book. These limitations are also contained in the individual license agreements recorded on the Software Media. These limitations may include a requirement that after using the program for a specified period of time, the user must pay a registration fee or discontinue use. By opening the Software packet(s), you will be agreeing to abide by the licenses and restrictions for these individual programs that are detailed in Appendix E and on the Software Media. None of the material on this Software Media or listed in this Book may ever be redistributed, in original or modified form, for commercial purposes.

5. **Limited Warranty.**

   (a) IDGB warrants that the Software and Software Media are free from defects in materials and workmanship under normal use for a period of sixty (60) days from the date of purchase of this Book. If IDGB receives notification within the warranty period of defects in materials or workmanship, IDGB will replace the defective Software Media.

   (b) IDGB AND THE AUTHOR OF THE BOOK DISCLAIM ALL OTHER WARRANTIES, EXPRESS OR IMPLIED, INCLUDING WITHOUT LIMITATION IMPLIED WARRANTIES OF MER-CHANTABILITY AND FITNESS FOR A PARTICULAR PURPOSE, WITH RESPECT TO THE SOFTWARE, THE PROGRAMS, THE SOURCE CODE CONTAINED THEREIN, AND/OR THE TECHNIQUES DESCRIBED IN THIS BOOK. IDGB DOES NOT WARRANT THAT THE FUNCTIONS CONTAINED IN THE SOFTWARE WILL MEET YOUR REQUIREMENTS OR THAT THE OPERATION OF THE SOFTWARE WILL BE ERROR FREE.

   (c) This limited warranty gives you specific legal rights, and you may have other rights that vary from jurisdiction to jurisdiction.

6. **Remedies.**

   (a) IDGB's entire liability and your exclusive remedy for defects in materials and workmanship shall be limited to replacement of the Software Media, which may be returned to IDGB with a copy of your receipt at the following address: Software Media Fulfillment Department, Attn.: *Creating Web Pages For Dummies,* 3rd Edition, IDG Books Worldwide, Inc., 7260 Shadeland Station, Ste. 100, Indianapolis, IN 46256, or call 800-762-2974. Please allow three to four weeks for delivery. This Limited Warranty is void if failure of the Software Media has resulted from accident, abuse, or misapplication. Any replacement Software Media will be warranted for the remainder of the original warranty period or thirty (30) days, whichever is longer.

   (b) In no event shall IDGB or the author be liable for any damages whatsoever (including without limitation damages for loss of business profits, business interruption, loss of business information, or any other pecuniary loss) arising from the use of or inability to use the Book or the Software, even if IDGB has been advised of the possibility of such damages.

   (c) Because some jurisdictions do not allow the exclusion or limitation of liability for conse-quential or incidental damages, the above limitation or exclusion may not apply to you.

7. **U.S. Government Restricted Rights.** Use, duplication, or disclosure of the Software by the U.S. Government is subject to restrictions stated in paragraph (c)(1)(ii) of the Rights in Technical Data and Computer Software clause of DFARS 252.227-7013, and in subparagraphs (a) through (d) of the Commercial Computer–Restricted Rights clause at FAR 52.227-19, and in similar clauses in the NASA FAR supplement, when applicable.

8. **General.** This Agreement constitutes the entire understanding of the parties and revokes and supersedes all prior agreements, oral or written, between them and may not be modified or amended except in a writing signed by both parties hereto that specifically refers to this Agreement. This Agreement shall take precedence over any other documents that may be in conflict herewith. If any one or more provisions contained in this Agreement are held by any court or tribunal to be invalid, illegal, or otherwise unenforceable, each and every other provision shall remain in full force and effect.

Installation Instructions

● ●

See Appendix E for complete information on installing the CD and the programs it contains. Here are the instructions in a nutshell.

Using Microsoft Windows

To install the items from the CD to your hard drive, follow these steps.

1. **Insert the CD into your computer's CD-ROM drive.**
2. **Windows 95 users: Click the Start button and click Run.**
3. **In the dialog box that appears, type** D:\SETUP.EXE **and click OK.**
4. **Read the license agreement and click the Accept button.**
5. **Click anywhere on the Welcome screen that you then see to enter the interface.**
6. **Click on a category's name to see a list of items in that category.**
7. **For more information about a program, click the program's name and read and follow the information that appears.**
8. **To install the program, click the appropriate Install button. If you don't want to install the program, click the Go Back button to return to the previous screen.**
9. **To install other items, repeat Steps 6, 7, and 8.**
10. **Click the Quit button to close the interface.**

    Eject the CD and carefully place it in this book's plastic jacket.

Using the Mac OS

To install the items from the CD to your hard drive, follow these steps.

1. **Insert the CD into your computer's CD-ROM drive.**
2. **Double-click the CD icon that you see to show the CD's contents.**
3. **Double-click the Read Me First icon and read the information that appears; then double-click a folder icon to see the programs in that category.**
4. **To install most programs, just drag the program's folder from the CD window and drop it on your hard drive icon.**
5. **Some programs come with installer programs — with those, you simply open the program's folder on the CD and double-click the icon with the words "Install" or "Installer."**

    Eject the CD and carefully place it in this book's plastic jacket.

If you have trouble installing the items from the CD, see Appendix E. If you still have problems, please call the IDG Books Worldwide Customer Service phone number: 800-762-2974 (outside the U.S.: 317-596-5430).

WWW.DUMMIES.COM

YOUR ONLINE RESOURCE

Discover Dummies Online!

The Dummies Web Site is your fun and friendly online resource for the latest information about *...For Dummies*® books and your favorite topics. The Web site is the place to communicate with us, exchange ideas with other *...For Dummies* readers, chat with authors, and have fun!

Ten Fun and Useful Things You Can Do at www.dummies.com

1. Win free *...For Dummies* books and more!
2. Register your book and be entered in a prize drawing.
3. Meet your favorite authors through the IDG Books Author Chat Series.
4. Exchange helpful information with other *...For Dummies* readers.
5. Discover other great *...For Dummies* books you must have!
6. Purchase Dummieswear™ exclusively from our Web site.
7. Buy *...For Dummies* books online.
8. Talk to us. Make comments, ask questions, get answers!
9. Download free software.
10. Find additional useful resources from authors.

Link directly to these ten fun and useful things at
http://www.dummies.com/10useful

WWW.DUMMIES.COM

For other technology titles from IDG Books Worldwide, go to
www.idgbooks.com

Not on the Web yet? It's easy to get started with *Dummies 101*®: *The Internet For Windows*® *95* or *The Internet For Dummies*®, 4th Edition, at local retailers everywhere.

Find other *...For Dummies* books on these topics:
Business • Career • Databases • Food & Beverage • Games • Gardening • Graphics • Hardware
Health & Fitness • Internet and the World Wide Web • Networking • Office Suites
Operating Systems • Personal Finance • Pets • Programming • Recreation • Sports
Spreadsheets • Teacher Resources • Test Prep • Word Processing

IDG BOOKS WORLDWIDE BOOK REGISTRATION

Register This Book and Win!

We want to hear from you!

Visit **http://my2cents.dummies.com** to register this book and tell us how you liked it!

✔ Get entered in our monthly prize giveaway.

✔ Give us feedback about this book — tell us what you like best, what you like least, or maybe what you'd like to ask the author and us to change!

✔ Let us know any other ...*For Dummies*® topics that interest you.

Your feedback helps us determine what books to publish, tells us what coverage to add as we revise our books, and lets us know whether we're meeting your needs as a ...*For Dummies* reader. You're our most valuable resource, and what you have to say is important to us!

Not on the Web yet? It's easy to get started with *Dummies 101*®: *The Internet For Windows*® *95* or *The Internet For Dummies*®, 4th Edition, at local retailers everywhere.

Or let us know what you think by sending us a letter at the following address:

...*For Dummies* Book Registration
Dummies Press
7260 Shadeland Station, Suite 100
Indianapolis, IN 46256-3945
Fax 317-596-5498

BUSINESS AND GENERAL REFERENCE BOOK SERIES FROM IDG

COMPUTER BOOK SERIES FROM IDG

FOR Dummies COMPUTER BOOK SERIES FROM IDG

Creating Web Pages For Dummies, 3rd Edition

Cheat Sheet

HTML Tags

Below is a list of the most-used HTML tags for quick reference. To see the tags in use, refer to the sample Web page on the other side of this Cheat Sheet.

See the tables in the section in Appendix C called "HTML 2.0-Compliant Tags" for a longer list of widely used tags — with examples.

Formatting

Headings: `<H1>Top heading</H1>`, `<H2> Next-level heading</H2>`,…`<H6>Lowest heading</H6>`

Bold: `<B>text</B>`

Italic: `<I>text</I>`

Paragraph: `<P>`

Bulleted List: `<UL> <LI> text <LI> text </UL>`

Numbered List: `<NL> <LI> text <LI> text </NL>`

Linking

Links to external Web pages:
`<A HREF="http://www.dummies.com">The ...For Dummies Web page</A>`

Links within a Web site, same directory:
`<A HREF="myres.htm">my resume</A>`

Links within a page:
`<A HREF="#nextline">Jump</A>` to the next line.

`Here is the next`
`<A NAME="nextline">line</A>.`

Graphics and Multimedia

`<IMG SRC="myphoto.jpg" ALT="My photo!">` See the embedded photo to the left.

Click `<A HREF="myphoto.jpg">here</A>` to download the photo.

`<EMBED SRC="mymovie.mov">` See the movie playing to the left.

Special Character Codes for Web Page Creators

To put special characters in your Web pages, enter the escape sequence or entity reference shown below. Test your special characters in several current Web browsers to make sure they display consistently.

Character	Escape Sequence	Entity Reference
"	`&#34;`	`&quot;`
'	`&#39;`	`&apos;`
•	`&#165;`	`&bull;`
$	`&#36;`	`&dollar;`
¢	`&#162;`	`&cent;`
%	`&#37;`	`&percnt;`
®	`&#174;`	`&reg;`
&	`&#38;`	`&amp;`
©	`&#169;`	`&copy`
<	`&#60;`	`&lt;`
>	`&#62;`	`&gt;`
@	`&#64;`	`&commat;`
à	`&#224;`	`&agrave;`
é	`&#233;`	`&eacute;`
ê	`&#234;`	`&ecirc;`

For more information and a complete list of characters used in different languages, see this Web page:

`http://www.bbsinc.com/iso8859.html`

IDG BOOKS WORLDWIDE™

...For Dummies: #1 Computer Book Series for Beginners

Creating Web Pages For Dummies, 3rd Edition

Cheat Sheet

Quick Reference — A Sample Web Page in HTML

```
<HTML>

<!-- Text between <angle brackets> is an HTML tag and is not displayed
directly. Most tags, such as the <HTML> and </HTML> tags that surround the
entire contents of a page, come in pairs; some tags like <HR>, for a hori-
zontal rule, stand alone. Comments such as the text you're reading are not
displayed. The information between the <HEAD> and </HEAD> tags is not dis-
played. The information between the <BODY> and </BODY> tags is displayed.-->

<HEAD>

<TITLE>Enter a title, which is not displayed</TITLE>

</HEAD>

<!-- The information between the BODY and /BODY tags is displayed.-->

<BODY>

<H1>Enter the main heading, usually the same as the title.</H1>

Enter some text, such as an introduction of yourself and your business.
Be <B>bold</B> about stating your key points. Put them in a list: <P>

<UL>

<LI>The first item in your list

<LI>The second item; <I>italicize</I> key words

</UL>

Improve your image by including an image. <P>

<IMG SRC="http://www.mygifs.com/rose.gif">

Then add a link to your favorite <A HREF="http://www.myfave.com/">Web site
</A>.

Break up your page with a horizontal rule or two. <P>

<HR>

And finally, link to another local page in your own <A HREF="page2">Web
site</A>.

<!--And add a copyright notice.-->
&#169; IDG Books 1998

</BODY>

</HTML>
```

List Your Favorite Web Authoring Resources Here

_____
_____
_____
_____
_____
_____

...For Dummies: #1 Computer Book Series for Beginners